Council of Forest Industries of British Columbia

How to Plan, Buy or Build Your Leisure Home

American Plywood Association

RESTON PUBLISHING COMPANY, INC.
A Prentice-Hall Company
Reston, Virginia

Harry Wicks

How to Plan, Buy or Build Your Leisure Home

Technical illustrations by Don Evans

Library of Congress Cataloging in Publication Data

Wicks, Harry,
  How to plan, buy or build your leisure home.

  Bibliography: p.
  Includes index.
  1. Summer homes—Handbooks, manuals, etc. 2. House buying—Handbooks, manuals, etc. 3. House construction—Handbooks, manuals, etc. I. Title.
TH4835.W52   643   76-7501
ISBN 0-87909-345-5

10 9 8 7 6 5 4 3 2 1

PRINTED IN THE UNITED STATES OF AMERICA

To Maureen, who made it possible

Table of Contents

Preface

It is estimated that better than 3,000,000 Americans now commute between two homes. It is also projected that roughly 200,000 people join the ranks of second-home owners each year. Leisure-home ownership is not just a current or passing fad: There are good reasons for wanting your own home in the country, and it is a pretty safe bet that you are already aware of one or more of them.

In order to earn a living, many of us are forced to spend most of our time in a pressurized atmosphere. Thus we yearn to escape to another environment where we can re-establish our roots with nature. For many, this escape is best when it is to a rural setting—a home by the shore, in the country or on a lake. When enjoyed regularly, such visits are emotionally and physically rewarding. In my opinion, the change of scene alone is a tonic.

But don't let projected enjoyment of the benefits of leisure-home ownership cloud the fact that buying or building a second home is a complicated undertaking. From the beginning, know that you will be ahead of the game if you have reliable and expert information to guide you as you go. You owe it to yourself to get the most for your money. The information in this book is intended to help you do just that.

I have tried to provide the answers to the questions which are most likely to baffle neophyte homebuilders and buyers. In many cases, you will see that avoiding a costly mistake is simply a matter of consulting the right person or agency at precisely the right time.

You will find information on site selection, legal and architectural aspects, mortgage know-how, and more. This pertinent home-buying information will prove extra-valuable as you become involved in each of these phases. The idea is to let this know-how help you to correct any mistakes you may have already made: If you have not yet started on your second-home venture, this book will help you avoid various—and costly—pitfalls in the first place.

The basics of building are also included. You will need this information

—obviously—if you plan to do your own building. On the other hand, if you hire a professional builder to erect your home, you will be way ahead of the game if you know what good building is all about. This way you can make certain that you are getting both the quality and quantity that you are paying for.

I will feel that I have succeeded in what I hoped to accomplish by writing *How to plan, buy, or build your leisure home* if any snags or frustrations that you may encounter will be solved or—at the very least—minimized through help you find on these pages.

In the final analysis, your aim is to live the good life as soon as possible; mine is to help you do just that.

*   *   *

Since you are about to become your own builder, it makes sense that you learn the builder's language as soon as possible. Thus, you will find trade terms used throughout so you will quickly, and painlessly, come to learn how various building terms are used.

If you are not familiar with any of the terms used in the book, simply refer to the glossary at the back of the book. Here you'll find all trade words clearly defined.

H.W.

Acknowledgments

The more I progressed on this book, the more I realized how fortunate I was to have so many good and valued friends—in and out of the publishing business. It didn't take me long to realize that it would have been just about impossible for me to turn out a book—containing as many elements as this one does—all by myself. Those who helped this book into print are listed below.

From the start, there were several people who were extra-involved, in one way or another, with the creation of this book. I feel that failure on my part to recognize and publicly acknowledge their efforts would be ingratitude of the grossest sort.

Thus, my very special thanks to: my friend and colleague, John Pearson, who read the initial manuscript, made suggestions, and assisted with the galleys and page proofs; my daughter, Patti, who suffered her father's scribbled editing in silence in order to type the finished manuscripts; my wife, who uncomplainingly listened to and shared my troubles and anxieties without ever making a demand that took me from my typewriter; and Peter Sweisgood, for being a friend when I needed one.

OTHERS WHO HELPED. . . . .

Bonnie Ackley, Juhl Associates, Inc.; Pamela Allsewood, California Redwood Association; Kenneth J. Beimly, Kingsberry Homes—Boise-Cascade; Edward Benfield, The Stanley Works; Merlin Blais, Western Wood Products Assn.; Harry Bond, Harry Bond Consulting Engineer; E. Harold Boyles, Eljer Plumbingware; R. E. Bracelin, Burks Pumps; Louise Brennan, American Olean Tile Co.; Tom Bross, Acorn Structures, Inc., Leonard Burton, Nevamar Div., Exxon; Dan Butler, Mobile Home Manufacturers Assn.; William J. Carey, Georgia-Pacific Corp.; Clarence Casson, Building Supply News; David Chase, Lennox Industries, Inc.; Phil Coyle, Stanmar, Inc.; Betty

Cristy, National Assn. of Home Builders; Ed Douglas Cunningham-Walsh, Inc.; A. E. Eggers, Thomas Ind., Inc.; Kriston Elliot, GAF Corp.; Pete Fetterer, Kohler Co.; Marian Finney, Nutone-Scovill; Leo Flores, Selz, Seaboldt & Associates, Inc.; Richard French, Caterpillar Tractor; Don Henry, Jacuzzi Bros., Inc.; William Gamble, Rockwell, Mfg. Co.; John Gaynor; Gerald J. Granozio, Leviton Mfg. Co., Inc.; Irene Grattano, John Moynahan & Co.; Ordon D. Hierlihy, Jr., Vacation Land Homes, Inc.; Michael Isser, Mekler/Ansell Associates, Inc.; John Jervis, LaFond, Jervis and Assoc.; Judi Kroeger, Lewis & Gilman; Roger MacLeod, Ward Cabin Co.; Debbie Martson, Young, White & Roehr, Inc.; Gerald P. Mullins, Formica Corp.; Martha Nold, U.S. Plywood; D. R. Norcross, Teco Corp.; Keith J. Pitcher, GMC Truck and Coach Div.; Hildegarde Popper, Sumner, Rider & Associates, Inc.; Kenneth Rajek, Weston Homes, Inc.; Ralph Rittenour, Home Building Plans Service; H. J. Schierich, Schierich Cabinetry; Hal Schwartz, National Assn. of Realtors; Eugene P. Souther, Seward & Kissel; Glen Spoerl, Sears, Roebuck and Co.; Carl Starner, Black & Decker Mfg. Co., Inc.; David Thomas, Tension Structures, Inc.; Anthony E. Vallace, Chemical Bank; Mary Ann Warwick; Franklin C. Welch, Ayer Baker; Tom Wheeler, Wheeler, Knight & Garcy, Inc.; Donald A. White, Jenn-Air Corp.; Richard Ziff, 3M Co.

*How to Plan, Buy or Build
Your Leisure Home*

1

The Second Home Syndrome

*   About second homes   *   Other reasons for buying a second home   *
Today's second home   *   Don't buy hastily   *   Getting a second home
*   Building your own house with a contractor   *   Manufactured homes   *
Vacation communities   *   Consider an older house   *   Mobile homes   *
Roughing it   *   That certainty—taxes   *

ABOUT SECOND HOMES

Shorter work weeks, holidays linked to weekends, and longer vacations mean that Americans have more leisure time now than ever before. With all this leisure time and steadily rising incomes, we are a society spending an all-time high on recreational pursuits.

We all have different ideas, though, about how we should spend our leisure time. For some, a trip by plane or boat—at home or abroad—is the perfect vacation. Others are happiest when loading up the car, camper, or recreational vehicle to head for a private or public campsite.

But, for several good reasons, more than two million American families have decided that they would rather be committed to one location, preferably in a home of their own. For these people, the second home is the only way to go—a dream spot that will be theirs after 180 or more monthly payments.

A second home is less costly than living in a lodge, motel, or resort, and the place is always there for the using. With a minimum of inconvenience (packing and the like) you can make a spur-of-the-moment decision to pick up and go, because shelter and recreational facilities are waiting at the end of your auto trip. Those who want these advantages feel that this is the only way to a better life—a place of escape when the pressures of everyday urban living seem intolerable.

1

In the dunes, by the sea . . .

Figure 1-1 *This octagonal-shaped vacation-house design adapts beautifully to a plot of ground that boasts a view in every direction. It's perched on poles to prevent water damage from occasional high tides, but it can also be built on a conventional foundation. For maximum beauty, the exterior walls are of textured plywood, permitted to weather gracefully. If local scenery dictates, plywood panels can be painted appropriately bright colors to suit a gay, beach atmosphere.*

Figure 1-2 *The optional prefabricated fireplace creates a focal point in the living room and takes the chill out of damp beachfront evenings. The exposed ceiling beams soar dramatically toward the center of the structure to create a feeling of spaciousness.*

Four different floor plans make this dwelling suitable for either two-, three-, or four-member families.

Getting there is easier than ever too. Better roads shorten travel time, and the continually expanding networks of federal and state superhighways have therefore been a blessing for leisure-home enthusiasts. Many areas once considered inaccessible (because it took too much time to get there) are now contenders for your buying consideration. In fact, because of the travel situation, many "veteran" leisure home owners are selling their closer homes at substantial profits, and buying or building farther out.

Since almost one quarter of a million people buy vacation homes and sites each year, the supply of choice leisure land is dwindling rapidly. Some real estate experts gloomily predict that prime-location recreational properties will be virtually nonexistent in the early 1980s. So if you have been undecided about whether to buy, the time might be now or never. Some years ago, Will Rogers told us that "they" just aren't making any more land. Now in the last quarter of the twentieth century, they still aren't.

Environmental concern is making its mark on the second-home scene too.

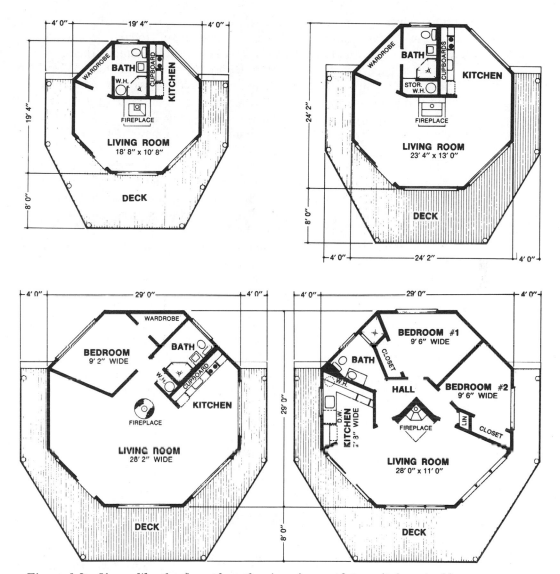

Figure 1-3 *If you like the floor plan, the size of your plot won't be a problem. Plans for three sizes are available—309, 482, and 695 sq. ft. There are two designs for the 695-sq.-ft. version: one rearranges the floor plan to add another bedroom, creating a hallway effect around the fireplace. All details for this home are available from Design No. 110, American Plywood Association.*

Not too long ago, a person could erect just about any type of house on a piece of property. In most areas today, this is no longer true. The hordes of would-be buyers descending upon rural areas with hammers and building plans in hand have forced many communities to reexamine and update building laws and ordinances. Although these changes are usually for the better, restraining overdevelopment immediately around you, they signal a change of lifestyle in Vacationland, U.S.A. In fact, many of today's leisure-home developments and communities have a very suburban look about them.

Builders have migrated into the leisure home market too. Wealthy developers and realty corporations acquire hundreds of acres at a time. It is difficult if not impossible, for an individual to bid on one acre or less against a competitor who can plunk down cold cash for several hundred acres. Thus, in many areas you are left with no choice but to buy your site from a developer.

Most developers subdivide their acreage in order to squeeze the maximum allowable number of houses onto that ground. Frequently, if current ordinances prohibit such cluster housing, the erection of condominiums, or other rental units, the developer has enough political clout and financial backing to secure zoning changes favorable to the investment.

More often than not, these homesteads quickly take on the look and social climate of your primary-home neighborhood. Among other things, for example, the manicured lawn becomes an occasion for keeping up with the neighbors. Frequently, such neighborhoods create a cocktail circuit, inevitably leading to weekends of partying instead of relaxing.

When searching for your site there is far more to think about than just the view. In fact, selecting the site can be more important than picking the house itself. What to look for, and what to guard against, is outlined in Chapter 3. You are well advised to arm yourself with this knowledge which has been gleaned mostly from those who have already invested in second homes. Knowing what to look for can save hours of time because some sites will automatically eliminate themselves under certain guidelines. More important, you might just be spared the disaster of buying an unusable piece of land— one upon which you cannot build due to environmental or local ordinance restrictions.

OTHER REASONS FOR BUYING A SECOND HOME

An investment in a second home may be considered a wise way to squirrel away a portion of your earnings. During periods of inflation, investment in real estate is one of the best hedges to protect what is yours. As interest rates and incomes rise, you pay off your mortgage note with inflated dollars.

Equally important, if the home is bought or built with care on a carefully selected site, your investment is sure to appreciate. This is important should a financial squeeze force you to sell. Unlike other investments that rise and fall with the dollar, real estate values appear to be on a scale that is steadily upward.

Furthermore, if you compare the earnings on real estate with those of the stock market, you will find a big dollar difference. In the ten years from

January 1960 to January 1970, the Dow Jones' Industrial average rose from 688 to 800—roughly, a 16 percent increase in 10 years. On the other hand, in 1960, the average sales price for a single-family house (in suburban areas of major cities) was $18,307. A decade later, the average price had risen to $27,022—or, an appreciation of 47.6 percent. Nationally, real estate values increased only about 32 percent—a somewhat less dramatic figure, but still twice the growth of the Dow. In this decade, the trend in favor of real estate seems to be, if anything, greater than ever.

Even if eventual sale is not your aim, the second home becomes the first home for many owners during retirement. Those who plan their leisure home for retirement are advised to buy or build with the future in mind: A house requiring minimum maintenance and running expenses should be selected. For instance, the excessive use of trim and architectural gingerbread, and such nonfunctional accoutrements as false shutters, should be avoided on the exterior if at all possible. These frills require periodic painting and other maintenance when you can least afford the expense or exertion.

Similarly, for inside the house, ask yourself *now* which design features will be best for you *then*, in retirement. For example, though esthetically pleasing and currently the vogue, rooms with cathedral ceilings cost more to heat; they also require more effort to clean, paint, and refinish. Extensively glassed walls also run up the heating bill, and your window-cleaning chores are all the greater.

Examine all the details of the house now—before you buy—and make changes where necessary to come as close as possible to a maintenance-free home. Years from now, you will be glad you did.

The mortgage should be arranged so that your home will be free and clear of debt upon retirement—when you must live on a fixed income. Ideally, in those years, the only cash outlay for the house should be for utilities, property taxes, and minimal upkeep (heat, electricity, and the like).

TODAY'S SECOND HOME

In past years, the second, or vacation, home was basically a no-frills shelter intended to provide little more than a place to sleep and eat. The idea was to rough it for a month or so each summer. Interior walls were usually unfinished. Indoor plumbing and electrical conveniences as we know them today were rarely enjoyed. And since the cabin or cottage generally was used for summer vacationing only, it rarely had heat. Come Labor Day, the house was shuttered until the next year.

Today's second-home owners have more sophisticated demands when it comes to leisure living. In all likelihood, they will use their homes for weekends, holidays, and even overnight trips, as well as for vacations. They generally don't want a pioneer-like, bare-necessities cabin in the woods or cottage by the lake. By choice, even though they may accept less for a while, they

A snug chalet for snow country . . .

Prowed Flair Manufactured Home by Stanmar, Inc.

Figure 1-4 *A handsome example of a manufactured house, in the Prowed Flair series of homes by Stanmar, Inc., is this modified A-frame—a practical and spacious design with glamour. Its steeply pitched roof sheds snow loads quickly—a must feature for homes in cold-weather climates. It is set on a concrete foundation provided by the owner.*

Prowed Flair Manufactured Home by Stanmar, Inc.

Figure 1-5 *The wall design utilizes the same economy of construction as an A-frame—without wasting space as an A-frame does, because floor space is usable right up to the walls. The kitchen is a generous size; the view from balcony over the living area, dramatic. In all, a welcome change of pace from most primary-home designs.*

Prowed Flair Manufactured Home by Stanmar, Inc.

Figure 1-6 *The glass wall should be located with both view and energy-saving kept in mind. Because of the two-level economy in the Prowed Series, the house can usually be completed with a touch of luxury such as the handsome fireplace shown here.*

Figure 1-7 *The interior walls of a Prowed Flair are paneled to eliminate periodic painting and wallpapering chores. The exterior walls are fully insulated. All versions of this Stanmar dwelling feature the loft—note the ladder at upper right.*

Prowed Flair Manufactured Home by Stanmar, Inc.

Figure 1-8 *The deluxe model has a third level, i.e., a ground floor or basement. This can be added economically, if your lot is a sloping one, by using a full foundation and building a two-story structure. The back of the house is simply tucked into the hill. The basic two-story Prowed Flair sells for about $40,000. If you opt for more space, you can choose a three-level model—which can be used on any terrain and which ups the price about $10,000.*

LOFT LEVEL

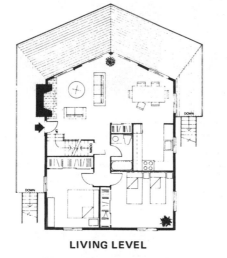

LIVING LEVEL

LOWER LEVEL

eventually bring along those amenities to which they have grown accustomed. Thus we find that today's typical vacation home is well-designed and built to assure maximum comfort. In many cases, the owner's second home surpasses the first both in quality and livability.

It is heated, has all electrical conveniences, and is esthetically pleasing in architectural detail. The well-planned home has its interior and exterior finished as completely as possible with attractive, minimum-care materials. The wide range of home designs makes it fairly easy to erect a "luxury" second home within a prescribed budget. Judicious selection from the wide array of exciting new building products now available makes the second goal —minimum maintenance—an achievable one.

Now second homes are equipped with labor-saving devices that add to the good life in the country: indoor plumbing, year-round heating, electricity, and usually a number of modern appliances. Ironically, the very conveniences that people bring along on their exodus to the country can do much to preserve the environment we value so highly. Efficient plumbing, for example, helps to keep precious lakes and streams clean. Thus fish and other wildlife are permitted to continue to thrive, and the balance of nature is retained.

DON'T BUY HASTILY

Unfortunately, many people jump into second-home ownership inadequately prepared. These adventurous, perhaps foolhardy, types think it unnecessary to take the time to acquire reliable knowledge before becoming entangled in planning, buying, or building a home. Armed usually with instant and meager information gleaned from newspaper and magazine articles, they leap hastily into the leisure home scramble—almost certainly headed for financial disaster.

Be wary of any material that focuses its attention either on pretty scenery or on lavishly appointed interiors and exteriors, while failing to acknowledge, or barely touching upon, the real problems of site selection, mortgaging, building, and the like. Chances are better than average that the house you adored in the striking picture was custom-designed by a competent architect, and built by a high-priced custom-house builder. The owner, in all likelihood, was probably not troubled with such absurdities as a tight budget and could entertain any whim. (Notice that the rule in articles of this type is to scrupulously avoid mentioning complete costs.)

Unless your financial picture realistically matches this one, stick to a feet-on-the-ground approach when building your leisure home. Assemble an idea file by saving those pretty magazine pictures, along with other good and valid ideas. Often, they can be used as design springboards to reality, ideas that can perhaps be incorporated or customized to suit your overall plans.

To make certain that you get the most for your money, there is no substitute for know-how. The lack of it can mean that you as buyer or builder may be forced to sell when a sale will spell a loss. Avoid a lark-like approach to what may be the single biggest investment of your life. Hopefully, this book will provide the know-how you will need.

GETTING A SECOND HOME

For some, acquiring title to second-home property comes easily. A house and its surrounding land in the family for a generation or more, for example, is passed down by inheritance. But, unless you are one of these fortunate few, you will have to employ one of these conventional methods:

1. buy property and erect the house yourself;
2. buy property and have a contractor build the house;
3. buy property and purchase a manufactured house;

4. buy an older house;
5. buy in a vacation community; or
6. buy a mobile home.

Note that the key word is *buy*.

Building Your Own House. You may elect to be your own contractor and erect a home using conventional construction methods. In the building trades, a house framed with studs, joists, and rafters is called a *stick-built* house. You can go it alone from start to finish. Or, from a more practical point of view, you can hire professionals for some of the work. The first route saves money, of course, but the second eases the chore considerably and lets you start enjoying your house a lot sooner.

Since you can build a house for about one-third to one-half of the cost of the same house if built by a contractor, the temptation to try your hand is financially justifiable. But, don't let thoughts of anticipated savings cause you to spend more than your budget allows for the house. If that happens, you are sure to get in well over your head.

You will also have to own or be able to rent the full complement of carpenter's tools, plus many of the tools used by other building trades. But what you will save on labor will more than pay for the necessary quality tools.

Perhaps the most serious demands when building a house are the physical and emotional fatigue, as experienced do-it-yourselfers know. Ask yourself honestly whether you are in shape physically and mentally to take on the (at times monumental) work of such a large-scale project. Will the cash savings justify the effort?

As your own contractor you will have to wear many hats—designer, carpenter, plumber, purchasing agent, and bookkeeper, to name just a few. The builder's role puts a strain on anyone's nervous system—make certain you and your work schedule are up to it.

Timewise, for instance, do not attempt to build a house using weekends only. Remember that weather plays an especially important role in the construction business. One rainy month during the summer can put your timetable back a year, assuming the winter weather in your area will halt construction also. If you make yourself a weekend-only contractor, you put an unfair burden on yourself and your family. To ease the strain, plan to use at least one or more summer vacations on the project. Actually, although from start to finish three or four years is an honest estimate of the project's duration, your own building experience will determine exactly how long the job will take.

If you can swing it financially, hire professional help for such heavy work as the digging and pouring of foundations, plumbing, framing, and applying siding and roof shingles. Also, since family safety is involved and the local building department inspector will have to make sure the electrical installation is up to standards, you should have a licensed electrician rough-in all electricals and install the main service panel. Obviously, a local electrical contractor knows the local and national codes.

Another task you must perform as a builder is the coordination of all subcontractors and supplies.

It is up to you to call in the subcontractor trades (such as the electrician or plumber) as they are needed. Hopefully, they will come quickly after your call, but that is usually not the case. Remember, you are a builder on a one-time basis. These subcontractors are in the business year-round and must keep their regular customers, the local builders, satisfied. You will probably be squeezed in between jobs for their regular people.

Similarly, you will have to compute the quantities of materials needed, order them, and check the materials when they arrive.

For obvious reasons, it is best if suppliers of materials are located within a reasonable distance of your building site. In most parts of the country, if unduly long hauls are required to deliver materials, the supplier tacks on a delivery charge. It is also your responsibility to assure access to your site from the road. If none exists, materials will be dropped where your property meets the road, and you will have to haul them in from there.

On your end, of course, the hours you spend shuttling materials back and forth are nonproductive. Each time you leave the job, if even to pick up some thing down by the road, all work ceases. Thus, when you are your own carpenter, the quicker you get back from the lumberyard or from the drop-off point, the sooner production is resumed.

Often, by pledging your full order to your local lumberyard, you can secure builder's prices on materials. Since this is the closest you will ever come to volume buying, you owe it to yourself to try for that discount.

Before you start to build, visit the local lumberyard with your plans and building specifications, and the lumber prices will be based upon the quantities listed in them. Don't let the supplier talk you into substituting unknown brands for materials listed by name in the plans. If the dealer does not carry a listed brand, make sure you get something equal in quality. The architect who drew up the plans indicated certain brands for specific reasons—your best bet is to stick with his judgment and expertise.

Once prices are agreed upon in writing, the purchase agreement should be initialled by you and the supplier. Next, try to work out a delivery schedule to assure that the dealer will have what you need—when you need it. Some materials are hard to get nowadays, and there is no reason to expect them to become more available in the foreseeable future. The dealer is within his rights to hold you to the shipping schedule, and it's your responsibility to be ready for the materials when they arrive.

Besides builder's prices, also try to get the dealer to give you the discount allowed to the trades for *cash* sales. A transaction is a cash sale if the entire balance due is paid within ten days of the billing date. For example, if you have a $200 bill during the month of June, the bill dated July 1 should be paid in full by the tenth of July. If it is, you can automatically deduct two percent or $4.00 for cash payment and remit $196.

If there is more than one building materials supplier in your area, visit the others to make price comparisons. It's a competitive business, and you should take advantage of that. But don't be guided by price alone because there *is* a difference in the quality of lumber. You can't compare prices on utility grade stock (which you don't want in your house in the first place) with standard grade (or better) lumber.

Finally, pay all bills promptly upon receipt. The quickest way to turn off your suppliers and subcontractors is to make late or partial payments. They are in business to make a living and will always service their quick-paying customers first.

Building with a Contractor. If you decide to have a contractor (builder) erect your house, you can use either stock plans, a design by a reputable architect or architectural firm, or the builder's plans. You will have to visit the building site periodically to make sure that the building is being erected in accordance with your contract and specifications. This arrangement works if inspection trips are made regularly, and the owner has some knowledge about the building of houses. A reputable contractor is also a must.

Neophyte homebuilders are well advised to hire an architect to oversee all aspects of the project. For his fee, usually 15 percent of the total cost to build, the architect takes over all phases of the project and "hires out" to you his building expertise. (See working with an architect, Chapter 4.)

Manufactured Homes. In the building trades, manufactured homes are generally referred to as *prefabs* (short for prefabricated homes). Though several types are available (discussed in detail in Chapter 14), they are all alike in that they are built primarily at the factory for assembly on the job-site.

The number of styles depends upon which type prefab you select—shell, modular, or panelized. The variety, though limited when compared to the custom-designed stick-built home, is quite good. The parts, or sections, are built to various degrees of completion in the factory, and then trucked to the site for assembly on your foundation. Other than a mobile home or older house, prefabs are the quickest way to get into your second home.

Vacation Communities. With the cost of land spiraling ever upward, more and more country real estate is being gobbled up by large developers. These corporations have the resources and know-how to convert mediocre properties into vacation paradises.

Ideally, such communities are located close to nature's facilities—a lake, a stream, or an ocean. In the mountains the developer carves out man-made ski trails, and equips them with snow-making equipment to extend the ski season. Well laid-out golf courses, for use by community residents only, are generally featured. For many, a championship-type golf course is reason enough to buy into such an area.

The advantage of a vacation community is that all services are usually

Contemporary cluster house in lake country . . .

Figure 1-9 One way to build on a budget is to choose a design that lets you add modules as time and money permit. The four basic building blocks for this cluster plan are all the same size. The difference is in the utilization of the interior living area, worked out to fulfill the basic requirements of different sites and budgets. (See Figure 1-10 on page 14.)

operative. The advantages, though, are reflected in the higher price of the site and house. Taxes are also generally higher to provide for all those man-made amenities that engaged you in the first place.

Such communities are also easy to get into. You simply pick and buy a site. If you plan to be your own builder, make certain you are allowed to do so before signing the contract for the land purchase. In some communities you must erect your home within a prescribed time, which is spelled out in the contract of sale. Other communities allow you to leave your property unimproved. For your sake, however, a time limit on nondevelopment is best because success of the recreational facilities is frequently dependent upon all sites being occupied by active and involved community-association members. In most cases, the building must be erected by the developer.

Like any business, the vacation-community scene has its share of snake oil sales persons. Beware of them. Chances are, either you have seen ads in

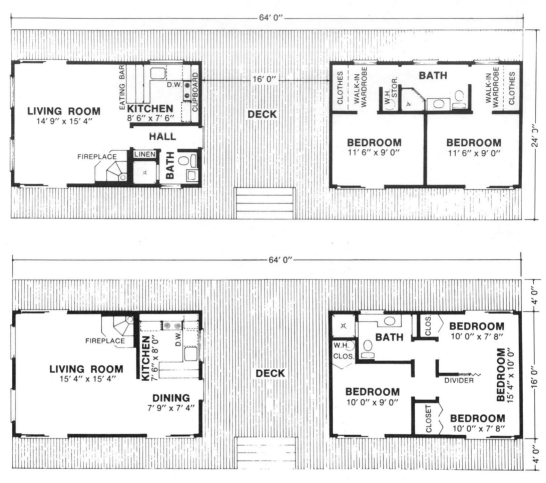

Figure 1-10 Floor plans show two different versions of a starter unit. If you use the one without a bathroom, provisions for sanitary facilities must be made while the second block is being erected. The two layouts of the sleeping-area module illustrate the home's flexibility of design to suit most families.

the Sunday newspaper supplements proclaiming idyllic leisure-land paradises, or you have been courted through the mails to come and see for yourself what a developer is offering. Because the market for the vacation-home dollar is highly competitive, such advertisements generally contain a variety of inducements—free meals, gifts, travel, even overnight stays—to visit the site. Though such offers do not automatically imply fraud, be wary of overly generous lures; cases of misrepresentation and fraud are more common than you might suspect.

Above all, don't ever invest in a site without first seeing it.

If you have any doubts about the advertising statements, or if you are wondering about misrepresentations in land sale contracts, pass up the land.

Design No. 117, American Plywood Association.

Figure 1-11 *The interior view of the starter unit without a bath. The prefabricated fireplace can be installed by a do-it-yourselfer. Like most vacation homes, walls are finished with textured plywood paneling. All exterior walls should be filled with adequate insulation to conserve heat.*

Or, at the very least, consult with your attorney before putting your signature on the dotted line. If the developer is using interstate transportation or communications—including the U.S. Mail—you are protected by the Interstate Land Sales Disclosure Act, administered by the Department of Housing and Urban Development. You may check with that agency to clear up or confirm your doubts. On a local basis, consult the Better Business Bureau. If complaints about a builder or developer have been frequent and justified, these agencies will know about it.

Consider an Older House. In your search for a second home, don't automatically discount the possibility of buying an older house. Often a well-built existing house can be the fastest and least expensive route to satisfied second-home ownership. Frequently, an old house can be remodeled and modernized at a lower cost than it would take to build a new home of comparable value and square footage.

Big savings are possible because of the presence of certain services and attachments. For example, utilities are already run-in and connected. You therefore save the cost of the installation of electricity, drilling for water, waste disposal, and telephone service—more than $3,500 at today's prices. Further, chances are that the house is already fitted with storms and screens —a savings of $20 or so per window. The house very likely contains a refrigerator and cooking range—another $600 to $800 saving. Additionally, the

Traditional home in the country . . .

Figure 1-12 *The advantages of an older home are obvious in this photo of a gracious 100-year-old house in New York's Catskill Mountains. Accessible all year round via well-paved and maintained roads, it came with complete landscaping, appliances, storms, and screens. The small outbuilding in the right-rear background was a bonus—a ready-made storage place. The owner estimates that he would have had to spend at least 50 percent more than the purchase price of this structure to get an equal amount of living—and space—in a brand new home.*

grounds will be acceptably landscaped; you won't have to dig into your wallet to plant trees, shrubs, and lawns that may be needed for erosion-saving as well as for esthetic reasons.

You can consider it a bonus if the old house has a garage, or if the seller is willing to leave behind still-usable miscellaneous furnishings and yard tools.

A big advantage is that you will know exactly what the property taxes are. Unlike new construction, where you won't know your exact tax for sure until the structure is completed, a quick look at the older home's recent tax bills gives an accurate picture of what you may expect to spend for taxes now and in the future.

Mobile Homes. With a jazzier name for the camper or trailer of yesteryear, mobile homes are the fastest way to get into a *new* vacation home. Fully built at the factory (finished inside and out), the mobile home is rolled to your site on wheels and placed upon foundation piers.

Its big advantages are flexibility and price.

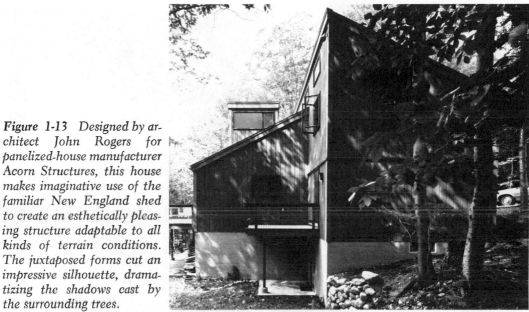

Figure 1-13 *Designed by architect John Rogers for panelized-house manufacturer Acorn Structures, this house makes imaginative use of the familiar New England shed to create an esthetically pleasing structure adaptable to all kinds of terrain conditions. The juxtaposed forms cut an impressive silhouette, dramatizing the shadows cast by the surrounding trees.*

Figure 1-14 *Treetop viewing is a luxury gained with the lookout perched above the shed adjacent to the decking. Because of this feature, the home is aptly called the "Crow's Nest."*

Figure 1-15 A bold, angular inside design lends itself ideally to contemporary living. The shed-type construction blends comfortably with modern, easy-to-care-for furniture.

Figure 1-16 Living room activity centers around the fireplace constructed of used brick. The mood is dramatized by the wall paneled with used barn-siding.

You are, first of all, almost completely flexible as to where you live. You can, if you desire, simply rent property in a mobile home park, relocating in different areas from time to time. The moves are not cheap because you may have to hire help at both ends to lift the home on and off foundations. In all likelihood, you will also prefer to hire a trucker to do the over-the-road hauling as well.

The complete-package price, however, is what makes the mobile home an attractive buy for many. They sell for anywhere from $4,000 at the low end, to about $18,000 for a luxury version. Prices for mobile homes include the works: you get kitchen appliances, basic furniture, and carpeting on the floor. Square footage of the mobile homes varies. Some as small as 650 square feet are available, and dwellings up to about 1,400 square feet can also be found. Considering the lifestyle you get for the cost, mobile homes are a good buy.

But, there are disadvantages too.

First, the home size perfectly acceptable for a childless couple could be a living nightmare for a young family with two or three energetic youngsters.

Figure 1-17 *For many second-home owners, a deck is a must. Here, it is installed at the rear of the house beneath the Crow's Nest.*

The feeling is crowded, and there is just no room for spreading out—unless you buy a second mobile home and attach it to the first. If yours is a growing family, make certain before buying that you carefully evaluate your family's needs when it comes to privacy.

The second big disadvantage is that, in many leisure-home areas, mobile homes are not welcome. In fact, some communities have laws preventing their use. Thus, if you already own land, you should ascertain whether or not you will be able to park a mobile home on it.

Rear Elevation

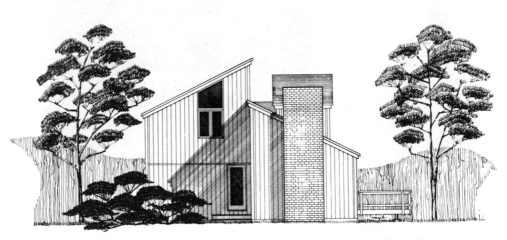

Right Elevation

Figure 1-18 *A well-designed house is suited to any environment; like many second homes, its exterior is finished with wood siding (treated with clear preservative) and left to weather naturally. The exterior walls and roofs of Acorn Structures come fully insulated.*

Roughing It. Some couples—knowing that they won't have the funds to build with for several years—still buy land as soon as they can swing it financially. Carrying costs are generally low because in rural areas taxes on unimproved properties are traditionally moderate. Such a move lets you get the piece of ground you have your heart set on before it is snatched up by another buyer.

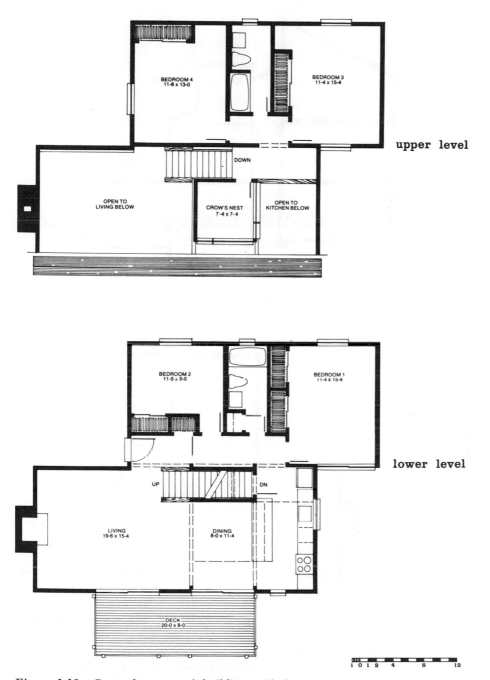

upper level

lower level

Figure 1-19 *One advantage of building with house parts, over a house completely finished at the factory, is the flexibility of design changes. Walls can be relocated to customize a dwelling to suit personal needs and preferences. The floor plan shown is one version recommended by the maker.*

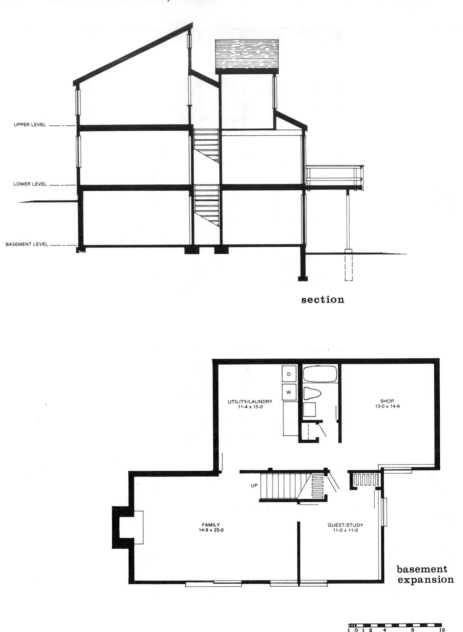

section

basement expansion

Crow's Nest House Manufactured by Acorn Structures, Inc.

Figure 1-20 *Though the Crow's Nest is equally comfortable perched atop a wind swept sand dune, its design lends itself particularly well to hilly terrain. Ingress/egress at the basement level is through a pair of sliding doors located in the family room. As do most manufactured-home firms, Acorn Structures limits house shipments to one section of the United States; its homes are available only in the northeast.*

The usual course is to eliminate vacations that cost a great deal so that cash can be put aside in a house-building fund. For vacations, the family usually erects a tent or parks a rented camper on their piece of ground. Often, if the owner plans to build the house himself, construction work progresses during these vacation and weekend stays. Generally, the entire family pitches in; rarely does Pop go it alone these days.

You should first acquire a generator for powering lights, appliances, and power tools; then install a waste disposal system (a septic tank). Next, the water well would be driven so your needs can be taken care of without bothering the neighbors (who might be miles down the road anyway).

A sensible course is to build the garage during the first summer, using it for living quarters until the house itself is completed. With a little planning, the investment you make in kitchen and bath facilities in the garage won't be wasted. Many house plans make that portion of the garage containing these fixtures a permanent guest area. Scores of plans are also available for expandable homes—homes that start small and grow according to your needs. These are shown in detail in Chapter 4.

Ward Cabin Company.

Figure 1-21　*The popularity of log cabins, similar to those our ancestors lived in, is on the increase. Today's cabin, of course, boasts all the modern amenities—it's the look outside that appeals to romantics. This model comes precut and ready for assembly on the owner-poured foundation.*

THAT CERTAINTY—TAXES

It is important to thoroughly analyze the local property tax picture, especially if you intend to retire to your leisure home. Do this for each site under consideration. Now, while you are still working, any periodic increases in property taxes are offset and absorbed by higher earnings. But later, on a fixed income, you could get priced out of the area, if taxes are on the high side or if they have been rising steadily in recent years.

Check the history of the local taxes. Through conversations with local merchants, bankers, real estate agents, and native residents, try to determine what the long-range plans are for the area. Will things remain pretty much as they are? Or are changes in local ordinances in the works? Is cluster housing (condominiums, apartments, and single residences on small plots) permitted? Find out, if possible, whether light or heavy industry is destined to invade the area. If so, it will mean more homes, which in turn demand the expansion and staffing of additional educational facilities. If this happens, taxes will be raised to pay the bills.

An invasion of industry can also change the face of the area. New roads may have to be built, or existing roads widened. If more land is paved and covered with buildings, will the area retain the charm that lured you there in the first place?

The obvious conclusion to be reached—based upon the material discussed in this chapter—is that there are many facets to building or buying a second home. To assure getting the most leisure house for your money, it is a must that you be in the position to make the best possible decisions as problems arise. How to get top value for your efforts and investment is discussed in the next chapter.

2

Getting Financial Help

The home-building picture in the mid-seventies was a bleak one.

Nationally, residential housing starts dropped 30 percent from 1973 to 1974. And, according to estimates from various sources, the average price of a single-family dwelling rose 10 to 20 percent between June 1973 and June 1974.

At the same time, mortgage ceilings across the country crept slowly upward: In New York, the rate was hiked to a then-record 8½ percent; in New Jersey, the ceiling was established at 9 percent. In all likelihood, we haven't seen the end. In April 1974, the rates of FHA-insured mortgages were upped to 9 percent (from 8½ percent). Some bullish economists are not ruling out 12 percent rates in the not-too-distant future.

The problems are obvious, but the solutions aren't. Traditionally savings and loan associations have paved the way to home-building with accessible mortgages and equitable interest rates, but they have had serious problems of their own, particularly with depleted mortgage money pools. Investors withdrew savings in record amounts, bankers claim, to try their hands at higher-yielding investments.

On the other hand, some of the nation's top economists have predicted that mortgage money will again be plentiful, reckoning that lower earnings on other investments would channel money back into the savings and loan associations—thus back into the mortgage pool.

PLANNING WHAT A SECOND HOME WILL COST

The Land. Though there are still some leisure properties in desirable areas selling for $200 to $500 per acre, the plot you will want will more likely cost $5,000 to $10,000—or even more.

Cost of Construction. The house itself, of course, is the single biggest cost factor, and its price can vary considerably depending on what you want in it and how you construct it. Though building costs vary slightly from one area to the next, you should assume for estimating purposes that it will cost you approximately $35 per square foot of living space to have a contractor erect a stick-built house. By selecting a factory-made house, you can knock that figure down to about $25 per square foot. If you build the house yourself, your cost per square foot will be somewhere around $15 to $20. Thus, if you need a house with 1,000 square feet of living space, you can realistically expect to pay about $35,000 to a contractor, $25,000 for a prefab version, or $15,000 to $20,000 for a do-it-yourself job.

These figures do not allow for any extras or fancy features. Plush extras—perhaps a sauna, sunken bathtub, or swimming pool—will cost you plenty. Similarly, any departure from the architect's plans, or from standard building practices, into the heady world of custom building, is a surefire way to push your building costs into the stratosphere.

Keeping Up the Place. Don't overlook or minimize upkeep and maintenance chores either—such chores as painting, lawn maintenance, boat upkeep, snow removal, and raking and bagging of leaves each fall. They can become costly if you pay to have them done by local service people, and you should make certain your estimated budget includes these carrying charges.

A few years ago, a couple bought slightly more than one acre in an area abundant with deciduous shade trees. Though the husband enjoys the leafy shade during the hot months, he will go to almost any extreme to avoid raking the leaves once they have dropped. At the end of their first summer, he unhesitatingly called in a local nurseryman to attend to yard cleanup. He was shocked when he received a three-figure bill for the services; unfortunately, he hadn't budgeted for such maintenance assists. As a result, every autumn since, his wife can be found doing the raking and bagging of leaves. His miscalculation is now costing her.

Panelized house: Built in a factory, assembled on your lot . . .

Figure 2-1 Not all prefabs have to look alike. This dwelling, called Mountain Haus, can be varied by adding to or subtracting from the number of modules used. The house shown consists of four 12' × 14' modules.

The Cost of Getting There. An important cost item, often overlooked or minimized by second-home buyers, is the cost of transportation between their two homes. If the family is going to stay the summer at the second home, the head of the family may need a second car, if public transportation in the vacation area is not adequate or available. Regardless of the mode of travel, the trip is going to cost. When using your auto, don't look at gas and oil as your only costs. You may also have to shell out for highway and bridge tolls, plus the cost of snacks if the journey is of a duration that justifies stopping for supper or a cup of coffee. The increase in annual mileage not only shortens the lifespan of your car, but can also up the cost of your car insurance.

FIGURING WHAT YOU CAN CARRY

Once you have set aside enough cash for the down payment, you should try to come up with an honest estimate of the monthly cost to carry the place. As an example, let's assume that you have decided to buy or build a $30,000 house with a $10,000 down payment and a $20,000 mortgage. We will also assume that your mortgage is a reasonable one by today's standards —15 years at 8½ percent. A quick look at Table 2–1 shows your monthly mortgage payment to be $196.95.

But the expenses don't stop there. More realistically, your monthly outlay will probably look something like this:

* Mortgage payment	$197
* Property tax	25
* House insurance	8
* Utilities	20
* Heat	15 *
* Escrow fund for maintenance	40 **
* Transportation	40 †
* Extras: entertaining, telephone, club or association memberships	$ 50 ‡

* Varies from area to area.
** Based upon about $500 per year.
† Varies depending upon distance and mode of travel.
†† Depends upon lifestyle.

What was to be a modest little place of escape will probably cost you a not-so-modest $395 per month—almost $5,000 a year. Can you afford it?

Obviously, the single biggest item is the mortgage payment. Thus it is to your advantage to borrow as little money as possible, and it's apparent that the less you have to borrow, the easier your payments will be. In broad terms, there are three basic ways to keep your mortgage payments down:

1. Be content with less. Be realistic about what you can afford. Establish a budget and stay within it.
2. Put off buying for a year or so, and increase the amount you are squirreling away so you will have a heftier down payment.
3. Start modestly and improve what you have as you can afford to do so on a cash basis. Begin with an expandable, modest home that lets you start using your vacation property quickly.

Hidden Costs—the Way You'll Live. When picking an area to settle in, make certain you check out the community's lifestyle: Does it coincide with

TABLE 2-1: MONTHLY MORTGAGE PAYMENTS *

Amount of mortgage	Amount per month over 10 years			
	8%	8 ½ %	9%	10%
$10,000	$121.33	$123.99	$126.68	$132.16
$15,000	182.00	185.98	190.02	198.23
$20,000	242.66	247.98	253.36	264.31
$25,000	303.32	309.97	316.69	330.38
$30,000	363.99	371.96	380.03	396.46
$35,000	424.65	433.95	443.37	462.53
$40,000	485.32	495.95	506.71	528.61

Amount of mortgage	Amount per month over 15 years			
	8%	8 ½ %	9%	10%
$10,000	$ 95.57	$ 98.48	$101.43	$107.47
$15,000	143.35	147.72	152.14	161.20
$20,000	191.14	196.95	202.86	214.93
$25,000	238.92	246.19	253.57	268.66
$30,000	286.70	295.43	304.28	322.39
$35,000	334.48	344.66	355.00	376.12
$40,000	382.27	393.90	405.71	429.85

Amount of mortgage	Amount per month over 20 years			
	8%	8 ½ %	9%	10%
$10,000	$ 83.65	$ 86.79	$ 89.98	$ 96.51
$15,000	125.47	130.18	134.96	144.76
$20,000	167.29	173.57	179.95	193.01
$25,000	209.12	216.96	224.94	241.26
$30,000	250.94	260.35	269.92	289.51
$35,000	292.76	303.74	314.91	337.76
$40,000	334.58	347.13	359.90	386.01

* Typical monthly repayment schedules are for different self-amortizing mortgages with various interest rates, principals, and terms. The monthly installments do not include fire insurance premiums or any real estate taxes, although it is a common banking practice today to add these figures on to the monthly mortgage charge, rather than leaving them for separate payment by the homeowner.

Mountain Haus, Vacation Land Homes, Inc.

Figure 2-2 Quality prefabs are designed to blend with almost any site and location. Here, a four-module house, with a crawlspace foundation and reverse board-and-batten siding, sells for about $27,000 complete—exclusive of lot. The cost includes a well and septic system allowance.

your way of life? Often, for an accurate appraisal, it pays to rent a home for a season or two. In many communities, for example, constant partying is the pastime. For a failure to recognize and participate in this scene, you're almost certain to be ostracized. In such areas, you simply won't make it unless you host your share of cocktail parties, join the country club (for which you may have no need), buy a boat, or engage in whatever the local customs demand. Careful observation reveals that many vacation communities are dotted with rundown, poorly maintained homes because the owners are spending all they have to keep pace with their social obligations.

Beware the Freeloaders. If the experience of veteran second-home owners is any criterion, soon after moving into your vacation retreat you may expect a plethora of uninvited house guests. Unfortunately, once you are comfortably settled in your snug home by the lake or shore, scores of friends and relatives (who had "other commitments" while the work was going on) will be eager to help you enjoy what you've built. And these unexpected visits can cost a great deal more than you might suspect.

As the host, you will foot the bills for the food and drink and, very often, for the fees charged for the use of community or private recreational facilities.

Figure 2-3   Inside the house, it is warm and cozy, boasting fully insulated walls clad with prefinished paneling.

Figure 2-4   Appliances and electrical fixtures come in the package too. Although the quality of the hardware has a direct bearing on the house's total price, most buyers stick with the equipment offered by the manufacturer.

Often, club rules allow only the member (you) to sign the tab. Unless money is no object—and make no mistake about it—a visiting family of four or more can create havoc with your weekly budget.

Set the record straight—from the outset—as to just what your house rules for guests are. Many experienced second-home owners make it clear that overnight (and longer) visits are by advance invitation only. If your weekly budget is tight, but you want certain friends and relatives to spend some time with you each summer, openly discuss just what you expect your guests to chip in, or pay, for. Your real friends will insist upon kicking in anyway, and it is only right that you give them an accurate and reasonable figure. Those that are offended by such directness shouldn't be missed at all.

WAYS TO BUY A SECOND HOME

Of course, it is important to consider carefully just how you will pay for your leisure home. Though some families still build homes on a cash basis, they are the exception rather than the rule. Most of us—without a fat inheritance or a lucky lottery ticket—simply do not have the out-of-pocket resources to buy or build.

Joint Ownership. For many, second-home ownership is made possible only through joint buying: Relatives or even close friends get together and pool their assets to make the purchase. For a number of reasons, this approach may be impossible for some families. Maybe the youngsters in the families don't get along—even though their parents are the closest of friends. Or perhaps opinions on where to locate are in sharp contrast: One family prefers the shore; the other, lake property.

If joint ownership seems advantageous for you, work out all the details regarding usage, financing, and legal matters before consummating the purchase. It should be decided when each family will use the dwelling, for how long, and the condition that the property is to be left in when each family departs. Responsibility must also be delegated for various maintenance and upkeep chores, or decisions reached on the payment of fees for service people. You must also determine how the title to the property is to be taken. Consult with your attorney and follow his recommendations on how to proceed.

The biggest problem with two-family ownership seems to be disagreement on house management. Differences and disputes may range from cleaning up after dinner to how much time and money should go into maintenance, upkeep, and improving the house. If you decide to get into your second home sooner through joint-ownership, be ready to relinquish a certain amount of privacy and decision-making.

Another way to buy jointly is for two or more couples to band together and purchase a large tract of land. After the purchase, the land is subdivided to give each couple a plot of similar value. The advantage, of course, is that the price per acre is considerably cheaper when a large parcel is bought.

The important thing to check here is the local building code. Make certain that, if your group does buy a piece of land, each of you will be able to build upon the subdivided parcel.

Another point to remember is that owning a large tract of virgin forest, or flat farmland, means you will have to come up with the money to install paved roads and adequate storm drainage.

Consider Renting. If two-party ownership is out of the question for you, but money is tight, consider seasonal rental of your property. If your place is within a two-hour commute—by public transportation as well as by auto— you should be able to rent out the property for a month or so each season. Of course, you lose the use of your place during the rental period, but for many this is a cheap price to pay for sole ownership.

Some second-home owners are lucky enough to be able to rent their places during the off-season. Generally, off-season renters consist of teachers and executives from a nearby university, college, or corporate training program office. If you are blessed with such a possibility, you may be able to earn rental income on your leisure home and still enjoy it during the seasonal months.

Have a Rental Agreement. If you do decide to rent, have your attorney draw up a model lease, spelling out clearly who is entitled to live on the premises during the tenant's occupancy. Many seasonal landlords have had the unhappy experience of renting to an individual or couple—only to find that it is the tenant's practice to invite a half-dozen or more friends to "their" place each weekend, or to sub-lease to a half-dozen or so others. Such traffic—called "groupers" these days—takes its toll on the structure. You pay for the repairs and upkeep.

There are other important points about renting. First, make certain that the area where you plan to buy or build permits rentals. Even though it is perfectly legal to rent in some areas, you may find neighbors who hope to discourage the practice by frowning upon it. If you disregard such attitudes and rent anyway, hostile feelings—with you at the butt end—could result.

Finally, you should discuss your plans of occasional renting with the institution that will hold the mortgage. The lending institution should know and approve of the rental idea, because there may be a clause in your mortgage agreement forbidding the practice.

THE INS AND OUTS OF FINANCING

Money is a commodity. The price we pay for borrowed money—interest—is determined partially by supply and demand and partially as a result of the Federal Reserve Bank's estimate of economic conditions. When people don't deposit part of their incomes in the bank, the money available for loans is quickly depleted. Money is said to be "tight." If the demand is brisk, rates will be high. If and when money is ample, the rates drop correspondingly, usually with the Federal Reserve rates acting as a barometer. In the mid-seventies, to say that money was difficult to come by was to border on understatement. But taking the inflationary seventies into perspective, they constitute simply one more "hard time," another swing of the economic pendulum.

No matter what type of financing you decide to use, the money lender will probably take these three steps:

1. A credit check will be made on you to determine your credit rating.
2. An appraisal, or evaluation, of the property you plan to buy will be conducted to learn if the price is a fair one.
3. The lender may or may not verify your employment.

Credit Check. The bank's check of your credit standing is to determine your record of bill payments. If your record shows you pay your bills only after several notices, or as a result of continued hounding, you will be passed by. An A-1 rating means that you pay your bills promptly and in full.

Besides having an A-1 credit rating, you should plan on having enough cash for a 30- to 40-percent down payment. Though most banks will lend up to 90 percent of the purchase price of a primary-home, it's a different ball game with second homes: The general rule is to lend 60 percent, and in some cases 70 percent. You must supply the difference.

Those who plan to build sometimes prefer to buy the property outright for cash and use it as collateral to obtain a mortgage. But the cash percentage still has to equal at least 30 percent. For example, if you buy a piece of ground for $10,000, and plan to erect a $30,000 house, your investment equals only 25 percent of the total value ($40,000). Thus, you may expect a request from the bank to come up with at least five percent ($2,000) more.

The Appraisal. Appointed by the bank, the appraiser (a local real estate and building expert whose experience can be depended upon) determines the property's true value. To do so, he checks the quality of construction, local codes and ordinances, and the area in general.

What the appraiser concludes can benefit you as well as the bank. For example, suppose you're ready to put up $15,000 cash for a $40,000 home; you've requested a $25,000 mortgage, but the house is appraised at $35,000. *You* have to add another $5,000 to the down payment, because the lending institution will not put in cash beyond the property's value. (If this situation arises, your best bet is to either negotiate a new purchase price with the seller, or look elsewhere.) By the same token, if the house appraises higher than the seller's asking price, the lending institution will lend you the money, and you make an instant paper profit.

Verification of Employment. Basically, this is done to check out two points:

1. your reliability (i.e., length of employment and prospect of continued employment), and
2. whether you earn enough to carry the mortgage payments.

WHERE TO GET MONEY

Once you have enough cash for the down payment, you have to find a lender who will advance the balance of the purchase price. Stated simply, the idea is to get your hands on a large sum of money that you can repay over a period of years, usually in monthly installments. In broad terms, there are seven basic ways an individual can finance second-home construction:

1. a mortgage,
2. a loan on a life insurance policy,
3. a personal loan,
4. refinancing of the mortgage on your primary home,
5. a second mortgage,
6. a mortgage arrangement directly with the seller, or

7. a builder's mortgage until completion, when you can convert to a conventional mortgage.

A Mortgage. Financing a second home is an example of money begetting money: The more cash you can afford to sink into the venture, the easier it is to get your hands on mortgage money.

Basically, the same principles that apply to the mortgage on your first home apply to the mortgage on your leisure home. But be aware that there are some important differences.

The primary difference is that you will be required to come up with a larger down payment—probably at least 30 percent of the purchase price.

Your best bet is to obtain a mortgage from a local bank, rather than from the bank at home where you usually do business. The local institution is familiar with the area, its land values, and the building codes and ordinances. It also has an interest in solid growth and development of the area and is therefore more inclined to give a mortgage with terms more favorable to the borrower. It can also offer valuable counseling and services to the borrower.

On the personal side, since you will soon become a member of that community, it pays to have a good financial contact close at hand should you ever want to expand the dwelling or buy additional property.

In general, it is easier to obtain a mortgage in a leisure-home development than it is for an isolated dwelling. For a development, the builder has probably arranged for financing, and you need only meet the requirements for eligibility. When it comes to financing do-it-yourself ventures, however, most banks are gun shy. You shouldn't be surprised by such a reaction. If something happens to the do-it-yourselfer, for instance, who completes the house? Though it is not likely that you'll get a mortgage on a do-it-yourself project, such considerations as financial position, personal contacts, and the kind of life insurance you carry might alter the bank's thinking.

You will also find that for certain types of leisure homes, such as houseboats, mobile homes, and dwellings in high-risk areas, you will not be able to secure a mortgage at all. Happily, most manufacturers of the first two types of homes have plans for financing, or are able to help you secure money from a lending institution. But payments are usually steep because the notes generally run for five years or less. Homes in high-risk areas, such as a parcel of oceanfront property, usually have to be financed entirely by the homeowner.

Many banks also frown upon lending money for the land purchase, although personal circumstance can alter this situation too. A bank, however, will probably not advance cash to help you buy a piece of unimproved ground, the feeling being that, if you can't afford to make the land purchase on your own, you are probably in over your head anyway.

Leisure-home mortgages also differ from primary-home mortgages in length. Most banks give shorter-term mortgages on leisure homes. Chances are, your first home is financed with a mortgage of 25 or 30 years' duration, whereas the typical leisure home note is for 15 years. Consider yourself lucky if your bank is willing to extend it to 20 years. The shorter life of the mortgage means, of course, that your monthly payments will be higher.

In all probability, there will also be a slight difference in the interest rate too. You can expect to pay at least 1 percent more than you would pay for the same money if used to purchase a primary home. Currently, mortgage interest rates are going at 8 to 10 percent. Don't be surprised if that bank "in the sticks" asks for 9 to 11 percent to mortgage your place in the country.

If at all possible, try to arrange your loan when money is not unduly tight, thus cheaper. A fraction of a percentage point, every month, can add up to a considerable amount over 180 or 240 installments.

The best money lenders to consider turning to for mortgage money are savings and loan associations, savings banks, commercial banks, and life insurance companies—all listed in the phone book. In general, you will find that commercial sources are quicker and less formal to deal with than other money lenders.

SOME MORTGAGE FEATURES
TO LOOK FOR

Prepayment Clause. If possible, try to obtain a loan contract with a clause that lets you prepay the loan at any time without penalty. The advantage is obvious: If and when a more favorable loan situation arises, you can take action immediately to refinance at lower interest rates and pay off the first note.

Open-end Mortgages. The open-end mortgage is desirable in that, with it, you can borrow money (later on) up to the value of the original mortgage. For example, if you have lived in your house for 10 years and paid $10,000 against the principal, you can borrow that $10,000 again to finance a remodeling job or an addition to the house.

The new loan, depending upon the terms, will either increase your monthly payments or extend the life of the mortgage.

Package Mortgage. Where these are legal, they are worth consideration. A package mortgage may cover not only the house and lot, but several of the major appliances, carpeting, storm windows, and the like. But keep in mind that, with the payment of interest over the term of the mortgage, the cost of the items will be much greater than what you would have paid in cash. Also, the useful life of the mortgaged items usually runs out long before the loan is paid. For example, if you must buy another refrigerator with five years remaining on the loan, you will, in effect, be paying for two appliances—one of which is no longer in use.

Of course, if a package mortgage is the only way you can get what you want in a home, then the advantages and desirability of doing so have to be weighed against the total extra costs.

Borrowing on Your Life Insurance. If your policy has a loan value, this is an easy way to obtain financial assistance. Some life insurance policies offer rates as low as 5½ or 6 percent against your built-up cash value; others are considerably higher. There are a couple of advantages here: (1) the money is easy to obtain—because the insurance company doesn't care what you do with the money—and (2) you don't have to make monthly payments.

Frequently these advantages backfire to become, in effect, disadvantages. Many borrowers fail to make payments to reduce the outstanding loan balance, thus reducing the face value of the policy. You may actually wipe out what insurance protection you think you have in this manner.

Most of us also find it easy to skip the interest payments on such notes. Again, this doesn't bother the insurance companies. After the stipulated grace period, the interest amount is simply added to the outstanding loan balance (the principal). You are then paying interest on interest, and thus enhancing the profit picture of the insurance company.

If you have the self-discipline to make periodic payments to reduce the principal, an insurance loan can be a good financing route to follow. Lacking this control, you are better off using one of the alternative methods of financing.

A Personal Loan. Provided you don't need a large loan, this is a good way to raise funds. The amount you can borrow varies from state to state, limited by state laws. The money is borrowed on a personal note from a commercial bank, savings and loan institution, or credit union.

You should consider several facts concerning personal loans. First, you will need an A-1 credit rating, and the money will probably have to be paid back in two to eight years, depending upon the terms of the loan. Further, the interest rate is higher than that for a conventional mortgage, usually somewhere around 12 or 14 percent. Finally, the note will probably be discounted, meaning that the interest will be deducted in advance from the amount you borrow. For example, to borrow $5,000 for five years, you will have to actually sign a note for about $6,000.

Refinancing Your Present Mortgage. When you refinance your house, you actually create a new mortgage. In the transaction, you repay the original amount in full and enter into a separate long-term commitment for the new total at current interest rates. The equity in your first home becomes the collateral for the new mortgage. In all likelihood, the equity you have in your first home represents a larger nest egg than you realize.

The equity in your house is the difference between what you owe on the real estate and what it is worth on today's market. For example, suppose you have $15,000 left to pay on your mortgage for a home on which you originally made a $10,000 down payment. Assuming you could sell the home for, say, $35,000, you would have $20,000 equity in the home ($35,000 minus $15,000). Note that the equity includes not only your down payment, but the appreciation in market value. Even if you bought quite recently, the equity may have increased substantially by reason of improvements you may have made, inflation in general, and mortgage money shortages.

There are two advantages in refinancing:

1. You can do with the money pretty much as you please. The bank has your first home as security and doesn't care what kind of vacation home you build or in what area it goes up.

2. You can often arrange for a longer repayment period. This, of course, lowers the payment amount and, you, happily, have two houses on one note.

The biggest disadvantage is in dollars and cents. Refinancing ultimately costs more—you pay back many more dollars of interest. When you remortgage, you pay the current, invariably higher interest rates; you might be swapping a 6½ percent loan for one that is costing you 8 or 9 percent or more. Unless money is no object, professional money lenders advise against surrendering a low interest rate for a higher one.

Placing a Second Mortgage. In a second mortgage, often called a *homeowner* or *equity* loan, you also pledge the equity in your property as collateral. It differs from refinancing in that it is a separate loan on top of your primary mortgage. In the event of default, the claim of the second mortgager comes after that of the primary mortgager.

(Incidentally, there's no need to suffer any embarrassment because of a second mortgage; it does not mean a family is in debt up to the ears. It is, in fact, one of the more flexible resources for large loans, and its use is growing in popularity and availability.)

A second mortgage is limited to a percentage of the equity you have in your first home. Some lenders loan up to 75 percent of equity, others go up to 100 percent or even more. How much you will be able to borrow depends upon your credit rating, the borrower's philosophy, and the condition of your real estate.

One advantage of a second mortgage is that you can repay on any mutually agreeable schedule, thus creating significant savings on interest when compared to refinancing. Keep in mind that the faster you repay your second mortgage, the greater the savings you'll enjoy. Also, the cost of obtaining the second loan is almost nonexistent.

The main disadvantage of second mortgages is that they generally involve interest rates higher than for first mortgages, because the second note usually represents a greater risk. Although most second-mortgage money is available through regulated agencies, including banks, sometimes the seller will carry a second mortgage himself. If this setup is available to you, it may eliminate the need to borrow on your present real estate. Often developers of vacation home communities give second mortgages just so you can make the purchase to begin with. In effect, they are lending back the cash for you to use as your down payment. At the closing, along with the commitment for the first mortgage, you will be presented with the payment schedule for your second mortgage—usually for a term from one to five years and at a whopping 18- to 20-percent interest rate.

Be aware, though, that some "low monthly payments" loans conceal a *balloon payment provision.* In short, you are committed to pay off one or more huge sums of money near the end of the contract. A balloon clause should be avoided by most people, since it would likely create future financial problems.

A second mortgage is a risky way to enter into second home ownership. You will have two notes to pay each month. If you need this much help to get into your second home, take another long, hard look at your financial position. Realistically, you probably should not be considering the buy in the first place. In fact, second mortgages are recommended for short-term use only—perhaps to bridge the gap between the purchase and a lump-sum settlement of an estate or other windfall. You must be able to pay back the note *effortlessly* and in a relatively short period of time.

A Financing Arrangement with the Seller. Often, the seller is more than happy to take back the mortgage on the transacted property. His main reason, usually, is to spread out his income from sale of the property over a number of years to keep his income tax down.

This arrangement is fine provided the seller's loan conditions are the same as those offered by the local bank. If you are shopping for a leisure home in a vacation community where this practice is fairly common, check out the offering against what the local banks will give on the same house. The seller's interest rates should be equivalent to the bank's, and the term of the mortgage should be a reasonable 15 or 20 years—not five years or less.

Generally speaking, however, borrowing from the seller costs more than borrowing from a lending institution (whose primary business is money).

A Mortgage with Construction Loan. Often called a *builder's loan,* this kind of note provides the funds for renovation or construction of the home. When the work is completed, the note converts to a conventional mortgage

a good financing arrangement when you are buying an existing home. Since the lender will want an accurate estimate of the cost of what is to be done, figures from a builder will probably be required. Your guess will not be adequate.

IDEAS FOR GETTING MORTGAGE MONEY WHEN IT'S TIGHT

To say that the availability of mortgage money is "uncertain" when the economy is in an up-and-down period borders on comic understatement. As interest rates soar, some lenders, depending upon ceilings imposed by federal and state governments, withdraw almost entirely from the mortgage market. During such periods, lenders commonly demand hefty down payments. This requirement was prevalent in the financial community in the mid-seventies.

During economic downturns, you may find the going rough when it comes to getting financial assistance. But there is hope. There are a number of potential money-lenders—mutual savings banks (in some areas), savings and loan associations, mortgage banking companies, and commercial banks. You should check out all (or, at the very least, two) of these sources for mortgage money.

Certain methods of obtaining mortgage money have been used successfully by others; and most banking experts agree that—especially in times of tight dollars—you should explore every possibility.

Get Personally Involved. Make an in-person application for the loan rather than using the mails. Since the lenders approve only a percentage of the loan applications received each month, you stand a better chance of getting the loan if you have personally impressed the lender. Assuming you pass all credit investigations, it is harder for the lender to say "no" to your face than it is by mail.

Try to Get the Loan Where You are Well Known. When money is scarce, money lenders tend to still remember their old customers. If it is against the policy of your primary bank to lend money for country real estate, perhaps it can help you deal with the local bank. The banking community is smaller than you might suspect, and a word from the big-city bank may work wonders.

Don't Hesitate to Call on Others. The seller is probably known at the local bank; if necessary, get him involved. He is just as interested as you are in the sale of the house. Also, there are others who stand to gain by your getting a mortgage: your lawyer, broker, architect, and builder, for example. Any or all of them might do business with you once you get your hands on mortgage money.

Often a well-timed call from a large depositor does the trick at a local bank.

Consider Using the Seller's Lender. Because this institution has already loaned money on the house, it is practically impossible for it to say that it doesn't approve of the house or grounds. And this lender will have to come up with less cash than any other institution. For example, suppose you plan to buy a $35,000 house with a $10,000 down payment and $25,000 mortgage. If the seller has reduced his mortgage loan to $15,000, his lender would have to supply you only $10,000 cash.

Can Your Employer Help? Often, a large corporation can supply the muscle needed to obtain a mortgage. Remember, the people in your company's comptroller's office are money experts too. Take the time to discuss your mortgage situation with them and to learn if the company can offer assistance.

Do You Have a Friend at the Bank? If so, don't underestimate the power of an individual. Banking experts say that most people have at least one friend somewhere in the money business. You may be surprised at how much leverage this friend can exert in your favor.

Put Up More Collateral. In your negotiations with the bank, don't forget your other assets—real estate, securities, life insurance cash value, and the like—as a way to obtain an otherwise impossible mortgage. Often, by using such assets as collateral or as a larger down payment, there is no problem in getting the mortgage.

Buy in a Development. Finally, buying a home in a vacation development can be far easier, financially, than going it alone. Because of their position in the financial community, large builders are able to arrange for a mortgage commitment before they turn the first spadeful of earth. If your credit record is a good one, and your income is within the prescribed formula (i.e., one week's pay should cover the monthly mortgage payment), getting the mortgage is almost a formality.

When the house leaves the factory . . .

Figure 2-5 Typical building is loaded at the factory and ready for delivery. Notice crane over-cab for on-site unloading—also used to assist with erection of wall units.

Mountain Haus, Vacation Land Homes, Inc.

Figure 2-6 The house being erected consists of three 14′ × 26′ modules formed of factory-built panels. A qualified three-man crew can complete this structure in just three days.

Mountain Haus, Vacation Land Homes, Inc.

Figure 2-7 *The truck is pulled as close as possible to the job and stabilized with outriggers to unload the second exterior wall. The foundation is erected by the owner to suit exact specifications detailed by the prefab manufacturer.*

A WORD ABOUT INTEREST . . .

Long-term lenders face the problem of charging the same interest rate over fifteen to thirty years, even though interest rates on other investments (bonds, short-term notes, and the like) gradually exceed the interest on the long-term loan. As the borrower makes more and more payments, he or she is usually paying off the debt with highly inflated (or "funny") money. Therefore, not only is the money earning less than it could elsewhere, but the money loaned (the principal) is losing worth as the result of inflation.

Thus, many financial institutions are pushing for *variable rate mortgages,* meaning the interest rates on home mortgages should be adjusted periodically—usually every four or five years. Theoretically, this system would do away with the feast-or-famine cycles typical of mortgage money since the mid-sixties. Some lenders believe that if the going interest rate—the rate determined by competition with all other demands for money—can be obtained, a steady supply of mortgage money will be available. Many also feel that adjustable interest rates would do away with the point system.

Mountain Haus, Vacation Land Homes, Inc.

Figure 2-8 *The sheathed walls are up, and a carpenter crew begins installation of ceiling joists and roof rafters.*

As to whether this will be the accepted mortgage practice in the near future, the Federal Government has the final say.

THE CLOSING

At the closing, usually at the lending institution, the loan is settled, all monies change hands, and the title is transferred to the buyer's name. It is, in effect, the consummation of the entire transaction.

When you purchase a home, there are costs other than the initial expenses that can, and do, add considerably to your down payment. Closing costs—a catch-all category including attorney fees, land survey and inspection costs, mortgage service charges (points), recording fees, and transfer taxes—must be paid in full at the settlement.

For instance, points, an integral part of the mortgage service fee, are charged when the interest rates are at the maximum set by the state and are a legal way for the lender to get extra money for his services. Make certain

Mountain Haus, Vacation Land Homes, Inc.

Figure 2-9 *The last step: windows, doors, and garage doors are slipped into place and fastened. The deck goes up last; it, too, is supplied with the house and is predetermined as to size and style.*

that the points have been reduced in accord with the present availability of mortgage money. Ask your lawyer to check this out.

Although costs can vary widely from area to area, as can the total number of services for which the buyer pays, the most common closing costs, and the fees charged for them, are listed below. The amounts are for a typical closing on a $20,000 house in 1971. This list is based upon a survey taken by the Department of Housing and Urban Development and Veterans Administration.

Title Examination (***Search***). This consists of a check through property records by the buyer's representative to determine that the seller is the legal owner of the property and that there are no encumbrances or liens against it. (A lien is a claim filed on the property by another party—usually to settle an outstanding debt.) The average cost of this service is $115.

Title Insurance. A protection policy that, in effect, guarantees to defend the buyer's claim to ownership should any claims arise against it. Frequently, the title insurer also handles the title examination, in which case one payment covers both services. Occasionally, the buyer must pay for title examination and insurance separately. The typical cost of title insurance is $150.

Land Survey. Unless your lawyer recommends otherwise, have a licensed surveyor check that the boundaries as stated in the deed are accurate. The surveyor will also check the locations of the house and other structures on the property to make certain that they are in accordance with local ordinances. Depending upon the area and the amount of property to be surveyed, you can expect to pay between $50 and $100 for a land survey.

Home Inspection. When buying an older home, have a qualified contractor or engineer make an inspection of the premises to determine the soundness of the structure itself, and the condition of the plumbing, heating, and electrical systems. Charges for such a building inspection will vary with the value of the house, but you can expect to spend between $50 and $100.

Especially when buying an old home, it makes sense to have a termite specialist make an inspection. Since the usual rate for a termite inspection is $20 to $25, it pays to have it done even for newer structures. If termites are found, the treatment should be paid for by the seller.

Attorney's Fees. The attorney in a land transaction may be selected by the bank or lending institution. But since his primary job is to represent the buyer's interest, it makes good sense to obtain separate counsel. The attorney's fee usually involves title-related activities such as the preparation of documents. Chances are, however, your relationship with the attorney will not be confined to the closing. Throughout this book, it is suggested that you confer with your counsel for answers in other areas.

Whether the attorney at the closing is retained by the buyer or the bank, the buyer pays the fee. The fee at closing will probably run in the neighborhood of $200 (1% to 1½% of purchase price), but if you have consulted your attorney on other matters as well, the fee will be adjusted upward.

Additional Costs. These can include various charges made by the bank for having performed an appraisal on the house, a credit check on the buyer, and the processing of the mortgage. Fire and life insurance premiums must also be paid to satisfy the bank, and, more often than not, various notary and recording fees must be met by the buyer.

You have to square away the property taxes with the seller as well. If the seller has already paid the taxes for the year in full, you will have to pay him a prorated share. Further, if the seller has left heating fuel in the tank, this too is measured and paid for by the buyer.

It is not unusual for these additional costs alone to amount to several hundred dollars.

Total closing costs of $500 are not uncommon on a $20,000 house. If you have any questions regarding exact amounts, question the charges levied by the bank before you pay them; you may be able to save yourself some money.

For instance, if there has been a recent land survey, termite inspection, or both, you do not want to pay for an unnecessary duplication of these services.

Under no circumstances should you attempt to represent yourself at a closing. Your attorney's presence is a must.

As we have seen, there are many ways to obtain financial help. Even in times of tight money, however, loans and credit often come too easily. Self-discipline and a carefully devised budget are your only defenses against "getting in over your head." When you are considering any financial plan, be certain of your ability to make payments. Consult an accountant, if need be.

Once you have a sound financing plan, based on a *realistic* payment schedule, you are ready to look for your private Shangri-La.

3

Finding Your Shangri-La

Since the boom in vacation home buying is certain to continue in the
foreseeable future, you can anticipate some difficulty finding the land that
will satisfy your needs exactly. Demand has pushed land prices upward at an
alarming rate. In fact, it is not unusual to find land located within two hours
of an urban center selling for $15,000 or more per acre.

Basically, there are two types of land you can buy: unimproved and
ready-to-build. The first type is ground that hasn't been touched by man. In
all likelihood, it is covered with virgin forest that you must clear away before
you can build. The second type is generally found in vacation community
developments or in rural areas where farms have been subdivided into plots
for residential use. Before buying either kind, you must first determine
whether or not the land is "buildable" property: That is, if you buy, will you
be able to build your house on the land and install the sewage disposal system
necessary for it?

ISOLATED OR COMMUNITY LIVING?

Once you have ascertained that the property is usable, there are other factors to be considered before plunking down cash for real estate. Though most of us want a leisure home in order to enjoy the quiet life, few want to lead the life of a hermit—for economical, recreational, and emotional reasons.

If your aim is to find yourself a peaceful spot for periodic returns to nature, you will not likely find it in a commercially developed area. But living off by yourself frequently creates expenses not found in community living. For instance, you will have to dig, drill, or drive a water well, instead of simply hooking up to the local water company's line. This can cost upward of $1,000. The electrical hookup can cost better than a thousand too, if you have to ask the utility company to bring power into a presently unserviced area. Finally, you'll have to make provisions for sewage and install a septic tank and field—adding at least another $1,500 or so to your costs.

Further, if you enjoy an afternoon in a boat or other solitary activities, an isolated place may be what you are looking for. But what about the family? Do they enjoy more social activities?

Even more importantly, if you or your family members are socially inclined, a week—or even a weekend—under the same roof with "nothing to do" could result in boredom and eventual bickering. A sound appraisal of your personal and family needs may avert such problems.

Settling in a planned vacation community may eliminate many of these potential problems and expenses, but, again, you should make certain that the community's lifestyle is what you all want. Some areas are very heavy on social activities, while the use of surrounding natural facilities is deemphasized or, as I have seen in some areas, completely ignored. In extreme cases, the community can become a virtual commune. Be aware that to be happy in a planned community, you should want the type of living that exists there. In general, carefully check the scene before you buy. Pulling out of an undesirable situation can be discouraging and costly.

PICKING THE AREA THAT SUITS YOU BEST

Before you can zero in on the perfect plot, you must, of course, decide which general area can best fulfill you and your family's recreational needs. Early in the game you have to decide what kind of activities your family wants the most, and how far they are willing to travel for them. It is pointless to find a site "that couldn't be better," if it means excessive travel to the golf, swimming, tennis, or other recreational pursuits that interest you most.

Although many second-home owners are willing to travel up to 200 miles to reach their second homes, the majority prefer to locate within 100 miles of their first homes. The reasons are obvious. Even with today's superhighways, it takes about two hours to travel 100 miles once you have left congested city streets. And, usually, two hours is the limit for a couple of restless youngsters in the back seat. Also, if you can buy or build your leisure home within a reasonable distance of your primary home, you stand to get more use from it. The family may stay at the summer place for the entire summer, while the working member commutes via public transportation for weekend stays. Often, an overnight trip during the work week is possible, if the breadwinner can steal away from the office an hour or two earlier than usual to make the break to the country.

So before piling into the car to start the hunt, sit down and compose a list of your family's preferred activities. Let each member of the family have a say in this discussion; now is the time to decide just what activities have top priorities. When all preferences are listed, rearrange the entries so that the most-wanted facilities are at the top; activities of diminishing importance should be farther and farther down the list. Some sacrifice may be necessary and, if it is, those recreational activities that interest the family least should be the first to go.

Next, use a compass to draw a circle on a map of your area. Your primary home should be at the center of the circle, and the radius should be equal to the maximum distance your family agrees to travel. Remember, of course, that the radius may not be perfectly accurate in traveling *time* all the way around the circle. The availability of high-speed highways, traffic congestion, topographical features and public transportation, among other things, may speed up or delay travel in different directions. Now, within that circle, zero-in on those areas that provide most, if not all, of the recreational facilities important to your family.

WHERE NOT TO LOOK FOR LAND

If public lands fall within your circle, forget them. You can discard the notion that Federal lands are a ready source for a building site. According to the U.S. Department of Agriculture's 1973 *Handbook for the Home*, "forget about a mining site unless you are a bonafide miner. There's little chance of staking out a mining claim and building a cozy cabin while you pretend to find gold. The U.S. Mining laws require legal proof of a valid claim before a mining patent can be granted; building occupancy of non-patented lands is illegal."

As it stands now, neither will the U.S. Forest Service lease private recreational sites in the National Forest System. A few unoccupied lots may be available in some already established residential tracts, but you will have to search these out.

Beware of any firm that advertises having agents with a "connection" who can give help in acquiring Federal lands. Generally, such agents are exploiting the myth that abandoned mining claims are available. Because of reports of high-pressure tactics, as of 1969 Congress requires that developers file a Statement of Record and furnish the buyer with an approved Property Report before a contract is signed. Your lawyer can advise you on this.

HOW TO LOOK FOR YOUR PIECE OF PROPERTY

Finding just the right spot can be a wearying chore, but you can take steps to make the task easier. Basically, there are four approaches to buying second-home property. In some cases, the methods overlap each other slightly; in general, however, they come under these headings:

1. Work through real estate agents.
2. Place an advertisement in the local newspaper.
3. At the same time, scan the local paper's classified ads for house sales.
4. Search and negotiate.

Real Estate Agents. For your protection, you should use only those realtors who are members either of the local real estate board or of the National Association of the Real Estate Boards (NAREB).

Discuss in detail with the broker exactly what kind of property you are looking for and precisely what you are willing to spend for it. With the assurance that you are, in fact, intent on purchasing—and not just window shopping—he will be on the alert for you. When he believes he has found what you are looking for, he will contact you. If, after a call or two, he finds that you fail to show for a site inspection, he will validly suspect that you are just a "looker," not a serious buyer. By the same token, the agent should not bother you with calls about parcels of property that he claims to be "close to what you are looking for"—which frequently turn out to be not so. To avoid such misunderstandings, make certain your needs are clearly understood.

Newspaper Ads. Some second-home buyers have done well by placing ads in local newspapers servicing the prospective sections or communities. In your ad, you should spell out your needs and price range, to advise local property owners that you are a potential buyer. If this method works for you, you will save the real estate agent's commission by dealing directly with the seller.

County officials can be of help with information about zoning, title encumbrances, easements, rights of way, and similar questions, but you will be on safer ground if your lawyer reviews the offering. To be safe, do not sign papers or make a deposit until your attorney approves the move.

Using Classified Ads. Simply subscribe to the local newspaper(s) and follow the classified section(s) on property sales. Similarly, large metropolitan newspapers generally have a thick real estate section, under farms and vacation properties, in their Sunday editions. In classified sections you will also find ads placed by brokers and real estate agents in the areas in which you are interested.

Search and Negotiate. The fourth method is time-consuming, but, in some cases, it can be pleasant and preferable. With one eye on your budget, make weekend trips into potential areas to look for the property firsthand. Each time you make such a trip, your first stop should be to pick up the local newspaper to learn what is available.

By spending a Saturday night or two at motels, you will be able to spend more time looking and less time traveling. Use this time to consult with local bankers, merchants, and leisure-home owners, to learn if they know of any property up for sale. Also, if you keep your eye peeled, you might spot a "FOR SALE" sign tacked up on a piece of property every so often.

This approach is favored by those who are not in a rush; for them, the property search is just one exciting part of the whole leisure-home adventure.

TYPES OF LEISURE PROPERTIES

Basically, there are five kinds of recreational properties: (1) lakeside, (2) oceanfront, (3) mountain, (4) country (or rural), (5) snow-and-ski. Construction problems vary from one type of area to the next, so you should be aware of what each locale demands in the way of house-building. It can also be more expensive to build in one area than another because of access to property, house-building techniques, availability of help, and the like.

In any event, study the homes in the area you choose, and benefit from what you see. Certain features or materials you may have wanted in a home may have to be discarded; your first concern should be to erect a house that will wear best under the local conditions.

Lakeside Property. The rural and mountain regions of the United States are dotted with thousands of lakes. Owning lake property means you can swim, boat, water-ski, fish, and enjoy the advantages of semi-country living. In many lake areas, the major means of support for the native residents are the armies of summer residents who invade the area between Memorial and Labor Days. The local population is usually geared to servicing the temporary residents, and you will find that most of what you need to make you comfortable is close at hand.

You should beware, however, those areas that are overdeveloped commercially. If the neighborhood is bursting with motels, restaurants, sightseeing spectacles, and the like, you may find yourself summering in a frenetic climate very much like, or worse than, the urban scene you are trying to escape from.

What to Check When Selecting a Lake Site. Since a lakefront site is usually more expensive than interior property, a couple of things must be determined before the additional cost is incurred. Is a parcel directly adjacent to the water, in fact, the best piece of ground for you?

For one thing, mosquitos are generally concentrated near the water, where the ground is almost always moist and the air still, and less active than on higher ground. Often, when the air is motionless at the water's edge, you will find a gentle breeze half-way up the hill.

Also, though damage from high water is far less likely on a lake than it is at an oceanfront, the possibility does exist. On some lakes, fast-moving waters can cause quick erosion. Frequent local storms also increase the incidents of damage from water. If you own a boat, a lakefront plot is sure to be your first choice. Make every effort to choose it with care.

Further, the "lay" of the land has an effect on *every site* you may be considering: Your home can be battered by water from more than one direction, depending on where it is located. For example, never buy a piece of property that appears to be a dried-up stream or lake bed; there is too much possibility of it again becoming water-covered. With the same thought in mind, don't invest in property that appears to be the former site of a stream juncture with the lake.

Try to determine the area's prevailing winds and then buy property on the lee, instead of the windward, side of the lake. The best approach is to study carefully the existing homes encircling the lake; their relative conditions will tell you on which side of the water a house weathers best. Otherwise, high wet winds will take its toll on the exterior of your home.

Like mountain and country properties, trees should play a part in your selection too. Carefully consider house placement to obtain the best possible view with a minimum number of tree eliminations. As much as possible, try to keep the trees intact when building, but prudently thin them out to assure a good air flow. If you doubt your knowledge in this area, retain an architect to recommend placement of the house, which trees should be left standing, and which ones should come down. The time to be concerned about "the view" is before you build.

Oceanfront Property. In recent years, desirable shorefront building plots have become increasingly difficult to obtain. The inevitable result is that current asking (and getting) prices are literally out of sight. Don't be surprised, if you are looking in the most-wanted waterfront spas, at prices as high as $30,000 per acre.

The prices are high, though, for reasons other than scarcity. At the sea, you can swim, boat, water-ski, fish from boats or the surf, dig for clams and scallops, hunt for seashells, sunbathe, and more. Children are especially fascinated for hours with a search for items washed ashore by recent, and not-so-recent, storms. Every so often on many beaches, something appears at the water's edge—perhaps from a schooner that sank a century or more ago. Many waterfront homes are filled with these salty objects d'art that give these vacation communities a feeling all their own.

More likely than not, beach plums grow wild, there for the taking to make your own beach plum preserves. Here you can virtually live off the land by enjoying your daily catches from the deep.

California Redwood Association

Figure 3-1 *Exterior materials should be chosen carefully to suit area climate, as well as personal taste. Here, a redwood plywood house by the sea nestles comfortably against a rugged coastline; its shed-like roof lines seem to follow the land's contour. The exterior is finished with saw-textured redwood plywood grooved 12" on-center. The wood is finished with a water-repellant containing a mildewcide; a reapplication of the preservative every two or three years maintains the wood and protects its natural color, allowing it to age slowly and evenly.*

BUILDINGS ARE DIFFERENT AT THE SHORE

The scene at the typical seashore settlement is a cluster of houses ranging from ultra-modest squatter's shacks, lived in by non-taxpaying natives, to super-elegant $60,000-and-up country homes, occupied by the wealthy.

All of the dwellings, however, are constructed to one degree or another to combat the especially drastic climatic conditions of the shore. Most oceanside dwellings, for instance, are low-profile structures, to better withstand the battering of the elements. The higher-profile, multilevel dwellings are generally expensive, custom-designed, and planned to suit a site within the esthetic and functional requirements of the owners.

Any beach house should be built with materials that can best withstand the severe elements, and, quality construction techniques should be used to assure a snug house that will provide comfortable living regardless of weather changes. For example, salt water, aided by sand blown in alternating directions by night and day, quickly deteriorates paint. Most beach homeowners, therefore, opt for wood siding left to weather naturally. (See Figure 3-1.) And the summer sun can beat down unmercifully to turn a home's interior into a veritable sauna bath. A sudden change in wind direction or a damp evening can drop the thermometer reading enough to require the use of blankets for sleeping. The daily extremes—hot dry days, and cool damp nights —discourage some from vacationing at the shore. For others, it is the only way to go.

The most serious dangers to your seaside home are hurricanes, tidal damage, and erosion. Striking beaches all over the world, hurricanes batter a house with high winds, torrential rains, and eroding sands. To minimize damage from this threat, try to pick a site with a dune between it and the water. Preferably, the dune should be covered with a heavy growth of grass, or it is likely to disappear in the next heavy storm.

The chance of your property washing away by tidal wave or erosion can be roughly determined by checking the history of the area to ascertain how much erosion took place in previous years. A constantly shifting shoreline can mean you may be without a second home in a relatively short time.

And be aware that erosion does not occur on sandy beaches only; rocky cliffs overlooking the water frequently wear down, crumble, and wash away. Check the history of erosion in these areas too, and if there is any evidence of geological instability, of course, do not buy the land.

Mountain Country. A location on a rugged mountainside offers leisure-time adventure for the hardy, for the weather can be as rugged as the mountain your house will stand on. A mountain location offers privacy, closeness to nature, and, in many cases, hunting.

Like the seaside, however, erosion is one of the primary concerns when selecting a site. You must therefore be concerned not only with the site but also with what is above and below it. Make certain you pick an area that is well protected from land, rock, and ice slides. Also watch out for evidence of ice accumulation above the parcel; such ice packs cause slides when the spring thaw hits. Even when "safe" areas can be found in pockets or on ledges, they must be checked for geological stability. In general, a site on higher ground is the best choice in the mountains, but make certain you carefully check the terrain for any indication of erosion. If you have any doubts about the land, it is well worth the fee to have a geological engineer study the land and provide you with a report of the findings.

Also, carefully inspect access to the property. Are the roads in good shape and maintained year-round? Or does winter bring snowfalls and impassable drifts that will prevent you from using your property a good part of the year?

Further, since hiking and backpacking have gained tremendously in popularity in recent years, check out whether or not the property is surrounded by public or private trails intended for such use.

For safety and peace of mind, also determine whether hunting areas are adjacent to any property under consideration.

The mountains have their weather extremes too, and a house in such a locale should be built to stand the stress. In general, you'll find that, architecturally, two types of dwellings are common: the simpler homes that tend to

Figure 3-2 *Dome structures are in demand for use as second homes by those who want an economical, but different, structure. Building economy is the prime advantage, while the main disadvantage for some is getting accustomed to living with curved walls. The model shown, "The Executive" (a basic one-bedroom), comes with one 8' sliding glass door (a second door can be added for convenience if desired), one window, and a kitchen unit that includes refrigerator, four-burner range, oven, cabinets, and a sink. Shipped anywhere in the U.S., this house is built with two layers of tough fiberglass sandwiching a core of insulating foam. The manufacturer claims these materials create an all-weather, maintenance-free home. The typical cost of 25 footer is $5,000. Write the maker for the nearest dealer and an estimate of shipping costs. (See Appendix A.)*

blend in with the surrounding landscape, and the grand-scale structures of the wealthy who have more of a desire to outdo than to enjoy nature.

Mountain country is rugged, thus you should plan on building a house to suit. Make certain the site you choose will permit you to securely anchor your structure to the ground because you can expect heavy snow loads to be dumped on the house during the height of winter. Your house should be built to take such abuse.

If possible, of course, select high ground so snow accumulations will be at a minimum. Though some opt to build mountainside homes of bright colors, the rule, more often than not, is to build using native materials as much as possible. This not only keeps costs down, but more or less assures that the dwelling will blend with the surrounding landscape.

Since maintaining a home on a steep plot of ground can create more

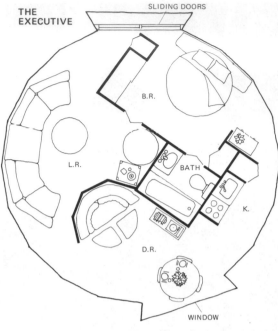

THE
EXECUTIVE

SLIDING DOORS

B.R.

L.R.

BATH

K.

D.R.

WINDOW

O'Dome House, Tension Structures, Inc.

Figure 3-3 Each O'Dome is a 20-sided polygon that sits on a 25½'-diameter base, giving about 530 sq. ft. of unobstructed floor area. The floor plan for the executive model, shown here, includes all the essentials for comfortable living. Several modules can be connected to create a cluster effect. The wall configuration is such that it permits working room to within 15" of the sides for an average-size adult. The height is 10' at the center.

than the ordinary share of maintenance work, try to keep architectural details on your house to a minimum. If possible, leave sidings and the like to weather naturally (to avoid having to paint every few years). This can be achieved by using either redwood or cedar—that is treated with preservative only—wherever lumber is used on the exterior.

Country or Rural Property. Though country property is less in demand than seashore or lakefront, it should not be automatically discounted. There are several advantages to living in the country. For one thing, land is generally less expensive; thus you can acquire a larger parcel to assure privacy in the years ahead. For another, the climate is often more stable than the other areas. Hurricanes, heavy winds, and the accompanying erosion problems are not likely problems. In practical terms, a milder, more temperate climate usually means less house maintenance and fewer demands if you plan to build your house.

But you still have to study the area's land conditions—to determine, for instance, if it is swampy or arid, or subject to flooding during the rainy season.

Because of the less restrictive weather conditions, you have more latitude when building a house in the country thus you can build it pretty much to please your tastes. Unlike vacation homes at sea or lake, where weather and (frequently) community tastes demand a particular style or class of house, you can concentrate on picking the house you have always wanted. About the only general requirement is to clear your house plans with local building authorities to make certain its design, size and location on the building site are legal.

FOR SKIERS—SNOW COUNTRY

Sites in a ski community provide what skiers want most—protected properties, easy access to ski runs, and roads that are accessible during the ski season.

Again, like mountain and oceanfront property, a snow-country site should be selected with a full knowledge of weather and erosion conditions. A visual inspection of existing homes will confirm that they are rugged and built to withstand the sometimes excessive snow loads on their roofs. The A-frame dwelling works well in snow country because its sharply sloped roofline quickly sheds accumulations. (See Figure 3-4.)

Also, since group living is a way of life for many skiers, a good-sized dwelling must be built. Keep in mind that a three- or four-bedroom A-frame structure occupies a considerable chunk of land. So make certain the parcel you like will accommodate the size house you plan to build.

Figure 3-4 *This classic chalet for the high country is actually a spin-off of an A-frame design. Like the latter, its steeply-pitched roof makes it a perfect choice for snow country.*

Figure 3-5 *Inside, the dwelling is sure to suit most ski buffs. The contemporary fireplace and raised hearth, paired with the exposed stairs and beamed ceiling, create an atmosphere of the rugged, happy times that are synonymous with the winter season.*

WHICH SITE FOR YOU?

Once you have decided upon the area, your search is quickly narrowed down to picking the best site for you in that locale. In broad terms, there are seven considerations when buying a piece of real estate for second home use:

1. accessibility,
2. convenience,
3. utilities,
4. security,
5. climate,
6. zoning laws, and
7. lifestyle.

Accessibility. Imagine buying a piece of property only to find that it cannot be reached during certain months of the year because of heavy rains or

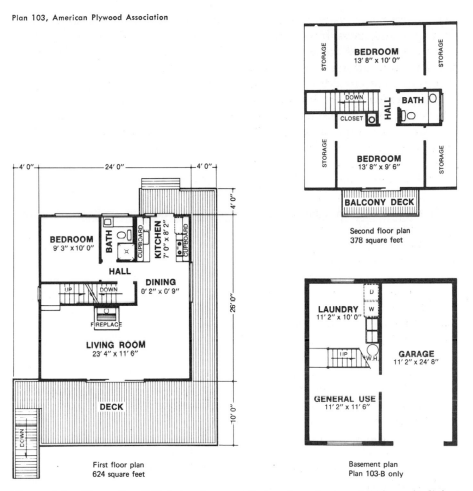

Plan 103, American Plywood Association

BEDROOM
13' 8" x 10' 0"

STORAGE

STORAGE

DOWN

BATH

HALL

CLOSET

STORAGE

STORAGE

BEDROOM
13' 8" x 9' 6"

BALCONY DECK

Second floor plan
378 square feet

BEDROOM
9' 3" x 10' 0"

BATH

CUPBOARD

KITCHEN
7' 0" x 8' 2"

CUPBOARD

HALL

DINING
0' 2" x 0' 9"

UP   DOWN

FIREPLACE

LIVING ROOM
23' 4" x 11' 6"

DECK

DOWN

First floor plan
624 square feet

LAUNDRY
11' 2" x 10' 0"

UP

W.H.

GARAGE
11' 2" x 24' 8"

GENERAL USE
11' 2" x 11' 6"

Basement plan
Plan 103-B only

Figure 3-6 Floor plan 103-A (no basement) boasts a spacious 1,002 sq. ft. living space. If more room is desired, use Plan 103-B which gives you a garage with laundry and storage space beneath the main structure. Wrap-around deck adds outdoor living area.

snow. You have two alternatives: either pay to keep a private road cleared from November through March. or stay home till the road opens up again.

If possible, rent a place in the general area of your choice for a whole season. You can then study the plots under varying weather conditions. As noted earlier, weather is a most important factor in site selection: Does the property drain well? If so, does it drain off onto someone else's lot? Or will you have a rice-paddy after the first storm? Being around under *all* conditions will help you answer these questions.

A plot can also be rendered inaccessible because it is completely surrounded by other peoples' property. In order to reach such real estate, you need an easement guaranteeing you the right to use a particular strip of land for ingress and egress. If possible, avoid such land parcels. But if the real estate you want the most comes burdened with easement problems, make certain you have your attorney assure you that your usage rights are protected even if the easement property should change hands.

Convenience. It is desirable, of course, to have as many facilities as possible within walking distance. Dependence upon an auto for use of the beach, the golf course, supermarkets, and the like can discourage any family. Thus it makes sense to buy a site where the recreational and shopping facilities can be reached by foot or bicycle.

Check out promised rights to beaches, marinas, and other commonly held recreational facilities. Have your lawyer review your sales contract, or check with state and local agencies to make certain that you will, in fact, have complete use of the facilities without retstriction.

Most important, you want to know how convenient medical service is— particularly in an emergency. Find out whether there is a hospital located within a reasonable distance, as well as dentists and general practitioners.

Utilities. Determine the availability of water. If the water is piped in, fine. But if you have to drive or drill a well, find out the depth, flow, and purity of nearby wells. Regardless of its source, water should be tested for pollutants by local authorities or the State Department of Health.

Find out, too, whether homeowners on nearby properties have had problems with septic tanks. Remember, your drain field must be approved by local authorities. In many areas, you will not even be issued a building permit until all sewage disposal standards have been complied with.

Though it may seem minor, also learn how trash removal is handled in the neighborhood. Is there a periodic collection by the town sanitation department, or will you have to pay a private collector to have rubbish and trash hauled off? In many areas, you will find neither: *You* remove the trash with periodic visits to the town dump.

If electrical power is not available from a local power company, you will have to shoulder the expense of installing and maintaining your own generating system, or learn to live totally with bottled gas. If it is available, and if the run from the utility company's main line to the house hookup is less than 200', electricity is neither a problem nor a great expense. If the distance is greater, however, it is likely that you will be charged for all footage over 200'.

Security. It is important to determine (1) whether police and fire protection are nearby and (2) the quality of such protection. An effective police force can reduce, and possibly eliminate, losses due to vandalism and theft. A responsive fire department will keep the cost of fire insurance within payable range. In fact, if your site does not have fire protection, fire insurance will likely be prohibitively expensive.

Another thing to check out for the sake of security is the availability of telephone service, if it is desired.

Climate. Perhaps the biggest climatic problem is erosion. Under no circumstances should you buy eroding land. As a rule of thumb, check for this especially near beaches, streams, and lakes; shun property that is low-lying. If you doubt a land's resistance to erosion, make a careful inspection of the land's condition: Caution flags are up when the ground is furrowed and has little or no ground cover. Also, look at the trees: If the roots are exposed, there is good chance of more soil washing away with each additional rain.

If you have any doubts at all about the geological stability of a piece of ground, have the property inspected by a geological engineer. Consultations with state and local agencies may also prove helpful.

Zoning Laws. Make no mistake about it: Area zoning is beneficial. Without it, virgin forest today could easily become an area overpopulated by housing developments, motels, gas stations, and other contingent businesses. The intrusion of such facilities would reduce, and eventually eliminate, the forest wildlife that give so much pleasure.

Happily, environmental standards are being adopted and strictly enforced in many areas. You should search out such localities and confine your selection to communities that are concerned with the environment. In such communities you will find strict building and zoning laws that work in your favor in two ways: (1) substandard houses are taboo, and (2) commercial development is kept to a realistic minimum.

Not so incidentally, you should also take the time to become familiar with the local plumbing codes. For example, is modern plumbing required? Or can wastes be diverted to septic fields and the like with the eventual pollution of lakes and streams? And, if so, is this an agreeable solution to your waste problem?

As beneficial as zoning laws are, realistically speaking, they can be—and, unfortunately, often are—bent or changed to suit an individual or business with a profit-making ax to grind. With enough money and political clout, changes will inevitably come.

One way to learn how the winds are blowing in a particular area is by subscribing to the local newspaper. Through it, you familiarize quickly with the local prime movers in politics. If necessary, seek out these people and ask questions. You should also consult with county authorities for help in interpreting zoning ordinances.

When you have decided to buy, all the answers you have gotten should be reviewed and verified by your attorney. In the final analysis, he will know whether the laws are actually foolproof.

Another point you should ask your attorney to clarify is whether the community has rigid setback requirements, which can make a good site difficult or impossible to build upon.

Lifestyle. Suffice it to simply repeat what was said before: Each vacation area has its own particular way of life. Many go the route of constant social activity, while others tend toward a family-centered way of life. In general, lake or ocean areas are usually preoccupied with social intercourse—a route you will be expected to follow when you buy or build.

Approval or disapproval of either way of life is not suggested here. Rather, just be aware that social climates vary from one area to the next and consider that fact carefully before buying or building in *any* area.

Moreover, if your financial picture doesn't appear to match that of the current residents, your best bet it to steer clear. If you buy into an area where your neighbors earn considerably more than you do, you will buy yourself the position of the little fish in the big pond. Renting a place in the prospective area for a season, therefore, makes sense for two reasons: First, while living there, you can make an appraisal of the area to determine if the social climate is, in fact, what you seek; and, second, you will be able to spend a great deal of time narrowing the search for your site.

Incidentally, unless your budget is unlimited, you should be aware of vacation-area economics. In most vacation communities, higher prices for just about everything not-so-coincidentally arrive with Memorial Day, and they don't come down again until after the "city folks" have departed on Labor Day. The differences in prices between your primary and second homes can be significant—even on such mundane items as faucet washers and detergents. So bring along as many staples as possible from your primary neighborhood stores.

By now, perhaps, you have a better idea of what you want in a second home and where you want it. Hopefully, you're better equipped to start the search.

The next thing you need to know, once you've selected your site, is what to do in order to erect the home itself. How much can you do by yourself? Which professionals should you rely on for how much? These and similar questions are answered in Chapter 4.

4

Working With Professionals... the Lawyer, Architect, Builder, and Broker

Picking a lawyer * *Lawyer-client relationship* * *Legal documents* * *Working with an architect* * *The architect's services* * *Finding an architect* * *Designing your leisure home* * *The architect/builder* * *Renovating an older home* * *Selecting and working with a builder* * *Narrowing down a group of builders* * *Putting the job up for competitive bidding* * *Legal agreement with a contractor* * *The payment schedule* * *Binding agreement* * *Cooperating with a contractor* * *Making changes in building plans* * *Final inspection* * *Settlement of payment* * *New protection for new homes—HOW* * *Use a broker or deal directly with the seller?* *

WORKING WITH A LAWYER

Regardless of the dollar amounts involved in your real-estate transaction, it is of prime importance that an attorney handle *all* the legal aspects related to the purchase. Make no mistake about it—buying real estate can be a complicated business, one in which even shrewd investors occasionally make costly errors. All things considered, a lawyer's fee is a kind of insurance against such errors. Further, since the fee in all likelihood will be set according to the purchase price, you will only short change yourself on legal expertise if you try to keep your attorney's fee down by minimizing the number of consultations. And, most importantly, the time to hire an attorney is *before* you sign *any* agreement or write a check.

Picking a Lawyer. Unless you already have an attorney, or a lawyer friend who handles your legal matters, your best bet is to retain a "country lawyer"

—an attorney whose shingle is hung in the vicinity in which you are buying. Chalk up a big point for your side if the local "pro" is held in high esteem by the members of the community.

And the surest way to get the most for your legal dollar is to hire someone who specializes in real estate: he or she will very likely suit your needs perfectly. Such specialists are usually as thoroughly familiar with local, county, and state building laws and ordinances as they are in the town and county clerks' offices. Because of their experience in the area, they can not only quickly find out if you can use the property being considered the way you intend to, but also give considerable assistance in the mortgaging process.

Finding a reputable attorney is not difficult. Perhaps an attorney in your home area can suggest someone in the locale in which you are buying. You can also check with local real-estate brokers, with the mortgage officers at the financing bank, and with other homeowners in the neighborhood. If one name comes up repeatedly, it makes sense to use this person—regardless of the fee.

The Lawyer–Client Relationship. The first rule is to always level with your lawyer: *Never* withhold a fact, no matter how insignificant it may seem. (You may be sure that any conversation between you and your lawyer will be held in strictest confidence.) It is essential that he know exactly what you plan to do with your property. For example, if you are buying in the country with the idea of erecting a small antique shop along the highway for seasonal or retirement income, let your lawyer know. Such a structure (or venture) could be illegal on the property you are considering. So if you don't tell your lawyer what you are up to, you run a high risk of buying a piece of ground that will not suit your purpose. To avoid such a costly mistake, make sure your lawyer is fully informed of your plans. He'll be able to tell you whether or not they are legal and workable, or if you should pass up the parcel in question and look for another.

Rule number two is to settle on a fee. The lawyer has a lot to do to complete the transaction and is going to charge you for the services. Some attorneys have a standard fee for a real estate transaction; others base the charge upon the property's value. Realistically, you can expect to pay somewhere between $200 and $600 for complete legal services.

Once you have an attorney, consult him or her on every legal problem concerning your second home—rule three. Several lawyer friends have assured me that they prefer the client who alerts them to all the facts, as opposed to the one who withholds problems they think are unimportant to the lawyer. Let the lawyer decide whether a fact is important. You're paying for the knowledge and experience, so you owe it to yourself to utilize your lawyer's talents to the fullest.

Legal Documents. Your real estate transaction starts off with a document called an *agreement of sale,* basically a contract between you and the seller. Since everything thereafter hinges on what is written into this agreement, you can see the importance of having an attorney early in the game. Obviously, he or she must review and approve the agreement of sale before you put your signature on the dotted line. If nothing else, if you are going for a mortgage, make certain the agreement of sale contains a clause stating that you will get your down payment back if you are not able to obtain a satisfactory loan within a specified period of time.

Besides checking the agreement of sale, there are many other chores for your attorney. He or she makes the title search of the property to assure that it is free of any liens and encumbrances, which can be claimed against you as the new owner, as well as possible rights-of-way or easements. The attorney also determines whether the dwelling you want can be built on the site, or whether septic tanks can be installed and wells drilled. These are facts you must know before you buy.

The attorney also protects your interests at the closing by reviewing various fees and charges and making certain the builder delivers all guarantees and warranties for appliances, equipment, and structural members.

It is also important that the builder supply a waiver of lien from any contractor or subcontractor who has not yet been paid. Lacking the certification and waiver, a subcontractor who has not been paid can, at a future date, file a lien against you for the unpaid amount. Legally he could require you to pay him under threat of forced sale. Make certain your attorney reviews these items and is convinced that you are reasonably protected against such liens.

You can take title to the property either in your own name (in which case your spouse has certain legal rights) or jointly with your spouse (either with or without a right of survivorship). Since the manner in which you take title will affect transfer, inheritance, and other taxes, handling of the title should be decided beforehand in consultation with your attorney.

Finally, for your protection, your lawyer will make certain that the deed is recorded.

Even if you choose to build rather than buy a second home, a lawyer will help you finalize a contract with a builder and later protect your interests as represented by that contract. The lawyer's role when you build will be discussed more fully later in this chapter.

WORKING WITH AN ARCHITECT

If, after poring over designs from building plan firms, literature from makers of manufactured houses, and plans that your builder has to offer, you cannot find exactly what you want, you know you have to engage an architect. For a fee, usually 15 percent of the total cost to build, the architect will custom-design a home to suit your particular needs, and then take charge of construction to make certain the dwelling is built as designed.

The Architect's Services. When you consult an architect, you deal with a person who knows every aspect of homebuilding from utilization of the site

Figure 4-1 Mr. and Mrs. Ted Van Dorn of Timber Grove, California, commissioned West Coast architect Ernest E. Lee, AIA, to design their lake country home. This small dwelling features economical garden-grade native redwood on a deck that was installed to emphasize vacation living as envisioned by the owners. The exterior is sided with Clear All-Heart redwood in a board-on-board pattern. The owners wanted a home that would complement rather than compete with nature. To get that feeling, Mr. Lee used vast expanses of insulated glass to let the outdoors in.

to the best materials for the job. This person knows how the building should go up, and the best builder to get the job done. Today's competent architect is in tune with what's happening now. The architect's sharp eyes and ears are always attuned to new ideas, materials, and suggestions, and he or she has the expertise to reject the bad ones and incorporate the good ones into future designs.

In simplest terms, the architect's job is to make certain that you get what you pay for. The fee includes handling the entire job and, if you desire, help in the selection of the site as well.

Before retaining an architect, ask to see some previous work. Look over the sample sketches in the office, and then ask for the addresses of some examples of recent work. A competent architect will be pleased that you want to see firsthand several of the homes he or she has designed and built. You owe it to yourself to ask past clients if they were satisfied with the work and with the performance of the architect's builder.

Because you and your architect will have a close working relationship, it's also important that you like the architect as a person, as well as a professional. It will be just about impossible to have a successful relationship unless there are good "vibes" between the two of you.

Figure 4-2 To strengthen the relationship with nature, architect Lee used only wood on the exterior. The large-size rafters permit greater spacing than the conventional 16 in. on center to increase the aesthetic feeling wanted by owners.

Finding an Architect. When looking for an architect, you may, of course, confine your search to the Yellow Pages. However, keep your eye open in outlying areas for recent architectural school graduates who might even work for a lower fee in order to build up a portfolio of designs. Many of these young people are extra-competent and have located in the country because they felt their creative skills would be stifled in a big-city office. You may also find successful city architects who have traded in the big-town rat-race for quiet offices of their own in the sticks.

As with your attorney, discuss a fee with the architect you'd like to retain. When you talk about the fee, make certain the architect's duties are clearly spelled out and understood by both of you. Since inspection visits, progress reports, and similar functions are of prime importance to you, don't leave details such as these to chance.

At any rate, fee alone should not be the determining factor when picking an architect. Through conversations with local natives—preferably real estate brokers, bankers, builders, and other members of the professional community—you can quickly ascertain an architect's credentials.

California Redwood Association

Figure 4-3 Far-out ideas do much to customize a second home; for example, note the centrally-located, suspended fireplace here. You can realistically expect such imaginative attention to details when you work with your own architect—particularly if he specializes in leisure-home architecture. (Innovative thinking is maintained on the structure's exterior, as can be seen by noting the chimney detail in Figure 4-1.)

Designing Your Leisure Home. Three or four meetings with your architect will be necessary, prior to hitting the drawing board, to discuss fully just what you expect from your second home. For example, the architect should know whether you entertain frequently or not at all, whether a large family or a couple will reside in the home, whether the home will be used just for the summer or year-round—as well as a million other details. The architect can do a better job of designing a house, *just for you,* if thoroughly familiar with your style of living. Thus he or she has to know your eating and sleeping habits, as well as your social life. How your family lives determines to a great degree how your floor plan should be laid out and your house styled.

Your architect must also know how you plan to use the property itself, for how you use it can have a bearing on how the house will be positioned on the plot. For instance, do you want to be able to park a boat alongside the house? If so, speak up now, so that storage space can be provided on the site plan. Do you eventually want to add a swimming pool and bathhouse? Let the architect know now, so the house is located accordingly. Or, if you are starting small, do you intend to add on later? Let your architect in on your thinking. Your future plans will affect the design of the structure now, as well as that which will follow.

Naturally, the style of home you want should also be discussed. You should have a pretty solid idea of what you want, be it extra-contemporary or New England Saltbox. By immediately zeroing in here, you will cut down the amount of time the architect spends making preliminary sketches.

Finally, don't misrepresent the amount you can afford to spend on the house. You're only kidding (and hurting) yourself if you exaggerate your means. Level with your architect from the outset, so he can concentrate on designing a dwelling that can be built within your budget. By the same token, don't deliberately understate what you can spend either. If you do, the plans will be for a house that is somewhat less than you can afford or want in the first place. To get the house you really want and can afford, you'll wind up tacking on expensive extras later on.

Generally, a reputable architect will keep costs down on a second home by eliminating fancy frills, excess trim, and the like—the labor for which costs plenty these days.

The Architect/Builder. It is best to follow the architect's advice when selecting the contractor (builder). A good architect knows how all local builders perform and is sure to pick only a reliable one, because the proper selection means less headaches for everyone concerned. The architect recognizes the importance of a mutual respect between himself and the builder for each other's work. On a project as large as building a house, all parties must be compatible—architect, client, *and* builder. By all means, try to stick with the architect's selection of a builder.

In this three-way relationship, be sure to distinguish who is responsible for what. In effect, the architect draws your dream house on paper, and the contractor turns that dream into reality. The builder answers to, and takes orders from, the architect alone. When you have an architect overseeing construction, don't butt in on the job, though you will be tempted to. The architect will handle inspections and have the builder correct any deficiencies. Should you make an inspection visit, remember that you have no right to make on-the-spot changes without consulting the architect. Chances are, the builder will not make a change anyway except on orders in writing from the architect. Under no circumstance should you ever order the contractor's workers or subcontractors to make any change from the plans or specifications.

Neither is it necessary to constantly badger the architect. He or she will make sure that the building is going up in accordance with the plans and specifications; and you will receive periodic inspection reports by mail. If your presence is required on the job, the architect will request a jobsite meeting.

When the building is completed, you must tour the dwelling with the architect to determine whether or not everything has been delivered as called for in the plans and specifications and to your satisfaction. Point out deficiencies, and the architect will have them corrected. (This relationship with

Figure 4-4 *One way to keep design costs down, yet acquire a somewhat custom-built house, is by choosing a manufactured house that boasts flexibility. In Barn II, American Barn's designers work with home buyers to assure that interior space best fulfills the owners' needs. The cost of such a home is about $26,500 for an erected shell, $35,000 up to the rough-finish stage, and $45,000 for a completely finished structure. These prices include up to 100 miles of transportation.*

the architect and builder, and the possible money consequences will be discussed later in more detail.)

RENOVATING AN OLDER HOME

Don't overlook the possibility of using an architect to coordinate remodeling if you plan to buy an older home. As in new home construction, he or she will come up with ideas and suggestions you may never have thought of to make your home more attractive, as well as more livable.

If you've decided on renovating an older home, you should retain an architect before signing the agreement of sale on a house. Before you commit yourself, the architect can make an inspection of the premises to determine if your intended changes can be brought about within your budget. (See Chapter 6.)

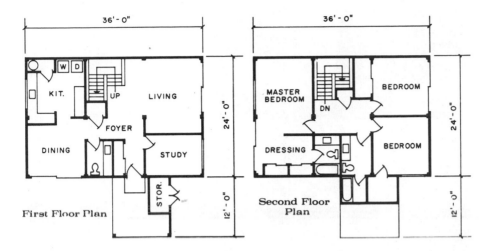

Figure 4-5 Because Barn II is of true post-and-beam construction, an infinite variety of floor, window, and door arrangements is possible. You can utilize the second floor as living space as shown, or leave open a portion to achieve a dramatic cathedral ceiling effect in the living room.

WORKING WITH A BUILDER

Selecting a Builder. To save the cost of having your own architect, you may opt for a stick-built house from stock plans. If you're not building it yourself, you will have to pick the builder. Since the building trades, like most industries, have their share of fast-buck operators, you are well advised to exercise caution when picking the contractor.

The quickest way to find out the number of builders in the area is to simply look in the Yellow Pages. But keep in mind that the classified directory tells you only who is available, not who is best.

Basically, there are three things to concern yourself with when selecting a builder:

1. *Reputation.* Ideally, the outfit you choose will have a spotless record, a company respected for its honesty, workmanship, and delivery record. Obviously, stay away from any builder who leaves behind a string of customers complaining about unfinished jobs.

   You can get a line on reputation by checking with the local Better Business Bureau and by talking with neighbors and members of the business community. Don't be afraid to discuss builders with those who are most likely to do business with them—electricians, plumbers, masons, and other subcontractors, as well as building materials suppliers.

Figure 4-6   Inside, the walls are finished with ½-in. plasterboard or rough-sawn boards —all beams are left exposed. Obviously the Barn can be altered to suit a variety of tastes and still retain its charm.

2. *Credit standing.* An honest businessperson will not be insulted if you ask the name of the company's bank for the purpose of checking its financial standing. In fact, a reputable contracting firm will be pleased to have you check its credit rating because a good standing indicates reliability, stability, and solvency.

Though some are embarrassed to ask for this information, you shouldn't be. Keep in mind that you were carefully checked before receiving approval on your mortgage.

3. *Work performance.* A sincere contractor will have readily available a list of satisfied customers. Request this list of names and addresses so that you can inspect the craftsmanship firsthand and talk with past customers. Visit at least half a dozen homes that the contractor has constructed, ideally ones that cover a wide range of styles and budgets. If you are lucky, the contractor will specialize in second-home construction and thus have full knowledge of what can be eliminated to keep costs down—without sacrificing quality.

Beware of contractors who say they can't seem to find any names of satisfied customers in the immediate area. Be equally wary if they claim that such records are unnecessary, and that they don't bother to keep them. Either negative response can be interpreted as a signal that you're dealing with a fly-by-nighter, a suede-shoe salesperson, an operator out to make a fast buck. If you don't want that "fast buck" to be yours, dismiss these types early in the game.

Competitive Bidding. Though in some remote areas you may not have much of a choice, there are usually a couple of contractors whom you can

Figure 4-7 *This arrangement features sliding glass doors to the deck, which is positioned alongside a massive stone fireplace. The charge for design consultation with the manufacturer is included in the price of the house. American Barn services a geographic area from Maine to Illinois to Georgia.*

invite to submit bids. A bid is the actual figure for which a contractor will build your house, not an estimate, which is merely an educated guess as to construction costs.

If at all possible, adhere to standard practice: Invite at least three contractors to bid competitively on the job. In fairness to yourself, as well as to the builders, make certain that all are bidding on exactly the same house. All bidders should be working from identical sets of plans and specifications that clearly and accurately spell out how the house is to be built and with what materials.

My experience in the home improvement and building businesses has led me to conclude that too often the homeowner merely asks contractors to give a price without spelling out details. Then, they are generally overwhelmed and confused by the wide range of prices the various builders submit. What the homeowner is not aware of is that the lowest bid might be based on using the lowest-quality materials. The high bidder on the other hand may have included first-rate materials throughout. Unless all builder's figures are based upon exact and identical criteria, there's no way you can evaluate competitive bids fairly.

Even if the bidding is based on equal criteria, you may not select the

Barn II, American Barn Corporation

Figure 4-8 A uniform framing system is used in all American Barn models: The building width is maintained at 24 ft.; the roof pitch, a constant 9 in 12; all framing timbers, 8 × 8 in.; and the post and lintel framework carries all loads in the structure. Thus, each 12-ft. wall section can include any combination and number of doors, operable windows, and fixed glass.

The design was conceived in 1971 in conjunction with the Watertown, Massachusetts, architectural firm of Sasaki, Dawson, DeMay Associates, Inc. The concept is based upon an actual early American barn of the type prevalent in the Deerfield, Massachusetts, area.

lowest bidder. You may have learned in your pre-bid investigations, for instance, that the outfit with the lowest bid never seems to meet completion dates or never quite finishes the job. What you save on the lowest bid could be used up when the attorney has to come in and mop-up money settlements, so another contractor can be called in to finish the job.

In fact, based upon reputation and high praise from those you've questioned, your decision may be to go with the highest bidder with the hope of getting your second home built with a minimum of aggravation.

Once your choice has been made, don't forget that you will become a member of the community in the months ahead. Exercise good business practice and write letters to all bidders, informing them as to which contractor has been selected to do the job and thanking those not selected for their time and interest.

Figure 4-9 *This snug house by the sea was designed by Architects Etcetera, Portland, Oregon. Shed-like roofs are dramatized by the use of boards installed diagonally on walls. Like many modern vacation homes, the exterior is treated with clear finish so the wood's beauty can be appreciated as it ages. The architect located windows to conserve energy, used large expanses of walls without fenestration to cut down heat gain during warm months and heat loss during the winter.*

Architects Etcetera Photos

Figure 4-10 *The aim here was to keep the property looking as close to its natural state as possible. Thus, paved walks and parking areas were not used. Instead, the designer specified decking (at left) that blends with surroundings to serve as the parking area.*

Legal Agreement with the Contractor. Once a contractor has been selected, you and your attorney should huddle with him or her. At this meeting an agreement should be reached with regard to what features should be included in house costs, completion dates, payments, warranties, and the like. All such terms must be included in the contract, which, once signed, should remain unaltered unless your attorney reviews and approves any builder-requested changes.

Ask your attorney about a clause in this agreement that will allow part of the final payment to be held in escrow until the builder has corrected any and all faults found on your final inspection.

The *payment schedule* must also be discussed and included in the contract. For the most part, this schedule is controlled by the money lender; standard practice calls for payments to the contractor in a number of installments at various stages of completion. Usually each payment equals 25 percent of the total cost. The first payment is made upon completion of the foundation; the second when the house is up and closed-in to the weather; the third when all subcontractors have finished their installations. The last payment is made upon final inspection and acceptance. In some contracts, a fifth step—work completed by the painters and paperhangers is added. In this schedule, of course, each payment equals 20 percent of the total cost. Regardless of the number of installments, the terms of payment should be clearly defined in the contract (exactly how much is to be paid, after how much work is completed), so there is no chance of misunderstanding.

Binding Agreements. Besides the contractual agreement discussed above, there are two other instruments that will prevent any misunderstanding between owner and builder:

1. *Plans.* These should consist of a full set of an architect's working drawings, elevations, and details covering the construction of the house in its entirety. A complete set of plans also includes mechanicals—drawings that spell out exactly how and what plumbing, heating, and electrical systems are to be installed. The contractor's responsibility is to see that all subcontractors perform their jobs according to the plans and specifications.

2. *Specifications ("specs").* A good set of plans includes specs listing all pertinent data: for example, what type and size wood to use where; specific hardware detailed by brand name; colors, types, and makes of paints; and so on. Even appliances should be listed by names and model numbers. In short, the specs are a word outline of all parts of the house.

Never let the contractor make substitutions for any item listed in the specs unless you first give approval. Beware of the contractor who is constantly looking to make changes; often, this type of builder will substitute an unknown brand for the brand-name item called for.

These two documents are the only ones that bind a contractor to deliver as promised. Your attorney will tell you that the builder is not legally obligated to include any features that are not detailed or mentioned in these contract documents.

California Redwood Association

Figure 4-11 Working closely with the owners in Bear Valley, California, Mc-Donald Planners and Architects of San Francisco designed this contemporary chalet to suit the terrain and elements. In fact, through such styling, this firm hopes to evolve an indigenous American-chalet style. The house is sided with redwood plywood and heavily trimmed with redwood boards. The rafters are doubled-up and rounded at their ends; this detail adds considerably to the chalet feeling (while providing adequate support for the roof).

Snow in the area is frequently so deep that the only possible entry is through a second floor bridge, not visible in photo. Thus, bedrooms and utility rooms are on the ground level while living areas and the master suite occupy the level above.

Cooperating with a Contractor. In fairness to the builder, who is erecting the house for an agreed-upon sum, never halt construction on the job by talking, questioning, or interfering with any of the tradesmen or subcontractors. Keep in mind that the contractor is paying their salaries and is therefore the only one authorized to instruct them how to perform their tasks. Interference by a meddling homeowner can cause serious dissension between owner and builder, which can be avoided, of course, if the homeowner takes all questions directly to the builder.

You should also know that the builder has a justifiable claim to be reimbursed for expenses incurred as a result of homeowner's meddling—telling one of the workers, for example, to add a little something extra on a particular job.

Making Changes in the Plans. Any change that may come up should be written into the contract and initialled by both the owner and contractor. If the change includes substituting one product for another (usually because of shortages), make certain that the replacement product is of equal or better quality than the item originally listed in the specifications. All changes should be approved by your attorney.

Your architect, if you have one, will review and approve all requests for changes. If you're your own builder or if you're working directly with a contractor, it may be worth the charge for an office visit to meet with an architect to discuss changes either that you have to make or that are proposed by the builder. If the changes are of a structural nature, consult a professional engineer.

Capricious changes—taking a wall out here, adding a wall there, installing an extra half-bath, and the like—can create havoc with your building budget. Once construction is underway, the cost of such changes is left entirely to the builder's discretion. A builder will make any change, provided it's within the building codes and it doesn't involve tearing out completed work. But a reputable contractor has a schedule of his own, however, and would like to finish your job on time to meet the next building-start date.

Final Inspection. When the builder advises you that the dwelling is completed, you should conduct an absolutely thorough final inspection. Go slowly from room to room. List any and all items that you question. In the building trades, the final-inspection checklist is called a "punch list." On a project as large as building a house, it is not unusual to find 30 or 40 items on a punch list. (Usually, the items are small and easily corrected, but don't be surprised to find some large items too, such as a missing kitchen cabinet.) At any rate, your punch list should be complete enough to include the exterior and garage. Check everything in sight: Make certain all doors swing and fit properly. Try all windows for operability and fit. Even go to such lengths as to squirt water on the roof to make certain that gutters and leaders disperse water runoff as they should. Try the drawers and doors in kitchen cabinets, all sink faucets, toilets, and every piece of mechanical equipment in the house. Also, carefully check craftsmanship. Look for such things

California Redwood Association

Figure 4-12 *This handsome redwood lodge in West Bethel, Maine, was designed and built by owner/architect Andrew Daland of Cambridge, Massachusetts. The exterior is 8-in. reverse board and batten, keeping detail rugged to suit mountain environment. To hold down exterior maintenance, paint was not used on the wood siding. Instead, redwood siding was allowed to weather naturally. Every three years, it is treated with a clear preservative to protect it from attack by decay organisms and to maintain its resistance to insects.*

as poorly taped joints in plasterboard, open miters in trim carpentry, and the like.

In many cases, the builder will accompany you on your inspection tour, to explain various points that you may think give you just cause for grievance but, in fact, don't. Whether or not the builder accompanies you on your inspection, always take the time to write down the items rather than trusting your memory or the builder's.

You should then send the builder a typewritten, dated letter listing all the items found on your inspection. Keep a carbon copy, of course, for your records. You are not expected to (and should not) make the final payment until all items are settled to your satisfaction. By the same token, don't try to get something for nothing out of the builder at this point by slipping claims for extras into the list. An alert builder will catch such items and, in all likelihood, your lawyer will hear from his lawyer.

Next, the builder will send the necessary workers or subcontractors back to the job to correct those items on the list that are valid. If an invalid claim —such as for shrubbery when none is listed in the specifications—is on the punch list, the builder will advise you.

When the builder has corrected all items on the punch list, make another inspection with the builder. This time, you simply check those items that are on the list. The builder will want you to initial and cross out each complied-with correction on the list as you review it.

Finally, it is the contractor's responsibility to call the subcontractors and utilities to make the connections for gas, water, electricity, and sewage. You are now ready to make final settlement.

Final Payment. At this meeting, the contractor turns over to you the warranties and instruction booklets for all mechanical equipment in the house. For your protection, you should fill out these warranty cards yourself and mail them to the various manufacturers.

Once you have made final payment, the property is totally and irrevocably your responsibility. There is no way that you can force the contractor to do any more work. Your association with the builder is finished.

New Protection for New Homes. To minimize the effects of getting stuck with a shoddily built house, a new kind of buyer protection, called Home Owners' Warranty (HOW), is now offered in many areas. Before too long, it should be available throughout the United States. This coverage can pay in more ways than one. At least one mortgage-money institution is offering interest rate reductions of ⅛ to ¼ percent on homes covered by HOW. It is anticipated that other money lenders will follow this lead.

When you buy your house, HOW coverage is included in what you pay. The rate is $2 per $1,000 of purchase price, with a minimum total premium of $50. For example, for a $40,000 house you pay $80; for a $20,000 house, you pay the $50 minimum. You pay the premium only once.

Coverage is as follows: During the first year, the builder warrants that materials and construction meet the approved standards for your area. These standards are usually based upon local building codes, as approved by HOW, dealing with mechanical systems—plumbing, electrical and heating—as well as with structural concerns.

In the second year, the builder warrants the overall performance of systems except when problems result from the failure of individual components. Coverage still includes defects caused by work that does not comply with approved standards, such as inferior piping, wiring, or septic tanks.

From the third through tenth years, coverage is limited to structural defects and is provided by HOW's insurance carrier, not by your builder.

To obtain full information on the HOW program and to learn whether or not your state has received clearance required for HOW's insurance coverage, write the HOW Corporation, National Housing Center, 15th and M Streets N.W., Washington, D.C., 20005. (See Appendix E for the names and addresses of other associations that may be of help to you.)

John Gaynor Photo

Figure 4-13   Planned periodic meetings at the jobsite between architect and owners is a must to keep work progressing smoothly. Though owners can visit the project as often as desired, they should never, of course, interfere with the builder, or with the builder's employees or subcontractors. Such intrusions waste time, cause confusion, and can lead to ill will between owner and builder.

Save all questions, complaints, and praise for your scheduled jobsite meetings with your architect, who will pass the word on to the builder. Keep a list of any and all questions you may have for on-job consultations—don't waste the architect's time with a lot of phone calls. The architect's fee is based upon a certain number of visits to the jobsite—not undivided attention to your project.

WORKING WITH A BROKER

Though a real estate broker's fee is included in the selling price, the services rendered can save as much or more in time and money. A reliable broker is able to provide you with expert information about the community—taxes, facilities, zoning, and building ordinances. When he or she knows what you are looking for, you won't waste your time (mostly weekends) looking at real estate that doesn't fulfill the specifications that you have established.

And sometimes you may not have to pay the full fee. Since, usually, lots and homes are listed with more than one broker, you might come across a broker who is willing to reduce his commission in order to make the sale. If he does, you'll pay that much less for the house. You owe it to yourself, therefore, to check a particular real estate offer with more than one broker.

If possible, choose a real estate broker who is a member of a local real estate board; such members adhere to a strict code of ethics. You may, however, have difficulty determining membership because not all communities have "local" boards and because many have boards that cover wide territories. One way of picking a board member is to look for the trademarked 'R' for REALTOR in advertisements or in office windows. This is certification that the broker is a member of a board, the state association, and the National Association of Realtors.

If the community does not have a Realtor member, you might contact one in a neighboring community or through the National Institute of Real Estate Brokers (see Appendix E).

Buying or building a second home is a tremendous project for most people. Generally, you need all the help you can get, and you can't beat the kind of help you get from the "pro's" in the business. If your budget allows and if you want to minimize the confusing decision-making, you should put together a team of individuals who can push the project through for you, efficiently and economically.

5

Building an Energy Saving House

*   Position your house with care   *   Design a functional house   *   Select
materials   and   workmanship   to   conserve   energy   *   Materials   *
Workmanship   *   Insulation   *   Get   top   efficiency   from   appliances,
mechanical equipment, and fireplaces   *

Building a house that will conserve as much energy as possible isn't particularly difficult. Our ancestors knew how to do it, and so do we. But until recently, we did not consider it necessary to be concerned with how much energy we consumed—or how much we wasted through lack of planning. The mid-seventies energy-crunch changed that outlook.

Now, as electric and fuel bills spiral upward steadily, we must find ways of reducing the amount of energy consumed while maintaining comfort. Like any commodity, the cost of energy is directly related to consumption: the more we use, the more we pay.

Though a new house with energy-conservation features generally costs more than one without them, your initial cash outlay—and more—will be returned in the form of savings on heating bills. For example, once the house has been closed in, you can provide insulation in exterior walls only by chopping holes in the walls around the house perimeter, and blowing the material in. The job is costly, and it doesn't provide thermal resistance equal to a blanket or batt installation (Figure 5-1). And, your house will still lack a vapor barrier, which is essential to keeping moisture out of the walls. The time, therefore, to think of saving energy is in the planning stage, not after construction has started.

In broad terms, there are five planning steps you can take to save as much energy as possible:

1. position of the house on the site with regard to exposure and all the elements;
2. design the home for efficiency and function;
3. select materials and workmanship that will conserve energy;
4. plan the use of insulation; and
5. get top efficiency from appliances, mechanical equipment, and fireplaces.

10 ways to save energy when building a new home

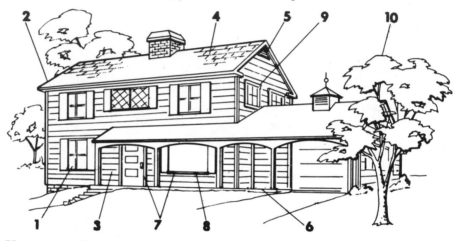

Here are ten things you can do to help keep fuel bills down:
1. *Use double-glazed windows throughout to reduce heat transmission up to 50 percent.*
2. *When choosing a house style, favor multi-level designs, with their proportionately smaller roof areas for a given amount of space, over ranch homes.*
3. *Insulate exposed walls with material having an R-value of at least 11 (3½-in. mineral wool batts or the equivalent), and ceilings with material having an R-value of at least 19 (6-in. thick material).*
4. *Use light-colored shingles on the roof to reflect sunlight and thus assist cooling equipment.*
5. *Adequately ventilate attic to lessen solar heat gain.*
6. *Use a minimum of 1-in. thick perimeter insulation for on-grade slabs and footings.*
7. *Accept only tight installations of windows and doors. Cracks between frames and rough openings should be packed with insulation and sealed with appropriate vapor-barrier material.*
8. *Caulk around all joints between windows, doors, and siding with a high-quality latex or butyl caulk compound.*
9. *In extra-cold climates, use storm windows. Tightly-fitted ones can reduce air infiltration by 30 to 50 percent.*
10. *Preserve as many trees as possible for reasons explained in the text.*

Figure 5-1 *Fiber glass insulation is available in batts and blankets as well as in rolls, as shown here. The material is stapled between studs; face paper is then scored with a knife at the desired length and simply torn.*

POSITION YOUR HOUSE WITH CARE

The basic idea is to use the natural terrain to protect the house from the elements (see Figure 5-2). For example, can your house be built in a valley instead of on top of a hill? Or can you locate it on the protected side of a hill or on the sunny side of a slope? Also, remember that you can obtain a degree of insulation by building your house partly *into* a hillside.

And don't make the mistake of arbitrarily clearing all rocks and vegetation from the site. Look for this fault particularly if buying a contractor-built or vacation-community home. Many builders and developers find it cheaper to build if just about all trees are knocked down and the land is leveled. When the land has been treated this harshly, you, the homeowner, pay in the end. Trees and protruding rock formations block cold winds in winter and provide cooling shade in summer.

If you are fortunate enough to own a site with a stream running through it, don't cover it or fill it in. What you have, in effect, is nature's air-conditioning; during the hot months, a site that boasts running water will be cooler than a dry one.

Always keep sun and wind in mind when locating your house on a site.

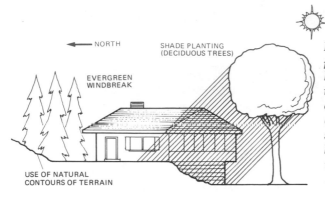

Figure 5-2 Landscaping should protect your property as well as beautify it. A row of evergreens to the north breaks the wind, while deciduous trees to the three other directions provide shade in the summer and allow warming sunlight through in the winter when they are bare. Use of terrain is also helpful.

In cold weather areas, winter winds usually come from the north, so it makes sense to face the walls with maximum insulation and minimum glass area in that direction. Additionally, if the house design and property layout permit, the shortest wall should face toward the north.

In much of today's architecture, especially in leisure-home designs, large areas of glassed walls seem to be almost mandatory. By siting your house so the glass walls face south, the low winter sun will shine into them during most of the daylight hours and ease the load on the heating system (Figure 5-3). In warmer areas, where cooling is of primary concern, the glass areas should also face south. With properly designed overhangs (often called "eyebrows"), little or no sun comes in during the summer when the sun is high. By contrast, if these windows are on the east or west sides, they pick up heat almost half the day, thus putting a strain on the house cooling system.

You can get protection as well as beauty from landscaping too. A row of evergreens planted to the north or northwest of a house can be an effective wind barrier. (Figure 5-2).

Tall deciduous trees should be retained or planted to the south, west, or east of the house to provide cooling shade in the summer. In winter, after the leaves have fallen, these trees do not block the roof and walls from the warming rays of the sun (Figure 5-2).

Figure 5-3 Discuss the function of roof overhangs with your architect. Correctly designed ones shield walls from the high summer sun, yet expose the same walls to the winter sun which is at a lower angle. Following that line of thinking, you can see how an attached porch, carport, or patio roof also serves to protect the walls.

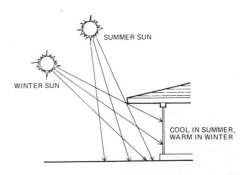

DESIGN A FUNCTIONAL HOUSE

Use plain common sense when picking your house—don't be guided by esthetics alone. If you question your knowledge in this area, an architect should be consulted.

First, make sure your house is designed for the climate it will be exposed to. For example, a house with a sprawling layout and large areas of glass walls might suit the climate perfectly in the southwest region of the U.S. But park the same house in the northern reaches of Maine, and it becomes an energy-guzzling monster to heat.

The house should be practical to heat and cool. The design feature to key in on is the ratio of wall area to floor area (Figure 5-4) : The lower the ratio, the easier it will be to heat or cool the house. Though a look at the drawing shows that a round house is the most efficient in this regard, that shape is a difficult one to build and to live in. Next best is a square house and, after that in decreasing efficiency, the simple rectangular, L, H, and T shapes.

Figure 5-4 The key to heating and cooling is the ratio of roof to floor areas. Since most heat is lost through the roof, and in a two-level house there is a lower proportion of roof to floor area, you can save up to 15 percent in fuel consumption with a multilevel house.

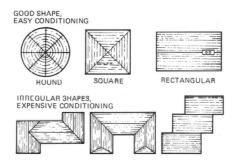

GOOD SHAPE, EASY CONDITIONING

ROUND SQUARE RECTANGULAR

IRREGULAR SHAPES, EXPENSIVE CONDITIONING

In colder climates, a two-story house makes good sense. Since most heat is lost through the roof, a two-story house saves money because it has a lower proportion of roof to floor area. You can save as much as 15 percent in fuel consumption by having living areas on two levels instead of sprawled out on one. Give careful attention also to your floor plan. Grouping common living space in one part of the house and sleeping quarters in another facilitates zoned heating and cooling (dual thermostats, one for each area) and allows the closing off of a section when it's not in use. If possible, family rooms, kitchens and dining rooms should face south and west so they are warmed by the afternoon sun. Bedrooms should be oriented to the morning sun so they can be easily cooled off for comfortable sleeping (Figure 5-5).

Well-planned ventilation in a home can reduce the need for cooling (Figure 5-6). In fact, many architects agree that in some regions, air-conditioning is totally unnecessary if the house is properly ventilated. Along these lines, a courtyard or atrium (enclosed or open) can be used to create better ventilation; even though an atrium adds wall area, it may cut the cooling load. If your home is custom-designed by an architect, discuss the possibil-

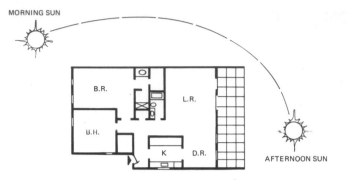

Figure 5-5   Give considerable thought to your floor plan too: Keep common (or active) living space confined to one part of the house and sleeping (or inactive) rooms in another, thus facilitating the use of zoned heating and cooling. Active rooms may be warmed by facing them toward the afternoon sun, and inactive rooms kept cool by facing them toward the morning sunlight.

ity of including a courtyard in your home. And, by all means, make certain that the house has cross-ventilation.

Don't automatically opt for large expanses of glass—the single largest cause of heat loss. Windows should be positioned and located with more than just a view in mind. Too often, windows are included for esthetic reasons only and are not operable for ventilation. In my opinion, windows that can't be used to ventilate a house don't make any sense at all: When a warm spell hits, you have no choice but to cool the house mechanically. Often, when the cooling system is spinning the meter at a dizzying speed, the house could be cooled by merely opening and closing the right windows.

Cathedral ceilings are dramatic and currently in vogue. But be aware that such ceilings can bring with them serious heating problems. Energy is wasted in conditioning a large volume of air in high unused spaces. And, since warm air rises, it is especially difficult to heat high-ceilinged rooms.

Old architectural standbys can still be used to save a lot of energy. Attached porches, carports, and decking can also serve to protect windows and doors from the direct rays of the sun if they are carefully laid out. If your architectural design allows, consider using operable shutters over windows to screen out the direct rays of the sun and cold blasts of wind.

When you compromise function, you're almost certain to compromise good design.

Figure 5-6   If possible, use ventilating fans to help reduce air-conditioner loads. A good attic or ridge-type ventilator can often entirely eliminate the need for artificial cooling.

SELECT MATERIALS AND WORKMANSHIP
TO CONSERVE ENERGY

Materials. Under no circumstance should you allow yourself to be talked into compromising materials. When selecting materials, consider their thermal properties—as well as price, maintenance and esthetics.

For example, you should use double-glazing on all windows—either insulating glass or storm windows. Many experts now agree that single-thickness glass should not be installed anywhere, because double-glazing can be just as effective in warm climates as cold ones. (See Figure 5-7.) Double-glazing, therefore, should be an integral part of the structure, instead of a purchase that's high on your "things-to-do" list after you've moved in. Though placed high on such a list, other unexpected expenses come along all too often to delay their purchase for another year or two. You'll pay for such procrastination with greater fuel consumption.

Though initially it costs more to install insulated glass than storm windows, the former will save you more in energy bills in the long run. Second, insulated windows eliminate the twice-a-year bother of taking down and putting up of storms and screens. And, you won't have to be concerned about storage space either: You'll appreciate this advantage especially in your retirement years.

Quality aluminum siding is another functional feature. Not only is it easily maintained, but it holds down heat flow. But, if it is installed directly over sheathing without using a thermal guard to keep building costs down, the initial savings are eventually eroded by higher heating costs.

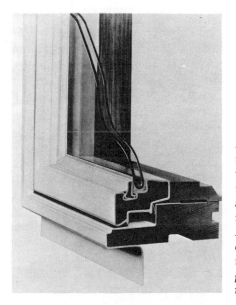

Figure 5-7 Use of double-pane insulating glass eliminates the need for storm windows in many areas—and the annual nuisance of putting up and taking down storms and screens. Top-quality windows may preclude the need for painting. Here, a cross-section drawing of an Andersen Perma-Shield window shows how rigid vinyl sheath over treated wood core provides window components with protection from weather.

To further conserve heat and air-conditioning, install weatherstripping on all doors and windows, if they are not so equipped by the manufacturer. Since both seldom fit perfectly in their jambs, properly installed weatherstripping is a quick and easy way to make them fit tightly. And don't install any metal window that does not have a thermal barrier. Thermally conductive metal frames cause condensation and heat loss, and make it almost impossible to achieve balanced heating.

Workmanship. One of the first questions to ask a contractor's former customers is if their heating bills fall within the range that was promised when they contracted for the house. Inspect several houses he has built to learn if they're tightly built.

Also, while at these homes, tactfully inspect the craftsmanship—or lack of it—in building details. Poor workmanship is a big clue to a builder's qualifications. Sloppy molding and trim work, for example, will quickly indicate that the builder is not concerned with accurate work. Try to determine whether or not windows slide freely and if doors swing and close as they should. In your house you should settle for nothing less. If shoddy work is obvious and glaring, then work that is concealed from view is probably of substandard construction also.

Look outside too. Are joints around windows, doors, chimney, and wall caps well-caulked? Try to determine whether the contractor used low-costing, oil-base type caulks or longer-lasting, more-serviceable types such as acrylic-latex or butyl. You can conclude that if he economizes where it's only a matter of pennies, it's wise to question his thinking on the high-cost items.

INSULATION

The basic purpose of insulation is to resist the flow of heat—that is, heat escaping from the house in winter or entering it in the summer when it's not wanted. Proper insulation, installed correctly, not only significantly reduces the amount of energy used in heating and cooling a home, but reduces air pollution as well. Since about one-fifth of our energy is used for residential and commercial heating purposes, it makes sense to insulate adequately so both individual and collective savings can be achieved.

In the past, the value of insulation was measured in inches of thickness. But the physical characteristics of today's insulating materials—mineral wool, fiberglass, Styrofoam, and the like—varies so much that thickness alone is no longer accurate. A better system has therefore come into use, which gives the user a more accurate indication of the degree of resistance to heat flow a particular insulation product offers. Insulation materials now have "R" numbers, usually printed on the vapor-barrier, or room, side. R values reflect the resistance to heat through a material: the greater the R number, the greater the insulating value. The R values of all building components—studs, sheathing, siding, inside wall covering—can be added up to find the total resistance of a wall, ceiling or floor. (Also see Figure 5-8.)

Figure 5-8 Where to insulate a home. Since all fuels are now expensive—and often hard to obtain—insulation should be used in every new home to eliminate any chance of fuel waste. All walls, floors, and ceilings between conditioned (heated or cooled) and unconditioned spaces should be packed with insulation. Additionally, walls in basements should also be fully insulated (unless they are more than 2 feet below ground level). Walls in finished basements should be fully insulated and sealed with a vapor barrier. The floors over unconditioned crawlspaces and basements should be insulated at least as much as the walls. In slab-on-grade construction, most heat loss occurs at the slab's perimeter; use at least 2 in. of rigid perimeter insulation (Styrofoam or its equivalent). A crawlspace foundation should also receive perimeter insulation.

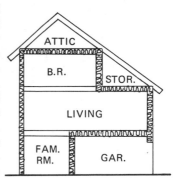

How Much Insulation? In April 1971, the Federal Housing Administration increased its minimum property standards for insulation. These standards now specify an R-11 value in ceilings and R-7 in walls; translated into everyday language, that means materials about 3½ in. thick in ceilings and 2 in. thick in walls. This is really not enough. Instead, use 6 in. material in ceilings and 3½ in. in walls to obtain values of about R-19 and R-11, respectively. You will reduce fuel bills by about 30 percent.

If your home is electrically heated, the R-19 and R-11 figures should be considered the absolute minimum thickness. Check with the local utility company to learn the minimum insulation recommended for electrically heated homes in the area.

Where to Insulate? All walls, floors, and ceilings between conditioned and nonconditioned areas should be fully insulated (Figure 5-9). Other areas include:

1. basement walls that extend less than 2 feet below grade,
2. vented and unvented crawlspaces,
3. all cracks between jambs and framing,
4. in back of band or header joists, and
5. around the perimeter of an on-grade slab.

If you install a forced-air heating system, make sure ducts are fully insulated. Savings through adequate use of duct insulation can be significant because any heat lost through the ducts inevitably lowers the temperature of the entire house.

Insulation Materials. There are four basic types: blanket, batt, loose, and rigid.

The first two, blankets and batts, are most commonly used and can be either fiberglass or mineral wool. The area to be insulated usually dictates which is the better choice. Blanket insulation is manufactured in rolled

Figure 5-9 Insulating an attic floor can be a simple procedure. Here, 6-in. thick batts are simply laid between joists (vapor-barrier side down). Note the apparel on the do-it-yourselfer to protect eyes, arms, and hands from scratches from fiberglass material.

Certain-Teed Corporation

Johns-Manville

Figure 5-10 Pouring wool may be used in unfinished attics by emptying the bags evenly between ceiling joists. When using pouring insulation, adhere to the manufacturer's recommendations for proper thickness and coverage per bag. Use a wood slat or garden rake to level the material and make certain that the eaves' ventilation openings are not blocked. Lay boards across joists to work from, so as not to step through the ceiling below.

widths to suit standard stud and joist spacing. Available in thicknesses of 1 to 3 in., the covering sheet on one side is treated to serve as a vapor barrier. In some cases, the cover sheet is surfaced with aluminum foil or other reflective material.

Batts are made of the same fibrous materials as blankets but are available in thicknesses of 2 to 6 in. Widths of 15 and 23 in. and lengths of 2, 4, and 8-ft. are common. Batts are available with a single cover (for use on the room side) or with both sides covered. Like blankets, some come with vapor-barrier covers, and some do not. These also are available with foil-faced covering.

Loose insulation comes in bags and is used primarily for pouring between joists in an unused attic. Loose fill is usually made of either glass, wool, rock, shredded redwood bark, vermiculite, or powdered gypsum (Figure 5-11).

The rigid insulation ordinarily used in residential construction is installed over, *not between*, studs. It is available in a wide range of sizes from 8 in.

Figure 5-11 A typical insulation installation on a masonry wall consists of 1 in. × 2 in. or 2 in. × 4 in. furring strips, spaced either 16 or 24 in. on center, fastened to the wall with masonry nails or anchors. Masonry wall blankets are then wedged between the furring strips, and a separate polyethylene vapor barrier is stapled over the insulation.

If 2-by-4s are used for furring, thicker blankets, with a vapor-barrier on one side, can be used instead. With these, simply staple the flanges to the face of the 2-by-4s as is done in the conventional installation of framed walls.

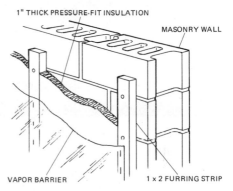

square tiles, to sheets 4 ft. wide by 10 ft. or more long. Thickness is usually from ½ to 1 in. Though it comes smooth on one side for finish painting, insulation board is most often used for roof and wall sheathing, subflooring, and slab floors. It should not be confused with plasterboard, which is thinner and not intended for sheathing use.

The perimeter insulation most often used is Styrofoam. Of varying thicknesses, it is installed around the perimeter (inside the forms) before the slab is poured. It should also be used in heated crawlspaces that serve as return plenums.

No special tools are needed to install insulation. A stapler and box of $\frac{5}{16}$-in. staples, a large shears or utility knife, and a ruler complete the toolkit. You do need goggles, though, to protect your eyes, a respiratory mask to avoid breathing the particles and a long-sleeved shirt to keep your arms free of scratches.

Insulating Tricks. When insulating between ceiling joists, start at the outside (wall top plate) and work across the room. When insulating joists in the attic, be sure that the insulation does not block ventilation at the eaves.

Regardless of where insulation is going in, leave space for ventilation between sheathing and insulation material. (See Figures 5-12 through 5-18 for the basic steps in insulation installation.)

Vapor Barriers. A vapor barrier is a membrane through which water cannot pass. Use an insulation with a vapor barrier applied on the "warm" side of the walls, the side heated in the winter. If no vapor barrier is attached to the insulation, separate vapor barriers are necessary (as illustrated in Figure 5-15). Properly installed they protect floors, ceilings, and walls from moisture that originates within a heated space.

CRAWLSPACE INSULATION

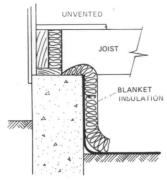

Figure 5-12 To insulate crawlspace walls, first lay a ground cover (the heavy, dark line in drawing), taping its edges to the walls. Next lay insulation blankets of appropriate width longitudinally along the wall, and tape the top flange to the wall. When the sill plate is fastened later, the insulation will be permanently secured. If desired, use bricks or stones at the bottom to hold blankets in place there.

JOIST OVER VENTED CRAWLSPACE

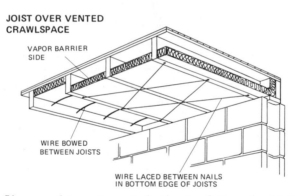

Figure 5-13 If a crawlspace is vented, the insulation should be installed at header joists and between floor joists. The vapor barrier should face up toward the heated room. To hold the insulation in place, use either heavy-gauge wires bowed and wedged between joists, or wires laced between nails in the bottoms of joists. Use either 55-lb. roll roofing or polyethylene as a vapor-barrier ground cover.

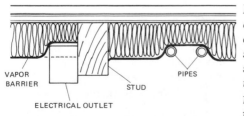

Figure 5-14 When obstructions, pipes, ducts, electric boxes, and the like, are located in wall cavities, push insulation behind them, to the cold side in winter, before stapling the flanges to the studs. You can also pack such spaces with loose insulation or cut a piece of blanket insulation to fit the space: If you do either, cover the area with polyethylene.

VAPOR BARRIERS

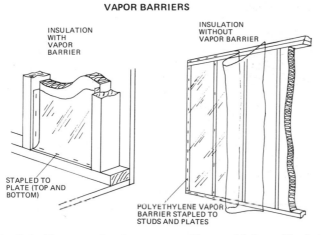

Figure 5-15 Suitable vapor barriers are usually provided on blanket insulation. Here, blankets are pushed into the stud spaces so the flanges can be stapled to the sides of framing members. Space the staples about 8 in. apart and cut the blanket slightly overlength so the barrier can be fastened to the top and bottom plates by compressing the insulation.

When no vapor barrier is attached to the insulation, cover the wall with 2-mil. thick polyethylene stapled to the top and bottom plates. Unroll a sheet to cover the entire wall area—including window and door openings, then cut to length. Staple polyethylene to plates and several studs, cut out openings, then staple around openings.

Repair any major rips or tears in the vapor barrier by stapling new material over the area, or by taping the torn sections back into place.

Figure 5-16 To install blankets in ceilings, staple the flanges from below. When blankets are stapled to the joists, the insulation should be extended over the top plate of the wall (but not so that it blocks ventilation of the eaves). Keep the insulation as close as possible to the plate; if the fit is not a tight one, stuff loose insulation between the blanket and plate.

Blankets and batts without vapor barriers are held in place by pressure-fit between joists without fastening. Plasterboard, which follows, makes certain the insulation stays where it's put.

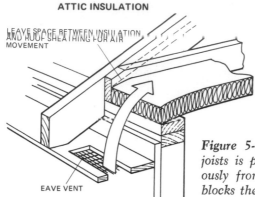

ATTIC INSULATION

LEAVE SPACE BETWEEN INSULATION
AND ROOF SHEATHING FOR AIR
MOVEMENT

EAVE VENT

Figure 5-17 *Insulation between the ceiling joists is placed so that air can flow continuously from eave to attic vent. If insulation blocks the airflow, venting is rendered useless.*

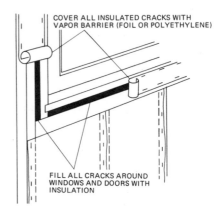

COVER ALL INSULATED CRACKS WITH
VAPOR BARRIER (FOIL OR POLYETHYLENE)

FILL ALL CRACKS AROUND
WINDOWS AND DOORS WITH
INSULATION

Figure 5-18 *Scraps of insulation are stuffed into all cracks between rough framing and door and window finish frames. You can fill the narrowest cracks by forcing pieces in with a putty knife until they are filled. All such loose insulation should then be covered with a polyethylene vapor barrier fastened to stud faces with staples.*

Vapor barriers are necessary because the temperature inside an insulated structure is higher than the temperature outside during cold weather. Blankets or batts are *always* installed with the vapor barrier facing into the heated area, to prevent the moisture that originates in the heated space from moving through to the cool side where it will condense and become water.

The following materials have been found to be satisfactory vapor barriers:

1. polyethylene sheeting, 2 mils or thicker,
2. waterproofed, laminated asphalt-coated paper, and
3. foil-backed gypsum board.

Any vapor barrier that is damaged during installation should be repaired with waterproof tape or, if the damaged section is large, by replacing the entire section.

VENTILATING ATTICS

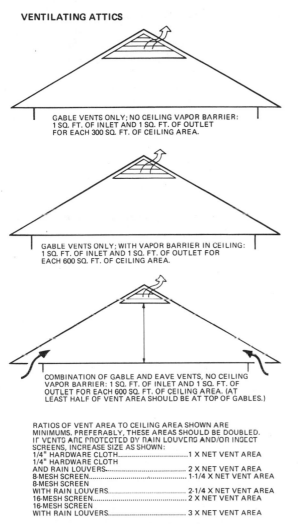

GABLE VENTS ONLY; NO CEILING VAPOR BARRIER:
1 SQ. FT. OF INLET AND 1 SQ. FT. OF OUTLET
FOR EACH 300 SQ. FT. OF CEILING AREA.

GABLE VENTS ONLY; WITH VAPOR BARRIER IN CEILING:
1 SQ. FT. OF INLET AND 1 SQ. FT. OF OUTLET FOR
EACH 600 SQ. FT. OF CEILING AREA.

COMBINATION OF GABLE AND EAVE VENTS, NO CEILING
VAPOR BARRIER: 1 SQ. FT. OF INLET AND 1 SQ. FT. OF
OUTLET FOR EACH 600 SQ. FT. OF CEILING AREA. (AT
LEAST HALF OF VENT AREA SHOULD BE AT TOP OF GABLES.)

RATIOS OF VENT AREA TO CEILING AREA SHOWN ARE
MINIMUMS. PREFERABLY, THESE AREAS SHOULD BE DOUBLED.
IF VENTS ARE PROTECTED BY RAIN LOUVERS AND/OR INSECT
SCREENS, INCREASE SIZE AS SHOWN:
1/4" HARDWARE CLOTH.....................................1 X NET VENT AREA
1/4" HARDWARE CLOTH
AND RAIN LOUVERS...2 X NET VENT AREA
8-MESH SCREEN..1-1/4 X NET VENT AREA
8-MESH SCREEN
WITH RAIN LOUVERS..2-1/4 X NET VENT AREA
16-MESH SCREEN..2 X NET VENT AREA
16-MESH SCREEN
WITH RAIN LOUVERS..3 X NET VENT AREA

National Mineral Wool Insulation Association, Inc.

Figure 5-19 Ventilating Attics Ratios of vent area to floor area shown here are minimums. Whenever possible, vent areas should be twice the area of the figures indicated. It is important that vent sizes be increased according to recommendations if they are protected by rain louvers or insect screen.

Ventilating. Attic ventilation is as necessary in winter as it is in summer. During the warm months ventilation carries off warm air; in winter, the insulation keeps that costly heated air within the house while open vents let moisture escape.

Two vent openings are the absolute minimum in any attic, located so that air will flow in one, pass over the insulated area, and out the other vent. A combination of vents at the eaves and ridge (or high in the gable ends) is best. If it is difficult to achieve natural ventilation, power ventilators can always be installed (Figure 5-20).

The vent area (the size of the opening) is determined by the size of the area being vented. The ratios are shown in Figure 5-19. If at all possible,

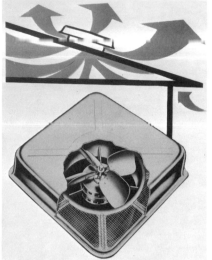

Kool-O-Matic Corp.

Figure 5-20 *Power ventilators effectively help to condition the house and save energy. The thermostat for this model is preset at 100°F.; it will start the fan automatically when the attic temperature reaches that figure and shut it off automatically at 85°F. The thermostat is adjustable and can be reset for warmer climates. The suggested setting for the adjustable humidistat is 90 percent. The fan starts when attic moisture reaches 90 percent, shuts off automatically at 86 percent.*

This unit, which installs on the roof exterior, is completely weatherproof.

VENTING CRAWL SPACES

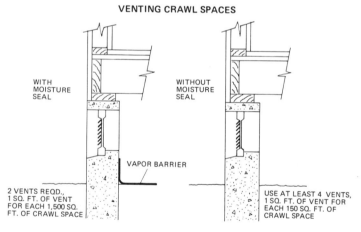

WITH MOISTURE SEAL

WITHOUT MOISTURE SEAL

VAPOR BARRIER

2 VENTS REQD., 1 SQ. FT. OF VENT FOR EACH 1,500 SQ. FT. OF CRAWL SPACE

USE AT LEAST 4 VENTS, 1 SQ. FT. OF VENT FOR EACH 150 SQ. FT. OF CRAWL SPACE

Figure 5-21 *Since a ground cover—an effective vapor barrier—significantly helps keep relative humidity at a low level, crawlspaces so protected will require less net area of venting than unprotected crawlspaces.*

vent sizes should be increased over those shown. (Actually, doubling these sizes is desirable.)

Crawlspaces. The ratios, shown in Figure 5-21, of square feet of vent to area of crawl space ground are minimums. They should be exceeded whenever possible. Because a ground cover helps to keep humidity at a low level, less vent area is required when a vapor barrier is installed.

Two materials that serve adequately as ground cover are 4-mil (or thicker) polyethylene sheet and 55-lb. asphalt roll roofing. Regardless of which type is used, the material should be overlapped a minimum of 3 inches.

At least two vents should be used in a crawlspace, located on opposite sides if possible.

Screening. Vents should be protected by screening to keep out insects, and louvers to keep out rain. When screening is installed over any vent opening, the opening size should be increased as shown in Figure 5-19.

INFORMATION ABOUT "R" VALUES

"R" values are the measure of *resistance* to heat flow (in or out). The higher the "R" value, the greater the material's insulation value and the less the heat loss. Here are several "R" values for window components; the variance makes it obvious why windows should be selected with care whether your second home is in a hot or cold climate.

Component	"R" Value
Metal sash	.85
Wood sash	2.57
Single glass	.89
Insulating glass (¼" air space)	1.64

* Without a specific thermal barrier.

GETTING TOP EFFICIENCY FROM APPLIANCES, MECHANICAL EQUIPMENT, AND FIREPLACES

Nearly 20 percent of our electrical energy supply is used in the home—13.8 percent for home and water heating, and 5.3 percent for major appliances. Thus, it makes good sense to choose all your home equipment with care. Listed here are some common-sense suggestions for conserving energy through the careful selection and use of home equipment. If we all change our energy consumption habits slightly, we are certain to reduce our ironic dependence on a servant—electricity.

Heating and Cooling Equipment. Choose the heating plant and system to suit the house. Too often, oversized heating and cooling systems are utilized, usually because the exact size needed is not available, or because a larger unit is needed to compensate for poor system design.

Note also that all units are not equally efficient. Make certain you choose one that is rated for high efficiency. The efficiency ratings for most systems are available; check them with your architect or plumbing contractor before making a purchase.

Some heating and cooling systems include other energy-saving ideas. There are heating models, for example, featuring retrieval systems that capture heat that might otherwise be lost; the heated air is recirculated through the system, or used as a sort of insulation around the heat source itself. There are also cooling systems that boast open-air cycle devices: These automatically compute whether the indoor or outdoor air can be cooled more efficiently—and then use whichever is cooler and less humid.

The air-conditioning unit itself should be positioned so that it doesn't waste energy. If it is set in the afternoon sun, it is forced to do double duty; it has to work harder to cool warmer air and keep it cool. Place the condenser on the cool, shady side of the house for greatest efficiency.

In a larger home, zoned heating should be considered as essential. This permits conditioned air to be channeled where you want it when you need it there. For example, a living room does not require the same heat at night, when everybody is sleeping, that it does when the room is in use. Conversely, there is no need to condition the air in bedrooms all day when it takes only a couple of hours to get them comfortable for sleeping.

Use ventilating fans. Often, a good attic or ridge-type ventilating fan can completely eliminate the need for a cooling system at all. An unventilated attic can reach temperatures of 130 to 140° F. or more, and much of this heat is radiated down into the living area. A properly utilized ventilating fan can pull that temperature down to below 100°, thus reducing the load on the air-conditioning system if you have one.

For best use of a ventilating fan, position is again important. The fan should draw air from the cooler, shadier side of the house and expel the exhausted air as high up as possible. Exhaust fans placed in the kitchen and bath save the cooling system too. Lacking proper ventilation, these rooms usually become the hottest areas in the house, affecting nearby thermostats accordingly.

But the fans should be used correctly. A large powerful kitchen fan left running for 30 minutes could pull most of the heated or cooled air from a one-story house. Turn on a fan to remove heat, odor, steam, and smoke and then, as soon as the air is cleared, turn it off.

Fireplace Planning. Unlike our ancestors, we tend to think of our fireplaces as an esthetic feature—rather than as a functional source of heat. Most of us like to watch and listen to crackling flames, but give little thought to the wasted heat that is wafting up the chimney. Today, however, there are fireplace units that have ductwork systems to distribute heat among two or three other rooms. Often (in chilly, rather than cold weather) this is just enough to keep the thermostat from activating the heating system.

Ideally, a fireplace should be located on an inside rather than outside wall, so heat moving up the chimney will be radiated to the walls in other rooms, instead of to the great outdoors.

Using Appliances More Wisely. Since better than five percent of your electric bill is generated by the use of appliances, you should know how to use the most common appliances to the fullest—while cutting back your electric bill:

The refrigerator. A refrigerator/freezer doesn't cool by blowing cold air in; rather, it cools by taking warm air out. Thus, here are two things you can do to assure more efficient use:

1. Install your refrigerator away from the range and heater. If possible, put the refrigerator in the coolest spot in the kitchen. It has been estimated that a 15-cu.-ft. frost-free refrigerator will consume about 24 percent more electricity when the room temperature is at 90° then at 70° F.

2. Anytime you leave your second home for a week or more, turn off your refrigerator. Use up or discard all perishables before you leave, clean the unit, and insert an open box of baking soda. Before leaving, make certain that the door has been propped open and that the refrigerator is turned off.

Ranges and ovens. Don't ask these appliances to perform tasks they are not intended for. For instance:

1. In cold weather, never use the oven or surface units to warm the kitchen. Besides being an expensive way to get some heat, they circulate air poorly and consume an inordinate amount of oxygen.

2. If your oven has a self-clean feature, during the cool season use it in the early morning hours instead of in the evening.

3. Thaw out all frozen foods at room temperature before cooking. Putting a frozen roast directly into the oven requires an estimated two-thirds more cooking time.

4. To be operating properly, the flame on a gas range should be blue. Traces of yellow usually indicate clogged burners. When the unit is cool, these should be cleaned with a pipe cleaner—not a toothpick which can break off and make things worse.

The laundry center. Washers and driers are heavy energy users, but a little common sense can keep down your energy consumption considerably.

1. To minimize heat lost through excessive runs of piping, locate the washer as closely as possible to the water heater.

2. A good percentage of the energy used in doing the wash goes to heat the water. Whenever possible, use cold and warm water cycles—rather than hot water—to cut down consumption.

3. Washers with adjustable water level controls—used to select the water level to suit the load—contribute significantly to energy savings.

4. Always keep the dryer exhaust duct free of lint. Besides being a possible fire hazard, a clogged exhaust duct lengthens drying time.

Dishwasher. This appliance is most economical when used at full capacity. Accumulations from several meals (to assure full loads everytime) is the best course to follow. And if your dishwasher has partial load and short wash cycles, use the shortest cycle that will clean your dishes. Finally, use the kind of dishwasher detergent recommended by the manufacturer for maximum efficiency.

OTHER ENERGY-SAVING IDEAS TO USE INSIDE

1. Insulate all hot water pipes to reduce the loss of heat.
2. Locate the water heater as close as possible to the point of use, that is, near the laundry center, kitchen, bathroom, and so on.
3. Install only thermostats that will automatically set back room temperatures at night.
4. Use fluorescents wherever possible; these are much more efficient than incandescents. Try to use low-voltage lighting systems for night lights and outdoor lighting to lower electric consumption even more.
5. Insulate all heating and cooling pipes and ducts to prevent waste by heating or cooling air in unconditioned spaces.
6. Close and seal all spaces between unfinished attic and conditioned spaces, such as cracks around the attic door or in the access panel in the ceiling.

Estimating How Much Insulation to Buy. In order to estimate insulation needs, two factors (obviously) must be known: (1) Where you want to insulate, and (2) What "R" number you have selected.

According to the Johns-Manville Insulation Center, to find out how much insulation you need to cover an area—whether wall, ceiling or floor—multiply the total area (*do not* deduct for joists, rafters or studs) by .90, if framing members are 16 in. on center (O.C.). If framing members are 24 in. O.C., multiply by .94.

For example, suppose you wanted to insulate 1,000 sq. ft. of ceiling area with joists spaced 16 in. O.C. The multiplication would be 1,000 x .90 = 900 sq. ft. of insulation.

Since a roll of blanket insulation measuring 15 in. wide by 32 ft. long provides about 40 sq. ft. of coverage, you will need 23 rolls to complete the job (900 sq. ft. divided by 40 = 22.5, or 23).

Radio and Television. Never let either entertain an empty room. Contrary to popular belief, a blaring radio or television does little to discourage thieves from entering—they quickly detect no other sounds or movement.

If your TV has an instant-on feature, unplug the unit whenever it is not going to be used for an extended period of time. This feature draws current, even when the set is turned off.

Energy conservation is important to us as individuals and as a people. Perhaps insulating a pipeline, cleaning lint from a dryer duct, or turning off a TV may seem silly, even futile. But it seems more and more that these small tasks are the price we must pay for modern conveniences based on energy consumption. Until the day that energy becomes limitless, we will have to take measures to use it sparingly—for the sake of lower monthly bills *and* the overall benefit of the country.

6

Buying and Remodeling

Statistics show that two out of three buyers choose a used rather than
a new house. (That statistic represents all home sales, not just second
homes.) Since there are advantages as well as disadvantages in buying and
remodeling an older home, you should weigh your decision carefully.

The major arguments favoring such a move include:

1. Generally you get more space in an older home than in a brand-new
    dwelling of the same price.

2. Often, especially in the more developed vacation areas, it is the only
    way to get the most desirable real estate.

3. If the house is in reasonably good, livable shape, you can start using
    it immediately. Repairs and renovations can take place later as your
    time and budget allow.

4. The grounds often require little, if any, investment in landscaping.

5. There may also be extra value in the form of outbuildings—a barn,
    shed, oversized garage, and the like.

6. Finally, it is generally easier to obtain financing on a piece of property that has a structure on it.

There are some disadvantages in buying an older home, though, and these factors should be weighed against the pluses. For instance,

1. You will likely have to compromise your "dream house." It's not probable that you'll find the exact house you had in mind when you started out on your second-home venture.

2. Remodeling can be costly. It's a safe bet that the changes you want to make, and the repairs that will *have* to be implemented, will cost more than you originally estimated.

3. Finally, there's always the possibility that your second home can become more drudgery than recreation. If you buy a home in need of major overhauling, you are likely to find yourself spending weekends and summers engaged in heavy labors, rather than relaxing as your original plans called for.

WHO SHOULD REMODEL?

Unless you fall into one of two categories, buying a house in need of extensive repairs should be avoided. To make that scheme work, you'll have to be either: (a) an extra-ambitious, talented do-it-yourselfer, or (b) in a comfortable enough financial position to have much or all of the work done professionally.

A do-it-yourselfer needn't have unlimited funds, but neither should money be so tight that work will grind to a halt frequently because of a scarcity of cash. To buy and remodel on a close budget is possible, of course; many couples do it. Usually, however, those who go this route are prepared to sacrifice comfort for awhile. This means that you might have to haul water from a spring until you can afford to drill a new well. Or you might have to live without a washing machine (and dryer) for a few years—not a terrible hardship these days, since most vacation communities boast at least one laundry center.

Those in need of professional help needn't be armed with an unlimited amount of cash either, but their financial condition should be such that they will be able to obtain a home improvement loan—and handle the payments— with little difficulty.

PLANNING A REMODELING JOB BY OTHERS

The best move, if you can afford it, is to hire an architect to plan and oversee the renovations. As with new-home planning, discuss and agree upon a fee so that there will be no misunderstanding on that count. You should tell the architect exactly what you can afford to spend, neither overstating nor minimizing the amount, or you are almost certain to end up with a house that is either outside your financial reach or less than you wanted.

A qualified architect will suggest renovations that are within your budget and see that you get the highest possible value for every dollar you invest. For the fee, he or she will supervise the contractor's work and shoulder all responsibility for the remodeling.

Before retaining the architect, visit some houses he has renovated. You want to be certain that his tastes and preferences coincide with yours.

ABOUT BUYING AND REMODELING

In such a venture, don't lose sight of the value of the house in relation to its surroundings. You should aim to keep the value of the house within a realistic price range for the neighborhood. For example, let's suppose you can "steal" a home for $15,000 that would likely sell for $30,000 after it has been properly restored. The ceiling amount for remodeling is, obviously, $15,000—the difference between the purchase price and the true market value. If the required work pushes the cost of remodeling beyond that figure, your best bet is to forget the house and look elsewhere. For example, if you spend $30,000 remodeling the house, and then you are forced to sell within a relatively short time, you will find it difficult to peddle a $45,000 home in a neighborhood filled with $30,000 houses. You will probably have to swallow the $15,000 loss.

Before buying an older home, therefore, consider retaining an architect to inspect the premises and provide you with a written report of the findings. For a modest fee, he or she will check all structural aspects and, if you spell out your family's specific needs, render an opinion as to whether the house will fulfill those needs.

Logically, once you decide you'd like to buy a house, you make the seller an offer. If the seller believes or knows that the price offered is a realistic one, he will probably not haggle. If, on the other hand, the house obviously requires renovating, the sale price is likely to be negotiable. In any event, the price you pay for the dwelling—plus the cost of remodeling—should not exceed the dwelling's fair market value.

Once purchase price is agreed upon, you and the seller must then negotiate the terms of the sale contract. Since this contract is binding upon both parties and should spell out exactly what comes with the house, there are several items you should make certain are included:

1. that the contract is conditional upon the house meeting the local building and health codes,
2. that a termite inspection has been made and the house is termite-free,
3. that a free and clear title is obtainable, and

4. finally, the sale should be conditioned upon your being able to obtain financing for the purchase, allowing you a reasonable amount of time to do so.

You can, if desired, record a real estate purchase contract and thus prevent the seller from selling the home to another buyer. Basically, you and the seller must decide whether to record the contract. Follow your attorney's advice and local custom on this score.

Are the Renovations Needed or Just Desirable. The word "remodel" means different things to different people. Basically, work on older homes falls into one of three categories:

1. *Replacing undesirable features with desirable ones.* These tasks are usually of the "must-do" variety, such as a rotted porch that should, for safety reasons, be torn out and rebuilt. Or perhaps unrepairable gutters and leaders that are causing a damp basement must be replaced. The jobs in this class should top the list of things to do for any house you might inspect.

2. *Renovations.* The renewal or replacement of outdated features, this type of approach includes projects like tearing out a dated—but still usable—kitchen and replacing it with a fully equipped modern one. It also includes jobs on the outside, such as re-siding over blistered and peeling siding rather than painting.

3. *Improving.* Under this heading come such chores as interior painting, wallpapering, refinishing floors, paneling walls, and the like—all of which are intended to improve the condition of the place. These projects are the least costly, usually nonstructural, and can be postponed indefinitely until you have the time to do them yourself on a pay-as-you-go basis.

NARROWING THE SEARCH

After one or two weekend excursions, you will quickly realize that time is your most precious commodity. Thus you shouldn't plan to make a detailed inspection of each and every home that your broker leads you to. In all likelihood, some homes will turn you off before you ever walk through the front door. For example, perhaps the architectural styling leaves you cold. Or if an isolated house in the woods is your passion, you won't want to waste time visiting dwellings lined up in a row on a busy street.

In the beginning, however, make at least a cursory inspection even of those homes that interest you least. By evaluating a number of houses, you increase your knowledge of what to look for and of what houses are going for in the area. The more homes you look at, the surer you will be of your final choice.

Figure 6-1 A charming house, with beach rights and an unimpaired view of the water, can cause potential buyers to overlook—or minimize—important aspects regarding the shape of the house itself. Here, for example, the absence of gutters and downspouts could cause water to accumulate in the basement. Additionally, since the cedar shingles have been covered with paint, periodic repainting will be a must because of ocean spray and strong sun.

Your first criterion, each time you look over a house, is whether it will suit the needs of your family. This prerequisite should remain foremost no matter how many homes you look at.

And don't expect to take in all the details on a first visit. Return to critically inspect those homes that interest you most.

Don't automatically believe all the claims that the broker makes for the house: Remember who is paying the broker's commission. But neither should you discount all he or she has to offer. A reputable local broker is well aware that once you buy, you will be a neighbor—and a potential source of good or ill will.

Some people can be very casual when making what might be the biggest investment of their lives. Many spend more time looking over a car than they do investigating a house before buying. At all costs, avoid such an attitude. If because of a hasty inspection you end up with a house that is a constant and perhaps expensive irritant, rather than a source of delight, you will have only yourself to blame.

WHAT TO DO BEFORE GOING TO AN INSPECTION

A good, initial house inspection is mainly a matter of common sense. Though you may not be able to conduct an inspection on a par with that of a professional in the home-building business, you can look carefully for good and bad points by following a logical inspection procedure.

First, purchase an inexpensive notebook to carry along on your house-buying search, to guard against a blurred memory distorting and confusing the homes in your mind. In this book keep a record of all impressions of each house you look at. Record such information as address, size of the land, price, taxes, heating bills, what comes with the house, and any special features. While still at the house, you should also write down what remodeling tasks you think are necessary.

Bring along a tape measure or rule so you can accurately measure rooms, to determine whether they will suit your intended use. Ask yourself such questions as whether or not your king-size bed will fit in the master bedroom. In many older homes, you will find it will not.

Be friendly with the owners but try to avoid an abundance of conversation with them. A lot of talk is sure to distract you from the primary purpose of your mission—a careful inspection. If possible, conduct the inspection without the owners trailing along. If they insist on staying with you—and they can do so if they choose to—don't continuously make comments about this or that fault. Rather, write down your impressions unobtrusively in your notebook. Later, in privacy, you and your spouse can discuss the house's strong and weak points.

WHAT TO LOOK FOR DURING AN INSPECTION

A good, initial inspection covers the points itemized for exteriors and interiors below. You don't need the help of a professional home inspector until you have decided on one home in particular.

In general, be wary of the "do-it-yourself specials" and other bargain homes. Often these turn out to be nothing more than a dilapidated shell whose remodeling is likely to require 100 percent of the owner's time and cash resources.

The Exterior. Make certain that the foundation walls rise at least 8 in. above grade and that the land is pitched away from the foundation to provide positive water runoff. A 6-in. pitch in a 10-ft. run is usually sufficient.

Walk around the entire house and check the foundation for cracks that usually indicate settlement.

While outside, visually inspect the roof from the ground. If height doesn't bother you, and the owner has an extension ladder you can borrow, use it to make a close-up inspection of the roof's condition. Note what type of materials were used, and ask the owner how long ago the roofing was applied. Also ask for a guarantee on the job if one exists.

Check gutters and leaders (downspouts). These are intended to carry rainwater *away* from the house—are they doing their job?

Inspect the condition of the siding and paint. If the house is freshly painted and you suspect that the paint was applied to cover faults, use your finger to poke at areas behind downspouts or where the siding butts

Figure 6-2 The house is also built too close to the ground. Because the bottom course of the clapboard siding is literally resting in the mud, termites have a ready-made attack route —direct from the soil to the wood in the house.

window and door casings. These are the places where water usually enters siding material to cause blistered and peeled paint. If this is a problem, the wood will be soft and spongy.

The Interior. Inspect carefully on the inside too. Spend considerable time especially in the basement and attic. In these locations structural members, rafters, joists, and the like, are exposed and available for close scrutiny. The two most serious house faults—presence of water and structural unsoundness—will be found here if either exists. If water gets into the house each time it rains, you are most likely to find evidence of the condition in either or both locations. Similarly, if framing is inadequate, it is here you'll spot sagging and cracking timbers. You must be completely assured that the structure is sound. Structural repairs can be prohibitively expensive.

1. *Termites.* The first thing to look for—in any home—is infestation by termites, which can be found in every state in the union except Alaska.

After the termites swarm in the spring, you should look for dropped wings around window wells, porches, or stoops, where termites generally attack. The presence of wings indicates that a swarm of the pests dropped them and burrowed into the ground at that spot. Ultimately, they will dine on the house itself.

Since they first attack sills, joist ends, and subflooring above sills, check these structural members carefully. Often, the presence of termites cannot be determined with the eye alone. Using an icepick or small-bladed pocket-knife, try to puncture the sill at several places around the house perimeter. If the blade or pick enters effortlessly and the wood feels hollow or spongy, it's a pretty safe bet that the house either has termites or is plagued with wood rot. Either problem is a major one that should be corrected before

TERMITE INFESTATION

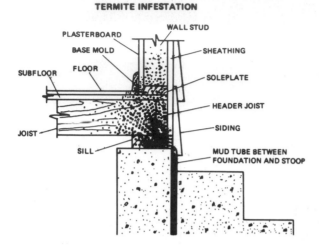

Figure 6-3 Subterranean termites are the most destructive of all insects. Preferring darkness and humidity, they'll construct mud tubes to span open spaces (from the crawlspace floor to the underside of joists, for example). A crack as thin as 1/64 in. can be used as an attack route. Once in the house, the pests chew their way through the dwelling, as shown here. If left unchecked, termites will eventually do serious structural damage to the house.

you consider purchasing the house. In fact, lenders will stop mortgage proceedings until they are.

Though a heavy infestation or existing termite condition can be easily spotted by an amateur, you must get an expert's opinion. In all likelihood, the lending institution will require a professional report anyway before you can secure a mortgage. An inspection by a professional exterminator typically costs $20 to $25.

2. *Check whether the structure is sound.* Using a level and steel square, carefully check the squareness of corners, the level of joists, and the plumb of exterior walls in the basement. If beams sag or drop and walls are badly out of plumb, it is a good sign that the house is subject to excessive settlement. Since this fault is a structural one, there is little (if any) chance that the faults can be corrected without great expense. You are well advised to steer clear of such structures.

3. *The heating plant.* Is it rundown or in well-maintained shape? If possible, find out who has been servicing the equipment so you can discuss the system with the serviceman. If the system looks doubtful, call in a plumbing and heating specialist for an estimate of just what repairs or replacements are called for and what both will cost. An expert can also give you a fairly accurate estimate on how long you can expect the heating system to last.

Equally important is the question as to how efficient the heating plant is. For example, is it sized to suit the house or must it run constantly to keep the house comfortable in winter? Also, if you plan to build an addition to the house, find out now whether the heating plant is capable of warming the contemplated addition. If it isn't, you'll have to figure on adding the cost of a new heating system to the cost of the addition itself.

4. *The basement.* Is it damp and musty? If so, it's a warning flag that problems exist. Many basements that appear dry during warm summer

months are under several inches of water each year when the spring thaw arrives. Carefully inspect the lower half of foundation walls to look for tell-tale signs of water penetration (that is, a watermark).

While you are in the basement, look for cracks in the foundation walls —signs of inferior workmanship, not only in the basement but likely in the remainder of the house as well.

If piles of debris, luggage, cartons, and the like, prevent you from inspecting foundation walls, ask the seller if you can move them so you can take a look. If permission is denied, you have reason to be suspicious. If there is no objection, make certain you put the pile back as it was.

5. *Poor plumbing.* All other features being equal, a home connected to a public sewer system should be selected over one serviced by a septic tank. Periodic replacement of a septic tank is an expensive proposition.

Check every plumbing fixture in the house including outside hose bibbs. If water merely dribbles from faucets, and the toilet takes an excessively long time to refill after flushing, the water lines may be filled with mineral deposits and may need replacing.

Fill sinks and bathtubs with water, then open the stoppers to see if they drain quickly and quietly. If drainage is slow, either the waste line is clogged or the septic tank may need replacing. A gurgling sink may indicate an improperly (and, in all probability, illegally) vented waste line.

Flush all toilets to make sure a single flush clears all waste from the bowl and that the water stops running when the bowl is refilled to the correct height.

It's a good idea to learn the name of the plumber who last serviced the house and have him check the water pressure. The plumber is also the logical one to ask whether the plumbing, in general, is in good shape and, if not, what it will cost to make it so.

6. *Electrical wiring.* First inspect the house service panel to determine if there is sufficient amperage to serve your needs: 100 amp., 220 v. is the recommended minimum. If the house has less, you can anticipate the expense of bringing its electrical service up to today's standards.

If the service has been updated recently and has blank circuits on the board (extra capacity), it is to your advantage. You will be able to add electrical appliances as you need them without fear of overloading wires or blowing a fuse.

You should also make certain that there are an ample number of convenience outlets. The National Electric Code requires an outlet for every 12 feet of running wall space. This requirement assures flexibility of furniture placement, enhances lighting, and minimizes the use of unsightly extension cords. If outlets have to be added, the job involves a lot more than simply calling in an electrician. In order to conceal new wiring, the electrician has to punch holes in the walls and, often, in the ceilings of every room in which work is done. Patching these holes can be an extensive and costly job.

Also, to be safe, request an inspection by the local government for electrical code compliance, thus assuring you that wiring is not worn, exposed, or dangerous.

7. *Insulation.* If the annual heating bill for a house seems to be on the high side, and the heating system checks out as an efficient one, the reason is probably poor insulation or no insulation at all.

First determine what insulating material was used and how it was installed. (See Chapter 5 for insulating basics.) A qualified heating expert can tell you whether or not the insulation comes close to providing recommended R-values in walls and ceilings. You can have this inspection done by an independent heating engineer, or ask the utility company (or firm supplying fuel oil) for its advice. Many energy suppliers give this service at no charge.

8. *Fireplace.* If you have visions of yourself parked in front of that charming old fireplace on white, wintry evenings, now is the time to make sure that it is, in fact, usable. If the fireplace is particularly old, chances are the flue lining should be cleaned and inspected by a contractor to make certain danger from fire doesn't exist.

Walk outside and look up at the chimney. Does it rise well above the ridge of the house? If not, downdrafts on the roof or nearby tall trees are almost certain to cause backdrafts into the room in which the fireplace is located. If the chimney doesn't sport a cap, you're going to want to add one.

9. *Interior decoration and finishing.* Inspect floor and wall tiles in the bath and kitchen. Make certain that they are well-adhered and not about to topple from the wall or lift from the floor.

In the kitchen, check the condition of cabinets and whether cabinet doors fit and close properly. Since the cooking range comes with the house, give it a going over too, making sure that all pilot lights and burners work.

In most older homes walls and ceilings are of plaster. Beware of bulges under wallpaper and large cracks in painted walls. Both are indications that the plaster has lost its key to the plaster lath beneath. Correcting the problem means taking down plaster and replacing it with new plaster or plasterboard.

About New Homes. If, after checking out older houses, you decide that a new home would better suit your needs, don't let newness cause you to buy without a careful inspection. New homes, as well as older ones, should be gone over with a fine-tooth comb before making a deposit.

WHY A GOOD INSPECTION PAYS

An inspection is supposed to uncover existing faults and let you know in advance what will have to be corrected. A cursory inspection defeats these aims.

Some shortcomings may have to be corrected before the lending institution will close the deal. If you have a hefty down payment tied up in the house, you'll need more cash to make the improvements before the bank will proceed with the mortgage. Thus, it may pay to retain either an architect or qualified builder to inspect the house before making a down payment. Both are qualified to determine the structural soundness of the dwelling and give you an estimate of what it will cost to make necessary repairs or desired improvements. An expert's fee is well worth knowing what you can realistically expect to spend if you buy the house.

WHAT COMES WITH THE HOUSE?

Generally, real estate is defined as the land and everything that is attached to it—buildings, trees, shrubs, and the like. Under normal circumstances, the buyer gets all of the real estate, but none of the seller's personal property. Problems can arise, however, when personal property becomes part of the real estate. When it does, it is called a "fixture" and passes with the real estate. Fixtures include shades, heaters, ranges, screens, storm windows, lighting fixtures, and the like.

To make the determination as to whether or not a particular item is part of the real estate, three tests must be satisfied:

1. Is the personal property permanently annexed to the real estate?
2. Was it intended to become a part of the real estate?
3. Can the fixture be considered as such in light of local custom?

Confusion can be avoided by communication. For example, if a seller has affixed an antique chandelier to the dining room ceiling, but does not intend to sell it with the house, he or she should either replace the fixture before showing the house or inform the potential buyer that the chandelier will be replaced by another fixture of agreed-upon value. Once property has been inspected by the buyer, *no* fixture should be exchanged without the buyer's approval. Disagreement can arise on such items as partially built-in hi-fi units, intercoms, window air-conditioners—all of which may or may not be anchored in some way to the dwelling.

The seller must accurately spell out in the sale contract exactly what he will give the buyer as part of the real estate. Clarity and full understanding at this point are musts. A misunderstanding at the time of closing can be serious enough to cause the purchase to fall through.

ESTIMATING REMODELING COSTS

With the inspection completed, you can get down to the nitty-gritty—can you afford the necessary remodeling? While lesser improvements—such as painting, wallpapering, and the like—can be handled by a do-it-yourselfer for the cost of materials, you will need a rundown on the major remodeling items. The following itemization is accurate, though costs can vary (usually insignificantly) from one area to the next.

* A *well:* About $1,500, but the total cost is dependent upon geological conditions.
* A *septic tank:* $1,500 minimum.
* A *roof:* Figure $600 to $800 depending upon the roof area. Roofers arrive at charges by billing $25 to $35 per 100 sq. ft.
* *Gutters and downspouts:* Materials, which vary widely, determine price. A first-rate job with quality guttering materials on a typical three-bedroom house costs about $600.
* *House painting:* The price is based upon three factors: (1) the size of the house, (2) the number of doors and windows, and (3) the quality of the paint used. You can expect to pay from $1,200 to $2,000.
* *Re-siding:* This varies for the same reasons that house painting does. For the cost of a good re-siding job with aluminum or vinyl, multiply the cost of a quality, professional paint job by two-and-one-half (2½).
* *Exterminating termites:* The cost depends on the size and type of house (basement or slab) and on the degree of infestation. A typical extermination job will run about $400 for a slab house, $350 for a house with a basement. A heavily infested and damaged house can raise expenses well over $1,000. If timbers must be replaced, a building contractor will probably take the job only on a time-and-materials basis.
* A *heating system:* For $1,600 to $2,500, you will get the basic heating unit—no cooling in summer. Before investing, make certain you read about heating systems in Chapter 12.
* *Electrical wiring:* A 100 amp., 220 v. panel costs about $250; a larger panel will be proportionately higher. Convenience outlets are priced at a rate of approximately $10 each, but that figure does not include the cost of patching walls and ceilings after the electrician has finished. Rewiring an entire house will cost anywhere between $600 and $1,200.
* *Kitchen remodeling:* $2,500 to $6,000, depending on the number of cabinets, and the quantity and quality of the appliances chosen.
* *Bathroom remodeling:* At least $1,500, though this amount will run considerably higher if a new waste line is needed, or if you prefer ceramic tiles on floor and walls. Bath remodeling can cost up to $8,000.

As you can see, the costs for basic remodeling projects quickly add up to an impressive figure. In many cases, remodeling costs can and do surpass the purchase price of the house.

S R & A, Inc.

Figure 6-4 Before: *After 60 years' exposure to seaside sun, spray, and winds, this stolid home showed its age. Since the house was in good structural shape, however, new owners were able to move in and confine their efforts, time, and cash outlay to esthetic changes.*

S R & A, Inc.

Figure 6-5 After: *The house was effectively modernized by closing in the dark porch facing the bay. The old, narrow jalousy windows were replaced with casements, to create windowed walls on three sides of the new sun room. Upstairs, floor-to-ceiling sliding doors lead out to a new second-floor balcony. The deck area in front of the sunroom is shaded by a plastic roof cover; this treatment also keeps down the cost of conditioning (heating and cooling) the house.*

Keeping Costs as Low as Possible. No matter how much of the work you plan to do yourself, there will be times when you will probably have to hire some professional help. To keep the cost for such services down, contract for them during the off-season as much as possible. Though tradesmen charge top dollar when the vacation season is in full swing, most have ample time on their hands between Labor and Memorial Days. During this period, their rates are lowest and they are dependably available.

Remodel in Logical Sequence. Once you have moved in, don't make the mistake of attacking remodeling chores in a willy-nilly fashion. Rather, you should have a long-range, overall schedule for projects to take place, so that work done last year won't be torn out for this year's project. If repairs and renovations are extensive, consult an architect. Besides assuring the use of

S R & A, Inc.

Figure 6-6 *Airy, bright, and refreshing, the remodeled porch is now the most active room in this updated seaside second home. The glass walls were designed around Andersen Corporation's Perma-Shield casement windows. This quality-built product features double-paned lights to save energy, and vinyl cladding to eliminate the periodic repainting chore outside.*

the latest and best materials, he or she can advise you as to which projects should take precedence over others.

In general, here is the preferred (and recommended) schedule of renovations:

1. *Correct plumbing deficiencies first.* Good water and waste lines are a must for livability as well as for health reasons. Since the repair of ancient plumbing systems often requires ripping out walls and ceilings, this overhaul should take place before any esthetic changes are made in the dwelling.

The bathroom should be the first room to be updated. It makes little sense to modernize a kitchen (ordinarily beneath the bath in a two-story house), only to expose it to serious damage from faulty plumbing overhead.

2. *House rewiring* should be done early in the remodeling game for pretty much the same reasons as plumbing renovation—torn-out walls, dust, dirt, and similar headaches. More important, inadequate, damaged, or exposed wiring is a safety hazard to your family. If the local building inspector determines that the house, in fact, must be rewired, the rewiring should be done before you move in.

3. *Kitchen renovation.* Usually, the kitchen is the hub of the home—

the center of family activity. Renovating a kitchen, therefore, is a major job, one wrapped up by a professional in two weeks but one dragged out by a do-it-yourselfer for six months to a year.

4. *Roof and siding.* Now that you've spent all that loot inside, protect your investment from the elements. A handsome exterior is not only extremely functional, it is what most folks see, a reflection of the people inside.

5. *Esthetic changes.* When the "must-do" jobs are taken care of, you can go to work tearing out nonbearing walls, installing picture windows for views, and refurbishing the interior in general.

The decorative projects can be spread over a number of years so they can be paid for either on a cash basis or with relatively painless monthly loan payments. And while these projects are underway, you'll be using and enjoying your second home.

This and That About Buying and Remodeling an Older Home. If you intend to make any of the typical improvements listed below, here's a rough idea of what you can expect such extras to cost:

* An in-ground swimming pool can run anywhere from $5,000 to $14,000.

* A quick but fairly reliable way to figure the cost of a kitchen is to estimate the kitchen cabinet cost, using $150 to $200 per lineal foot. You can also figure that replacement of inadequate plumbing and electrical wiring in the room will add another $2,000. A basic appliance package (refrigerator and range) will cost from $500 to $600. If you opt for such creature comforts as a dishwasher, garbage disposal, compactor, and microwave oven, the appliances will add up to $2,000.

* If you plan to build an extension on your house, run the longer wall against the existing house, if possible. Building two shorter (end) walls and one long wall is obviously cheaper than two long walls and one short wall.

* Before starting a house addition, check out local regulations concerning sewage and septic tanks. In some localities, minimum septic-tank size is based upon the number of bedrooms, so adding a bedroom may require a larger tank as well. If so, your addition can cost another $500 to $600.

* Finally, when choosing a contractor for remodeling work, try to pick one who is a member of a recognized trade organization such as the National Association of Homebuilders, Kitchen Dealers Association, or National Home Improvement Council. Members of such organizations stay in good standing only by performing as promised.

There are advantages to buying an older home. It is usually a more spacious dwelling with established landscaping, located on the best plot.

Further, it generally has had the little personal things done to it that a new home does not. It is also more easily financed.

But you must exercise caution with an older structure. Despite the generally appreciating values of real estate, you are buying a building that has been exposed to all the possibilities that time can bring. Keep in mind the measures outlined in this chapter, however, and you should have few, if any, problems.

7

Building in Stages...
The Expandable
House

* Planning is important * Getting started * Tenting out * Used
trailer * Temporary shed * Garage * Basement * Other choices
* This and that about on-job living * Security * Your power tools
* Building know-how *

Building and expanding a house in stages is certain to appeal to do-it-yourselfers. Building in this fashion, you stand a far better chance of staying within your budget and of avoiding a king-sized mortgage when the dwelling is finished. If you have a fair amount of common sense and some handyman skills, building in stages is a sound approach to second-home ownership. It is especially worth considering if you'd like to spread the cost over a number of years. Even if you plan to have all construction done by a contractor, an add-on house could be the quickest way to start using your country property —barring a prefabricated or mobile home. You can start enjoying your leisure-home property as soon as the first stage is up and closed-in. While living in the first stage, you can then add the remaining stages as time and money allow.

But there are other good reasons to consider an expandable house.

For one thing, the composition of a family changes: children are born, grow up, get married, and produce grandchildren; or close relatives—brothers, sisters, grandparents—move in. To accommodate such future growth, a house with expansion possibilities is a practical and wise choice. The house on pages 128–133 is a good example of a dwelling whose specifications take such changes into account. Future construction is taken into consideration and planned. For example, rough openings are provided in the walls so that the cost of alteration at a later date is kept to a minimum. Adequate service

121

utilities (plumbing, wiring, and heating) for the completed house all go in during the first stage, so that the following stages cost proportionately less on a square-foot basis.

Finally, a house with expansion possibilities is more marketable than one without, and resale is therefore generally easier.

Quite understandably, however, the thought of building a house frightens many. Such fears are not entirely without foundation when you consider the number of details involved in a project of this size and scope. Happily, you'll find that building in stages can do much to allay these fears. The project seems—and is—far less awesome when you concern yourself with only one stage at a time.

As the work progresses, your experience and knowledge will accumulate. You might be pleasantly surprised to find yourself completely capable of handling many tasks that you had suspected were beyond your skills. Conversely, you might find some jobs you figured on doing yourself are better done by others.

A question you will have to ask repeatedly is, "When is the right time to call in professional help?" Generally, you should count on outside help for such heavy chores as foundation and masonry work, and for those tasks requiring special knowledge and tools such as plumbing, heating, and electrical installation. Only you will be able to tell when it is wiser to subcontract the work. When you do seek professional services, keep the costs as low as possible by arranging your work schedule so that subcontractors are used during the off-season—when they are more readily available and usually charge less.

PLANNING IS IMPORTANT

Don't foolishly cut corners in an effort to save money in the first stage of building. An overall plan for the complete house, with all stages finished, is of extreme importance. Without long-range planning, you are very likely to end up with a lopsided structure that looks like it has been expanded indiscriminately—a cubistic abstraction of good house design. Happily, it is far easier than you might suspect to avoid such an end product: There are a number of expander-type house plans available on the market, such as the typical one on pages 128–133.

GETTING STARTED

First you have to provide some sort of on-site housing to serve your family's basic needs while constructing the first stage. You can:

1. live in a tent,
2. buy a used trailer,
3. build a temporary shed,

4. build the garage first and live in it, or

5. live in the basement.

If you plan to use either a tent, trailer, or shed as on-site housing, locate the structure with care. Don't select a low spot that is likely to collect and hold water each time it rains. Make certain there is good drainage *away* on surrounding ground so that you don't wind up living in a stream during a rain. For comfort, the dwelling should receive some sunlight during the day and shade during late afternoon.

Tenting Out. Though tenting is sure to get the youngsters' votes, Dad might have some reservations about the scheme if he is an ex-Army man. Living in a tent is roughing it for sure but, for romantics, it has a charm of its own. In my opinion, a family experiences an adventurous, pioneer-like spirit when living in a tent and erecting a house with their own hands.

Basically, you can use either one of two types of tents: the cabin type, in sizes to sleep from four to ten; and the two-person tent (A-shape). The first is available in prices ranging from $70 to $140, while you can get under cover in the latter type for $25 or less. A cabin-type is roomier and provides some walking-around space—a particularly welcome feature on days when rain halts job production. The smaller A-type is intended strictly for sleeping, useful for no more than two sharing the housebuilding chores. No matter which type of tent you buy, for comfort and health reasons, make certain it is fitted with adequate screening to keep bugs out.

Before investing money in camping paraphernalia, however, check with the local building department to make certain that you will be allowed to camp temporarily on your property. If you are off by yourself in the woods this question shouldn't present a problem. On the other hand, if your building plot is in a partially developed area, your neighbors—comfortably ensconced in their finished dwellings—may have plenty to say about the idea. And so may the local ordinances.

Wherever you are building, roughing it doesn't mean you have to be miserable. So *make your tent comfortable.* In fact, the lack of comfortable quarters will directly affect your work.

Try to erect your tent on a platform (see Figure 7-1) to get you up out of the mud and provide a barrier to prowling nocturnal animals. The platform materials will not be wasted: After you move into the first stage of your home, you can carefully dismantle the platform, strip all members of nails, and reuse the materials in the second stage.

For jobsite living comfort, you will have to bring along some creature comforts. Here's the minimum you'll need:

1. Energy. In the final analysis, you will come out ahead if you power your tent lights, heater, and cooktop with bottled propane gas. It is safer than fussing with liquid fuels for the various accessories, and each appliance can be connected with minimum bother. You buy L-P gas by the bottle (cylindrical tank) and simply connect lines to feed those appliances you have.

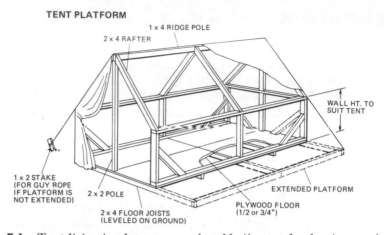

TENT PLATFORM

1 x 4 RIDGE POLE

2 x 4 RAFTER

WALL HT. TO
SUIT TENT

1 x 2 STAKE
(FOR GUY ROPE
IF PLATFORM IS
NOT EXTENDED)

2 x 2 POLE

EXTENDED PLATFORM

2 x 4 FLOOR JOISTS
(LEVELED ON GROUND)

PLYWOOD FLOOR
(1/2 or 3/4")

Figure 7-1 *Tent living is a lot more comfortable if you take the time to rig it up on a semipermanent basis by building a simple frame such as this one. Use nominal "two-by" stock (2-by-3s or 2-by-4s) to frame the temporary structure and cover the floor with exterior-grade plywood.*

Lumber can be reused when you move into the first stage of the house and chances are you'll recoup about half the cost of the tent. This type is available in sizes to sleep from four to ten.

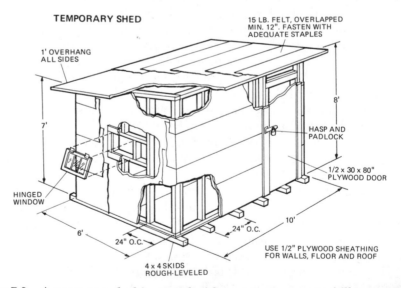

TEMPORARY SHED

15 LB. FELT, OVERLAPPED
MIN. 12". FASTEN WITH
ADEQUATE STAPLES

1' OVERHANG
ALL SIDES

8'

7'

HASP AND
PADLOCK

1/2 x 30 x 80"
PLYWOOD DOOR

HINGED
WINDOW

24" O.C.

10'

6'

24" O.C.

USE 1/2" PLYWOOD SHEATHING
FOR WALLS, FLOOR AND ROOF

4 x 4 SKIDS
ROUGH-LEVELED

Figure 7-2 *A temporary shed is erected without any unnecessary frills or expense. Walls are clad with the same material as the floor and roof—½-in. plywood sheathing. Install at least one screened, operable window as shown: Ventilation is a must if you plan to use L-P gas-powered appliances inside. Here, too, materials can be saved and reused in house construction. Before building your temporary shed, however, make certain they're allowed in your area.*

2. *Toilet.* Select one of the portable chemical toilets rather than the type that utilizes plastic bags. Porta-Potti, available at camping supply stores or Sears, Roebuck and Co., for about $100, comes with a detachable holding tank that stores the waste. Its design makes it gas-tight and self-cleaning. To empty it, you simply carry the holding tank to a permanent waste facility. A 50-flush water supply makes the unit a perfect size for weekend use by the family.

3. *Refrigeration.* If your work sessions are confined to weekends, an L-P powered refrigerator is not necessary; these are costly and short on storage space. Instead, use a quality ice-chest. During the week deep-freeze all freezable foods for the weekend. Come Friday, put the frozen and other foods in the chest along with an ample supply of ice cubes. If the chest is kept out of the direct rays of the sun, the food will be cooled all weekend.

Buy a quality ice chest for about $40—not the $1 Styrofoam types found in supermarkets (which are fine, perhaps, for a quick trip to the beach). In a tent, someone at some point will use the chest as a chair. The cheap, beach-type will crack and food will spoil.

4. *Stove.* A decent two-burner propane camp stove for about $30 will do the job. Chances are the stove will be used mostly for breakfast, coffee, soups and the like. More often than not, you will have sandwiches for lunch and charcoal-cooked foods in the evening.

5. *Heater.* For $30 or so, you can take the chill out of the tent with a catalytic heater, which is safer than a liquid-fueled heater since there is no pumping, priming, filling, or spilling. Though a catalytic heater is not as likely as an open flame heater to consume *all* the oxygen in the tent, it should still be used with adequate ventilation.

6. *Sleeping.* You'll need a cot and a sleeping bag for each member of the family. A sturdy camp cot can be bought for as little as $10—maybe less in a

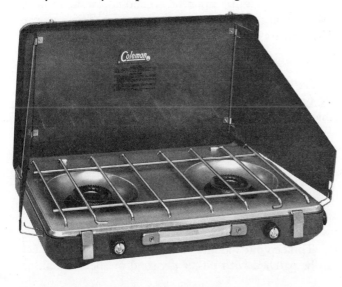

Figure 7-3 Model 5410-708 two-burner propane stove by Coleman Company features precisely controlled heat and easy cleaning. If desired, the stove can be connected to a large, refillable propane bottle as described in the text.

Priced at about $40, it's all the cookstove you'll need in your temporary quarters. Each of two large burners produces up to 10,000 BTUs of heat. The folding wind baffles protect cooking efficiency from drafts.

Figure 7-4 Some appliances stand double duty, as does this heater-cooker from Zebco Camping Appliances (about $40). Swing the heater head up and lock it in place for use as a catalytic heater or use it lying flat in its case as a burner surface for cooking.

Labeled Zebco 2700 Convertible, the unit has storage space inside for two disposable propane cylinders.

second-hand store. Sleeping bags are available in prices ranging from $8 for a youth size up to $80 or more, depending upon how good you want to be to yourself. There are two important points to watch for when selecting a sleeping bag: It should be machine-washable (for obvious reasons) and well insulated.

Used Trailer. Generally, living in an old trailer might be considered a step up from the tent. Some prodigious searching should produce a used one for $500 or less. At that price you can expect it to be in rough shape and lacking some or all usable amenities. But, after the summer or two you will use it, you can recoup part or all of your investment through resale.

The key points to check out when inspecting a trailer are:

* *Security*. Since you are likely to leave tools on the job, make certain the trailer can be either locked or fitted with a hasp and padlock.
* *Tightness against weather*. The trailer should be waterproof with no leaks in the roof or ill-fitting windows.
* *Holes in the body*. To keep out rodents and nocturnal animals, be certain any holes can be patched with either plywood or sheet metal.

Figure 7-5 *A portable charcoal broiler, fueled by propane, lets you enjoy steaks cooked outdoors while at jobsite (about $40). Tripper by Zebco is powered by an efficient 10,000-BTU burner complete with high-radiance permanent briquettes locked into place between double steel screens.*

Temporary Shed. Unless you plan the temporary shed to be a permanent outbuilding when your home is completed, don't overbuild it. Keep it simple and use construction-grade (or better) materials to build it; the materials here, like the tent platform, can be cleaned and reused in the second or third stage of construction.

A shed needn't be any more elaborate than the one shown in Figure 7-2. To protect the materials, you would be wise to give all the lumber used in the shed at least a prime coat of paint. Windows can be kept simple—a single sash hinged along the top edge to provide ventilation.

Wrap and cap the entire dwelling with 15-lb. felt, using an ample number of staples to make certain it won't be torn off in high winds. For extra protection on the roof, apply a second layer of felt at a 90° angle to the first layer. Overlap succeeding layers of felt a minimum of 12 inches.

If the shed is to remain as a permanent outbuilding, the exterior should be constructed to completion (siding, trim and shingles) to avoid duplication of effort and wasted materials.

Garage. If your plan calls for a detached garage, you might consider erecting the garage first and living in it.

Depending upon your ability to work, you may be able to dig the required footings for the garage, and form them out for the concrete pour, in

Three-Stage Construction: *The best way to go about building an expandable house is to approach it slowly and step-by-step. Plan to erect the first stage and live in it for a few seasons before going on to the next phase. This way you will have a better feeling for just how you want to utilize any additional space as it is added. Generally, an expandable house is built in from three to five stages. The home shown goes up in three. The design of Plan No. 108 (from the American Plywood Association) lends itself well to three-stage building.*

Stage One . . .

Figure 7-6 *Not a small home when just one-third complete, the first stage has a total of 922 sq. ft. of living space; 640 sq. ft. on the first level plus an additional 282 sq. ft. in the sleeping area of the second floor loft.*

one weekend work session. The following week, a mason contractor can do the actual pouring of concrete. If you decide to do this chore yourself, at the very least have two helpers and a pair of concrete-type wheelbarrows on hand. Use ready-mix concrete; that is, concrete ordered from a batching plant and mixed in the truck's drum while enroute to the jobsite; when it arrives, water is added, mixed for a prescribed period, and the pour proceeds.

My experience in building has been that often a mix appeared somewhat under the strength it should be. Whenever it appeared so, I made it a practice to board the truck and add a bag of Portland cement for every three to four cubic yards of concrete. On the other hand, if the supplier has not skimped on cement, none should be added: A bag or two of cement added to a correct mix will weaken—not strengthen—that batch. If your knowledge of concrete is limited, ask the building inspector for an opinion.

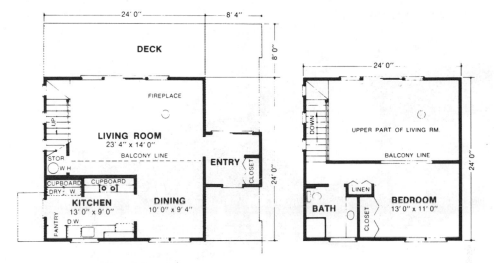

Figure 7-7 *The studio plan is laid out to give maximum efficiency; the high ceiling and clerestory windows give the illusion that the living room is larger than it really is. The second-floor sleeping space can be arranged to handle a pair of single beds or a double bed and bunks. The kitchen and second-level bath—initially the most expensive rooms in any house—are installed in the first stage. The freestanding factory-built fireplace can be installed immediately, or added later if money is tight. Outside, the decking is placed after the first stage is built. This will serve Phase 2 as well.*

Assuming you can complete the garage footing-and-slab pour on Saturday, you can "crack" the forms the next day (that is, carefully separate them *slightly* from the concrete).

On the third weekend, the forms can be stripped, and carpentry on the structure can start. Though it is possible, of course, to frame out the structure singlehandedly, the job goes a lot faster if you have at least one other pair of hands to help hoist the rafters or trusses into position.

If you opt for speed, hire a local two-man carpenter team to do the erecting while you serve as a laborer. With three men going full blast, you should be able to erect all framing members and install the overhead garage door in one Saturday. From there on, it is a relatively easy one-man job to apply sheathing to the roof and walls and finish closing the frame in with felt, siding, and shingles. The most time-consuming part of the job when working alone is the number of trips you have to make from the work location to the materials pile—with production halted while you walk.

Basement. If your house is to have a full basement, you can consider using it as temporary sleeping quarters. From the start, all the cash outlay, except for camping appliances, will actually be invested in the first stage. If you feel that the garage should be the last stage built, and money tends to be on the tight side, you will probably prefer this approach.

Second Stage . . .

Figure 7-8 When the second stage is added, living space is increased to 1,498 sq. ft. Though this may be all the house you will ever need, notice how Stage 3, the garage, unifies the total-design concept.

B-1

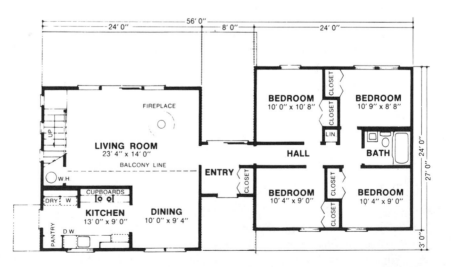

Figure 7-9 You will also note that in Phase 2 there are four alternative layouts for the bedrooms. The basic layout, B-1, gives four bedrooms and a bath.

Figure 7-10 B-2 shows three bedrooms and an oversized bathroom with space for a built-in vanity. Option B-3 is designed around a playroom or family activity area in addition to the three bedrooms and bath. Finally, alternate B-4 has two complete bathrooms, one of which is connected to the largest bedroom with a walk-in wardrobe and dressing vanity. When choosing the second-stage layout that best suits your family needs, don't forget that Stage 1 has sleeping space on the second level.

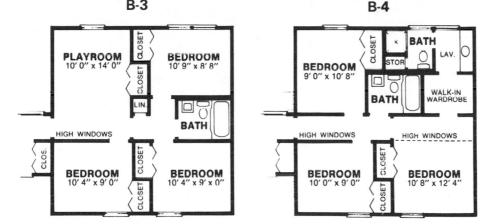

To live in the basement, the flooring system goes in once the foundation has been poured. The only variation from a standard construction schedule is that felt and/or polyethylene sheet must be applied over the subflooring so that the space below is waterproof.

Early in the game, your electrical service can be run in and connected to the entrance service panel in the basement. For convenience and practicality, you can have the electrician provide several temporary branch circuits, one or two for the living area and a couple more for your power tools. Choosing this route means that you can bring along that spare refrigerator, a TV, radio, and other appliances that you planned to use in your second home anyway.

For access to the basement, you might consider installing an outside cellar entry, and thus put off the building of the interior cellar stairs and a trapdoor for the time being. Many second-home owners consider outside cellar entries a boon during all building stages for getting tools and equipment in and out of the basement.

Third Stage . . .

Figure 7-11

Phase 3, which adds 576 sq. ft. of general and storage space, rounds out the overall design. More than just a double garage, it tends to complete the architectural feel of the house. It also provides automatic windbreaks that will function as pleasant suntraps on clear but windy days. Should the need arise in the future, the third phase could easily, and inexpensively, be converted to a "bunkhouse" for youngsters.

From a practical point of view, this design lends itself beautifully to execution in plywood. Dimensions are sized to keep cutoff and waste to a minimum when working with 4-by-8-ft. sheets. The illustrations here show the house skinned with Texture 1-11 plywood siding—panels with squared vertical grooves on two or four-inch centers. It would be equally handsome if executed in any of a dozen or more other exterior-type, textured plywoods.

Other Choices. If roughing it via one of the above methods is not for you—regardless of cost—you are left with either of two alternatives:

1. You can rent rooms at a nearby motel or rooming house. Though this is undeniably a comfortable way to go, it is also the most expensive.

   Besides paying premium, in-season rates, you'll also be forced to do most of your eating in restaurants, unless your motel room has

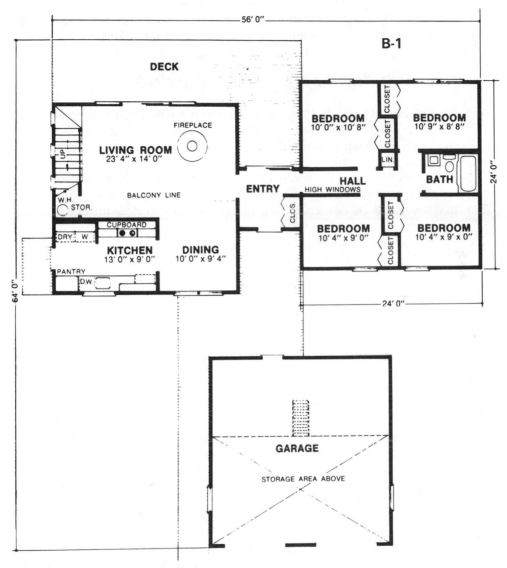

Figure 7-12

kitchenette facilities. The cost of a summer of all this pampered living could completely wipe out the savings you hoped to effect by building the house yourself.

2. Commute between your primary home and vacation home site—a poor plan if you have more than an hour of traveling time. You spend far too much time driving, loading, and unloading the car, and far too little time engaged in actual construction work. You'll also find the extra travel can be fatiguing with a resulting dampening of enthusi-

asm. Extra-slow progress has been known to defeat many do-it-your-selfers who started out with the sincerest of intentions.

THIS AND THAT ABOUT JOBSITE LIVING

Privation. If you do rough it, forget about a daily bath and privacy. For the time being—like those pioneers that you're emulating—you'll have to content yourself with washcloth baths or with a refreshing dip in the nearby lake, stream, or ocean.

Safety. During the warm months, you may prefer to knock off work during the hottest period of the day when the sun is overhead, and use this time to enjoy whatever your second-home property puts you close to. The time can then be made up in the cool evening hours when you can work harder without fear of heat prostration.

If it has been awhile since you had your last physical, see your physician before attempting a rigorous construction project. If your life up to this point has been a rather sedentary one, the labors to come just might be more than your system can stand. Play it safe and get the green light from your doctor before starting.

For safety reasons, neither is it wise to work alone off in the country. Should you have an accident—a fall from a ladder, for example—it may be many hours, or even days, before you are found. For example, an experienced builder, an acquaintance of mine, almost became an insurance statistic one recent winter. At the end of a day's work on his cabin in Vermont, he stepped out of the cabin to start the trip home. Totally absorbed in his work all day, he did not realize that the snow falling outside had reached near-blizzard proportions. As he exited the cabin, he dropped into a snow bank and sank to his neck.

Despite the fact that this man has above-average strength, he was help-less and could not extricate himself. Happily, several hunters, hearing his cries for help, rescued him from a certain frosty departure.

Security. Vandalism and pilferage in the sticks is at a much higher incidence than you might suspect. Thus, it is important that you provide ample protection for your tools and materials during your absences. One way is to build a sturdy toolbox about 3-ft. deep by 4-ft. high and 5-ft. long. The box's hinged lid should be pitched to provide positive water runoff, and the entire box should be covered with a waterproof material, such as 6-mil polyethylene or mineral roll roofing.

To prevent the box itself from being carted off, anchor it to a tree with a sturdy padlocked chain or bolt it to a post set in concrete. Done this way, the nuts holding the box to the post are inside and cannot be backed off without gaining entry to the box.

A better idea is to make arrangements to store tools in the garage of a cooperative neighbor. If you do, try to inconvenience your new friend as little as possible. Pick up and leave your tools at prearranged times convenient and agreeable to both of you.

The only other alternative is to cart the tools back and forth between your primary home and vacation home.

Your Power Tools. Unless you use the basement as temporary quarters, you will need a portable generator to provide power for your tools. Since you will need it on a one-time basis, it makes more sense to rent a generator than to buy one. If there are no tool rental outfits in the area, check the tool-rental stores in your primary area. Provided you put up a sufficient deposit, the renter may not object to your removing the tool from the immediate area. If that fails, talk to contractors in your second-home area to see if any has an unused spare lying about.

BUILDING KNOW-HOW

One way to get a good understanding of the building basics is by reading the Department of Agriculture booklet no. 73, "Wood Frame House Construction." See Appendix D for how-to-order information. The pamphlet is written in an easy-to-understand style and it details all the steps you can expect to encounter when building a home.

Besides the savings in building your own home, you can also derive a tremendous sense of satisfaction, of accomplishment, of achievement. The erection of a home can be every bit as personal and as creative an endeavor as painting a sunset or writing a story.

By the time you have driven the last nail, you will have spent a large portion of your waking hours going over plans, coordinating delivery dates, shuttling materials and family to and from—and watching your creation reach completion. No price may be placed on this joy.

8

So You Want to be Your Own Builder

By now you are aware that "doing your own thing" when it comes to housebuilding means one big investment of time. Besides filling literally all of your waking hours, the project is going to take a reasonable amount of know-how and more than a little muscle as well. Depending on how much of either you have, you can erect a stick-built house in one of three ways:

1. By hiring a contractor architect to handle the building. If an honest self-appraisal indicates that you may lack either sufficient knowledgeability or physical stamina, then you are probably better off going this route and confining your participation to jobsite meetings.

2. By being your own general contractor—and inheriting all the problems associated with that role. You'll have to coordinate all material purchases (and deliveries) and all subcontracted work in order to erect the house as quickly as possible. By being your own general contractor, you can save from 10 to 20 percent of the cost to build.

3. Or, you can go the do-it-yourself route. Besides serving as your own general contractor, you do most or all of the jobs that would otherwise be handled by subcontractors. Depending upon your skills in the various trades, which affect how much specialty help you have to hire, it is possible to save up to 50 percent by being your own builder. Since these savings are all in the labor costs, the more work you do yourself, the greater your savings.

137

You can see from the list above that the more duties and responsibilities you assume, the greater your savings. You can also save money, however, even if others do the work, by cutting down on the time spent on construction. A contractor-built stick house, for example, is the most expensive way you can get a home. That's easy to understand when you realize that a house is comprised of thousands of parts and cutting and assembling them on the job takes time—and time costs money. You can therefore lower the cost of a contractor built structure by about 20 percent if you select a manufactured house. Similar savings can be achieved if you have a contractor erect a shell that is finished outside and left unfinished inside. You then complete the interior yourself.

Whether you decide to be general contractor or builder/journeyman, you must arm yourself with know-how. I am amazed at the way many do-it-yourself books and magazines blithely reassure the reader with statements such as "*simply* cut the rafter to length" or "once started, the foundation pour goes *quickly*." The truth is that rafters aren't "simply" cut. Rather, after determining sizes and quantity needed by studying the plans, you must order the materials, lay them out accurately, and cut them carefully. Finally, you install them by nailing in a precise and prescribed manner. These are the necessary steps if the structure is to be built soundly and with craftsmanship. The story is the same for those "quickly poured" footings. The fact is, a proper pour also requires careful layout followed often by back-breaking physical labor—the pour itself. The physical part of the job calls for some thinking and common sense as well if you are to survive.

To avoid bitter disappointment and costly mistakes, take the time to acquire as much building how-to information as possible from reliable sources. Although major construction steps and basic pointers are covered in this book, you are advised to read other material on housebuilding, as suggested in Appendix D.

WHERE TO START: DRAWINGS AND PAPERWORK

Your first step is to select the building plans for your house from either an architect or plans-service firm. Stock plans offered by an accredited outfit are designed by competent architects with the do-it-yourselfer in mind. The cost of plans from the sources shown in Appendix B are reasonable and offer a solid way to save several hundred (or more) dollars on this aspect alone.

Plot Plan. In its simplest form, a *plot plan* is a rough (unscaled) sketch indicating the location of the house and other features on the building plot. In some communities, a *detailed* plot plan is required; on such a plan, the drawing is in scale, and elevations and bench marks are indicated. The complete plot plan (or topographic drawing, usually called "topo," for short) should give the exact description (location) of the plot and a scale plan indicating the surveyor-set stakes that outline the plot. Elevations at the plot's corners are indicated as are all buildings and sites for septic tanks and water wells (if these are required). The line drawing should also show all easements below, as well as on the surface of, the ground.

The local building department will review your plot plan and advise whether or not the house can, in fact, be built as you have sketched it. The biggest considerations are usually house setback (the distance from the building to your front property line) and the width of side yards. Setback is usually defined, to prevent the erection of oversized dwellings that would fill entire building plots. A continuity of appearance is thus maintained throughout the neighborhood. In many communities, side yards are also clearly defined. For example, requirements may call for "10 feet with a combination of 25 feet": This means that the minimum a side yard can be is 10 feet with the other side measuring at least 15 feet (the difference between 10 and 25 feet).

Often, the distance allowed between houses is also spelled out. For example, if the minimum distance between houses for a given locale is 25 feet and your neighbor's house is within 10 feet of the property line, the side yard on that side of your house cannot be less than 15 feet.

The cost of a topo can vary anywhere from $50 to $500 depending upon the time it takes to prepare it. For this reason, you are well advised to hire a local surveyor to do the job. With experience in the locale, he will probably have good files on the terrain, and a knowledge of the area will keep down his bill. You can save more money by having the plan done by the same surveyor who surveys the house for the mortgage institution.

When the house is finished, the mortgage lender will probably require pictures of the completed structure. Though generally the lender wants a photo of the house as viewed from the street, occasionally other photo needs come up. Black and white photos will do, as long as each snapshot is identified with the owner's name, house number and street, and mortgage number.

Insurance. Before starting any work, you must obtain adequate insurance coverage. Ordinarily, you will start with a builder's risk policy to protect you while the house is under construction. Keep in mind that a builder's risk policy *specifies* nonoccupancy. While the house is unoccupied, the policy protects against damage from fire, wind, and vandalism. Upon completion of the house, and after issuance of the certificate of occupancy, the policy is converted to a standard homeowner's policy. Be sure to discuss the possibility of a deductible clause with your insurance broker, to keep the cost of a builder's risk policy as low as possible.

It is just about financially impossible to carry insurance protection against theft on the jobsite, because thieves who rob construction jobs are rarely apprehended and prosecuted. Your best protection against heavy material thefts, therefore, is to close the place in as fast as possible, in the meantime asking the neighbors to keep an eye on the jobsite. The fastest way to close in a house is to work with a large crew of carpenters. If you are working alone, try to order only as much material as you will need for each upcoming weekend work session.

Workmen's Compensation Insurance. Never hire a subcontractor who does not carry Workmen's Compensation Insurance. The individual who builds a home without such coverage—and gets away with it—can consider himself more lucky than smart.

The risk of not carrying Workmen's Compensation is a great one. For example, a worker who is injured on the job can hold the owner of the property—*you*—liable for the injuries. Should the worker die, the estate has a legal claim against the owner. Large amounts of money, far greater than the value of the house and the property beneath it, can be involved. Don't, under any circumstances, risk building without compensation coverage.

Before hiring a subcontractor, have his or her insurance carrier supply you with a certificate of coverage for the workers on the job. Be aware of the fact that in the absence of such coverage you are responsible for the workers.

Perhaps the most common mistake made by do-it-yourselfers is the hiring of "uninsured moonlighters." If you decide to use moonlighters, consult with your insurance carrier and obtain insurance coverage for these employees on a daily or weekly basis, depending on how they will work on the job. Thus, besides requiring each subcontractor to provide proof of insurance coverage, you should plan on obtaining a special policy issued for those occasions when you hire someone who does not carry compensation coverage.

Liability Insurance. With compensation coverage secured, you're not through yet with buying insurance. Since you, your family, and other non-workers are not covered by the compensation policy, you should also provide some protection for when you make inspection tours or do some work yourself. This policy should be written to cover all outsiders who visit the job but who do not perform any work.

For two reasons, it makes the most sense to have the entire insurance program laid out and carried by one agency:

1. to make certain you have all the coverage you should have, and
2. to avoid possible confusion as to *which* company is liable for *what* should a claim arise.

Permits. The first thing you should do as a builder is find out from the local building department which permits are necessary to start construction. In heavily populated areas, this procedure can be complex and require the assistance of a professional engineer. For a fee of approximately $100 to $150, an engineer will prepare the drawings and applications as required and file for the permits. In underdeveloped areas, the system is often simple. Usually it is necessary only to notify the building department as to where the building is going up and what type it will be. Here, municipal interest is usually more for the sake of getting the house on the tax rolls than it is for strict compliance to building codes. You will also have to either get your plans for the well and septic tank approved, or pay for the sewer and water connections if your house will be serviced by municipal utilities. Generally, it is also necessary for the major subcontractors (plumbers, electricians, and the like) to secure their permits before the general contractor can apply.

When the above criteria have been met, the general contractor can apply for his permit. Unfortunately, permit approval can take anywhere from one week to three or more months. Just how long yours takes depends upon how complete your submitted plans are and what, if any, changes must be made and approved before the permit is issued. The amount of time also depends upon the degree of proficiency and bureaucracy at the local town hall.

SCHEDULING IS IMPORTANT

Since time is money, the job must run smoothly once work is started. Subcontractors (subs) must be lined up and ready to go when you need them; this usually calls for a tremendous amount of personal involvement and time on your part. I make it a practice to notify "subs" about two weeks before they can expect to work on the job, thus giving them a chance to schedule their work efficiently. Then, as the need for the notified sub approaches, I call again two or three days in advance and reconfirm the day and date. If the sub cannot make the date for any reason, you still have time to try to round up a replacement. If you cannot keep the deadline, or cannot find a replacement for a defaulting subcontractor, reschedule a new date as early as possible. Since weather and materials-supply exercise great control over work progress, a change of work dates is not uncommon in construction. Finally, the night before a sub is due on the job, call and confirm the next day's schedule.

One way to assure that subcontractors will show up as needed is to pay their bills promptly. As each stage of a sub's work is completed and accepted by you, pay the bill to date. And, if you advise all your subcontractors in advance of your intent to pay promptly upon the completion of work, chances are they'll quote you builder's prices.

PAYING AND DISCOUNTS

You owe it to yourself to use the best (not necessarily the most expensive) materials throughout your job. Whether working from custom-designed or stock plans, you will find a page called materials schedule in the house plans where all recommended materials and products are clearly spelled out. Stick with the specified materials and avoid handyman specials at the local

WORK SCHEDULE (PROGRESS)

Job	Subcontractor	Tent. Stg. Date	No. of Man Days to Comp.	Tent. Fin. Date	Reason For Delay
Survey					
Excavating					
Foundation					
Rough Carpentry					
Roofing					
Siding					
Prime-Paint Exterior					
Rough-In Electric					
Rough-In Plumbing					
Rough Heating					
Chimney					
Insulation					
Wallboard					
Masonry					
Floors					
Heat Registers					
Tinning					
Furnace					
Finish Carpentry					
Tile Floors					
Finish Plumbing					
Bath Tile					
Caulk					
Painting					
Install Kitchen					
Finish Electric					
Moldings & Trim					
Finish Floors					
House Cleaning					

Work up a progress sheet, and post a copy in a conspicuous spot on the job. If kept up-to-date, the progress sheet can be helpful in coordinating the subcontractors' time schedules. The form illustrated contains the minimum number of entries; you can make yours more specific by detailing *all* start and completion dates for all jobs.

lumberyard. If the local supplier does not stock a particular item in the plans, make certain that what you buy is of equivalent or better quality than the item being replaced.

You cannot expect to get builder's prices on materials for a one-shot deal. Even small builders who build 15 or 20 houses a year do not get the same prices as a large-volume builder. The local supplier will, however, generally give a discount if he is guaranteed the entire order. Discuss your needs with him and pin down the costs of materials item by item.

It is common practice in the building supplies industry to give a 2-percent discount for cash (that is, payment in full between the first and tenth of the month). The supplier usually sends out the bill so it is received on the first of the month. If you get your check in the mail by the tenth, you can automatically deduct 2 percent from the balance due. Conversely, many building materials suppliers charge a slight interest on any balance remaining unpaid after the tenth.

Since most building materials suppliers operate on a slight profit margin (perhaps 10 percent), there is no margin for any free extras. For instance, should your house be off in the woods and accessible only by unpaved roads, the dealer will in all likelihood specify that if you want delivery to the building site, you will have to assume responsibility for the trucking expenses. Should it get stuck in the mud, for example, you'll agree to pay the tow charge, an additional per-hour rate to cover the driver's salary, and truck charges while it's bogged down at your site.

Prices are similarly tight in the concrete transit-mix business. When you order concrete delivered, you have a specified amount of time to unload the truck and release it from the site. Thus, you should clock and sign a truck both in and out of the site. Most transit-mix outfits level a demurrage charge after the truck has been on the jobsite 30 minutes.

To keep your job running smoothly, it is an absolute must to pay all bills as soon as they are due. This requirement is as true for materials suppliers as it is for subcontractors.

JOB INSPECTIONS

The method and thoroughness of building inspection can vary greatly from one community to the next. On the one hand, you may find a building department pleasant to work with and efficiently organized, with qualified inspectors trained in the building of houses. In this case, as it should be, the building inspector can be a tremendous help. Since he or she has the final say about how each phase is to be built or installed, discuss all aspects of the structure with the inspector, heeding any advice you come away with. On the other hand, many small-town building departments are staffed with appointees who spend more time working at their political duties than they do at their desks in the department of public works.

Regardless of the type of building department you find yourself involved with, make certain that an inspection progress sheet (called a "weather sheet" by the building trades) is posted on the structure. Since the building code can, and usually does, call for inspections at many stages of construction, it is best to have this sheet signed and dated by the inspector as each inspection is made. Relying on the memories of those in the building department can prove disastrous.

I personally learned this lesson the hard way. Once in checking an extension to a home, the local building inspector looked over the rough plumbing and gave a verbal approval to close up the wall. Sometime later, during a final inspection, the inspector remarked that he had never seen the rough plumbing and that the wall would have to be torn open before he would give approval. Whether his memory was simply poor, or he was applying muscle for "consideration" was of little importance. I had no signed proof of the fact that he had indeed okayed the rough plumbing. One (heated) word led to another, with the result that I was forced to remove the plasterboard so the plumbing could be reinspected—a costly lesson. I now make it a point to see that the weather sheet is signed after each inspection visit.

Ask the local building department for an inspection schedule, since in some communities the local codes go quite far in requiring inspections. For example, inspections can be required on:

1. open footing,
2. steel (rods) in footing,
3. footing ready for backfill,
4. joists,
5. rough framing,
6. rough and finish electricals,
7. rough and finish heating,
8. insulation,
9. septic tank and field,
10. rough plumbing,
11. water test,
12. final plumbing,
13. all masonry work, and
14. final.

The above list is an approximation of possible inspections: In some communities, the number of required inspections is greater, in others, less. Often, after the building inspector comes to know your work, he or she will give approval without visiting the jobsite. This is an acceptable practice, as long as you remember to stop by the building department to have that entry on the weather sheet signed.

Each inspection listed must be conducted and the work approved before the next construction phase can start. All inspections are needed before the final inspection—which is a requisite for the certificate of occupancy.

CERTIFICATE OF OCCUPANCY (C.O.)

A C.O. states that the structure was erected in compliance with local codes and is suitable for occupancy. Generally, it must be obtained before the house can be lived in and before a homeowner's insurance policy may be obtained.

In some communities, however, it is possible to move in before the house is completed. This can be a boon when you are doing the building yourself or when the occupant's presence will deter or eliminate theft and vandalism. But don't plan on moving into an incomplete house before checking with and receiving approval from the local building department and your insurance carrier. (Ordinarily, a C.O. is necessary before you can get homeowner's insurance coverage, but your carrier may bend the rules a bit.)

DO-IT-YOURSELF BUILDING

One of your early moves should be to try to hook up with a local carpenter or carpenter crew. Often, you can get the name of such persons by asking around the lumberyard and real estate offices.

Teaming up with a carpenter makes sense in many ways. In remote areas, the local carpenter is often capable of performing more than carpentry, but be aware that only licensed tradesmen can perform much of the plumbing and electrical work (if such work is by other than the homeowner). The carpenter's familiarity with and knowledge of the local building laws can also save you a great deal of anxiety. The presence of an experienced tradesman on the job during the week, when you're not there, not only keeps things moving with subcontractors, it minimizes the incidence of theft.

Before starting, you should both agree upon compensation. Decide whether the carpenter will work as a salaried employee, on a time and materials basis, or for agreed-upon sums (that is, piece work). Further, determine whether the carpenter is willing to accept payments either as various stages are completed or on a weekly basis. For a weekly salary, the carpenter works a prescribed number of hours each week—including Saturdays with you, if desired. But, many tradespeople prefer to work on a time and materials basis. With this arrangement, at the end of a prescribed period (usually a week or two), the rate for the total hours worked is added to the cost of materials used. Then a fee is added in, usually 15 percent of the total for running the job, ordering and paying for materials, and physical labor.

Since you will be absent a great deal of the time, payment on a production basis is often the best arrangement. As each stage of the job comes up, you and your carpenter work out a fair payment for the actual work. When the carpenter completes a portion of the job, regardless of the time involved, you pay the agreed-upon amount.

You will also have to work out an agreement concerning materials. If agreeable to the idea, the carpenter can pay for materials and turn over the bills to you for reimbursement. Or, if preferred, you can establish an account at the local lumberyard and give authorization for the carpenter to sign for materials as needed. (Regardless of the method of payment for the materials used, you should require the carpenter to indicate on each invoice from the start exactly what the materials were for.) You should also work out an understanding for materials payments with all subcontractors.

BIDS AND ESTIMATES

Be aware that there is a difference, and often a marked one, between an estimate and an actual bid on a particular job. An estimate is exactly what the name implies—an educated guess as to just what a particular job may cost. A bid, on the other hand, is an accurate determination of what a subcontractor will do the job for. For example, suppose you ask an electrical contractor what it would cost to install an exhaust fan in your bathroom. He may quickly toss out, "Oh, about two hundred dollars." That's an estimate. If you then decide that you want to go ahead and install the fan, you would then lay out the job *exactly*, including the specification of the products to be used. With such concrete facts on hand, the electrician's bid to do the job may fall anywhere between $150 and $250.

The lesson: Never use an estimate as an ironclad cost figure. An estimate is only a "ballpark figure" intended simply to help you make a sound decision as to whether to proceed with a particular job.

COORDINATING WORK

Since you alone are responsible for assuring smooth sailing between the carpentry end of the job and the subcontractors, to avoid confusion with subcontractors, conduct all transactions in a businesslike fashion. If the subcontractor does not have a work agreement form, type up one of your own similar to the sample shown on page 147. Type it on a single sheet and have photocopies made. Complete all sections of the form with each subcontractor, making certain both parties sign the agreement and receive a copy.

So you've decided to be your own builder. You're letting yourself in for a lot of hard work, many a last-minute reshuffling of deadlines, aggravation

AGREEMENT WITH SUBCONTRACTOR

OWNER/BUILDER: _____ Date: _____

Address: _____

Job Address: _____ Plan No.: _____

Subcontractor: _____

Subcont. Address: _____

Workmens Compensation Ins. Co. & Agent: _____

Policy No.: _____ Expiration Date:_____

Liability Ins. Co. & Agent: _____

Coverage: _____ Policy No.:_____ Expiration Date: _____

Total Price: _____ ($_____) dollars

Payment Terms: _____

Work Dates: _____ Start: _____ Finish: _____

Work to be performed and materials to be provided:

(Use additional sheets if necessary, identify with page numbers, validate with subcontractor's and builder's initials.)

Subcontractor: _____

signature & title   *date*

Owner/Builder: _____

signature & title   *date*

A written agreement between you and a subcontractor will eliminate possible confusion about the work to be done or the monies paid. All details of a subcontracted operation should be stated in such an agreement. If the sub doesn't have such a form on hand, type up your own using the above as an example.

from time to time—not to mention a bundle of paperwork. But if you believe in doing things right and if your second home is the one thing you want done *right,* there's no other way.

9

Blueprints, Excavating and Masonry

* Building know-how * Building essentials * Blueprints and specifications: Plans, Elevations, Sections * Laying out the job * Excavation * Masonry and concrete * Footings * Wall forms * About concrete * Waterproofing the basement or slab *

The cost of professional tradesmen comes high these days, and it is certainly not going to get any cheaper. Though do-it-yourself headlines in newspapers and magazines may belabor the point somewhat ("Do-it-yourself and pay yourself those high wages!"), the message is a true one: Building your own home saves thousands of dollars. Homebuilding experts estimate that 20 to 25 percent of all second homes built annually are erected by do-it-yourselfers. Surprisingly, many of these builders have no homebuilding experience at all; they are building on a first-and-only-time basis simply to keep their costs down. Some of these hardy souls, however, "do it themselves" solely because that's the way they *want* to get their second homes.

BUILDING KNOW-HOW

But don't think you can charge into home building with little forethought, because other nonprofessionals have met with success. Although you needn't be afraid to take on the job yourself (as long as you have a fair share of common sense and a healthy appetite for work), don't let others' successes lull you into thinking that "you can't miss." Many have watched their life savings drain away when it became impossible for them to finish their homes. In such cases, the incomplete house may be sacrificed at a below-cost price, or lost completely through mortgage foreclosure. But an ample dose of common sense and a working knowledge of building basics can prevent this from happening to you.

The common sense you will have to supply. The building basics you can find in this chapter. Obviously it is impossible to present everything you need to know in a book of this type, so the illustrations in this chapter have been selected according to their ability to enhance textual descriptions. Other chapters (on such specialized subjects as plumbing, heating, electrical work, kitchens and the like) contain material geared to acquaint neophyte builders with a solid base of building know-how. Building terms, the trade vernacular, are used throughout—you may as well start off by talking "construction" as the professionals do. (So that you will, in fact, know what you are talking about, the terms used throughout the book are defined in the glossary at the end of the book.)

The information in this chapter is presented in an order that roughly follows a normal building sequence. For clarity's sake, there is some over-lapping of information. For example, in order to clearly discuss heating, some points about insulation must be reviewed.

Whether or not you finally decide to be your own builder, you owe yourself a solid understanding of just what good building is all about. It is the surest way to get the most house for your money.

BUILDING ESSENTIALS

There are three guidelines to follow:

1. Work only from well drawn plans and clearly written specifications.
2. Neither economize to the point of miserliness nor spend money wildly when selecting materials. Try to buy quality products only, but make it your practice to shop for the best price.
3. Use only sound building techniques and principles. Though you may be tempted from time to time to "fudge," stick to the best practices as shown in this book and in other fine building manuals. Don't allow yourself to be misled by well-meaning, but misinformed, friends who may have gotten away with all types of shortcuts. If they haven't yet paid the piper for their transgressions, they will sooner or later.

BLUEPRINTS AND SPECIFICATIONS

Don't make the mistake of creating a house design as you go. Those who try usually wind up with a house looking something like a Charles Addams cartoon. Since the investment in your second home is substantial, don't leave its success to chance. Either select a set of stock plans by a reputable plans service outfit, or have plans custom drawn by an architect. Good plans for do-it-yourselfers may also be obtained from various associations allied with the building materials industry; such organizations have the homebuilder's best interests at heart. A listing of good sources for plans is in Appendix B.

For the purpose of illustration, on the following pages we have used architectural drawings from typical plans marketed by Home Building Plans Service. The house shown is HBPS Number Four, a functional and spacious second home (see Figures 9-1 and 9-2). All good stock plans are as well drawn and as explicit as the ones on these pages. Do-it-yourself plans for houses of all styles are available to suit most tastes and budgets at a fraction of what it would cost to custom-design a house. But, keep in mind that you can still customize your house by making changes here and there. If you do, you will have to prepare a drawing in the same scale and submit it along with your plans when you file for the building permit.

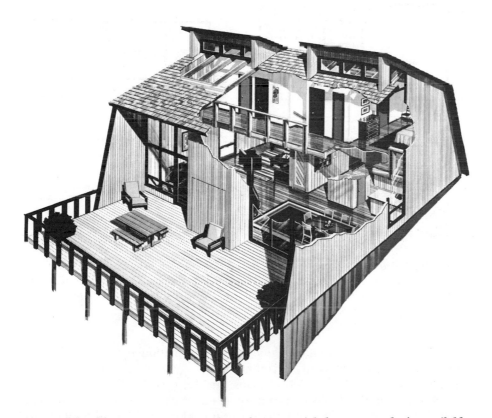

Figure 9-1 *Plans-service outfits alert the potential buyer to what's available through the use of three-dimensional illustrations such as this one. Plans for this home, Design Number Four by Home Building Plans Service, are shown in this chapter; they illustrate clearly what a good set of building plans is all about.*

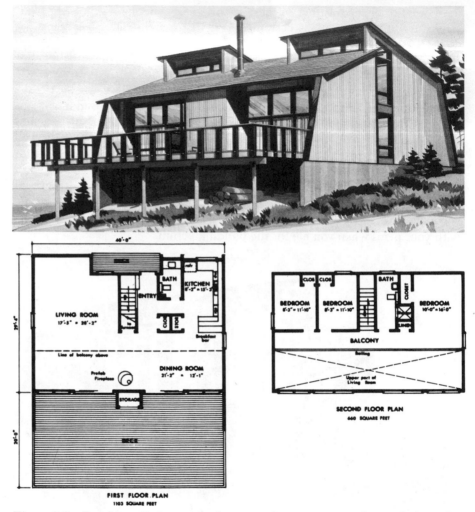

Figure 9-2 *Brochures listing stock plans contain an easy-to-understand view of a home's exterior and floor plans. How to build the structure is spelled out in the plans you buy. How to use the plans you'll get is explained in this chapter, using plans for this home as an example.*

To provide the tremendous amount of information required to build a house, every set of blueprints is comprised of a number of sheets. You will need at least four complete sets of plans: one set each for the local building department, for the builder and/or subcontractors, and for yourself. The fourth set will prove helpful if left with your contact at the local lumberyard.

Obviously, to work from a set of plans, you must have a reasonable working knowledge of architectual drawings—that is, a working knowledge of the architects' sign language, the drawing symbols (see Figure 9-3).

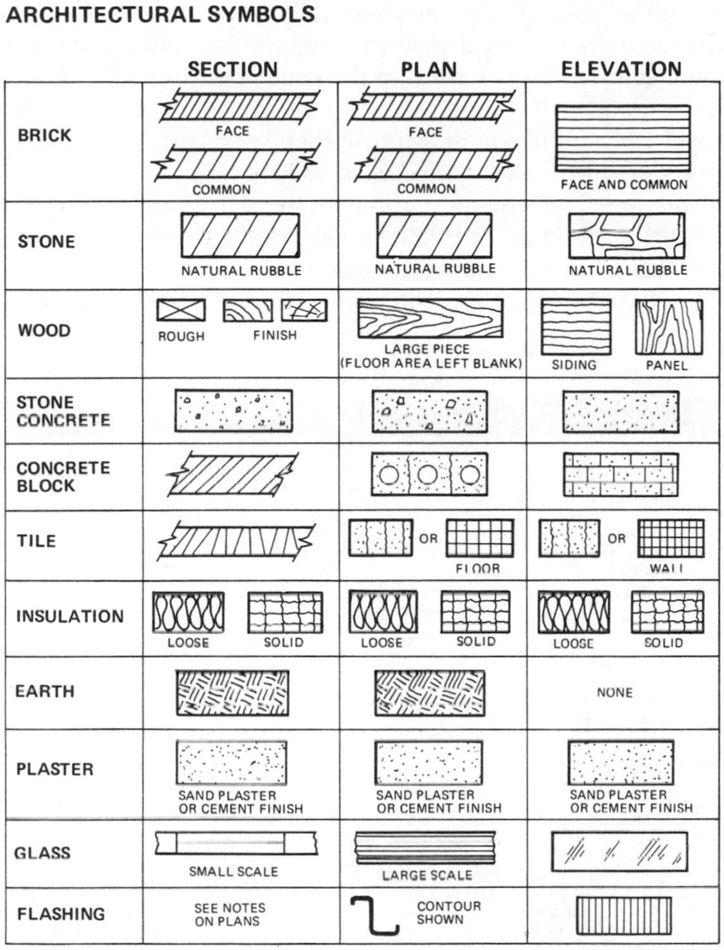

ARCHITECTURAL SYMBOLS

	SECTION	PLAN	ELEVATION
BRICK	FACE / COMMON	FACE / COMMON	FACE AND COMMON
STONE	NATURAL RUBBLE	NATURAL RUBBLE	NATURAL RUBBLE
WOOD	ROUGH FINISH	LARGE PIECE (FLOOR AREA LEFT BLANK)	SIDING PANEL
STONE CONCRETE			
CONCRETE BLOCK			
TILE		FLOOR	WALL
INSULATION	LOOSE SOLID	LOOSE SOLID	LOOSE SOLID
EARTH			NONE
PLASTER	SAND PLASTER OR CEMENT FINISH	SAND PLASTER OR CEMENT FINISH	SAND PLASTER OR CEMENT FINISH
GLASS	SMALL SCALE	LARGE SCALE	
FLASHING	SEE NOTES ON PLANS	CONTOUR SHOWN	

Figure 9-3 Architectural symbols are one of the reasons why such an enormous amount of information can be packed into so little space on a set of building plans. The symbols shown are the most commonly used ones in house construction: some are identical on plans, elevations, and section drawings; others vary from drawing to drawing. To save time, it pays to memorize the most common ones:

For one thing, you should work only from architectural plans that are drawn in scale. As a rule, residential plans are drawn to a ¼-in. scale (¼ in. = 1 ft.), which indicates, of course, that each ¼ in. on the drawing represents 1 ft. on the structure. Certain features of the building should be shown in larger scale for greater clarity, in which case the scale may be ½ in. = 1 ft. or larger. This larger scale is generally used to clarify esthetic or more complicated information, such as the molding details around a fireplace mantel, kitchen cabinets, and the like. Very often, the framing plans are drawn in ⅛-in. scale because rough framing is rather routine. If any details must be worked out, the framing carpenters generally solve these minor problems, as they arise, according to local practice. At any rate, always check the scale before proceeding with work because the scale often varies from one sheet to the next.

Basically, blueprints are drawn as either (1) plans, (2) sections, or (3) elevations. Here's what each is, and what to look for:

1. *Plans* show the size and outline of the structure, but they often contain other information as well. Dimension lines, locations and sizes of stairs, interior partition walls, windows and doors are all usually detailed on the plans, as well as the plumbing and appliance fixtures (see Figures 9-4 and 9-5).

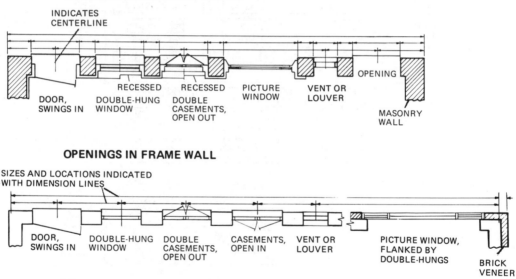

Figure 9-4   *Openings in masonry and framed walls are indicated as shown here.*

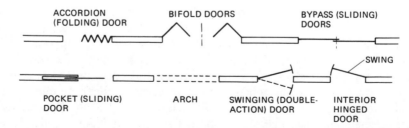

Figure 9-5   *Typical openings in interior partitions (walls).*

The *foundation plans* are generally combined with the basement plans and are similar in many respects to floor plans (see Figure 9-6).

A complete set of plans also includes a *plot plan*, which is required by the building department before you can get a building permit. If you are working from stock plans, you can either draw this yourself (with some assistance from the local building department) or have one prepared by a local architect, engineer, or surveyor (for nominal fee).

2. *Elevations* (Figure 9-7) are scaled drawings of the dwelling's exterior, showing windows, doors, and other details in position and to scale. Elevations also include grade levels, window and door heights, floor levels, pitches of roofs, the materials to be used on the walls and roof, the type of windows, and the like. Foundation and footing lines (below grade), if they appear on the plans, are indicated by broken lines.

Most plans also include elevations of any interior walls that require finish-detail work (for example, kitchen walls, a fireplace wall, and often bathroom walls). Interior elevations give you an accurate picture of what you can expect the finished walls to look like (if you use the materials specified). Walls that are simply clad in plasterboard, plaster, or paneling are not shown in elevation drawings.

Usually, the elevations are identified according to the direction they face on a given plot: north, south, east, west. However, when plans are not designed for a specific site, they are labeled "front," "rear," "left side," "right side."

3. *Section Drawings* (Figure 9-8) are intended to show how the building is constructed, and how the various parts fit together. For example, a particular section drawing may detail how a manufactured window is to be fitted into a wall of either frame or masonry construction. It should also list the sizes of framing lumber as well as the types of material that are to be used for insulation, sheathing, siding, interior wall finish, and the like.

Other Planning Tools. No matter what kind of plans you are working from, they should include the following items:

1. *Detail drawings* (Figure 9-8). When these are included, they supply the builder with specific construction information not covered by plans, sections, or elevations. Typically, such plans consist of detailed drawings for, say, the kitchen installation—what make and size cabinets are to be installed, which hardware to use, where to locate a certain vent, and other nonstructural information. The detail drawings are always labeled with titles to prevent confusion.

2. A *schedule sheet*. This spells out exactly which products are to be used —the size, make, and model number, for example, of every window.

3. A *materials list*. All materials, rough and finish, for the entire dwelling are spelled out here. Not all plans include a materials list, but having one is a definite convenience when it's time to start getting prices at your lumberyard.

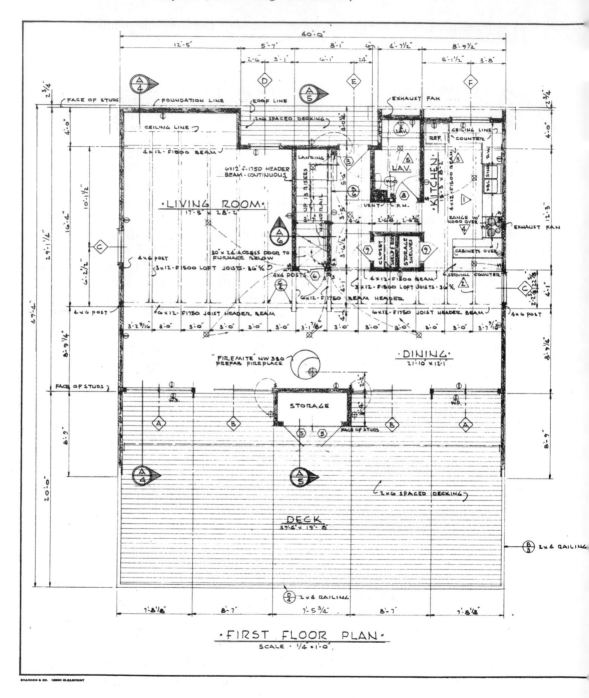

Figure 9-6 *A first and second floor plan.*

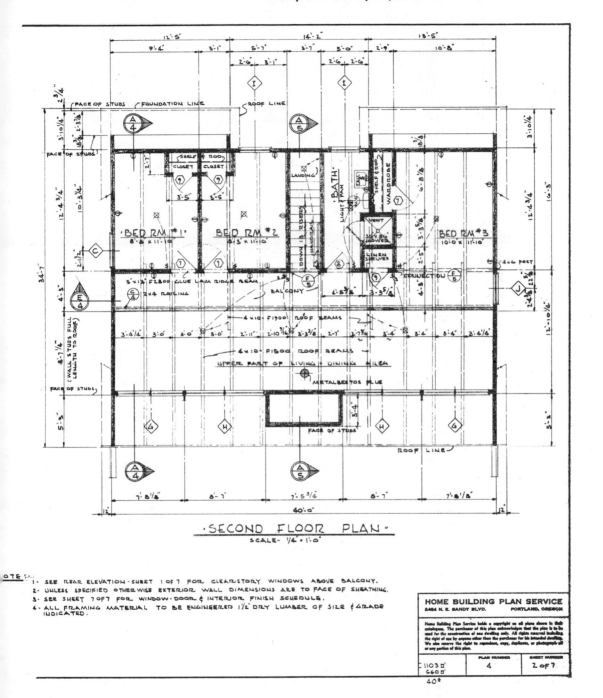

·SECOND FLOOR PLAN·
SCALE- 1/4" = 1'-0"

NOTE:
1- SEE REAR ELEVATION·SHEET 1 OF 7 FOR CLEARSTORY WINDOWS ABOVE BALCONY.
2- UNLESS SPECIFIED OTHERWISE EXTERIOR WALL DIMENSIONS ARE TO FACE OF SHEATHING.
3- SEE SHEET 7 OF 7 FOR WINDOW·DOOR & INTERIOR FINISH SCHEDULE.
4- ALL FRAMING MATERIAL TO BE ENGINEERED 1½" DRY LUMBER OF SIZE & GRADE INDICATED.

HOME BUILDING PLAN SERVICE
2464 N. E. SANDY BLVD.   PORTLAND, OREGON

Home Building Plan Service holds a copyright on all plans shown in their catalogues. The purchaser of this plan acknowledges that the plan is to be used for the construction of one dwelling only. All rights reserved including the right of use by anyone other than the purchaser for his intended dwelling. We also reserve the right to reproduce, copy, duplicate, or photograph all or any portion of this plan.

| 1103 □ | PLAN NUMBER | SHEET NUMBER |
| 660 □ | 4 | 2 OF 7 |

40#

Figure 9-6   A first and second floor plan.

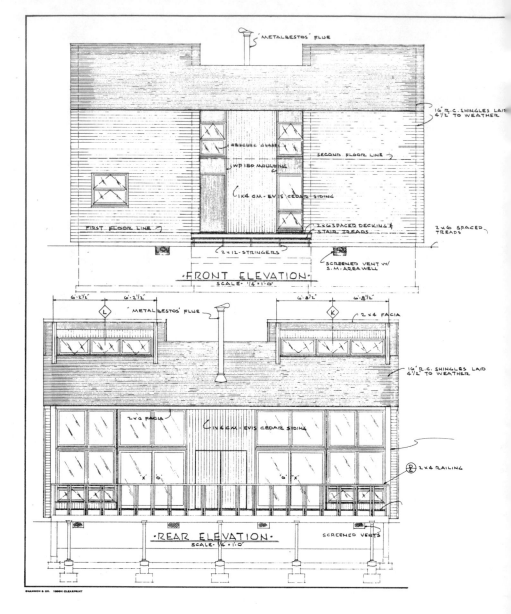

Figure 9-7 *Elevation drawings for exterior walls.*

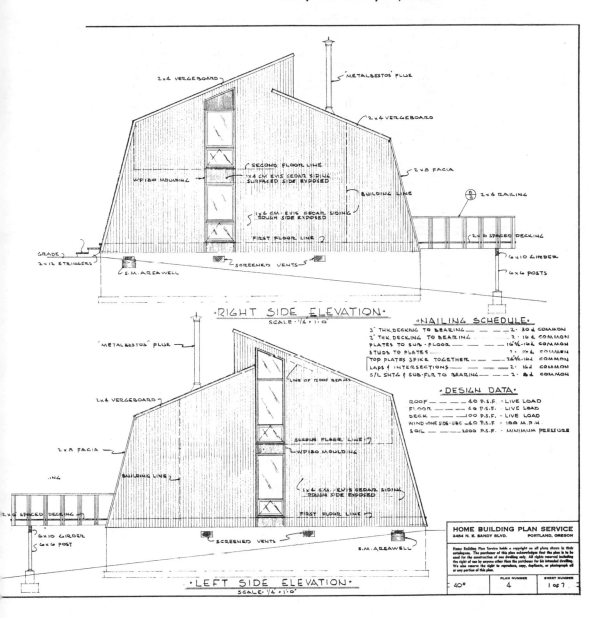

Figure 9-7 *Elevation drawings for exterior walls.*

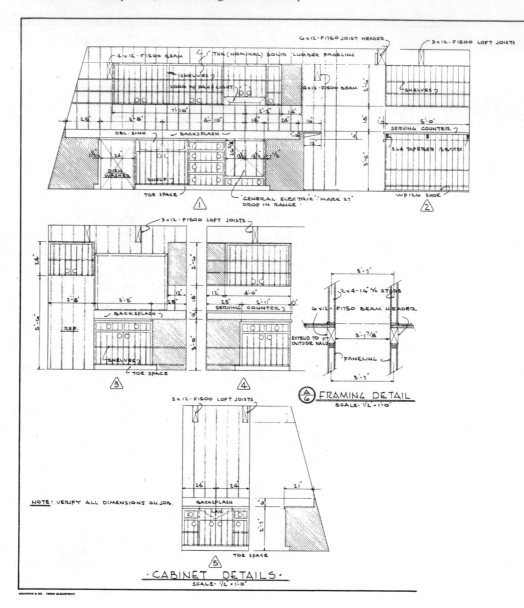

Figure 9-8 *The detail sheet clarifies fireplace, kitchen, and stair information.*

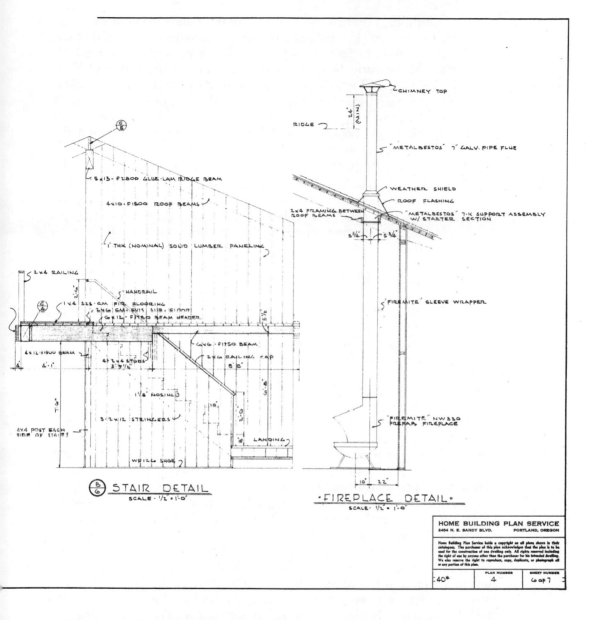

Figure 9-8 *The detail sheet clarifies fireplace, kitchen, and stair information.*

Building materials can and do vary from one section of the country to the next. For example, in an area abundant with good stone, you are likely to find many houses sided with this readily available material. Similarly, homes in heavily forested country will most likely be built of local woods (sawn and shaped at nearby lumber mills). The reason, pure and simple, is money. The cost of local materials is lower because long-haul trucking is eliminated. So check out what's available locally before you order materials; your neighbors and the local building department can give you the inside word here.

4. *Specifications*, called "specs" in the trades, contain supplemental information that, by its nature, cannot be included in the drawings. The specs list every item to be included in the dwelling (accurately detailed by size, make, and color) to avoid any chance of misunderstanding among owner, builder, and/or lumber yard.

LAYING OUT THE JOB

Before starting, it is a good idea to have test borings of the soil made by a local engineering firm. The borings will tell you whether any rock or water conditions exist that require special treatment before footings can be excavated and poured. The borings will also indicate whether the ground has been filled—an important fact because footings *must* rest upon undisturbed ground.

The results of this test may also help you decide on a particular type of foundation or structure. For example, in an area where water damage from high tides or post-rain flooding is a threat, dwellings are usually erected upon piles or poles. This type of construction is a common sight at ocean- and lakefronts because all but the low-lying sites are already occupied—many of which were once thought unfit for occupancy. Before you even buy a plan, find out whether homes in the area are built in a particular style due to climate or owners' preferences. In short, geography (not your personal taste) may determine what you can build on your site.

Next, the location of the house is determined and marked out with stakes. Either you or a surveyor can do this, but in any event the house location must conform to the plot plan you submitted to the building department. (Remember, to keep down the fees, you can have the surveyor lay out the building lines when he does the survey for your mortgage—assuming you are certain the mortgage will go through and that the seller has no objections.) Before laying out the foundation, however, do as the professionals do and take the time to clear the work area of any and all obstructions.

Further, since the house must eventually sit upon the footings you are laying out, use leveling instruments if you have them. If you don't, have a surveyor handle all layout work. At this stage of the project, 100-percent accuracy is a must. All corner lines must be absolutely perpendicular (at 90°

angles) to each other. To establish right angles, use the 6-, 8-, 10-ft. method shown in Figure 9-10. Keep in mind that each corner must be located precisely at the point where the outside surfaces of the foundation wall intersect.

ESTABLISHING EXCAVATION DEPTH

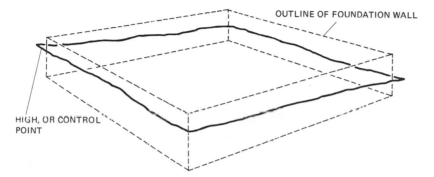

OUTLINE OF FOUNDATION WALL

HIGH, OR CONTROL POINT

Figure 9-9   To establish the depth of an excavation, use the highest elevation of the excavation's perimeter as the control point. The foundation wall should extend at least 8 in. above grade so that wood members are protected from soil moisture and termites.

A *foundation that is laid out correctly is protected from drainage problems too, that is, from rainwater runoff from adjacent properties.*

First, batter boards are erected at each corner to mark the foundation height; then, each intersection of the outside foundation wall is marked with a stake firmly anchored in undisturbed ground. The *exact* point of intersection is designated with a nail driven into the head of each stake.

When all building lines have been established, repeat the entire procedure to make certain there are no errors. Also, take the time to double-check the layout against the plot plan. Even if lines were established by a surveyor, corners should be verified for squareness and rectangles checked for accuracy (see Figure 9-10).

If your footing layout is inaccurate, you will have an out-of-square foundation wall, which can cause expensive construction problems throughout the entire job.

EXCAVATION

If the ground is fairly level, excavation can start immediately. On rugged or sloped terrain, you will have to first rough-grade the property so that the steps following will go smoothly.

Plan your excavation work carefully (see Figure 9-11). First, topsoil

STAKING AND LAYING OUT

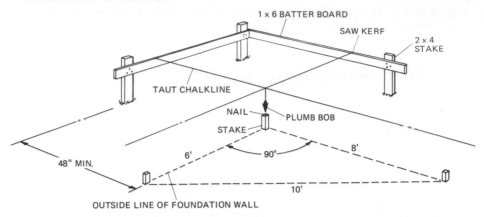

Figure 9-10 *Small stakes are precisely located and nails are driven into stake tops to indicate the outside line of foundation walls. Next, 2-by-4 stakes are driven a minimum of 4 feet outside the foundation wall lines. A mason's line is affixed to opposite boards so that each line falls exactly over the nail in the corner stakes at either end. Corners are then checked for squareness by measuring the triangle as shown. Use a ruler and move the lines until you get the 6-, 8- and 10-ft. ratio for the three legs of the triangle. The corner is then square.*

EXCAVATION LAYOUT

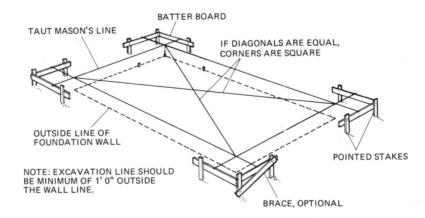

Figure 9-11 *Another good way to check whether a building line is laid out squarely is to measure the diagonal lines. The diagonals of a square or rectangle will be exactly equal if the corners are square. The hole to be excavated will be roughly 12 in. outside the dotted line representing the foundation wall line all around, thus allowing space for excavating and waterproofing operations.*

should be stripped and then stockpiled so it will not interfere with construction but will be readily available for finish-grading when the building is completed. Sand removed from the excavation should be selectively placed so that concrete transit-mix trucks or wheelbarrows can be easily brought to the forms for pouring. In many cases, when the sand is carefully placed, all concrete may be chuted directly from the truck to the forms. If sand is haphazardly placed, you can plan on transporting a great deal of the concrete by wheelbarrow.

A bulldozer, front-end loader, power shovel, or similar earth-moving equipment will do the trick (see Figures 9-12 through 9-14). If the ground is stable and the house is to be built on a slab or over a crawlspace, a power trencher can be used to excavate for the footings. In such construction there is no need for forming below grade; concrete is simply poured into accurately laid out and excavated trenches.

Typical Excavating Equipment

Caterpillar Tractor Company photos

Figure 9-12   D-3 Track-type tractor.

Figure 9-13   D-3 Track-type loader.

Figure 9-14   225 Hydraulic excavator.

When excavating a basement, excavate only to the top of the footings (that is, to the bottom of the basement floor), because some soils tend to soften when they are exposed to air and water. The final excavation for footings should be made immediately prior to the actual footing pour.

Keep in mind that your excavation must be wide enough to allow space for constructing and waterproofing the foundation. If your home is in a poor-drainage area, and requires drain tiles around the house perimeter, leave ample room for this operation to avoid having to redig.

When the excavation is complete, the building lines are then reestablished in the basement using the batter boards as shown in Figure 9-15.

Keep in mind that in cold climates it is important that the house foundation extends below the area frost line. This depth varies from one area to the next, and it should be determined by consultation with the local building department. In most northern climates of the United States (excepting Alaska), the frost line is about 4 feet.

ESTABLISHING CORNERS

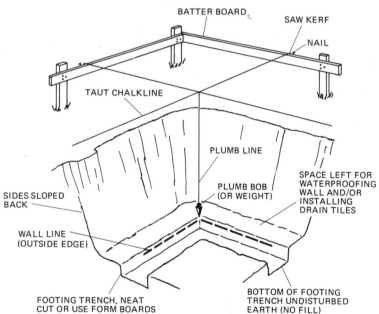

Figure 9-15   After excavation, the lines are replaced on the batter boards and the corner points are dropped to the bottom of the excavation using a plumb bob. Stakes are then driven at these points and, using a builder's level set up in the center of the excavated hole, the tops of these corner stakes are set flush with the top of the footing. Stakes are then connected with lines attached to nails driven into the stake tops, and an outside form board is constructed using this line as a guide. Footings should be excavated immediately prior to the pour because some soils soften with long exposure to air.

Also check with the local building department to learn the recommended building practices concerning foundations in the area. If you have a choice, select the superior method even though it may cost more initially. In fact, throughout the job, to protect the money you are plowing into your project, you are well advised to go with the better construction methods, if possible, whenever you have a choice.

MASONRY AND CONCRETE

Even if your home is in a remote area, chances are you will have your concrete delivered to the job by transit-mix truck, rather than mixing and pouring it by hand. The usual practice for ordering from a ready-mix outfit is to indicate (1) the number of bags of cement per cubic yard (cu. yd.) of concrete, (2) the desired aggregate (stone) size, and (3) water content. A five-bag mix is the minimum you should accept for a residential pour. If there will be reinforcing steel in your concrete, up the standard to a six-bag mix (see Table 9-1).

The size of the gravel, or aggregate, is important; the normal is considered to be between 1½ and ¼ in. As a rule of thumb, if the gravel size is smaller than the norm, say a 1-in. maximum, you should add a quarter of a sack of cement to a five-bag mix (for a total 5¼-bag mix). When there is a greater variance in gravel size, say a maximum of ½ in., discuss the concrete mix with the building inspector and follow his recommendations. If in doubt, write to the American Concrete Institute (its address is listed in Appendix E).

Footings. *Footings* are those members of the below-grade structure upon which the foundation walls rest. Since their function is to transmit the superimposed load of the house above to the soil below, footings must be poured upon undisturbed soil. If your land has been filled, therefore, all fill materials must be removed before pouring the footings.

The design of footings is dictated by local conditions. Regardless of the requirements by local authorities, footings must be wide enough to distribute the imposed load over a sufficient area to prevent any chance of settling. Since most residential-dwelling designs impose a minimal load upon footings, a standard formula (shown in Figure 9-16) based upon wall thickness is the accepted practice in most areas. You should know, however, that this formula is intended for standard conditions: In the final analysis, all footings must be designed to suit the load capacity of the soil beneath. If the soil has a low load-bearing capacity, wider footings may be called for. Reinforcing steel may even be needed.

Wall Forms. You can erect wall forms in one of two ways: One is to rent steel forms from a masonry supply house; the second, perhaps more economical way, is to build your own forms. You can definitely save dollars by building your own forms, but you pay the price for such savings with your labor.

TABLE 9-1 CONCRETE MIXES FOR SMALL JOBS

Approximate weight of solid ingredients
in pounds per cubic foot of concrete

| Mix desig- nation | Maximum size of aggre- gate, in. | Cement | Sand* | | Coarse aggregate | |
			Air- entrained concrete†	Concrete without air	Gravel or crushed stone	Iron blast furnace slag
A	½	25	48	51	54	47
B		25	46	49	56	49
C		25	44	47	58	51
A	¾	23	45	49	62	54
B		23	43	47	64	56
C		23	41	45	66	58
A	1	22	41	45	70	61
B		22	39	43	72	63
C		22	37	41	74	65
A	1½	20	41	45	75	65
B		20	39	43	77	67
C		20	37	41	79	69
A	2	19	40	45	79	69
B		19	38	43	81	71
C		19	36	41	83	72

* Weights are for dry sand. If damp sand is used, increase tabulated weight of sand 2 lb and, if very wet sand is used, 4 lb.

† Air-entrained concrete should be used in all structures which will be exposed to alternate cycles of freezing and thawing. Air-entrainment can be obtained by the use of an air-entraining cement or by adding an air-entraining admixture. If an admixture is used, the amount recommended by the manufacturer will, in most cases, produce the desired air content.

Select the proper maximum size of aggregate. Use Mix B adding just enough water to produce a workable consistency. If the concrete appears to be undersanded, change to Mix A; if it appears to be oversanded, change to Mix C. If the sand is moist or wet, make the corrections in batch weight as prescribed in the footnote. The water content should never be enough to make the mixture overwet: Concrete should slide, not run, off a shovel.

Adapted from American Concrete Institute Data.

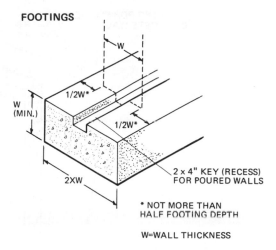

FOOTINGS

W (MIN.)

1/2W*

1/2W*

2XW

W

2 x 4" KEY (RECESS) FOR POURED WALLS

* NOT MORE THAN HALF FOOTING DEPTH

W=WALL THICKNESS

Figure 9-16 *The shape and size of footings depend on soil conditions. The footings should be wide enough to spread the imposed load over a sufficient area so there is no settling. A satisfactory footing design for most residential dwellings is shown here. The footing width is twice that of the foundation wall; the thickness equals that of the foundation wall—usually 8 inches. The recess in the top of footing is made by pushing a strip of wood into the concrete, thus creating a key that the foundation wall can lock into.*

You can figure several weekends (or longer, depending upon your carpentry experience) to construct the forms, and several more weekends to disassemble and clean the wood after stripping the forms from the poured (see Figure 9-17) walls. If you construct your own foundation forms, use sound construction techniques as outlined in the U.S. Department of Agriculture Handbook No. 73 (see Appendix D).

Today, job-built forms are generally of plywood, which is then cleaned and reused in the house as sheathing and subflooring. Because of the construction time involved, forms of sheathing boards are pretty much a thing of the past.

Regardless of which alternative you decide on, form walls must be tight enough to minimize water leakage and strong enough to withstand the great force exerted on them as concrete is chuted from the ready-mix truck.

About Concrete. The handling of concrete varies with the seasons. For example, in warm, dry weather it must be kept moist to prevent too rapid hydration (evaporation). Thus, to slow down drying time, freshly poured concrete is usually covered with wetted burlap while it cures. The burlap is sprinkled with water occasionally to keep it damp during the curing period. In cold weather, precautions must be taken to prevent freezing. Generally, antifreeze is mixed into the concrete. In some instances new concrete may even have to be covered with salt hay and kept warm by one or more salamanders (heaters) during the entire curing period. Your best bet is to check with your local building department regarding local practices in pouring concrete during weather extremes.

For many, calling in a masonry contractor is far and away the wisest move. Since much of the concrete work—erecting forms and pouring the mix —is really just bull-work, consider the practicality of farming out this part of the job in order to save your energy—and possibly your heart—for the pleasanter aspects of building.

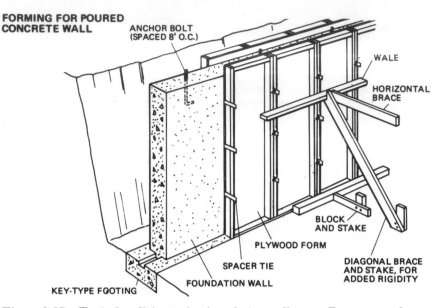

FORMING FOR POURED CONCRETE WALL

ANCHOR BOLT (SPACED 8' O.C.)

WALE

HORIZONTAL BRACE

BLOCK AND STAKE

PLYWOOD FORM

DIAGONAL BRACE AND STAKE, FOR ADDED RIGIDITY

SPACER TIE

FOUNDATION WALL

KEY-TYPE FOOTING

Figure 9-17   Typical wall forms for foundation-wall pour. Forms must be strong and securely braced to resist the pressure of plastic concrete. Pressure increases dramatically as the wall height increases. Thus, the ties are installed through the forms to provide additional bracing. After the forms are stripped, the ties are snapped off at the foundation wall. Wood ties can be used but commercially-made metal ones are easier to work with.

Waterproofing the Basement or Slab. If your area seems to be especially damp, invest a few bucks more and take the precaution of waterproofing the foundation walls (see Figure 9-19). Waterproofing is applied, below grade on the outside, with either a cement plaster or bituminous waterproofing compound. For maximum protection against water intrusion, install drain tiles as shown.

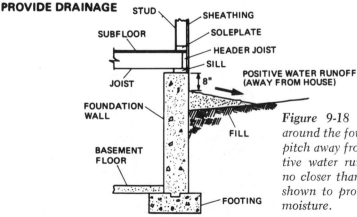

PROVIDE DRAINAGE

STUD

SHEATHING

SUBFLOOR

SOLEPLATE

HEADER JOIST

SILL

JOIST

POSITIVE WATER RUNOFF (AWAY FROM HOUSE)

8"

FOUNDATION WALL

FILL

BASEMENT FLOOR

FOOTING

Figure 9-18   When the soil is filled in around the foundation wall, the slope should pitch away from the house to provide a positive water runoff. The grade should come no closer than 8 inches to the house sill as shown to protect wood members from soil moisture.

DRAINAGE AT OUTER WALL

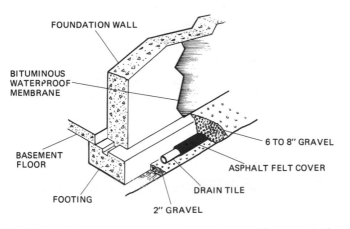

Figure 9-19 *If subsurface water persists in your area, it's a good idea to install concrete drain tiles (footing drains) around the house perimeter. Pipes are set in and covered by gravel and run alongside and below the tops of footings. The drains should lead away from the house foundation to an outlet that is always open. (In some areas, it is permissible to connect footing drains to the sanitary system.) The drain is sloped about 1 in. in 20 ft., and the lengths of pipe are laid with ¼-in. joints between. 15-lb. felt (tarpaper) goes over the joints before the gravel is placed in the ditch to cover the drain tiles.*

Slab-house construction, of course, is different from basement-house construction. Two types of slabs are used in residential construction: independent and thickened-edge (see Figures 9-21 and 9-22). The role of either type of slab, besides providing a floor, is to transmit the structural load to the footings, so that (just as in foundation-wall construction) footings must rest upon undisturbed ground.

SLAB CONSTRUCTION

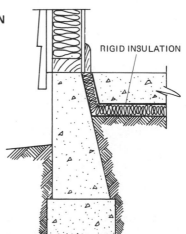

Figure 9-20 *In slab-on-ground construction, insulation and moisture control are essential. Use rigid insulation beneath the slab and at the perimeter of the house. Membrane damp-proofing—a polyethylene vapor barrier—goes in between the insulation and the concrete slab.*

THICKENED-EDGE SLAB

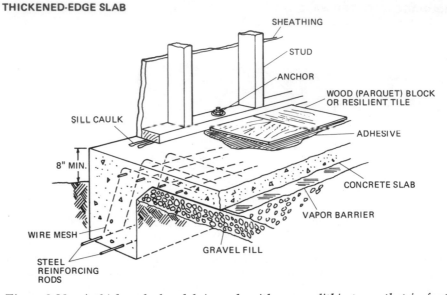

Figure 9-21 *A thickened-edge slab is made with a monolithic pour—that is, foot-ings and slab are poured at the same time. Steel reinforcing rods are suggested for strength in such construction. Notice that the top of the slab is also 8 in. above grade.*

Make certain you use a vapor barrier under a floor slab—don't let *any* masonry contractor tell you that one is not needed. The material you choose should have a good vapor-transmission rating, high resistance to moisture, and the ability to withstand tears and breaks during the pouring operation (see Figure 9-22).

Incidentally, if your slab is poured by others, try to be at the site to observe the entire operation. Unfortunately, I've seen unscrupulous contrac-tors and masons punch holes in the vapor barrier to allow water in the mix to drain off. Although this practice speeds up the drying time (making the contractor happy), it also negates the usefulness of the vapor barrier. The homeowner suffers later with a damp floor, separating tiles, and all the other problems of a damp slab.

The most common methods of installing a vapor barrier are:

* three layers of roofing felt with hot asphalt mopped on between layers,
* 6-mil or heavier polyethylene,
* 55-lb roll-roofing, or
* heavy asphalt-laminated duplex barriers.

At this point, your leisure home has gotten "off the ground," even if only a foot or so. Without underestimating the importance of the rest of

INDEPENDENT SLAB AND WALL

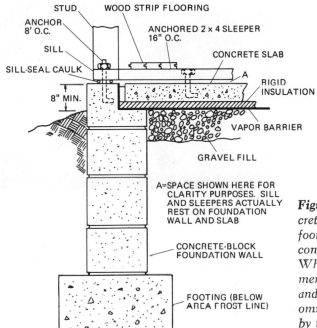

Figure 9-22 *An independent concrete floor slab. The poured concrete footing is below the area's frostline; concrete blocks are used for the wall. When a wood floor is desirable, 2-by-4 members must be anchored to the slab and the use of treated lumber is recommended to discourage infestation by termites.*

the project—the framing of walls, roof, and so on—I must say that you've made the remainder of your job a lot easier if you've taken pains with the planning of foundation and footings.

Next, you'll wear your carpenter's hat.

10

House Framing

GETTING READY

Once the foundation is in, you can start thinking about the rough framing.

But before doing anything else, take the time to make the jobsite as orderly and as free of obstructions as possible. Backfill the excavation and rough-grade the surrounding area, so that lumber deliveries can be stored where you want them—instead of being dumped wherever the driver can find room.

Getting It Together. When you are prepared to take deliveries, you can order the initial framing materials. Some building plans, such as those offered by the plans services in Appendix B, include a list of quantities and types and uses. Also, many lumber suppliers will put together such a list for you, free of charge as long as they are assured of getting the entire order. Since this list is a very technical one that should also include all windows, doors, and framing lumber, as well as all hardware appurtenances, you should take advantage of this service to save yourself considerable time and to avoid costly mistakes. These suppliers know at a glance what you would very likely have to look up and double-check in a building manual. Besides, if you wind up with the wrong materials, you can always take them back with little or no aggravation.

Finally, you must coordinate delivery dates with your planned work schedule. Weather, of course, can ruin a construction schedule, but you'll have to go on the assumption that all *your* weather will be clear and that work will progress smoothly. At this point, you should also have a clear understanding with the lumberyard on how payment for materials is to be made. Chances are, though, your first few orders will have to be paid C.O.D.; you will be able to charge materials on a monthly-payment basis after the lumberyard people get to know you and your paying habits.

Protecting Materials. To minimize the chance of theft, framing materials should be delivered to the jobsite on the day construction is to start, for once these tempting materials are parked on your property, the risk of theft is greater than when the masonry work was going on. Thus, one security measure is to make every effort to coordinate material deliveries with your anticipated production schedule. Ideally, have the lumberyard deliver on Friday those materials that you expect to install during your weekend work session.

Take other precautions too. If possible, ask cooperative neighbors to keep an eye on your place in your absence; instruct them to call the police if they observe any suspicious activity. Also, use common sense in construction. Since windows, in particular, attract thieves, install these in rough openings as quickly as possible. Finally, post signs on the premises offering a reward for information leading to the arrest and conviction of thieves.

Additionally, materials must be protected against the weather. The framing lumber should be stored off the ground on sleepers or skids, so air can circulate beneath it. And after each work session take the time to cover the lumber with a waterproof material, such as 6-mil polyethylene, and weight it down with cement blocks or rocks to prevent the wind from blowing it off. All uninstalled windows (including picture and bow windows), which don't go in until the roof framing is completed, should be protected with a prime coat of paint and covered also.

FRAMING YOUR HOUSE—SOME COMMENTS

If you are not already familiar with framing terminology, refer to Figure 10-4. The few terms in this illustration will help you understand the rest of the chapter and will be added to as we go along.

Of the two best known house-framing methods, balloon and platform, the latter is the more commonly used these days.

In *balloon framing*, the studs run continuously from foundation wall to rafter ends. In this method, the second-floor joists rest on a 2-by-4 ribbon let into the studs, and joists are then spiked to the studs. If you use balloon framing, you must install firestops in all bays (between studs), to prevent or at least slow down the vertical spread of fire. The biggest advantage of balloon framing is that because of that uninterrupted flow of space between studs, it is easy to snake wires, pipes, and the like from one floor to the next.

In the *platform method*, the floor joists are erected upon the foundation walls and then covered with subflooring to create a platform. The wall sections can then be assembled and lifted into place using the platform as an open-air workbench. Ordinarily, the first level is completely framed, the subflooring is placed over the second-level floor joists, and then the second level is added. Finally, the roof is framed to cover the entire structure.

Nailing. To provide the rigidity and strength to withstand heavy rains, snow loads, and windstorms, it is absolutely essential to properly nail framing members. Adequate nailing also fosters better performance of materials: for example, poor (or under) nailing in the framing inevitably causes cracked plaster or plasterboard or wide gaps between sheets of wall paneling. For good nailing practices and the platform structure, see Figure 10-5.

Framing Hardware. Many building experts have long felt that toenailing of structural members was an inadequate system and that better fastening methods for greater anchorage and strength were needed. As a result, a wide variety of connecting and strengthening devices are now available to either augment or replace standard framing fastening practices. Typical hardware, available at all well-stocked building supply outlets and lumberyards, is shown in Figures 10-1 through 10-3.

Sketches Courtesy Teco Company

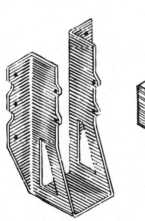

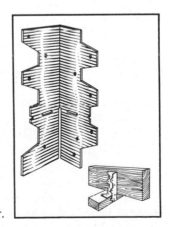

Figure 10-1   Joist-and-beam hanger.

Figure 10-2   All-purpose framing anchor.

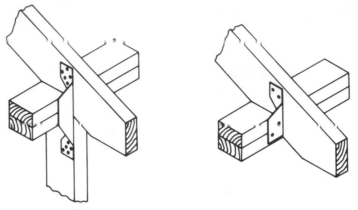

Figure 10-3 *Ty-down rafter anchors.*

FRAMING YOUR HOUSE—STEP BY STEP

Floor Framing. The first step, obviously, is to attach floor joists to the foundation and install the subflooring. Basically, there are three requirements to consider when selecting materials for use as floor joists:

1. The *strength* of the material needed depends upon the loads to be imposed.
2. The *stiffness* requirements place a limit on deflection when the floor is under load. The degree of stiffness also limits the amount of vibration from moving loads—a person walking across the room, for example.
3. *Superior nail-holding characteristics* in joists and in all other framing materials is a must.

Generally, joists are of 2-in. nominal thickness. Actually, if you measure the thickness of 2-in. stock you will find it to be only 1½-in. thick. Don't think that the lumberyard is ripping you off. The 2-in. designation is the nominal one, that is, the dimension established by lumber-industry standards. The actual dimension is what that particular piece of lumber measures after it has been dressed. The joist depth is usually either 8, 10, or 12 in. nominal; the depth you select, of course, is determined by the span. The span table for floor joists published by the Federal Housing Administration should be used as a minimum guide. In many instances, however, the local code requires materials of greater depth; when it does, you are obliged to conform to the more demanding requirements.

The most commonly used wood in framing is spruce and Douglas fir. The minimum quality you should accept is that rated as standard. Southern pine is also frequently used, but if you choose this species, accept only No. 2 grade or better. In fact, No. 2KD (kiln-dried) pine is your best bet here.

Once the floor framing is in and covered with subflooring, you have a convenient work platform.

Wall Framing. Wall framing actually includes all vertical studs as well as the horizontal members that support the floors and roof. In addition to this supportive function, it also provides a nailing surface for the finish walls inside and out.

Like joists and rafters, therefore, the materials used for wall studs not only should have good stiffness and nailholding power, but also should be free of warp and twist. Wall-framing lumber should be relatively free of moisture content—15 percent is considered desirable, with 19 percent the maximum. If the moisture content is greater, allow the framing material to reach serviceable condition before applying the interior wall finishes.

The species most commonly used for studs include Douglas fir, the spruces, various pines, and white fir. The conventional building practice is to

WALL FRAMING FOR PLATFORM CONSTRUCTION

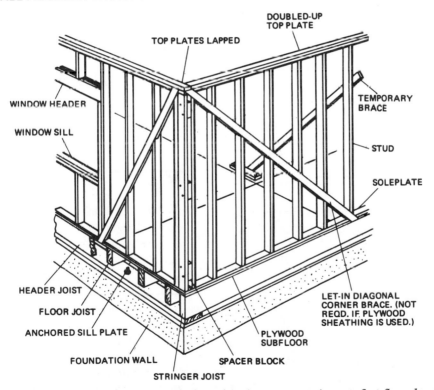

Figure 10-4   The details of a platform-framing construction at first-floor level. When there's a second level, the floor joists above rest upon, and are fastened to, the doubled-up top plates. Notice the ledge created at the top of the foundation wall by the sill setback; this dimension is equal to the sheathing thickness which, when installed, is flush with outside plane of foundation wall.

GOOD NAILING TECHNIQUE,
PLATFORM CONSTRUCTION

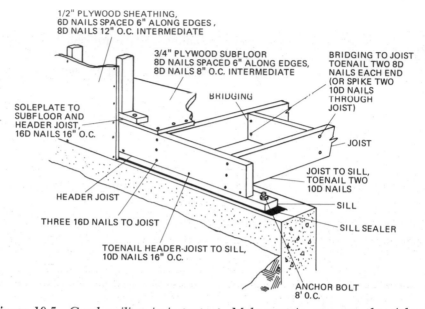

1/2" PLYWOOD SHEATHING,
6D NAILS SPACED 6" ALONG EDGES,
8D NAILS 12" O.C. INTERMEDIATE

3/4" PLYWOOD SUBFLOOR
8D NAILS SPACED 6" ALONG EDGES,
8D NAILS 8" O.C. INTERMEDIATE

BRIDGING TO JOIST
TOENAIL TWO 8D
NAILS EACH END
(OR SPIKE TWO
10D NAILS
THROUGH
JOIST)

BRIDGING

SOLEPLATE TO
SUBFLOOR AND
HEADER JOIST,
16D NAILS 16" O.C.

JOIST

JOIST TO SILL,
TOENAIL TWO
10D NAILS

HEADER JOIST

SILL

THREE 16D NAILS TO JOIST

SILL SEALER

TOENAIL HEADER-JOIST TO SILL,
10D NAILS 16" O.C.

ANCHOR BOLT
8' O.C.

Figure 10-5 Good nailing is important. Make certain you use the right-size nails at various connection points. Common nails—with heads—are used in all framing; if in doubt about which nails to use where, check with your local building department. Sill sealer material between sill and foundation is intended to take up any uneven spaces between these two members and serves as a sill stabilizer.

space 2-by-4 wall studs 16 in. apart, measured "on center" (O.C.). Top plates and sole plates are also of 2-by-4 nominal stock. Since finish floor-to-ceiling height today is generally 8 ft., it is common practice to rough frame walls to a height of 8 ft. 1½ in. (from the top of the subfloor to the top of the doubled-up top plate) to allow for finish materials.

Usually the walls are assembled in sections on the platform and then tilted up into position (Figure 10-6). (If you have enough helpers on the job, you can even raise a full length of wall at a time.) Each wall section contains rough openings for windows and doors (see Figures 10-9 and 10-10). All exterior walls are erected, plumbed, and braced before any construction of interior walls begins.

Wall frames should be solidly connected to the foundation below. To make certain they are, you can either install sheathing to make a tie with the foundation wall or use anchor bolts. In the first method, sheathing passes down below the sill plate and fits into a ledge formed when the concrete for the wall was poured. But installing anchor bolts is better. Here you install hook-shaped ½-in. bolts every 8 feet around the perimeter of the house. The

Figure 10-6 Once subflooring is fastened into place, the wall sections can be assembled on the platform, then tilted up into position for fastening. If you have enough helpers on the job to aid in the lifting, you can raise a full length of wall at one time.

anchors should be embedded at least 8 inches into concrete walls and 16 inches into block walls. The threaded end of each bolt is left to project at least 2 inches out of the foundation so that it can pass through the sill plate and be secured with washers and nuts.

The interior walls should be well fastened to any exterior walls with which they intersect or butt-join. All intersections of walls must also provide good nailing surfaces on both sides (that is, on inside and outside corners). How to assure such nailing is detailed in Figure 10-7.

Mod-24. Lately, a system, called Mod-24, that uses less framing lumber has been coming into use across the United States. Supported by the four major building code agencies and the Federal Housing Administration (FHA), the system advocates 24-in. spacing of floor joists, wall studs, and roof trusses. Field tests supervised by the National Association of Home Builders (NAHB) have proved that, from a structural standpoint, the wider spacing is fully adequate in home construction. Test buildings also showed that by using Mod-24, a savings of from $200 to $400 per house is possible. "Mod-24," a 16-page booklet that explains how the system is applied, is available free from the Western Wood Products Association (see address listed in Appendix D).

Ceiling and Roof Framing. Very likely you will choose one of the four roof styles shown in Figure 10-8. Each constructed by different technique, they are fairly standard for single-detached residential structures. For many, even some do-it-yourselfers who consider themselves rather sophisticated

TYPICAL INSIDE AND OUTSIDE CORNERS

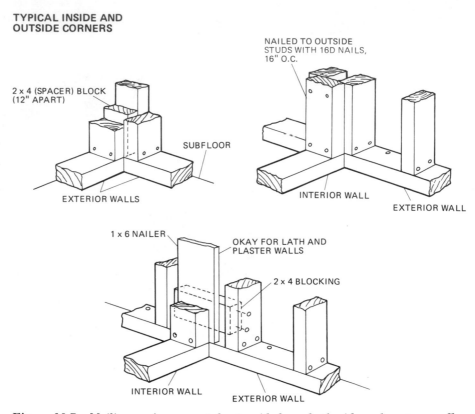

Figure 10-7 *Nailing surfaces must be provided on both sides when two walls intersect. Typical examples of interior partition butting an exterior wall are shown here: (a) Standard outside corner; 2-by-4 spacer blocks are used every 12 in. or so to assure a rigid corner. Stud placement guarantees nailing base for interior wall materials. (b) To provide a nailing surface inside, when an interior wall butts an outside wall, you can use double studs on the outside wall. (c) When a partition must fall between studs on a wall it intersects, create inside corners by adding a board as shown here.*

TYPICAL RESIDENTIAL ROOFS

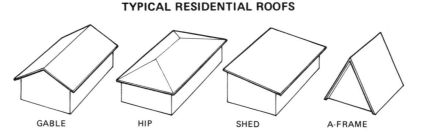

Figure 10-8 *Four roof shapes typical in residential construction. Each has its own special framing-technique requirements.*

TYPICAL WALL OPENINGS

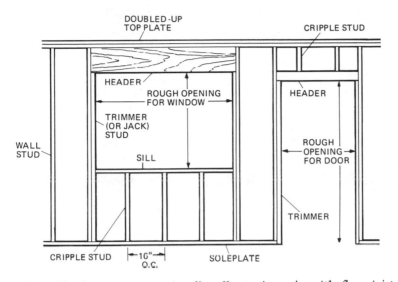

Figure 10-9 *Headers are a must in all wall openings. As with floor joists, the depth of material to use is determined by the span that the header makes. Whether or not the wall is a loadbearing one also makes a difference in header requirements.*

TYPICAL HEADER

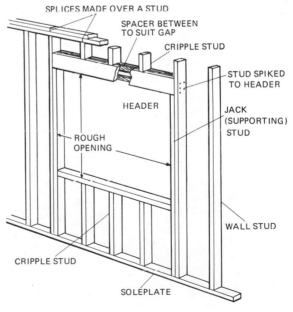

Figure 10-10 *A header is created by using two lengths of two-by stock with appropriate-thickness spacers in between; the header must be flush with both the interior and exterior surfaces of the wall that it's in. The two-bys are held together with 16d nails toenailed at an angle, or driven straight through and then clinched (that is, the protruding point is bent over securely against the header surface).*

carpenters, roof framing is the most difficult part of the job. I know professional carpenters whose roof-framing skills are questionable at best. So, since there is a great deal to framing a roof, you shouldn't consider the illustrations shown in this chapter as all-inclusive; rather, they are intended to illustrate typical framing techniques.

And if, after beefing-up your understanding of roof framing by reading building manuals and the like, you feel the task is still beyond your abilities, you needn't feel embarrassed because you have to call in a professional to do this part of the job. If possible, hire a local carpenter to frame the roof with you working as his assistant (to keep down costs). If you cannot set up such an arrangement, you will have to hire a local contractor. At any rate, it is important that your roof be properly framed, so don't penny-pinch here.

There are basically two types of roof-framing techniques. They are: 1. Joist-and-rafter, and 2. Truss.

1. *Joist and Rafter.* When all exterior and interior walls are framed, plumbed, and nailed, and after the upper (top) plate has been fastened in place, the ceiling joists go in (to tie the walls together). In most cases, these span the width of the house. The size lumber to use (determined by the span, type of wood used, and the load that will be imposed from above) should be specified in the blueprints.

Ceiling joists serve several purposes. First, they resist the outward thrust imposed upon the walls by the roof rafters. They also provide the nailing surface for the ceiling and floor finish treatments. Finally, they support the floor above. Because of this, joists must be securely nailed to the top plate

Figure 10-11 A good method for installing ceiling joists on—instead of over—a beam or girder is to use a 2-by-2 ledger strip as shown. The strip is solidly nailed so it is flush with the bottom of the girder; joists are then notched and installed sitting upon the ledger strip. Here, a carpenter checks the top of the joist with a framing square to make certain the plane is exactly 90° from vertical plane of beam.

ROOF AND CEILING FRAMING

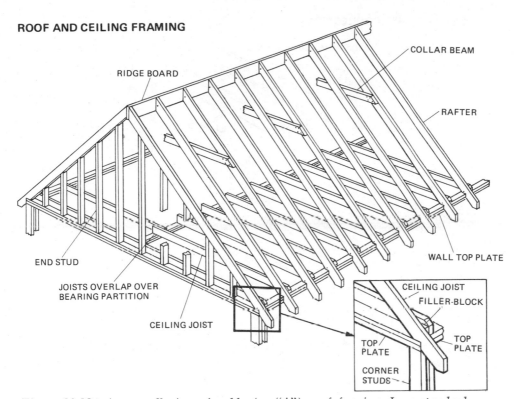

Figure 10-12 *An overall view of gable (or "A") roof framing. In a standard pitched-roof construction, ceiling joists go in after interior and exterior walls are framed and before rafters are installed (or the weight may cause opposite walls to bow outward). If the span across the house is great, ceiling joists should meet over a bearing partition. At this point, joists should overlap and be spiked together. Roof framing (that is, the cutting of rafters) is not a job for an amateur. Beginning do-it-yourselfers are well advised to hire a competent carpenter for at least this portion of the framing operation.*

of every wall that their ends rest on and to every load-bearing partition wall that they cross or join on. Finally, joists should be spiked to the rafters at the exterior walls.

In standard pitched-roof construction, rafters are installed after the ceiling joists are fastened.

2. *Truss Roofs.* Roof trusses, unlike joists, span the entire width of a structure. Mathematically, the principle that gives them the strength to do this is the inherent rigidity of the triangle. As shown in Figure 10-14, a number of triangles are built into the frame so that the stresses are parallel to the members of the structure. With this strength, therefore, trusses simply rest upon and are fastened to opposite exterior walls; further, the members may be spaced 24, rather than 16, inches on center.

CEILING JOIST CONNECTIONS

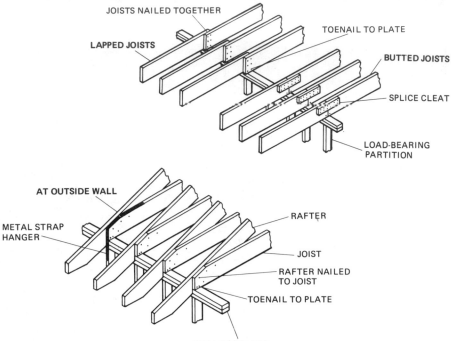

Figure 10-13   *Like the rafters, ceiling joists are normally placed to span the width of the house. If at all possible, interior partitions should be placed so that joists of even lengths (i.e., 12, 14 or 16 ft.) can be used without waste to span from exterior walls to interior (loadbearing) walls. Joists must be securely nailed and, when they join or meet over an interior partition, they should be nailed together using one of the techniques shown here.*

If your area is subject to heavy and frequent windstorms, it's a good idea to anchor walls and roof framing together using strapping as shown. Standard construction techniques call for fastening together of rafters and joists at outside walls.

The greatest advantage of a truss roof is that it eliminates the need for load-bearing interior walls. Thus, complete design freedom in the use of interior space is possible. Partitioning walls may be placed anywhere. The disadvantage is that attic storage space is obstructed by the diagonal members. If the choice of construction technique is up to you, you must decide between the free use of living space and the importance of storage space.

If you are going to install the roof yourself, you should also consider the fact that trusses are easier to install than rafters and the roof will therefore go up faster. You may also make the trusses yourself, although the wiser approach would be to have them made up and delivered to the jobsite by a truss manufacturer.

W-TRUSS

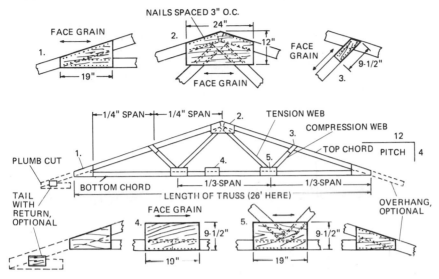

Figure 10-14 A W-Type truss is probably the most commonly used roof truss in residential construction. Because of the number of interior members, the distances between the connections are not particularly great. It is therefore usually possible to build these with lower-grade, less expensive lumber.

In construction of the 26-ft. truss illustrated, notice that the critical connection locations are spelled out as fractional distances of an overall span. Gussets over the connections are fastened with nails and glue; in damp climates, resorcinol glue should be used. Nomenclature for W-truss members: (1) Bevel-heel gusset; (2) peak gusset; (3) upper chord intermediate gusset; (4) splice of lower chord; (5) lower chord intermediate gusset. Notice that the grain direction for plywood is indicated for all gussets; this is important to assure maximum strength.

COVERING THE FRAMEWORK

After the entire structure has been framed, the roof and walls are completely closed in with sheathing. In addition to supplying a flat surface to which exterior materials are applied, sheathing gives the structure its rigidity and strength. If the wall sheathing was not applied to the wall sections as they were erected, it should be applied before the roof framing is added.

In some of the (more) temperate climates, the sheathing material can also serve as the siding. In such instances, a textured plywood is commonly selected to assure an esthetically pleasing appearance on the outside.

Sheathing. There are four types you should be familiar with:

1. *Wood sheathing* refers to nominal 1-in. thick boards of 6-, 8-, and 10-in. widths. Wider material is rarely used and is not recommended because of the high risk of warping and cupping. Sheathing boards are available in

SHEATHING BOARDS

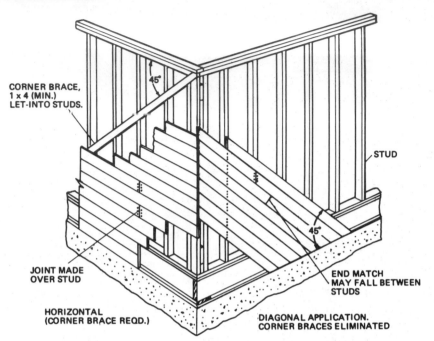

CORNER BRACE,
1 x 4 (MIN.)
LET-INTO STUDS.

45°

STUD

JOINT MADE
OVER STUD

45°

END MATCH
MAY FALL BETWEEN
STUDS

HORIZONTAL
(CORNER BRACE REQD.)

DIAGONAL APPLICATION.
CORNER BRACES ELIMINATED

Figure 10-15 Two methods of applying sheathing boards to framework. At left, horizontally fastened boards require the use of diagonal bracing at all corners. Of one-by stock, braces are let into studs and both plates. But if sheathing itself is diagonally applied as at the right, bracing can be eliminated. Though labor for this step is then saved, diagonal sheathing obviously requires the cutting of all sheathing boards at a 45° angle at both ends—and that's a time-consuming way to sheath an entire house.

square-edged, shiplap, and tongue-and-groove patterns (Figure 10-17). Although the boards are commonly placed at right angles to the studs, they should be fastened diagonally for greater rigidity. Wall sheathing boards should be affixed to studs using three 8d common nails at each stud.

2. *Plywood sheathing* is in great use now for three primary reasons: (1) It gives excellent rigidity; (2) it speeds up the sheathing operation considerably (you cover 32 sq. ft. with each panel); and (3) it eliminates the need for diagonal corner bracing which must be let into the studs.

Standard sheathing-grade plywood should be used. The standard thickness today is ⅜ in.—perfectly acceptable as far as strength and rigidity are concerned. However, depending on the type of siding to follow, ½ in. plywood is often a better choice. Sometimes the thickness is determined also by the widths of factory-made window and door jambs. In many cases, to use a thicker plywood sheathing, jamb extensions have to be added on the inside to bring the jamb flush with the interior wall finish.

**PLYWOOD AND INSULATING
BOARD SHEATHING**

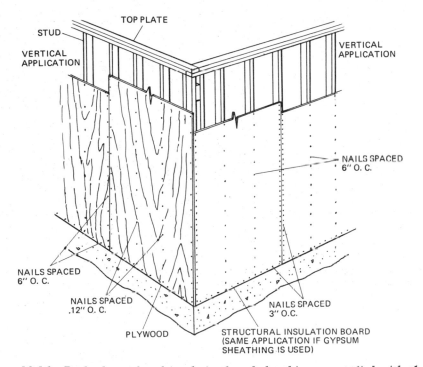

STUD
TOP PLATE
VERTICAL
APPLICATION
VERTICAL
APPLICATION
NAILS SPACED
6" O. C.
NAILS SPACED
6" O. C.
NAILS SPACED
12" O. C.
NAILS SPACED
3" O.C.
PLYWOOD
STRUCTURAL INSULATION BOARD
(SAME APPLICATION IF GYPSUM
SHEATHING IS USED)

Figure 10-16   Both plywood and insulating board sheathing are applied with the sheet-length vertical because perimeter nailing is then possible. Diagonal bracing is not a must with either type of sheathing. Plywood can be applied horizontally, but it will not be as efficient from the standpoint of rigidity and strength. When sheet-type sheathing is installed with its length perpendicular to wall studs, blocking between studs must be provided to obtain edge nailing and greater rigidity.

Nails should be spaced along the edges and on interior studs as shown in the drawing; with both types of sheathing, allow about ⅛-in. space between the sheets as you install them (for expansion).

As with all sheathing, the plywood must be well nailed. The nails should be spaced 6 in. O.C. along the edges and no farther than 12 in. apart on intermediate studs. 6d nails should be used on ⅜-in. plywood, 8d on thicker (½-in.) material.

3. *Structural insulating boards* are impregnated with asphalt to provide some resistance to water; they are therefore not damaged by an occasional rain during the course of construction. But the material may not be left exposed to the elements indefinitely with no concern about possible damage.

Basically, there are three types of insulating board: (1) regular density, (2) intermediate density, and (3) nail-base. The first comes in two thick-

MOST COMMONLY USED SHEATHING BOARDS

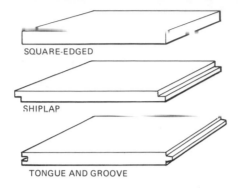

SQUARE-EDGED

SHIPLAP

TONGUE AND GROOVE

Figure 10-17   *If you use sheathing boards instead of a sheet material, chances are you will have to settle for one of these shapes. If it's locally available, choose the tongue-and-groove shape.*

PLYWOOD ROOF SHEATHING

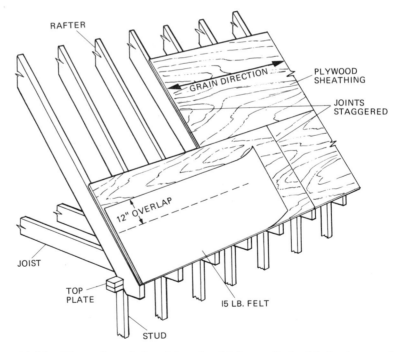

RAFTER

PLYWOOD SHEATHING

GRAIN DIRECTION

JOINTS STAGGERED

12" OVERLAP

JOIST

TOP PLATE

15 LB. FELT

STUD

Figure 10-18   *Plywood roof sheathing should be applied with its face grain perpendicular to the rafters. Generally, standard sheathing-grade plywood is acceptable, but in damp climates you are well advised to use exterior-grade plywood sheathing (the difference is in the glueline). End joints should always be made over the center of rafters and these should be staggered by at least 16 in. For good nail-holding power, ⅜ in. and ½ in. plywood are usually recommended as the minimal thicknesses of plywood to use on roofs.*

Figure 10-19 *Often, architectural style dictates the use of a ridge beam construction (low slope). Here, solid, glue-laminated beams spanning the open area are supported by the exterior wall at one end and an interior partition or post at the other. The beam is designed for the roof load for the span selected. The wood decking can serve as both supporting and sheathing. When ridge beam and decking are used, good anchoring methods are a must at ridge and outer wall. Usually, this is accomplished with metal strapping. It is also advisable to use long-ringed nails, as well as supplemental metal strapping, at both bearing areas.*

nesses, ½ and $^{25}\!/_{32}$ in., and in 2-by-8, 4-by-8, and 4-by-9 ft. sizes. The second and third types come in ½ in. thickness and 4-by-8 and 4-by-9 ft. sheets. The 4-by-8 ft. sheets are installed with their long dimension vertical; the 2-by-8 ft. pieces go on horizontally (perpendicular to the studs).

Diagonal corner bracing (as shown in Figure 10-15) is a must with insulated-board sheathing; and the bracing should be fastened with galvanized or corrosion-resistant nails. To fasten ½-in. insulated board to studs, use 1½ in. roofing nails; for $^{25}\!/_{32}$-in. board, use 1¾ inchers. Space the nails 3 inches apart along the edges, and 6 inches O.C. at intermediate studs (unless the manufacturer's instructions say otherwise).

4. *Gypsum sheathing*, often called "garage sheathing" by professionals, consists of a treated gypsum filler faced both sides with water-resistant paper. Some manufacturers produce gypsum sheathing with one long edge grooved and the other long edge V-shaped, to make its application easier

and to add some degree of tie between sheets. As with insulated board, diagonal bracing is required at corners.

Fasten ½-in. thick gypsum board using 1½-in. roofing nails spaced 3 inches apart along the edges and 6 inches apart on intermediates.

Covering the Roof. When the entire roof has been framed and all items that will project through the roof (chimney, vents, and the like) are installed, it should be sheathed as quickly as possible to protect all materials and work below.

Plywood is the most popular roof sheathing used these days. For strength, the sheets are laid with their face-grain perpendicular to the direction of the rafters and butted over the centers of rafters. These joints should be staggered by at least one rafter so there is no continuous joint-line from cornice to ridge board. It is also good construction practice to use H-clips on plywood edges between rafters for extra support.

Though ⅜-in. plywood is accepted by most building codes for use as roof sheathing, you are better off using ½-in. material. The added thickness gives superior resistance to rack from high winds and affords better penetration for shingle nails. Plywood roof sheathing is fastened with 6d common nails spaced 6 inches O.C. along the edges and 12 inches apart at intermediate rafters.

FINISHING THE EXTERIOR

Roofing Material. Once the roof and walls are closed in, the roof should be finished off as quickly as possible to protect the investment below from water damage.

There are two points to keep in mind when selecting roof-finish materials:

1. If large expanses of sloping roofs are visible from the ground, you should try to select a material that will contribute to the overall attractiveness of the house. Too often, an owner will select expensive siding materials and then downgrade the building's appearance with a cheap roof. Give careful attention to your roof; use materials that add color, pattern, or texture as desired.

2. Buy a quality roofing product. Since labor is most of the expense of a roofing job, don't make the mistake of picking shingles that will need replacing in less than 10 years. A quality product will last at least 20 years depending upon climatic conditions.

Typical roofing materials for a sloping roof include asphalt, wood, and mineral fiber shingles. Slate and tile can also be used on a sloping roof, but their high cost puts them in the luxury class these days.

Asphalt shingles are the most commonly used material on sloping roofs. Though there doesn't appear to be anything special about applying roof shingles, there are some important points you should know about.

Figure 10-20 Any and all holes in the roof should be cut, and fixtures installed, before shingles go on. Here, a Nutone roof-type exhaust ventilator is installed just prior to application of asphalt shingles.

Figure 10-21 Self-sealing shingles have a factory-applied sealant that is activated by heat from the sun. The sealant softens when warmed by the sun's rays and bonds the shingle above. Shingles that bear the U.L. label for wind resistance have been tested in 60 m.p.h. winds.

The standard three-tab shingle measures 12 by 36 in. and is usually applied with 5 inches exposed. Packaged in bundles of 27 strips each, three bundles will cover one square (100 sq. ft.) using the standard exposure. The amount of exposure on an asphalt shingle, however, can vary, according to the type of material and the roof's pitch, from 5 inches for a steep roof down to 3½ inches for a moderately flat slope. Many makers stamp exposure information on each bundle of shingles.

Pick a type that weighs at least 235 lbs. per square (100 sq. ft.). To minimize any chance of shingles lifting off due to high winds, select a brand which includes a self-sealing edge tab. These come with dabs of composition

Figure 10-22   *Texture on top seems to be the style today. Shown here are four different types—from four different manufacturers—each with a new, textured look. Top-quality shingles from all makers are wind resistant and fire retardant. You should settle for nothing less.*

applied on underside which, after the roof has been exposed to several days of sunlight, causes each shingle to adhere to the shingles below.

The material laid beneath asphalt shingles can be either 15- or 30-lb. saturated felt, applied so it is perfectly flat to avoid bulges on the finished roof. Under no circumstance should any nail other than standard galvanized roofing nails be used to install shingles.

Wood shingles. If, as many do, you opt for the natural look of wood shingles, use only No. 1 grade: all-heartwood, all-edge grain and tapered. Wood shingles are normally applied with 5 inches to the weather, and it takes four bundles of 16-in. shingles to cover one square.

Regardless of shingle width (narrower ones are in the lower grades), use only two 3d rust-resistant nails per shingle. Locate these about ¾ inch from the edges and 1½ inches above the butt line of the following course.

The first course of shingles should be doubled-up; and, approximately an ⅛ to ¼ inch of space should be allowed between all shingle edges to allow for expansion when wet. By using varying widths, joints in following courses are spaced so that they do not line up over a joint below.

Flat roofs. Flat roofs are actually pitched very slightly to provide positive water runoff. To obtain a continuous watertight surface on this type roof, a membrane system, consisting of several layers of felt with hot asphalt, is laid. A final application of asphalt is covered with a layer of crushed stone.

Outside Trim and Millwork. Exterior trim is that part of the exterior finish besides the siding, brick veneer, or other wallcovering. Based on this description, it includes window and door casings, cornice and cornice moldings, soffits, rake (gable-end) trim, and fascia board.

Today's homes are designed with a minimum amount of trim. A cornice, if on the house at all, is usually of the close type; and some contemporary architecture eliminates this detail completely.

Exterior trim material should be selected with care. It must have good weathering and painting characteristics and be entirely free of warpage. It is especially important that any material that makes contact at grade level, such as columns, have a high degree of decay resistance. Your best bet, regardless

NARROW BOX CORNICE

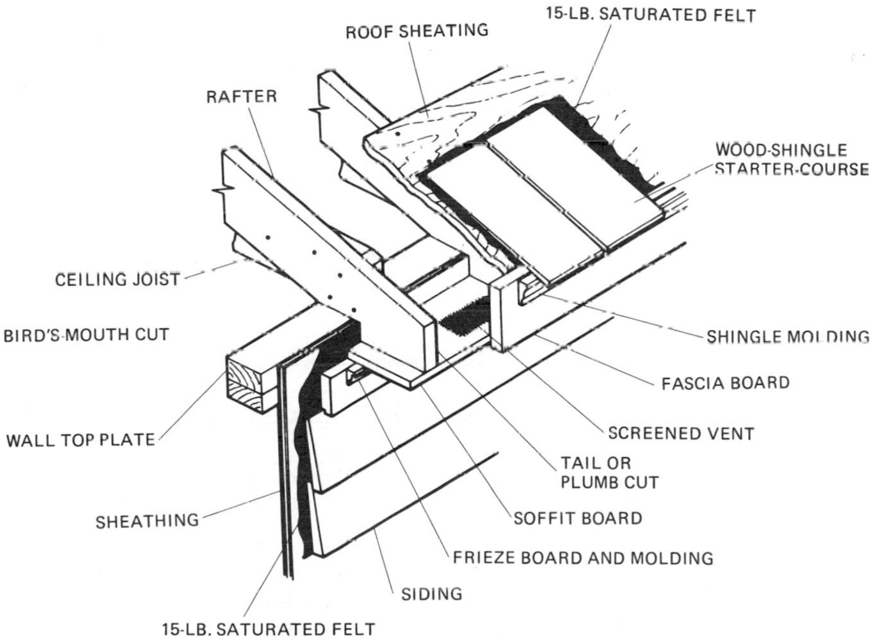

Figure 10-23   A cornice on a house is the projection of the roof at the eave line, that is, the joint between roof and side-walls. In a gable roof it is formed at both sides of a house while in a hip roof it runs continuously around the perimeter of the entire structure. Of several types, the narrow box cornice is shown here. The rafters project and serve as the nailing surface of the soffit as well as fascia trim. It is common practice to use a frieze board at the wall-soffit joint to terminate the siding at this point. The soffit, as shown, provides a good inlet for attic ventilation and also provides drainage should any water enter the enclosure due to ice dams or snow.

of the material used, is to treat all trim members for decay resistance before installation.

For two reasons, it's a good idea also to prime coat all trim *before* installing it on the house. For one thing, prime painting goes faster with pieces laid across a pair of sawhorses; also, those portions of wood members that will be out of sight when trim is installed will be protected against moisture penetration.

Framing for Doors and Windows. As a general rule, doors, windows, and their frames are usually factory-assembled, simply because sash must be equipped with weatherstrip and properly fitted to assure efficient operation. Additionally, most manufacturers treat the wood components of doors and windows with a water-repellant preservative to minimize the chance of warp during storage on the job.

When selecting windows, keep in mind that they are to serve two purposes—light and ventilation. For lighting purposes, although there may be some variation under your local code, the minimum glass area of a house

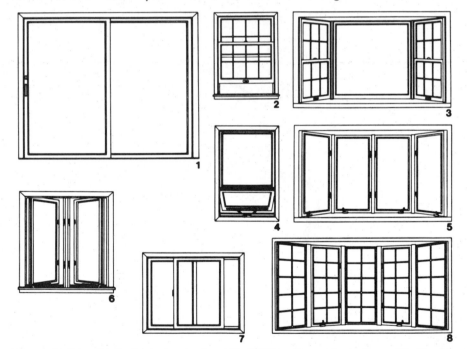

Figure 10-24   Typical window styles: (1) Gliding (bypassing) door; (2) Double-hung; (3) Angle-bay with center-fixed picture window flanked by operable double-hung windows (available in 30° and 45° styles; note the picture window flanked by double-hung units are also available for use on flat wall—i.e., without outward projection); (4) Awning window with fixed sash above; (5) Anglebay with operable casement windows—available in 30° and 45° styles; (6) Double casement window; (7) Gliding (bypassing) window; (8) Bow window with fixed and operable casements.

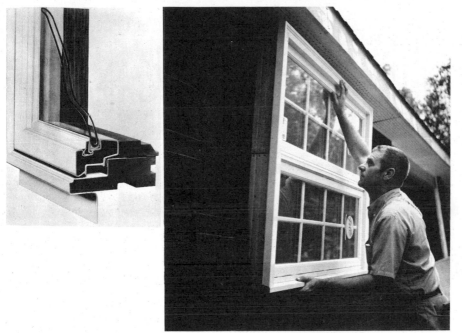

Courtesy of Pella by Rolscreen Company

Figure 10-25 *Once sheathing is covered with 15-lb. felt, windows can be installed. The type shown is slid into the opening until casings butt the sheathing on all four sides. Next, the window is checked for plumb and level, then fastened with nails driven through casings into the rough framing. Fin-type windows come with a flange for nailing to the face of sheathing (see inset).*

should be 10 percent of the floor area. To assure adequate ventilation, operable windows should equal 5 percent of floor area. The latter figure is flexible, of course, if the house is completely air-conditioned.

Types of Windows. Though many types of windows are available, you are likely to install one of those shown in Figure 10-24. Whether you should use metal or wood windows is mostly a matter of personal preference, often dictated by the architect who designed the home. But be aware that the heat loss through metal windows is far greater than through wood ones.

Insulated glass eliminates the need for putting up and taking down storm windows, and the periodic painting of them. But it does not eliminate the need for screening. If awning or casement-type windows are selected, the screening remains on the inside year round. Double-hung and sliding windows mandate screens on the outside, which should be taken down and stored each fall.

Exterior Doors. It is important to know that the front entrance door should be 3-ft. wide to assure being able to get furniture in and out at least one door. The rear and side entrances, on the other hand, are generally 2 ft. 8 in. wide.

Figure 10-26 *Pick your front door with care. Remember that most decorators feel that the front door says a great deal about the people behind it. Its look can be warm and inviting or cold and indifferent. Three typical styles are shown here—Colonial, Modern, and Traditional.*

Figure 10-27 *There are different styles to suit the different door needs in residential dwellings. Sliding doors are intended for places where space is a problem. They're frequently used for closets for this reason. Folding doors can separate one room from another without taking up much space because the door swing is cut in half. A Dutch door from kitchen to patio is a great way of letting fresh air in without letting small ones out. The combination door is used outside front and back doors. It's used to keep out the cold in winter months and, by exchanging a screened panel for the glass in summer, to keep your house insect-free. Since a combination door covers up most of that attractive front door you so carefully picked out, also choose it with a critical eye on design and quality. Patio doors— of glass—are intended to open up the wall and let the outdoors in. They're great if you have a view, should be passed up if you don't.*

Exterior doors are 1¾ in. thick (compared to 1⅜ in. thick interior doors). Exterior jamb material is also of heavier stock than interior jambs; a nominal ⁵⁄₄ in. stock (actual dimension, 1⅛ in.) is recommended. Quality exterior door frames have rabbeted jambs that automatically provide the needed door stop. For wear resistance, the sill should be of a hardwood such as oak.

Like windows, exterior doors are available in wide variety. Unless your house design is of an esoteric nature that demands a particular custom-made door, chances are you will select one of the door styles shown in Figures 10-26 and 10-27.

Both windows and doors should be specified in a schedule included in your plans; to see what they look like, check the elevation drawings.

Siding. When all exterior trim has been applied, the siding can go on. Though the installation varies with the type of siding, install all flashing first. A building paper, such as 15 lb. saturated, is then applied over the sheathing.

In broad terms, there are 10 sidings. Here, briefly, is a description of these types.

1. *Wood shingles*, often desired by second home owners because of their natural look and minimal maintenance requirements, are available in smooth and textured surfaces and with factory-applied stains and paints. If you have the loot, you may prefer to install rugged handsplit shakes, but bear in mind that they are more difficult to install. All wood shingles are durable and if finished with stain rather than paint, require little maintenance. To avoid black spots caused by fungus, wood shingles should be treated with a clear preservative every two or three years.

2. *Shake panels.* The same wood shingles are available in panel form. Each panel consists of individual shingles attached to a backing board at the factory. Like shingles, panels are available prestained and prepainted. If one of these is chosen, the panels should be applied using color matched nails. Natural shingles, like all nail-on sidings, are held with rust-resistant or galvanized nails. Though shingle panels give the same look as individual shingles, they are easier to install and go up faster. But, you pay for these benefits: Panels cost more than loose shingles.

3. *Horizontal siding.* One of the most popular sidings, the looks of horizontal wood siding blend with most styles of architecture, and the long horizontal shadowlines created by the butt edges give a pleasant look. The five most popular types of horizontal wood sidings are shown in Figure 10-28.

Bevel or clapboard, in a variety of widths, is probably the most commonly used siding. To minimize the chance of cracks and splits in siding, wider bevel-sidings generally come with shiplap or rabbeted joints. These kinds of joints permit the wood to lie flat against the sheathing instead of simply contacting at the joints only.

Drop and rustic siding are usually of heavier material, often used where sheathing has been eliminated such as on houses in moderate climates and on detached garages.

If you are using wood siding, choose a grade that is free of knots and other defects. And, handle the siding material with some care. Most wood sidings are of softwood, thus they can be easily damaged. Store siding indoors —perhaps in the garage—under a tarpaulin.

Use only zinc-coated steel or aluminum nails to fasten siding. Ordinary steel-wire nails are sure to rust and cause stains on the finished job regardless of how many coats of paint are applied. Horizontal siding is face-nailed to

FIVE MOST COMMONLY USED SIDINGS

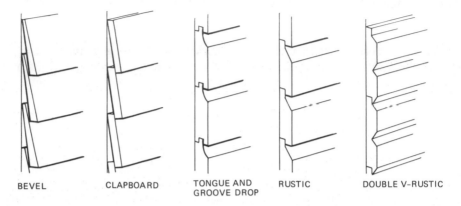

BEVEL   CLAPBOARD   TONGUE AND   RUSTIC   DOUBLE V-RUSTIC
                              GROOVE DROP

Figure 10-28   *Most commonly used wood (board) sidings; the ones shown here are intended for horizontal application. The essential characteristics to look for in siding are easy working qualities, good painting qualities, and a lack of warp. For these reasons, most wood sidings are of either the cedars, sugar pine, white pine, cypress, or redwood. Siding material should be of a high grade and free of knots, pitch pockets, and waney edges.*

each stud and the nail sizes vary with the thickness of the siding and the type of sheathing used below. To be sure that you are fastening your siding correctly, discuss the nailing techniques with your materials supplier as well as with the local building inspector. All wood sidings should be prime painted as soon as practicable upon completion of the siding operation. If rain wets the siding before you can get to the painting, make sure it is thoroughly dry before you prime the wood (unless you are using a latex paint).

4. *Vertical siding.* Matched boards installed vertically are often used for decorative treatment around an entrance, on a gable, or above brick veneer.

With vertical siding, good nailing other than into the sheathing must be provided. Install 2-by-4 cleats between studs, spaced usually not more than 4 feet apart, and fasten the siding (through the sheathing) to the cleats with two 8d nails per backer block (cleat).

5. *Plywood sidings.* Regardless of the style or brand of plywood siding chosen, make certain it is an exterior grade. In this type, the layers (or veneers) are bonded together using a waterproof glue. Douglas fir plywood siding is most commonly used when the siding is painted. For a natural-looking exterior, choose a cedar or redwood plywood that can be either stained or simply treated with a clear wood preservative.

Plywood siding comes in 4-ft. widths and lengths of 8, 9 and 10 ft. Generally, ⅜-in. thickness is used if the application is direct to studs. If plywood is applied over a sheathing approved by your local building department, ⁵⁄₁₆-in.-thick material can be used. The heavily textured, deeply grooved plywoods are thicker than both types mentioned above.

Figure 10-29 *The look of textured siding is an important part of the visual impact created in this house design. Here, the architect specified the use of Texture 1-11 plywood, which gives the wanted textured look yet is installed by the sheet.*

Though it is impossible to list or illustrate the entire variety of plywood textures and styles available in a book of this type, several of the more widely used finishes are shown in Figures 10-29 through 10-34. If you don't care for the siding that the architect has specified for your house, write to one of the manufacturers listed in Appendix C or to the American Plywood Association (see Appendix E) for information on what is offered today.

6. *Hardboard sidings*. Vastly improved manufacturing techniques of hardboard have increased the number of finishes to choose from. Be aware that hardboard does not have the dimension stability equal to plywood sidings. In fact, most hardboard manufacturers prescribe a spacing between members to allow for expansion and contraction due to moisture content.

If time is a factor, choose hardboard sidings prime-painted at the factory —though unfinished sidings are available at a slightly lower cost. Unfinished hardboard should be prime-painted *immediately* after installation.

To assure your being satisfied with a hardboard installation, follow the maker's instructions. And when hardboard siding is delivered to your job, stack it on 2 by 4 sleepers spaced a maximum of 4 feet apart, and cover the stack with a waterproof covering at the end of each work session.

Figure 10-30 *Rough-sawn fir, reverse board and batten.*

Figure 10-31 *Rough-sawn fir, lap siding.*

Figure 10-32 *Hardboard, reverse board and batten.*

Figure 10-33 *Rough-sawn fir, reverse board and batten.*

Figure 10-34 Closeup of texture 1-11 plywood siding applied vertically.

7. *Aluminum and vinyl systems.* The advantages of both is that once they're installed, there is practically no maintenance. The popularity of both is on the rise—a fact that is apparent when you note the number of older homes being re-sided these days.

Because specialized tools and knowledge are required to install either of these systems, have them installed by a professional. Here are some guidelines for selecting a quality job.

Quality. Aluminum specifications (alloy and gauge) are established by the FHA and the Aluminum Siding Association. If these standards are not clear to you, check out and discuss them with your architect and/or building inspector.

Craftsmanship. Make certain you retain a reputable installer to apply the material. It is common knowledge that this area in the construction field is overrun with high-pressure sales types with little or no construction experience.

As a precaution, get estimates from at least three contractors. Ask each contractor for a list containing a minimum of six satisfied customers. Automatically eliminate any contractor who claims it would be "difficult" to provide such information: If he can't remember for whom he has worked recently in the area, it's probably safe to assume that his is strictly a fly-by-

Figure 10-35 *Vinyl siding by Certain-Teed Products Corporation compliments architectural siding styles from traditional to contemporary. The prepunched nailing edge assures the concealment of nails for a perfect installation. The beauty of vinyl siding is that it eliminates the periodic repainting chore.*

night operation. Also, take the time to check the various contractors' performance records with the local Better Business Bureau; if a businessman's past performance has been shoddy, you'll find out.

Since aluminum siding can be energized by faulty electric wiring, a line downed by a storm, or an appliance, it should be grounded as a safety precaution. The Aluminum Siding Association recommends using a number 8 or larger-size wire with approved connectors. The grounding wire should be connected to either a cold-water ground or the house electric-service ground. Connectors should be Underwriter's Laboratories Approved and fastened to uncoated portions of aluminum stock (grounding is ineffective if clips do not make contact with bared metal). Make certain the siding contractor specifies grounding details in the contract.

8. *Brick veneer.* The term "veneer" implies a framed wall faced with masonry siding, unlike a masonry wall that supports weight from above. When a brick veneer is to be used, the foundation must be poured to supply a ledge upon which the brick rests. Metal ties are used between the veneer and framework to keep the former from toppling away. It is important to use a sufficient number of ties, usually spaced about 15 in. apart vertically and 30 to 32 in. O.C. horizontally.

There are many important aspects to applying brick veneer, such as the installation of flashing, provision for adequate drainage from behind the wall (weepholes), and the type of brick. If you plan to be your own bricklayer

Installation details

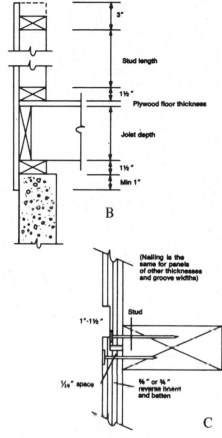

No diagonal wall bracing required with plywood panel siding

Insulation as required

Plywood panel siding

A

Georgia-Pacific 303 plywood siding

3"

Stud length

1½"

Plywood floor thickness

Joist depth

1½"

Min 1"

B

(Nailing is the same for panels of other thicknesses and groove widths)

Stud

1"-1½"

1/16" space

⅝" or ¾" reverse board and batten

C

Figure 10-36 *Quickie course in plywood siding installation.*
Stud spacing. *The manufacturer's stamp on the back of plywood panel siding (here Georgia Pacific 303) specifies either 16" or 24" o.c. for the stud spacing. Follow directions exactly; apply siding directly to the studs (see A) or as noted.*
Building paper. *It is not required if joints are either shiplapped or covered with battens or when siding is installed over sheathing. But it is required for unbattened square butt joints if panels are applied directly over studs. In all cases local building codes take precedence; follow them.*
Wall height. *Be sure, when assembling walls on a platform for tilting into position, to allow for a 1" lap at the bottom (over the top of the foundation wall) and a 1½" lap as covering for the second plate (at the top). See B.*

Nailing. *Hot-dipped galvanized or aluminum nails are a must to eliminate rusting and staining from weather and damp. For ⅜" and ½" thick panels use 6d box, siding, or casing nails. Drive them in every 6" along panel perimeters and 12" apart at intermediate studs. For thicker panels, 8d nails are recommended. For nailing shiplapped panels, see C.*
  IMPORTANT: all siding edges must be backed by solid lumber framing or blocking.
Spacing. *Always hold a 1/16" space between all ends and edges of panels. This expansion space must be left to ensure that panels stay flat under all weather conditions.*
Joints. *Caulk butt joints at all inside and outside corners, using high-performance polyurethane, thiokol, or silicon compounds. No caulking is needed for shiplapped joints or for joints backed by building paper.*

and have little masonry experience, you are well-advised to return to your building manual for a crash-course on bricklaying basics.

9. *Asbestos shingles.* Actually composed of mineral fibers, these shingles are more commonly called asbestos-cement shingles. Though durable and of a composition that requires little maintenance, they are not particularly attractive and should be avoided unless they are in wide use in the neighborhood.

10. *Asphalt shingles.* These stubbornly persist. Of two types, shingle and roll, they are usually embossed with a simulated brick or stone pattern. Asphalt wall shingles are applied in the same manner as roof shingles, except that a metal bead is used at the corners to prevent the intrusion of water. This siding material, in my opinion, should be saved for backwoods shacks inhabited by hermits and the like.

YOU CAN'T BE TOO CAREFUL

The information contained in this chapter is, basically, a quickie course in house framing and exterior-finish fundamentals. The intent here is to supply general know-how so you will be able to make a fairly sound decision as to whether you should build on your own or hire a contractor. Those who intend to do their own building should make it a point to acquaint themselves with the information contained in one or more of the building manuals listed in Appendix D. Additionally, you are cautioned to familiarize yourself with each step before plunging ahead.

Remember, mistakes will cost no one but you.

11

The Plumbing System:
Water Supply,
Waste Disposal, Fixtures

City water supply * *Getting water elsewhere: How much water do you need? Lake water, about wells, well water* * *Protecting your water supply: testing and purification of well water, other health precautions* * *Sewage disposal—sanitation: Percolation tests, septic tank, the septic field, septic failures* * *Plumbing fixtures: Rough plumbing, finish plumbing* *

In simple terms, a residential plumbing system consists of three basic components:

1. the water supply,
2. the sewage disposal, and
3. the fixtures (sinks, bathtubs, and the like).

All three are installed more or less at the same time; and the plumbing system is not usable until all components are in, tested, and approved by the local building inspector.

CITY WATER SUPPLY

Though some rural municipalities boast a city water supply, most do not. If you are fortunate enough to locate in an area with municipal water service, your plumbing installation is much easier. You simply run piping from your house to the main at curbside; the water company then makes the connection at the main.

207

In some cases, charges for municipal water are paid in quarterly install-ments and are generally based on the number of outlets counting the fixtures inside, and the hose bibs outside the house. Under such a billing system, quarterly charges remain the same regardless of the volume of water con-sumed. But in many areas the water bill is determined by usage; water con-sumed is clocked as it flows through a meter and you pay for it by the gallon.

If the municipality has a sewage system—and these days many locales require vacation community developers to include this service as well as a water supply—the sewage connection is as simple as connecting to the water supply. You provide the waste line from the house to the sewer trunk line. Usually, the homeowner pays a fee to the local government for a permit that allows the plumber to make the sewer connection.

Hooking your home up to a city's water supply and sanitation facilities is much cheaper, of course, than building your own independent systems.

GETTING WATER ELSEWHERE

Lacking a city water source, *you* must search for one. Perhaps you will be able to pipe in water from a lake, stream, or pond on your own property. Or maybe you can dig a well. In some cases, you can route water from a neigh-bor's property; but if you must, make certain your lawyer draws up and records an agreement of purchase of rights to its use. This agreement should contain complete information on easement rights (across the neighbor's property) for your pipeline. Such an agreement in writing assures continued availability of your water supply even if the current neighbor sells to an indi-vidual who personally is not inclined to be so benevolent.

Though quick and easy, getting water from a surface source (such as a stream, pond, or spring) is risky insofar as such sources are subject to almost overnight pollution. You should first have the water tested by the local health department to make certain it is fit for human consumption (see Figure 11-1). Water from a surface source is perfectly acceptable provided it is neither contaminated nor odorous and bad-tasting. If you plan to draw from a surface source, check with local building and health authorities to learn whether a permit is required. In some states it is. Very often, the determining factor is whether your property abuts the water source.

How Much Water Do You Need? Almost as important as a water source's sanitary level is its service. And don't confuse water requirements with water service. For example, 50 gallons is about the average daily requirement for an individual; averaged out on a hourly basis, that figure is slightly over two gal-lons per hour. But a system that delivers water at that rate must be considered inadequate. Imagine how long it would take for a toilet tank to refill after each flushing at that rate.

Though it is not likely that every fixture in the house will ever be in use at the same time, a system should be able to deliver to all outlets simultane-

POND WATER

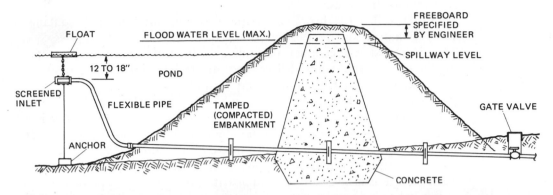

Figure 11-1 Surface water—a pond or lake— should be considered a source of water supply only if ground water sources are unacceptable. In many instances, in order to develop a pond as a water source, construction of an embankment with an overflow or spillway is required. You can get assistance in designing a storage pond from federal, state, or local health agencies. It is also possible to get help from the U.S. Soil Conservation Service but, in most instances, you are well advised to hire engineering or geological experts.

If a pond intake is too close to the bottom, the water is likely to be turbid; too near the surface, it may contain algae, floating debris, and the like. The best pond intake to use is the type shown here: a flexible pipe attached to a rigid conduit that passes through the pond embankment.

ously if such a demand does occur. To plan a good home water service, therefore, both the peak-minute and peak-day requirements should be considered (that is, those hours of the day when most, if not all, outlets are in use). Failure to think in terms of peak requirements will result in a shower that merely dribbles when the kitchen-sink faucet is on, or in a limp garden hose when the toilet is flushed.

If you have to live with an inadequate water supply you'll soon find that you will be forced to schedule all water-consuming activities—and then hold the family to that schedule.

Lake Water. To tap water from a lake, you need a shallow pump, enough plastic piping to reach from the house to the lake, and a foot valve to prevent the system from draining back into the lake when the pump isn't running.

If you plan to use your dwelling year-round in a cold climate, installing a system becomes a little more complicated. Since the water in the lake itself will freeze, the pipe must extend far enough and deep enough into the lake so that the icing above does not affect the system. And the run of pipe from lake to house will also have to be planted safely below the area's frost line.

About Wells. A direct well pumping system consists of the well itself, a pump controlled by a pressure switch, a pressure tank, and the distribution system. Usually a pressure switch set at 35 to 55 lbs. per sq. in. provides enough pressure for lawn sprinkling and laundry equipment as well as for conventional house use.

Often called the hydro-pneumatic tank, the pressure tank contains a small volume of water and a comparatively larger volume of compressed air. The air expands and contracts depending on the water pressure, thus supplying the energy necessary to deliver the water to household fixtures and eliminating the need for the pump to start with each small demand.

Frequently, intermediate storage systems are needed, between the supply source and the distribution pump, to assure good service. The water in an intermediate storage tank is at atmospheric pressure (that is, a free water surface at atmospheric pressure). An intermediate tank can vary in size from one day's supply to three days' supply. If fire protection is not close by, ample water storage is a must for your immediate protection. Low-producing wells —that have an adequate supply of water—can give excellent service if the

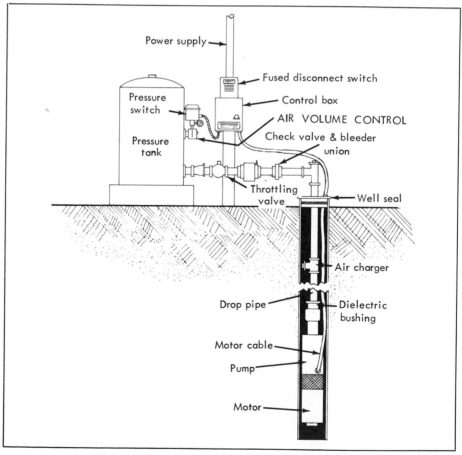

Water Systems Council Drawing

Figure 11-2   Typical submersible pump installation.

intermediate tank is filled during low-demand periods, so that water is readily available during the relatively short periods of peak demand.

These tanks must be carefully installed and built to guarantee water quality; they can be of fiberglass, steel, or reinforced concrete as long as they are constructed to deliver potable water.

The mineral content of the water must be taken into account too. "Hard" water (that is, water with a high mineral content) causes scaling and sludge, thus quickly clogging humidifier systems and greatly reducing the efficiency of the hot water heating system. Conversely, water that is too "soft" (that is, a low mineral content) tastes flat, because the minerals give water its taste, and quickly corrodes pipes as well. If the water is exceptionally hard (over 150 milligrams per liter), it may be advisable to install a water softener. Most experts agree that 80 milligrams per liter (4 to 5 grains per gallon) is ideal. Your local authorities can advise you on this score.

Well Water. In almost every case, a well of your own is the best water supply. Whether your well is shallow or deep, have it dug by a professional. (See Figure 11-3.)

Shallow wells. These are wells that are less than 25 ft. deep. They are less desirable than deep wells because they are more vulnerable to contamination. Additionally, during long heat spells, shallow wells are more likely to run dry.

Figure 11-3 *Single-stage centrifugal shallow-well pump.*

Burks Pumps Photo

Deep wells. How deep the well-digger must go before finding water determines the method used. For depths less than 50 ft., wells are usually dug or driven; from 50 to 100 ft., they are bored; and, for "super"-depths of 500 to 1,000 ft., they must be drilled. In sandy soils, jetting (hydraulic drilling) can be used, a technique that is usually impossible in rock formations.

Dug wells (Figure 11-4). A well can be dug either by hand or with power tools depending on its depth and the geological conditions. Generally, a dug well is three to four feet in diameter and less than 50 ft. deep. If constructed carefully, a dug well can be cased as tightly as other types of wells.

Driven wells (Figure 11-5). If local geological conditions permit, a driven well is an excellent and inexpensive way to obtain water. The system consists of coupled pipe sections with a screened well point on the end. To drive the point, it is struck repeatedly by a heavily-weighted length of pipe. The latter is generally fastened to a rope suspended from a large tripod.

DUG WELL

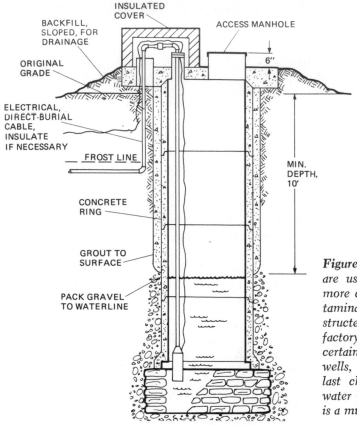

Figure 11-4 Wells dug by hand are usually shallow and therefore more difficult to protect from contamination. But if properly constructed, one can provide a satisfactory water supply. Because of certain advantages of other types of wells, a dug well should be your last choice. Grouting, to protect water from surface contamination, is a must.

Driving a well can be difficult in clay and hardpan formations and just about impossible in rock formations. Local water-supply equipment dealers can advise you as to whether this system is feasible in your area.

Drilled wells (Figure 11-6). This technique calls for the use of some pretty sophisticated equipment—some of it capable of reaching great depths through solid rock formations. There are two types of drilling methods used, rotary and percussion, either producing a well (for a residential water supply) that is usually 6 in. in diameter.

PROTECTING YOUR WATER SUPPLY

There are several safeguard measures you should take:

1. Install a storage tank that holds at least one day's supply of water. For a family of four, a 200-gallon capacity is the minimum size storage tank you should consider (see Figure 11-7).

Figure 11-5 The simplest and cheapest way to get a well is to drive one. Driven wells are constructed by driving into the ground a well point fitted to the end of pipe sections. The well is driven with a weight such as the weighted length of pipe shown.

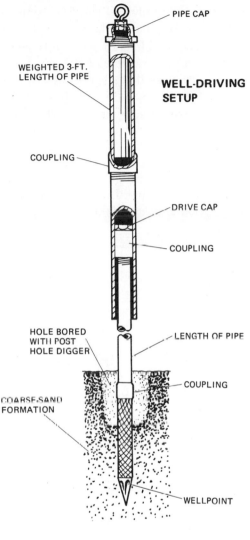

PIPE CAP

WEIGHTED 3-FT. LENGTH OF PIPE

WELL-DRIVING SETUP

COUPLING

DRIVE CAP

COUPLING

HOLE BORED WITH POST HOLE DIGGER

LENGTH OF PIPE

COUPLING

COARSE-SAND FORMATION

WELLPOINT

DRILLED WELL

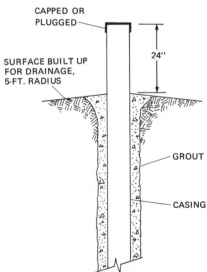

CAPPED OR PLUGGED

24″

SURFACE BUILT UP FOR DRAINAGE, 5-FT. RADIUS

GROUT

CASING

Figure 11-6 Drilled wells are generally accomplished by either percussion or rotary hydraulic drilling, depending on the geology of the site and availability of equipment. Cave-ins are prevented as drilling progresses by driving a casing (of slightly larger diameter than the bit) into the ground as the well's depth increases.

2. If physically and legally possible, fence in your water source (if it's a lake or pond) to keep out cattle and other animals.

3. You should also have tests conducted to determine whether your source is capable of delivering an adequate water supply under peak demand—that's figured at about 5 gallons per minute in a one-bathroom house with all fixtures in use at the same time.

4. Make an attempt to ascertain whether the water is likely to become contaminated in the near future. Discuss this possibility with your local building department and health authorities. A mushrooming population would signal an increase in the amount of sewage percolating into the ground. Intrusion by commercial facilities is another danger signal. In either event, the increased sewage makes contamination almost certain.

The cost of a well installation can vary for many reasons. The method

CONCRETE RESERVOIR

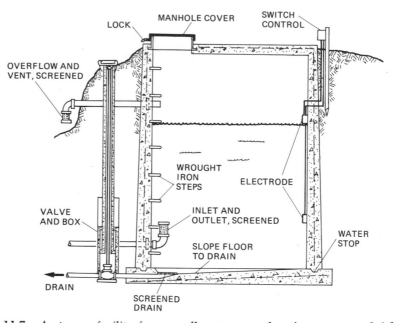

Figure 11-7 A storage facility for a small system can be of concrete or brick if the system is wholly below the surface. If the inside of the tank is to be painted, use only paints approved by the American Water Works Association. Federal, state, and local health agencies can also be consulted to learn the names of approved paint coatings for interior tank use. Domestic storage tanks should be completely covered and built so as to prevent any chance of pollution of the tank contents by outside water or other foreign matter. Notice the lock-type manhole cover to prevent access by unauthorized persons.

used, the depth reached, and the geological conditions are all obvious influences on cost. A perhaps not-so-conspicuous factor is the general level of affluence in your area. Well-diggers, like most in a service business, tend to charge what the traffic will bear. Typical charges by a professional run from $5 to $10 per foot depending on *all* the variables. Thus, the cost of the same well may vary from a low of $200 to a high of $1,500. Since the cost is so variable, get estimates from several well-diggers.

One final note: regardless of the type, the well must be positioned as far as possible from the septic system—under no circumstances closer than 100 feet.

More specific details on wells and water supply are contained in the books on the subject listed in Appendix D. (See also Figures 11-8—11-2).

BORED WELL

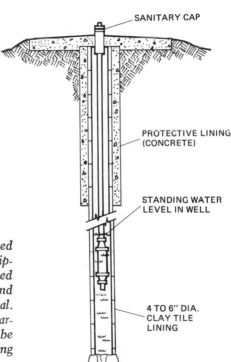

SANITARY CAP

PROTECTIVE LINING
(CONCRETE)

STANDING WATER
LEVEL IN WELL

4 TO 6" DIA.
CLAY TILE
LINING

Figure 11-8 Bored wells are constructed using either hand or power auger equipment. These wells are usually considered practical at depths under 100 ft. and when water requirements are minimal. Bored wells have the same general characteristics as dug wells, but they may be extended deeper into the water-bearing formation.

Testing and Purification of Well Water. According to experts in water engineering, nearly two-thirds of private water supplies have defects of varying degrees. Serious waterborne diseases such as typhoid fever, dysentery, and hepatitis occur rather infrequently, but they *do* occur.

The first step after installing your well should be to disinfect it with a chlorine solution of one ounce of hypochlorite (containing 70 percent avail-

Figure 11-9 Two systems from Jacuzzi Bros., Inc., each creating a complete water system when matched with proper pumps, are shown here. The compact Aqua-Genie eliminates the need for tank, tank house, tank pit, and air charger. The AquaGenie 80 (psi) is specifically engineered for use with jet and submersible pumps.

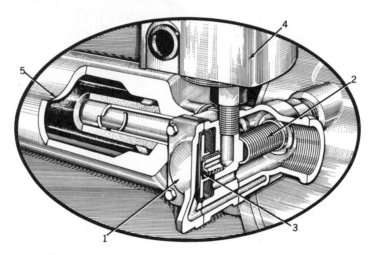

Figure 11-10   How the AquaGenie 80 works: The special valve (1) is comprised of a spring-loaded poppet (2) and trip-valve assembly (3), which controls system access to a standard pressure switch (4). The miniature cell (5) maintains pressure when there is no demand and, in conjunction with the valve, regulates the operation of the pump.

able chlorine) for every 50 gallons of water. Enough solution to fill the well should be added and permitted to stand at least 24 hours.

Next, before the well is put into use, pump it continuously until it is free of chlorine. Then a sample should be drawn into a sterilized glass jar for testing. Consult your local health department to learn where such testing is conducted in your area.

Figure 11-11 A deep-well jet pump by Burks Pumps.

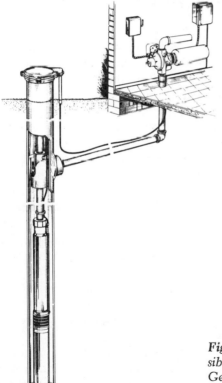

Figure 11-12 A typical submersible pump, connected to Aqua-Genie-200 control device.

Other Health Precautions. Steer away from obviously unsafe water sources. The risk of failure is too great with well equipment to leave safe water to chance. If you think that your system cannot be made safe, consult local authorities to determine what you can do to make it so.

Besides contamination from the water supply itself, there is always the

possibility of contamination from the surface. For a well to become contaminated in this manner, three elements must be present:

1. There must be a source of contamination.
2. There has to be a route for the contamination to follow.
3. There must be a medium by which it travels.

For example, surface contamination can penetrate a well via the wall
casting exterior, but such a path can be blocked by filling the space between
the pipe and earth with a cement grout during construction. A qualified
well-digger knows how and where to place the grout; you should make certain this safeguard is installed in your well.

SEWAGE DISPOSAL: SANITATION

Since it's more than likely that you won't be able to tie your house
waste line into a municipal sewer system, you will have to install a waste-
removal system of your own. Probably the least expensive and most commonly used sewage method today is the septic tank.

One of the first things you and your family will have to learn about living in the country—and about septic tanks—is not to waste water. Since
approximately 99 percent of sewage is water, the careless use of water causes
frequent septic-tank fillups. But don't worry about knowing when the tank
is full, you will: At the low end of the field, you'll find septic tank effluent
(liquids) bubbling out of the ground.

Though solid waste (the disposable organic type) comprises only one
percent of the sewage, all the sewage should be regarded as a health hazard.
Keep in mind that sewage contains all the viruses and bacteria common to
the household. For example, when there is illness in the family, these germs
turn up in the sewage. Thus it's obvious why a properly functioning system
is so important.

Percolation Tests. Before deciding where to place your septic sewage
system, the soil must be tested for porosity (the ability to absorb liquids).
Actually, it is in your best interest to conduct these tests before purchasing
the site.

Fairly simple, a percolation, or drainage, test consists of nothing more
than boring a number of holes where you plan to put the drain field. These
holes are then saturated with water to see how long it takes the water to
percolate away. Though it sounds simple, it's important that these tests be
done accurately. There are books available that give the details for performing a percolation test, but you should ask the county health department to
supervise your tests. With the results of the test on your property and a
knowledge of similar property in the neighborhood, the local authority will
be able to advise what size drain field should be put in. (Besides, in order to

build and install a drain field, you are required to obtain a permit. Whether the permit is granted depends partially on the results of the test.)

If the soil percolates slowly or not at all, there is likely either a high-water problem or rock formations below the surface. Both can rule out use of a septic system. If you are faced with this problem, visit the offices of the local and state government officials who have jurisdiction over water pollution and sewage control; these people will have the best solution—if there is one—for your problem.

No matter what size field is recommended as a result of the tests, increase the size by 50 percent if your property allows. For example, if your system calls for at least 800 sq. ft. of trench, it won't cost much more to put in 1,200 sq. ft. The nominal extra cost initially is well worth the peace of mind.

Septic Tank. Stated simply, a septic tank is nothing more than a holding compartment for solid waste that permits effluent to drain off to a dispersal field. A typical septic tank has from 750 to 1,000 gallons capacity; yours should be no smaller (see Figure 11–13).

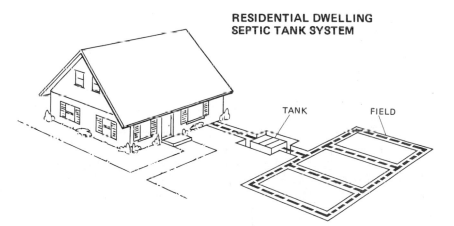

**RESIDENTIAL DWELLING
SEPTIC TANK SYSTEM**

TANK   FIELD

Figure 11-13   A typical septic sewage system for a residential dwelling should consist of a 750- to 1,000-gal. tank and field which allows effluent to drain into the soil. In an efficient system, effluent percolates into the soil at a faster rate than liquids are added to the system.

Waste flows through the tank slowly, often not flowing at all. Inside the tank, heavy solid waste settles to the bottom, while lighter grease and fats rise to the surface and form a scum. The tank's outlet is designed to prevent the passage of this scum: the effluent leaves the tank from a depth that traps sludge in the tank. Meanwhile, bacterial action decomposes and liquifies the solids, which can then flow out to the septic field.

The accumulated sludge, however, should be cleaned out periodically, usually every three to five years, though the frequency can vary with usage. When it is necessary to have the tank cleaned, openly discuss the fee beforehand with the tank cleaner. There are, sadly, unscrupulous operators in the tank-cleaning business who charge by liquid volume—then run the cost up by recirculating liquid or water to "clean" the tank. Don't be misled or overcharged—the tank does not need to be flushed; it needs merely to be emptied (see Figure 11-14).

SECTION THROUGH TYPICAL CONCRETE SEPTIC TANK

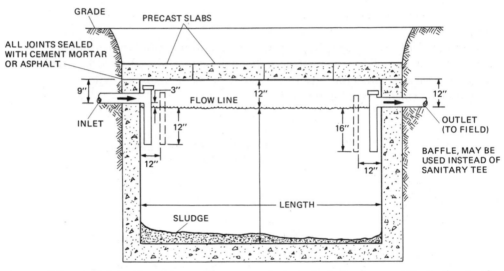

Figure 11-14 To measure the accumulation of sludge in a septic tank, simply lower a stick into the tank. Sludge adhering to the stick reveals the sludge depth. A septic tank does not need cleaning until the sludge is within 8 to 10 inches of the bottom of the outlet pipe.

The Septic Field. The effluent is discharged to a below-ground field, consisting of drain tile or perforated pipe, from which it then drains (percolates) into the subsoil. As long as the system percolates the effluent into the subsoil at a faster pace than the house discharges waste to the system, you have no problems. If discharge from house exceeds septic percolation, you are sure to find effluent floating on your lawn.

To keep the system in balance, all family members should be educated in water conservation. Water should not run continuously and needlessly. For example, Dad shouldn't let water run while shaving or brushing his teeth. And everyone should try to break bad habits that may have developed in the primary home, such as flushing a cigarette butt or tissue down the toilet: each flush adds about five gallons of liquid to the septic system. Also, don't tolerate a leaky faucet, which can add gallons of liquid to the system every day.

If your absorptive field must be located on ground higher than the septic tank, figure on adding a lift pump to the system between the septic tank and the field. The submersible pump is usually set to discharge effluent to the absorption field in spurts rather than in a constant flow. If you must use a pump, pick one that discharges at least 5 gallons per pumping.

Septic Failures. Assuming the septic tank has been cleaned regularly, a failure generally occurs in the absorption field. You can tell it is the field if effluent appears on the surface at the lower end of the system. Don't waste any time: get to work and install a new absorptive field. If you wish to use the original field again in the future, let it dry for a few months, and you will be able to do so. You can then switch back and forth between the two fields to prolong the lives of both.

If the absorption system hasn't failed, check the line between house and system for a blockage. Tree roots, disposable diapers, a collapsed sewer pipe, and the like are notorious troublemakers in waste lines.

PLUMBING FIXTURES

Rough Plumbing. After the rough heating pipes or ducts are in, rough plumbing is accomplished most efficiently if the plumber has an electrical source for power tools to ease the drilling and cutting chores. Under ideal conditions, two skilled and ambitious plumbers can rough-plumb a one-bath house in a single day. (This is the major argument for contracting-out work to the various trades by the job, rather than by the day.) Out in the boondocks, however, where the pace of life is admittedly and comfortably slower, the same plumbing job is likely to take three days. If you are looking for a slower, more relaxed pace, keep in mind that the rural way of life applies to work as well as to play.

Piping. Copper tubing is the most expensive piping you can install, but is also the fastest and best. Therefore, since by the hour or by the job, the plumber's time is reflected in the bill, the savings in time spent on the job make back some of the extra cost of copper.

Plastic pipe (CPVC and ABS) is gaining in popularity, because it is easy to work with and doesn't require expensive special tools. (But you must remember to leave play where pipes are fastened to studs and joists because of expansion and contraction due to temperature changes.) Though now permitted under many codes, check with the local building department before installing it.

Concerning waste lines. Since waste flow is by gravity alone—(waste lines are *not* under pressure), a trap must be installed beneath every fixture. Because traps always contain a fixed amount of water (in the curved U or P), they also serve to prevent gas odors from coming back into the house. Drain lines must also be vented through the roof (1) to permit the evaporation and dissipation of gases; and (2) because these let in air, to eliminate the chance of suction that could draw the water out of the traps.

Rough plumbing inspection. When all rough plumbing is in, lines are run to all fixture locations and the stubs capped. This is the time, before walls, ceilings, and floors are closed in, to inspect all runs (with the building inspector) to make sure that a shutoff valve is installed between the line and each fixture. In the years ahead, you'll be glad they are there each time you have to do some repair work on a particular fixture. All piping, stacks, and waste lines should be filled with water and every joint checked to make certain there are no leaks.

Finish Plumbing. When the walls are closed in and finished, the plumber can proceed to install and connect the fixtures. If all details concerning fixtures (make, color, model) are carefully and accurately spelled out in the plans and specifications, as they should be, there will be absolutely no confusion at this stage. Building from a good set of plans, prepared by a qualified architect or plans service outfit, should eliminate all guesswork. If a specified fixture is currently unavailable, make certain it is replaced with one of equal or better quality. Under no circumstances should you accept lower-quality plumbing than you contracted for.

In the basement. Though the code in your area may or may not require a basement drain, consider installing one. It is a great convenience. It should be routed to either a sump pump, sewer, or septic tank and located 10 or 12 feet from the hot water tank. For one thing, draining the water heater is a lot easier with a basement drain. A drain is a lifesaver, too, should a clothes washer overflow or a hot water tank rupture. At any rate, make certain you check with the local building department to learn its requirements for basement drains if you elect to install one.

But perhaps a basement drain is out of the question. Maybe the soil in your area is such that your absorptive field cannot accept any water from the basement via a drain. Perhaps, as it is in some areas, it is illegal to discharge basement water into a sewer—even privately owned ones (Figures 11-15 to 11-18). In place of a basement drain, then, consider installing a sump pump to handle possible water catastrophes in the basement.

A sump pump removes water from a basement and discharges it to locations other than a septic tank or sewer.

The usual method is to construct a dry well into which the sump pump discharges or, if the terrain permits, basement surface water can be discharged directly onto the ground outside.

The water heater. How much hot water your heater delivers is important. If it delivers too little for your family's needs, hot showers will suddenly turn cold or the family laundry will not all be done in a single day. The delivery of storage water heaters is rated two ways, and this information is usually imprinted on the tank's nameplate. One figure gives you the *capacity* of the tank, while the second number tells you the *recovery rate* per hour.

Figure 11-15 An automatic submersible sump pump.

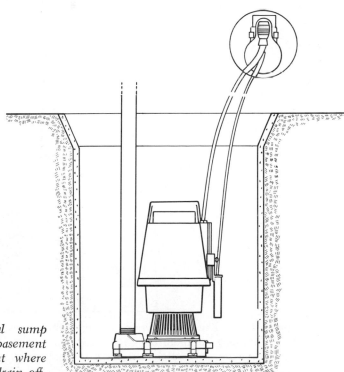

Figure 11-16 A typical sump pump location is in a basement sump or other low point where water will not otherwise drain off.

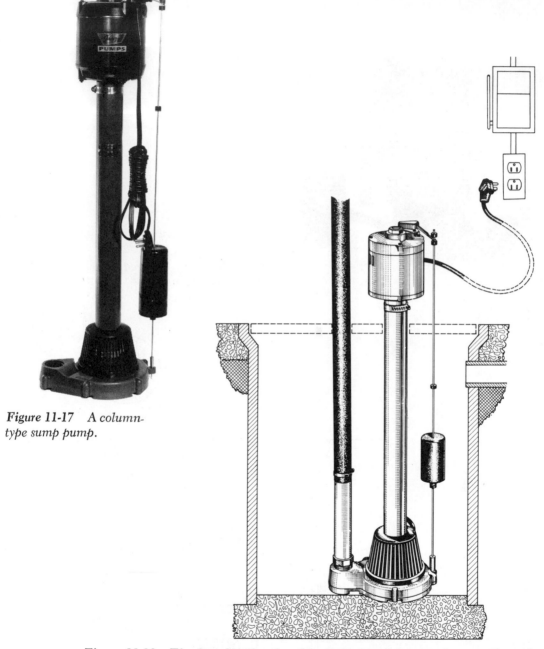

Figure 11-17 A column-
type sump pump.

Figure 11-18 The best location for this sump pump is away from traffic and
where the sump can drain the entire area. The sump should be provided with a
metal or wooden cover to guard against accidents and to prevent the accumulation
of dirt and rubbish. The area should be ventilated and clean for best operation.

Typical flared-tube fittings (copper tubing)

Typical flared-tube fittings

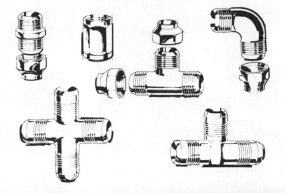

Figure 11-19 *Basically, there are 12 simple steps to make a solder joint: Although they are simple, they make the difference between a good joint and a poor one. For best results, none of the steps shown should be omitted.*

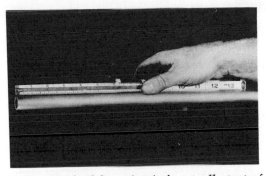

Figure 11-20 *Measuring isn't actually part of the soldering job, but inaccuracy here can affect joint quality. Tubing must be exactly the right length in order to seat properly in fitting socket.*

Figure 11-21 *Cut the tube to the exact length with a square cut. A tube cutter is generally used for pipe sizes up to 1 in. in diameter. Larger tubing can be cut with a hacksaw blade.*

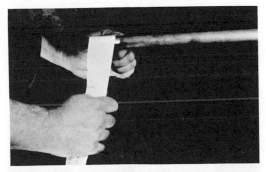

Figure 11-22 *The tube cutter leaves a small burr on the end of the tube; this should be removed using the reamer attached to the tube cutter.*

Figure 11-23 *The surfaces to be joined must be clean and free of oil, grease, and heavy oxide. The end of the tube is cleaned for a distance only slightly more than is required to enter the socket. Fine sand cloth (00) cleaning pads or special wire brushes may be used here.*

Figure 11-24 The fitting's socket is similarly cleaned.

Figure 11-25 After cleaning, apply a thin coat of flux to the surfaces to be joined. Here, the flux is applied to the tubing end.

Figure 11-26 Repeat the fluxing step with a fitting socket. The preferred flux is one that is mildly corrosive and contains zinc and ammonium chlorides.

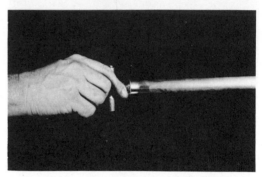

Figure 11-27 Assemble the joint by inserting the tubing into the fitting socket. Make certain that the tube is fully seated against the end of the socket. Then twist the connection to help spread flux evenly over the mating surfaces.

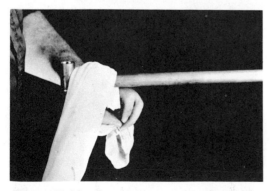

Figure 11-28 Remove any excess flux with a clean rag. The joint is now ready to be soldered.

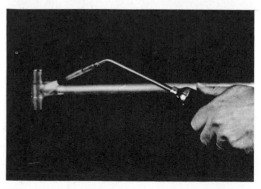

Figure 11-29 Apply heat to the assembly.

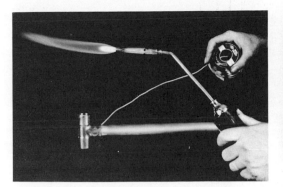 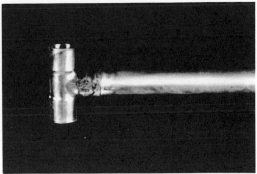

Figure 11-30 *The flame is removed and the solder applied. It is drawn into joint by a capillary action.*

Figure 11-31 *The finished joint should look like this.*

Figure 11-32 **About capillary action:** *To understand the principles of sweating (soldering) pipe, you should know how capillary action works. When the copper tubing is inserted as far as possible into a fitting, a small amount of space remains between the inside wall of the fitting and the outside wall of the tubing. When the fitting is heated with a flame and solder is applied around the tube at the outer edges of the fitting, the solder is drawn into this space by capillary action. The pipe and fitting are thus bonded tightly together. Such action results whether the piping is running horizontally or vertically.*

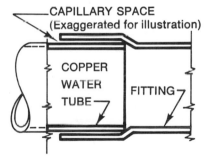

CAPILLARY SPACE
(Exaggerated for illustration)

COPPER
WATER
TUBE

FITTING

The sum of the two quantities is the number of gallons of hot water that a tank can supply in an hour. For example, a tank with a 50-gal. capacity and a 40-gal. recovery rate is capable of supplying 90 gallons of hot water per hour. Ninety gallons per hour is considered satisfactory for a family of five in a two-bath home with an automatic dishwasher and clothes washer.

A tank's recovery rate, therefore, is of far more importance than its storage capacity. Because most hot water heaters manufactured today have such rapid recovery rates, the storage tank you need may be a lot smaller than you figured. For example, a family of four with an automatic dishwasher and clothes washer is well served by a 30-gal. tank with a rapid recovery rate.

When you select a water heater, try to choose one that has a drain valve with a hose connection. This feature lets you drain the tank whenever desired with the least effort. Using a garden hose, the tank can be drained directly to either floor drain or laundry tub, whichever is more convenient.

The use of water and the disposal of wastes must be restrained for two reasons: first, a balance between intake and discharge makes for a dry lawn; second—and more important we must learn to live within the confines of the natural systems around us. The unlimited draining of a small pond, for instance, is irresponsible insofar as the pond supports other life in the area. Correspondingly, thoughtless, excessive percolation of sewage into the ground can eventually poison our own water supply. Therefore your plumbing systems should be constructed so as to least disturb the balance of nature as it stands just outside the door of your leisure home.

12

Heating

* To heat or not to heat? * Degree days * What should a heating system do? temperature, air-freshening capability, humidity, cleanliness, noise level, future needs * Which kind of heat is best for you? * Ducting versus nonducting * Nonducted systems * Ducted central systems * The total comfort system * Operating costs * Future cooling * How to get a good heating system * Initial cost * Basics of installing heat: rough heating, finish heating * Space heaters, stoves and fireplaces: gas heater, pipeless furnace, heat pump, electric space heaters, stoves, fireplaces *

During the planning and building sessions, a great deal of your time will be occupied with floor-plan efficiency, kitchen and bath details, the selection of paints and wallpapers, prefinished paneling, and the like. But don't let your concern for these items cause you to overlook or to minimize the importance of your heating system. Today more than ever new-home builders must choose heating and cooling systems with care.

Of course, the most obvious concern is for comfort. No matter how well you've designed and built your home, or how great a view you have, you will be unhappy in it if you are physically uncomfortable. Additionally, a good heating system can contribute significantly to your family's health; it can also help to keep housekeeping maintenance at a reasonable level. Beyond comfort, new homeowners are rightly concerned these days with the cost of maintaining and feeding the system they install. In other words, efficient space conditioning is a must if both winter and summer living conditions are to be affordable as well as enjoyable.

TO HEAT OR NOT TO HEAT?

How much to invest in a heating system and when it should be installed depend mainly on two things: (1) how you plan to use your second home and (2) the climatic conditions of the area.

For year-round use, for example, in a moderate climate, the warmth generated by a large open fireplace is usually more than adequate for those chilly, sometimes damp, mornings and evenings when you would appreciate just a touch of warmth. (In fact, many second-home owners install a fireplace whether it's needed or not; for these folks, logs burning in a fireplace is synonymous with their vision of a second home.) Even if the temperature occasionally goes below freezing, in all likelihood a fireplace or stove is all you'll need. Either type of heat source is adequate, too, for those who plan to use their second homes only during summer months, even if the winter conditions are harsh. As nominal heat sources, both are relatively economical because you can burn wood or coal. In many cases, wood is freely obtained either from your own property or from that of your neighbors, who are happy to be rid of the dead limbs and fallen branches. (Fireplaces and stoves are discussed in greater detail farther along in this chapter.)

If, however, you plan to use your second home year-round in an area with cold seasons, or eventually retire to your second home, your heating system should be installed while the house is being built. Of course, if because money is tight, installing the heating and cooling system during construction of the house is out of the question, you should at least plan for and accommodate the system that will follow. In short, use a little foresight.

A lack of such planning will, in all probability, force you to compromise your selection of a heating system later; in fact, you may be forced to live with a system that may have been your third or fourth choice initially.

You should install the hidden portion of the system while the walls, floors, and ceilings are open, thereby avoiding the nuisance of tearing holes in the walls later, or having to settle for a less desirable system because you don't want to rip open walls. The oil or gas-fired furnace can be installed any time, but the piping to radiators or baseboard convectors, or the ducting to vent-registers, should be installed before the walls are closed in. Later, when cash is available, the heating plant and radiators or convectors can be installed and connected to the pipes already in position.

Degree Days. Since most fuel-oil companies automatically schedule their deliveries based upon degree days, you should know what the term means if you don't already. Further, the number of degree days in your second-home area may help you to decide on whether to heat your home and on which system to select.

For one thing, degree days cause fuel costs to mount up. Simply a measure of how cold the heating season, one degree day is the numerical difference between 65°F and the average outside temperature in winter. For example, if the average temperature for a day is 20°F, the number of degree days on that day is 45 (65° minus 20). Obviously, the higher the number of degree days in a year, the more fuel you burn and the greater your annual heating bill is.

WHAT SHOULD A HEATING SYSTEM DO?

If you intend to use your home year-round, the heating system should do more than just heat the house. (Though cost is obviously an important consideration, it will be determined primarily by the type and amount of equipment you finally decide to install and it therefore should not distract you from your heating needs and system capability.) Basically, there are six facets of heating that you should concern yourself with:

1. The evenness of air temperature,
2. air freshening capability,
3. humidification,
4. cleanliness,
5. the noise created by the system, and
6. your future needs.

1. *Even-air Temperature* means a constant temperature throughout the house from one room to the next. Temperature levels during the day should have little fluctuation, and they should be constant within a fraction of a degree. The system should turn itself on and off to maintain a level temperature without your sensing it, and the variance in temperature from floor to ceiling should not be more than 2°.

2. *Air-freshening Capability* should be neither overlooked nor considered unimportant. Not too long ago, houses were pretty leaky as far as air infiltration was concerned. Windows and doors were ill-fitting and the use of weatherstripping was uncommon. In effect, the house was porous, so that air could leak in to keep the inside air relatively fresh. Modern house construction has changed that. Outside walls are leakproof; windows and doors are tight-fitting and weatherstripped; and insulation has an airtight vapor barrier next to the inside walls. A house built by today's standards simply does not "breathe."

Since air freshening and motion are essential, fresh air must be brought in mechanically. Will the system you select do that?

3. *Humidity* is as necessary as fresh air inside the home.

Relative humidity is the amount of moisture in the air compared with the total amount of moisture that the air is capable of holding *at a given temperature*. If, for example, the house air at 70° contains one-half the amount of moisture it could hold if saturated at that temperature, it is said to be at 50% relative humidity.

STATIC CAUSED BY LOW HUMIDITY

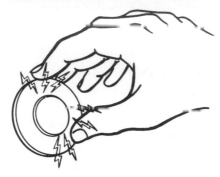

Figure 12-1 Low humidity in a house causes shocks. Additionally, dry air evaporates moisture from our bodies to cause discomfort for many.

Warm air has a greater capacity for holding moisture than cold air. At 1°F, one pound of air holds only 7 grains (.001 of 1 lb.) of moisture when saturated. At 75°F, the same pound of air holds 19 times as much moisture —132 grains. Given the same amount of moisture in the house, the air has a lower relative humidity because it is now *capable* (at a higher temperature) of holding more moisture.

The lower the relative humidity, then, the drier the air. And dry air, thirsty for moisture, will take it from any source—furniture, upholstery, and people. If the heat in the house is allowed to reduce the relative humidity, not only do noses and throats dry up, but furniture and flooring dry out, eventually becoming wobbly and squeaky. Low relative humidity also increases the number of static shocks you get when you walk across a wool rug and touch a metal object or another human.

Obviously as the heating system warms the air, it must also humidify the air to preserve comfort. But simply bringing in air from the outdoors does not necessarily add moisture to the indoor environment. If you bring in one pound of air at 0°F and heat it to 75°F, its relative humidity is drastically reduced. By heating it, its capacity to hold moisture will have been increased by 19 times but, because no moisture was added, its relative humidity is only 1/19th of what it was at 0°. Thus, it becomes obvious why there is a definite advantage in having a means of adding humidity to air inside the home.

4. Cleanliness. Most airborne dirt in homes comes in through open windows, not from the heating system. People also track in dirt on their shoes, some of which eventually gets into the air. Various household activities (a workshop, for example) add dust to the air. Cigaret, pipe, and cigar smoking also create airborne contaminants. And there is a certain amount of dirt attributable to the gases that escape up the chimney; if this kind of grit is present in the house, it got in only through open windows.

Some heat systems do filter the air inside the home. Why not pick one that does?

5. Noise Level. When installed properly, all well-made central heating systems are relatively quiet. In general, when you cut corners and select bargain-priced equipment, you can expect to pay the price in bothersome noises.

6. *Future Needs.* Equally important to the purchase price of your system is the long-term cost of operating it. Initially, your primary concern is for good heating but, as the heating plant ages, if laying out $100 or more for service calls becomes an annual affair, your original thrifty attitude will have been ill-advised.

There are other long-range aspects to consider too. You should know that many experts in the housing and mortgage-money industries estimate that in a few years, any house without central air-conditioning will be considered obsolete. The resale value of your home is greatly enhanced if it features central cooling, or if it is built so that air cooling can be added at any time at a nominal cost.

WHICH KIND OF HEAT IS BEST FOR YOU?

Ducting Versus Nonducting. Until fairly recently, local building custom generally dictated which system the new homeowner would live with; the choice of system was more-or-less left up to the builder and/or heating contractor. Though their intentions may have been of the highest order, they usually gave little or no thought to efficiency and new developments in the industry. In plain talk, most builders and heating contractors simply stuck with what they had been installing for years—with little or no complaint from users.

Thus we find that a heating system that predominates in one geographic area may be hardly used at all in another. For example, though the majority of homes in northeastern United States utilize either hot water or steam heat, hydronics are far less popular in the midwest where warm air systems are favored.

All central heating systems fall into one of two categories—ducted and nonducted. In a *ducted system*, one heating element is used for the entire home, or for all rooms in one zone of a house. A central blower moves air over the heating element or elements, and the warmed and conditioned air is then moved into the rooms via ducting. A *nonducted system* puts a heating element of some type in every room of the house. Heat is transferred from this element to the floor, furniture, and walls. When the air in the room comes into contact with these surfaces, it is warmed.

Each of these two very different concepts of heating has its advantages and disadvantages. Both types can be used with any fuel—oil, gas, or electricity—and both are compatible for use in homes of any size and type. However, though personal preference may be the deciding factor, larger homes are generally more economically heated by a nonducted system.

In any heating system, the source of heat (i.e., the radiator or vent) is always located at or close to the area of greatest heat loss (i.e., beneath windows and close to doors). Thermostats, on the other hand, are located at a point of minimum heat loss about 48 in. from the floor on an inside wall.

Before you decide upon a system, you owe it to yourself to become

Figure 12-2 An oil-fired burner from American-Standard was developed to meet requirements for forced hot-water, gravity hot-water, and steam applications. The controls, factory-mounted and pre-wired on packaged units, are mounted on the front of the unit for easy service and maintenance.

Courtesy of American Standard

familiar with what a good heating system is all about and to understand the pro's and con's of the basic ways to heat a home:

1. Nonducted:
    a. Hydronics (hot water or steam)
    b. Electric
2. Ducted: warm air

Nonducted Systems. The most common type is baseboard radiation, which uses either hot water (hydronics) or an electric heating element. The baseboard units are installed around a goodly portion of the perimeter of the room.

An older hydronic method is the use of cast-iron radiators placed near or under a window. Though there are now radiators available that can be recessed into the wall to make them less obtrusive, these are being replaced (in new construction) by more modern hot-water heating with convectors.

HYDRONIC

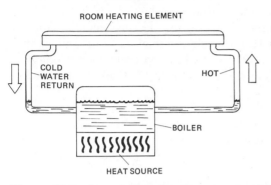

TOTAL COMFORT SYSTEM

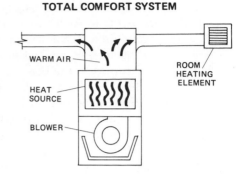

Figure 12-3 In a hydronic system, water is heated and circulated to elements in the rooms (i.e., radiators) to warm the room. In a ducted system, air is warmed and circulated via duct-work.

These new hot-water heating elements are also in a metal enclosure located under the window. Cold air enters at the bottom, is warmed as it contacts the heating element and rises to drift out grilles at the top. A majority of the heating is done by convection—heat is transferred to the room by natural circulation.

Hydronics, Hot Water. In a hot water heating system, the furnace heats water in a boiler and the heated water is then pumped through pipes to the various room-heating elements—either cast-iron radiators or baseboard convectors. The hot water warms the element which, in turn, transmits heat to the room by convection. When the water in the elements cools, it returns to the boiler via a second set of pipes.

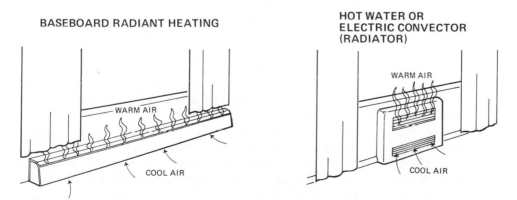

Figure 12-4   In nonducted systems, baseboard convectors or radiators are located at the points of greatest heat loss—beneath windows. Cool air along the floor travels to the heating element and is drawn in, warmed, and kept moving.

Steam Heat. A steam system also consists of a boiler, pipes, and heat elements in each room; but instead of heated water, steam is the heating agent. In a steam system, all piping between the heating elements and the boiler must be pitched so water that collects in radiators from condensation is returned to the boiler. A steam unit sends heat up faster than a hot-water system, but its room heating elements also cool faster than those in a hot-water system.

Humidifiers. With either hydronic system and especially steam, the use of a humidifier is recommended during the heating season. The best humidifier is the type that produces a reasonable evaporation with a whirling disc that mechanically atomizes the water so that it floats into the air for absorption.

The problem with humidifiers is that any solid matter in the water precipitates out from the suspension when the finely atomized water evaporates, thus creating a fine white dust.

Electric Heat is now available in heat panels that can be mounted on floor, ceiling, and walls. From a comfort standpoint, this type of heating is highly desirable when paired with a system that conditions the air year-round and cools it during the warm months. And the heating and other equipment require minimal space; a chimney, for example, is not necessary. Further, such a system requires practically no maintenance on the part of the home-owner.

On the other hand, an electric system is costly. The energy crunch has dimmed the sales outlook for many manufacturers of electric heating devices because current electric rates make electric heating the most expensive system to operate. Also, electric heating requires a maximum amount of insulation; the absolute minimum thicknesses you should consider installing are 6 in. in ceilings, 3 in. in walls, and at least 2 in. of rigid insulation under floor slabs and at floor perimeters. To be safe, check with your local power company; at no charge, it will inspect and evaluate your home and advise what insulation is required for maximum efficiency.

Ducted Central Systems. In such a system, the heating element can be direct or indirect. In a *direct-fired* system, either a warm-air furnace, a hot-water coil, or an electric heating element warms the air in a central location; the air is then moved to where it is needed. In a direct-fired furnace, the gas or oil fire is contained in a gas-tight steel enclosure. The fire heats the steel, and the steel in turn heats the air.

In an *indirect* system, the fire is in a steel or cast boiler, and heat is transferred from the fire to the metal to the water. Water is then conducted to a heat-transfer coil in the central system where air moving over the coil picks up warmth. Since there is one extra heat transfer through the water, this method is considered indirect.

The complications of this added transfer step add to the mechanical equipment needed and therefore to cost. As a result, the majority of residential homes served by ducted central heating systems use direct-fired heating sections.

DUCTED CENTRAL SYSTEM

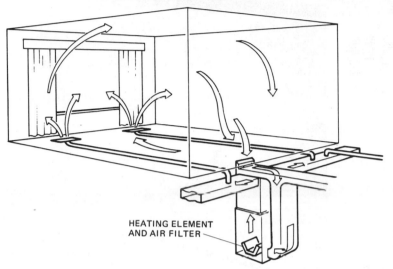

HEATING ELEMENT
AND AIR FILTER

Figure 12-5   In a ducted system, the heating element is remote from the room or rooms being heated. Ducts remove air from the room and bring it back to a centrally located blower. Here, air is filtered, conditioned, and moved back over the heating element before returning to the rooms via ducts. The heating element can be hot water, electric coil, or direct-fired heat exchanger.

The Total-Comfort System. A new development in home heating, the total comfort system is something different from the ordinary warm-air furnace—probably the one system that best satisfies all of those requirements of a heating system mentioned earlier.

In a total comfort system, the blower runs constantly. Unlike the ducted warm-air system, in which blowers are adjusted to run intermittently and only when the burner is operating, the blower in a complete system *never* shuts off. As a result, air temperature, humidity, and air freshness are constantly conditioned (warmed or cooled) to keep all three at a constant level.

Fast morning warm up. For sleeping comfort, as well as economy, most people like to reduce the room temperature at night by about 5°. With a total comfort system, in the morning you begin to feel warmth almost immediately after turning up the thermostat. The constant blower quickly moves heat from the heating element into the rooms. With a hydronic non-ducted system, you must wait after turning up the thermostat before you start to feel heat. A steam system sends up heat faster than a hot-water system does, but both are much slower than the ducted total-comfort setup.

Operating Costs. As mentioned earlier, both ducted and nonducted systems can be highly efficient if carefully selected and properly installed; there is no appreciable difference in operating costs between the two types.

A conventional warm-air system uses repetitive cycles—a blast of hot air followed by a cooling of the house—to condition the air. The blower's on-off

Figure 12-6 An OF Series oil furnace from Lennox can have central air-conditioning included initially, or added later at reasonable cost. The cooling coil fits right on the furnace, and the same duct-work and blower are used for both heating and cooling.

cycle creates considerable cost. With a ducted total-comfort system, ceilings tend to be cooler and floors warmer because of the active air circulation that pulls heat down from the ceiling. Fuel consumption is a little less than with a hydronic system, but it costs more to run the circulating blower continuously in a total-comfort system than it does to power the pump in a hot-water system. One factor more or less cancels the other with the result that operating costs are roughly the same in systems of comparable quality.

Future Cooling. A good total-comfort system is always designed for central-system cooling as well as heating. In most cases, the ducting used for heating is also used for the cooling operation. However, in order to handle cooling, the blower installed initially must have the capacity to accept the small increase in air volume that is generally desirable during the cooling cycle.

When you add cooling later, you will need the proper cooling coil in the supply plenum downstream from the heating section. You'll also need the proper sized air-cooled condensing unit on a slab outside the house. The two are interconnected with small-diameter copper tubing that handles the refrigerant. The addition of such a cooling system costs far less than the equivalent capacity in window air-conditioner units.

Window units, of course, are the only way you will be able to add air-conditioning to a house that is heated by hydronics. The cost of ripping out walls and ceilings to install the ductwork required for central air-conditioning makes such an installation an unfeasible one in most cases.

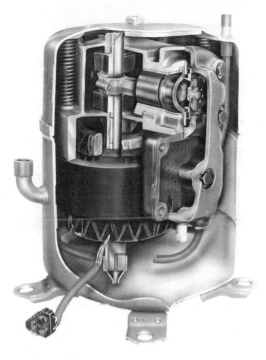

Figure 12-7 The core of the Crown Imperial Series total comfort package is the new 2500 Series high efficiency Power Miser 2 compressor line. Its maker, Chrysler Airtemp, claims the unit is significantly more efficient, reliable, quiet, and easier to service than previous models.

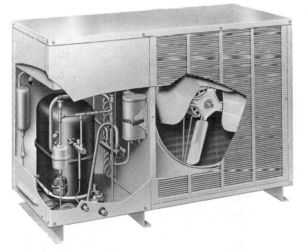

Figure 12-8 A heat pump does the work of two comfort systems— it air-conditions and it heats. Left, an outdoor heat pump by Lennox. This model connects by refrigerant lines to a matching indoor unit.

HOW TO GET A GOOD HEATING SYSTEM

The contractor you pick to install your heating system is of major importance. Unfortunately, not all sheet-metal contractors have the knowledge or skill to design and install a total-comfort system correctly. At the same

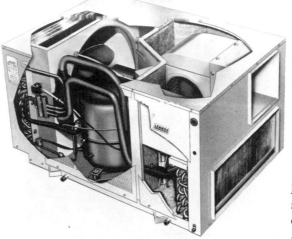

Figure 12-9 *This heat pump is a space-saving single package that installs outdoors. Lennox makes it.*

time, some plumbing and heating contractors have neither the knowledge nor desire to install a hydronics system correctly. Thus, regardless of the type of heating system you decide to install, it is important that you pick your contractor carefully. Here are three ways to make sure you do:

1. Consult the mortgage lenders who will carry your mortgage. These people are experienced and they are just as concerned as you are about the quality of heat in your house. They'll undoubtedly be able to supply a list of reliable heating contractors.

2. If there is an active local chapter of the National Warm Air Heating and Air-Conditioning Association in your community, ask them to help you with a list of qualified installing contractors and recommendations (see Appendix E).

3. If you have friends or neighbors with an efficient system of either type in their house, ask the name of the installer.

BASICS OF INSTALLING HEAT

Initial Cost. The cost of putting in any system is controlled by several factors: (1) the size of the house and its design, (2) the equipment chosen, and (3) geographical area. Once you have decided which system you want, you should invite several heating contractors to bid on the job. Depending upon the degree of sophistication of the equipment, you can expect to lay out anywhere from $3,000 to $10,000 for the job. $5,000 is a good guesstimate figure for an average house. As always, make certain all contractors bidding on the job figure on equipment of equal quality.

Figure 12-10 The Lennox supplementary electric heat coils can be installed in blower-coil units or in the ductwork. They are controlled by the heat pump thermostat and operate automatically only when needed. The long-lasting nichrome elements are exposed directly to the air stream for quick, efficient heating.

All work involving the heating system should be coordinated with the house carpentry. If you are your own carpenter, the heating contractor must be flagged in advance as to when to come in to do the rough and finish heating. Neither step takes a great deal of time when done by a qualified contractor, but the scheduling of work is of primary importance.

Rough Heating. The rough heating work can start once the roof has been closed in.

If you're installing a hot-air system, careful planning at this stage is a must. You'll have to make certain that all openings for ductwork are taken into account during the rough carpentry stage. The carpenter should handle all of the opening provisions so that wall and ceiling framing can be adapted to suit if necessary. In general, when these openings are left for the plumber's saw, you're likely to find holes and notches whittled in supporting walls, joists, and sills with little or no thought for the consequences.

A hydronics system requires practically no carpentry planning. The heating contractor simply installs all rough pipes before the insulation goes in and the walls are covered. However, be on hand—if you are your own carpenter—to do (or at least oversee) any cutting of plates, studs, and joists. You can make sure that no more is cut out from framing members than is necessary. You should also beef up any structural member that must be cut

How a heat pump works

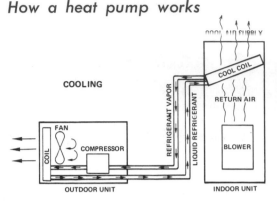

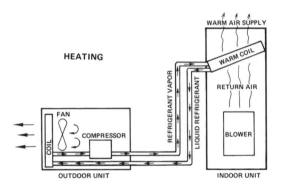

Figure 12-11 *The outdoor unit compressor feeds liquid refrigerant through its coil to the indoor coil. Warm indoor air is forced over the coil by the blower. The liquid refrigerant changes to vapor and absorbs heat, lowering the temperature of the indoor air blowing over the coil. The refrigerant then goes back to the outdoor unit where it is compressed and flows through the outdoor coil where its stored heat is released to the air. This is a continuous process as long as there is a need for cooling.*

Figure 12-12 *The changeover from cooling to heating is controlled by the thermostat which works through the heat pump controls to reverse the refrigerant flow. Refrigerant in the outdoor coil absorbs heat from the air—even when the temperature is quite low—and the compressor pumps it, in hot vapor form, to the indoor coil. Heat is then picked up from the warm coil by circulating indoor air. The liquid refrigerant returns to the outdoor coil to keep repeating the cycle as long as heat is needed.*

before the saw touches the wood so that the member will continue to perform the supporting role it is designed for.

Finish Heating goes quickly, particularly if it is simply a matter of installing registers for a warm-air system. Before floor registers can go in, the finish floor must be in place; wall vents are installed before the carpenter installs any trimming (casings and moldings).

With a hydronics system, the finish floor must, again, be in place before radiators or baseboard convectors are installed. Walls should also be closed in because it is impossible to fasten plasterboard or wall paneling behind the heating elements once they are secured.

When finish work is completed, the system should be fired up and inspected. Besides an occasion for a close inspection, a start-up before you move in gives you the opportunity to leave windows open to let out the smell created by the fire in the new system. These smells are caused by the burning off of oils and paints on the new surfaces.

At any rate, the furnace must be operable at the time that the building inspector makes his final inspection.

**THERMOSTAT FOR SYSTEM
WITH HEAT PUMP**

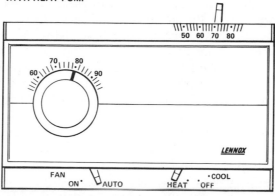

Figure 12-13 The thermostat is the heart of an electric total-comfort system. The Lennox version has a built-in temperature anticipator that senses slight heat changes and starts the heat pump to compensate—before you feel uncomfortable.

SUMMARY TABLE
COMPARISON OF NONDUCTED AND DUCTED HEAT SYSTEMS

Comfort Essentials	Nonducted Systems	Ducted System (Total Comfort)
Even air temperature	Good, except in rooms with large glass areas	Excellent
Air freshening	Very poor	Very good
Humidification	Very poor	Excellent
Cleanliness	Very poor	Good (Excellent with electronic air cleaners)
Future air conditioning	Very poor. Economically restricted to window units	Excellent. Whole-house airconditioning can be added any time at reasonable cost.
Quietness	Excellent in quality systems	Excellent in quality systems

Courtesy of Lennox Industries, Inc.

SPACE HEATERS, STOVES AND FIREPLACES

If your comfort wants in a second home are simpler than what you want for your primary home, a space heater will probably provide all the heat you want. Heaters are generally selected by those in unfinished cabins in the woods who more or less opt to rough it.

One important habit you should acquire if you equip your cabin with a small heater is to remember to check your fuel supply each time you leave your place. Be sure there is adequate fuel on hand for your next visit, especially if you usually arrive during late-evening or early-morning hours when the stores are closed.

Here are several heaters that hardier-type vacationers can choose from:

Gas Heater. Often referred to as a garage heater, this wall-mounted unit can be controlled either manually or by thermostat. Because it brings in its own supply of fresh air to support combustion and is vented to discharge fumes to the outside, a chimney is not required. Such systems may be fired with natural gas from a city supply or L-P (liquid propane) bottled gas. If you must use L-P bottled gas, you will have to live with the sight of the rather crude-looking tanks parked outside your home. Such a concession is slight, of course, if your house is alone in the woods. But to satisfy neighbors in a built-up area, you might consider installing attractively designed fences around the bottles to screen them from view.

Though it is possible to divert some heat from such a unit to peripheral rooms, each gas heater should be considered a single-room heater. What this means is that you may have to install one in each room for maximum comfort.

Pipeless Furnace. You may recall seeing one of these ductless units during childhood days spent in a country cottage. A pipeless furnace is one of the oldest heating systems around, and it is an inexpensive way to get heat in a summer cabin or hunting lodge.

The furnace is located in either the basement or crawlspace with an in-the-floor register located directly over it. The hot air rises from the furnace and circulates through the house by convection; cooler air returns to the furnace via the sides of the same floor register.

There are many disadvantages to this system. One is that the heating is spotty at best—warm near the register with the temperature getting lower as you move away from it. Also, since the heat is pretty much confined to the room where the register is located, privacy is sacrificed because doors must be kept open for air flow. And, the system is dirty: The grille must be removed frequently to clean inside.

Heat Pump. Perhaps less widely known than most heating methods, the heat pump is powered by electricity and is used both to heat and cool. During warm months, this device removes heat from the house to the outside in much the same manner that a refrigerator removes warm air from the compartment and dissipates it through its coils. In winter, the unit reverses itself to take heat from outside air and bring it inside. If the temperature drops suddenly and there is insufficient heat for the unit to transfer inside, resistance heating in the main duct may be cut in to increase the pump's output.

In some climates, the use of a heat pump entirely eliminates the need for air-conditioning.

Electric Space Heaters. Like gas heaters, these are wall-mounted, but electric heaters do not require venting. Most electric heat units are resistance-type heaters, creating heat when a high-resistance element heats as electricity passes through it.

Some electric heaters come equipped with blowers to push warmed air farther into the room. Others function by means of radiant heat, that is, by heating objects in the room, not the air.

Figure 12-14 *An auxiliary space heater can be a particular blessing in the morning—especially in the bathroom. This fan-forced model provides constantly circulating warm air. Its angled, anodized-aluminum 10-by-14-in. grille assures wide distribution of warmed air. From Nutone, this model is available with either automatic or manual controls.*

Another type of electric space heater is the electric blanket. Using one permits sleeping comfort while permitting you to lower the thermostat at night when it would be wasteful to heat the entire house just to have some warmth in the bedroom.

In many areas, use of electric heat is ruled out because of power-company rates. In any event, if you rely on electric heat of any type, you should have on hand a portable generator for emergency power. Power failures in remote country are almost routine after heavy snowfalls or storms.

And, with electric powered heat, maximum insulation on exposed walls and roof is a must.

Stoves. Because the fire is fully enclosed and the rate of burning can be controlled to some extent by a damper, a stove gives off roughly three times the heat that a fireplace does, burning the same quantity and type of wood.

Figure 12-15 Quick and relaxing, infra-red is another type of space heater. This heater, like the one shown in Figure 12-14, is installed between studs so it is flush with the finish wall. Nutone also makes ceiling model heaters that incorporate lighting and exhaust fan as well.

Design can vary from the type you'd expect to see in an old general store to the familiar Franklin stove.

No matter what type of stove you buy, make certain you follow the manufacturer's instructions for installing both the stove and the flue pipe. Any stove must be located on a fireproof surface, which varies depending on the stove. For example, stoves without legs will "explode" a concrete slab without an insulating barrier between. The flue must also be insulated with fireproof material at the point of exit through the roof or wall. Under no circumstances should a flue pipe be permitted to come into direct contact with wood members.

One big disadvantage of a woodburning stove is that it is hazardous to children. Its metal case is at a high temeprature when the fire is going and can cause severe burns if touched.

Fireplaces. A warm fire in the fireplace can be a sensible means of coping with the fuel-energy crisis. Of two basic types, masonry and factory-built, the first is best installed while the house is being erected. A factory-made fireplace, on the other hand, can be installed anytime.

Masonry fireplaces. Building a fireplace that draws properly is not a job for the average do-it-yourselfer. In fact, you shouldn't even hire a local mason to do the job until you have checked with the owners of several fireplaces that he has built to be certain that he produces satisfactory results.

Figure 12-16 *A conical freestanding fireplace, Regency by Majestic is a versatile design that can be used to accent any room decor. The unit may be mounted on tripod legs or on an enclosed base as desired. Available in a choice of decorator colors, this fireplace is sold in wood-burning and gas-fired versions. The unit is preassembled and shipped with screens, telescoping pipe and matching pipe to accommodate conventional 8-ft. ceiling heights.*

Figure 12-17 *Those who prefer built-in fireplaces can still choose from factory-built units. Here, it is possible to construct a complete woodburning fireplace without laying a single brick—unless you opt to face the wall with a brick veneer as shown here.*

Figure 12-18   If space is at a premium, yet a decorative fireplace is considered a must, a wall-hung model selected from Majestic's Apollo series may be the answer. Available in a wide variety of motifs in contemporary design, the hearth contains a thermostatically controlled 1,650 watt heater that yields 5,640 BTU. Ideal for small homes, this space heater plugs into 120 volts. Bonus, the fireplace can go with you should you ever decide to move: It's almost as easy as taking down a picture.

Possibly, a modest brick-faced fireplace can still be purchased for around $1,000 in some remote areas. But the cost of building a fireplace today, more likely runs anywhere from $1,500 to $2,500—more, if your design calls for a massive stone fireplace front.

A fireplace must be located especially carefully. If at all possible, it should be positioned on an inside wall so that heat from the chimney radiates through the walls and into other rooms of the house; placed on an exterior wall, all chimney heat is lost to the outdoors.

No fireplace, regardless of type, should ever be located near a door or between a pair of doors or windows where it will be subject to cross-drafts. Such air movement creates havoc with the chimney's draw.

THE ESSENTIAL PARTS OF A MASONRY FIREPLACE

The hearth front is the floor area in front of the fireplace which must be of a fireproof material such as tile. The back hearth is the surface upon which the fire is built; this usually has a drop (opening) to the ashpit below.

The fire chamber, or walls of the fireplace, should be made of fire brick. The sides and back are sloped slightly to reflect heat back into the room.

The damper is located toward the front and above the top of the fireplace opening. It is best if the damper is the entire length of the opening with a movable valve plate or adjuster hinged at the back (*not pivoted in the center*).

The smoke shelf, a horizontal surface just back of the damper, helps to prevent downdrafts from reaching the fire (which would cause smoking). Properly constructed, the smoke shelf and the damper valve plate turn the downdrafts back up the chimney.

The smoke chamber is a triangular area connecting the damper with the chimney flue which must be of adequate size and height to provide the necessary draft.

Note: Fire bricks should be laid in fire clay. The remainder of the chimney can be laid with cement or lime-cement mortar.

MASONRY FIREPLACE DESIGN

The dimensions of a fireplace opening are critical. Besides sizes, the relationship of one dimension to another is of paramount importance. Keep in mind that the larger the fireplace opening, the larger the flue has to be to provide the necessary draft.

A fireplace should be wide enough to allow the use of firewood 2 ft. long. This is the standard length for cordwood cut in half. The fireplace opening should also be high enough so that the fire may be tended conveniently.

TYPE	WIDTH	HEIGHT	DEPTH	FLUE LINING
	inches	*inches*	*inches*	*inches*
Small	28	28	16	8½ x 13 in. or 10 in. round
	30	30	16	Same as above.
Medium	34	30	16	13 x 13 in. or 12 in. round
	36	30	18	Same as above.
Large	40	30	18	Same as above.

Prefabricated fireplaces. You've seen this type of fireplace advertised in national magazines and are probably already aware that they come in a variety of designs to suit most home decors. Of metal, they can be installed along a wall or in the center of a room by a do-it-yourselfer—usually in less than a day.

The parts are engineered to assure perfect fires without smoke in the house as long as the unit is installed properly. Some units are suspended

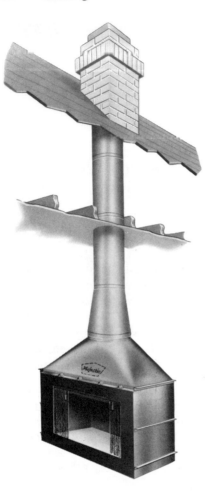

Figure 12-19 *This typical, modern prefabricated fireplace is an all-metal unit that comes complete from hearth to chimney top. The unit shown (by the Majestic Company) has triple-wall construction and allows zero clearance for combustibles, thus making any masonry work unnecessary. Flexibility of design makes it possible for you to install one of these in any location in any room.*

from the ceiling, others are floor or wall-mounted. If on the floor, make certain it sits on a base composed of noncombustible material. A simple, yet attractive, one can be fashioned by creating a box of redwood 2-by-4s, which is then lined with asbestos and filled with either sand or marble chips.

Since the fireboxes in most prefabs are small, logs must be cut slightly shorter and of a smaller diameter than customarily used in masonry fireplaces.

Most prefabricated fireplaces are U.L. listed and acceptable to local building codes. *But some are not.* Make certain that the unit you buy is approved by both authorities before plunking down your cash.

If you plan to do your own installing, pick a fireplace that comes with complete installation instructions. Follow the schedule to the letter, to keep warranties and guarantees in effect for the prescribed periods.

Fireplace fuel. From a fuel conservation point of view, having and using

Built-in fireplaces are easy to install

Figure 12-20 *This fireplace can be set in any location and enclosed with a 2-by-4 stud wall. Footings and foundations are not required below factory-built fireplaces.*

Figure 12-21 *Because of triple walls, the flue sections of this model may elbow and return in minimum space to clear obstructions.*

Figure 12-22 *Inside, flue and framework can be concealed with any type of wall material as long as it is U.L. listed for zero-clearance to combustibles.*

Figure 12-23 *When the exit point through the roof is pinpointed, the roof can be cut and flue sections added through the roof. Flashing is then installed.*

Figure 12-24 *Pipe sections are then terminated with the chimney cap section of your choice. Top line fireplace manufacturers offer a number of chimney styles to choose from.*

Photos Courtesy the Majestic Company

Figure 12-25 *The outside is completed with simulated brick-top housing and a flat rain cap.*

a fireplace makes a great deal of sense. When you use wood for heat you are burning a renewable fuel resource. And, often you can use wood in your fireplace that may be unusable in any other way. For instance, a good source for wood is trees that are considered undesirable; that is, those that are poorly formed or diseased. Fireplace wood can often be obtained for free from local dumps and landfill sites. Since many local ordinances no longer permit open burning of trash, huge piles of trees and branches downed by storms can generally be found here. By burning such material, you actually help the environment by reducing piles of waste which, when allowed to accumulate,

FIREPLACE CONSTRUCTION

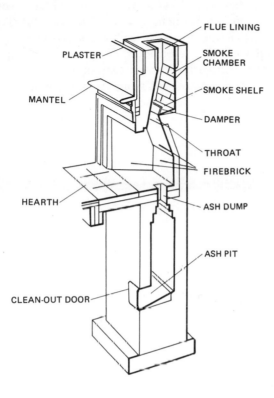

costs local government considerable sums of money to deal with. Lacking free sources of wood, you can purchase fuel from cord-wood dealers in rural areas.

Aroma and heat value from a fireplace vary with the types of woods. Softwoods, such as pine or spruce, ignite quickly because they are resinous; these burn rapidly with a hot flame. Softwood fires also burn out quickly and require frequent replenishment of wood. For longer-burning fires, use hardwoods such as ash, birch, maple, or oak. For aromatic fires, use the wood of fruit trees, such as apple and cherry, or nut trees, like pecan or hickory. Your best bet is to mix softwoods with hardwoods to obtain an easily ignited, yet long-lasting, fire.

If possible, use only seasoned (dried) wood in your fireplace. Certain resinous woods, such as larch, spruce, and hemlock, contain moisture pockets in the wood. When the wood is heated, trapped gases and water vapor build pressure in these pockets and pop with great velocity. These mini-explosions could cause serious accident to a nearby human, or fire in the home if sparks shoot onto a flammable rug.

Besides the climate, how you use your home, and money availability, perhaps the biggest factor in deciding on a heat system is *you*. If you are a hardy outdoors person, intent on an occasional weekend of skiing, ice fishing, or hunting, perhaps all you'll care to have is a space heater—just enough to take the tingle off your nose. On the other hand, if you enjoy sitting in an overstuffed easy-chair with a book in your lap or a ballgame on TV, you will probably want a system that is a bit more accommodating.

13

The Basics of Home Electricity

* Electricity in an older home * Planning a wiring system * How many branch circuits do you need? * How much service do you need? * Electrical installation * Do you need a permit? * Materials * Wiring basics * Some rules in general * Ground Fault Circuit Interrupters * How to have power when there is none *

Electricity contributes more than any other convenience to our high standard of living. Yet this valued servant, if installed or maintained improperly, can be the greatest safety hazard you and your family will have to live with. Therefore, when it comes to the wiring system in your home, don't play games about what you do or do not know; if you lack factual electrical know-how, plan on using a licensed electrician to do the job. Neither should you try to economize on materials and installation costs. Instead, if your budget is tight, save by pinching pennies in areas where safety is not a factor.

ELECTRICITY IN AN OLDER HOME

Most housing experts agree that few older homes have up-to-date service and safety. In fact, it is estimated that 90 percent of all existing homes need some rewiring in order to adequately serve today's needs. Thus, it is imperative that you make a careful inspection of the size of the electric service wires and service panel before buying an older home. Determine the capacity of the service as carefully as you check plumbing, roofing, and other facets. If the owner claims that the house has been rewired lately, the house will have a 3-wire, 150-amp. service—of much greater value than the older 2-wire,

ELECTRICAL PLAN SYMBOLS

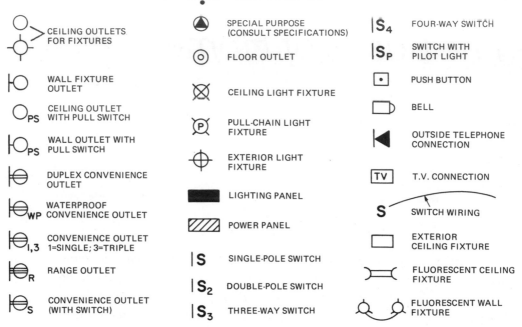

Figure 13-1 *Plan (blueprint) symbols for electrical installation.*

30-amp. service. You can determine whether the house service is 2- or 3-wire by counting the number of power company wires connected to the house at the service head. Each wire has a rain drip loop (see Figure 13-2).

PLANNING A WIRING SYSTEM

How Many Branch Circuits Do You Need? The first step is to determine your needs exactly so that the installed system will satisfy your electrical demands. There must be an adequate number of branch circuits for lighting and convenience outlets. A rule of thumb for calculating the number of lighting branch circuits is that all branches combined should provide about 3 watts for each square foot of building area. To determine the number of branch circuits you need for outlets, you can assume that eight to ten convenience outlets should be the maximum number on a 15- or 20-ampere branch circuit.

To accommodate larger appliances in the kitchen, laundry and workshop, it is a good idea to provide extra branch circuits in those rooms. Whatever the number of branch circuits you estimate you will need, install a service that will have several unused circuits (blanks) in reserve. Then, if

Figure 13-2 *Under no circumstance should do-it-yourselfers attempt to make the hookup from the utility company power lines which carry high voltage and are thus extra-dangerous. A properly planned "Service Entrance," as shown here, eliminates the annoyance and safety hazard caused by overheated wires. Installation of proper capacity wires assures top performance of tools, appliances, and lamps.*

In most locales, the utility company makes the connection down to the meter. From this point on, the bill is footed by the homeowner. It is common practice nowadays to have the meter located on an exterior wall and no higher than 6 ft. from the ground.

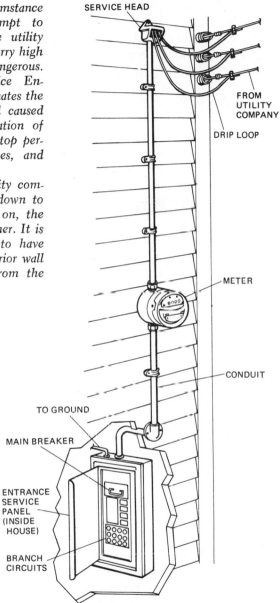

SERVICE HEAD

FROM UTILITY COMPANY

DRIP LOOP

METER

CONDUIT

TO GROUND

MAIN BREAKER

ENTRANCE SERVICE PANEL (INSIDE HOUSE)

BRANCH CIRCUITS

you decide to add other electrical equipment in the future, you will have the available capacity: costly updating of the house service won't be called for.

National Electric Code. For $3.50, you can obtain a copy of the National Electric Code from your local power company or by writing to the National Fire Protection Association, 470 Atlantic Ave., Boston, Mass.

02210. In the literature, you will find examples of methods used to calculate circuits, feeders, and main entrances.

How Much Service Do You Need? For modern living with full house power, the minimum service you should consider installing is 150-amp. 220v. If your home is equipped with a hot water heater, electric range, high speed dryer, and central air-conditioning, this capacity does the job. If you plan to add electric heat, you need at least a 200 amp. 220v. service.

It is far less expensive to install a larger capacity service initially than it is to install a small-capacity service that will ultimately have to be replaced. When discussing the job with your electrician, ask for figures on the various size services. You will be surprised at how little difference there is in the cost between a 150-amp. and 200-amp. service.

Under certain conditions, of course, you can put in a smaller service. The sizes most often include:

* *100-amp. service.* Under the National Electric Code, this is the minimum-size panel for any home of up to 3,000 sq. ft. Such a service handles all lighting, the hot water heater, and major appliances. It will not provide enough electricity to let you heat your home electrically.

* *60-amp. service.* Though for many years, this was the standard service installed, in most cases today it falls far below normal household demands. Such service provides capacity for lighting and portable appliances including a range, standard dryer, and a hot water heater. And that's it. You will not be able to add any major appliances or tools in the future.

* *30-amp. service.* This capacity service should be considered adequate only for temporary electrical needs (while building, for example) or for a one-room structure. A 30-amp. service supplies limited capacity for lighting and several smaller appliances: Before you can install any larger appliances, you will have to enlarge capacity.

When planning your electrical system, you can get help from the local power company, most of whom do not charge for such assistance. The power company will recommend the type of service you need, whether a yardpole is required, and how much of the installation it will handle and where your costs take over. In most localities, the power company makes the installation to the entrance head or yardpole, and you foot the bill from that point on. Only some power companies supply the meter.

Besides taking advantage of any help that the power company offers, and regardless of who makes the installation, make certain that the job is inspected by the proper authorities; when it passes muster you will receive a Certificate of Approval—which you will need to satisfy your insurance company (as well as for your own peace of mind).

The house service panel. Often referred to simply as the "fuse box," this

METHOD OF GROUNDING SERVICE

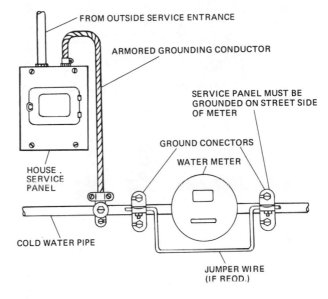

FROM OUTSIDE SERVICE ENTRANCE

ARMORED GROUNDING CONDUCTOR

SERVICE PANEL MUST BE
GROUNDED ON STREET SIDE
OF METER

GROUND CONECTORS

WATER METER

HOUSE
SERVICE
PANEL

COLD WATER PIPE

JUMPER WIRE
(IF REQD.)

Figure 13-3 The electric service is always grounded to either the metal water-supply pipe or to a grounding rod driven into the earth. When the water pipe is used, remember that the system must be grounded to the pipe on the street side of the meter. If the cable from the box does not reach past the meter, install a jumper (or bypass) wire as shown.

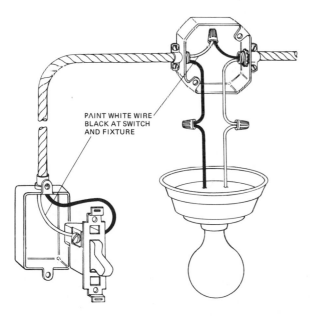

PAINT WHITE WIRE
BLACK AT SWITCH
AND FIXTURE

Figure 13-4 In electrical installations, the white wires are always neutral and the black wires are always hot. But in some switch installations, both white and black wires are hot. In this example, a wall switch installed at the end of a run controls a light fixture. The black feed wire is connected to the white wire from the switch. The black wire from the switch is then connected to the black wire on the lamp. Thus, the switch, in effect, is installed in the feed (or hot) side of the line between the fixture and the power source. Here, white wires should be painted black at the fixture and switch to indicate that they are hot.

element in the house's electrical system provides protection from electrical failure and overload. The house service panel is the link between the house system and the incoming power from the utility company. Two types of protective devices are used in home service panels—fuses and circuit breakers. Both are approved and supply adequate protection.

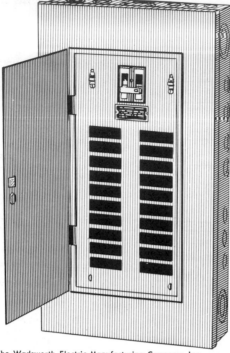

Figure 13-5 A 20-circuit breaker panel with main disconnect.

The Wadsworth Electric Manufacturing Company, Inc.

Any time you must work in or around the service panel, do so with care. Make certain the floor is dry and that you keep hands and tools away from the terminals to which incoming lines are connected. These incoming lines are always "hot" up to the point where they connect to the service panel. When you throw the main breaker or fuse, you simply cut off power from *that point on.*

The correct size of fuses or breakers should always be used on each branch circuit; generally, a 15-amp. fuse or breaker protects a No. 14 wire circuit while a 20-amp fuse or breaker is used with a No. 12 wire circuit.

When a fault such as an overload causes a fuse to blow, it must be replaced with a fuse of equal capacity. A tripped circuit breaker, however, merely requires the resetting of a handle or switch; because of the convenience of a circuit breaker system, it is the overwhelming choice of homeowners today. (Note: Before the circuit is reactivated, the cause of the failure should be determined and eliminated.)

ELECTRICAL INSTALLATION

Before starting you should have on hand accurately scaled wiring plans for the entire structure. If you are working from building plans prepared by a reputable architect or purchased from a reliable plans service, such details

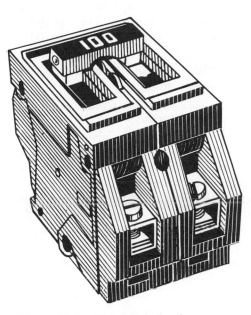

Figure 13-6 Circuit breaker boxes have one or two large breakers that control house power. Model C2100 by Wadsworth is a 100-amp. version.

Figure 13-7 A special-purpose breaker from Wadsworth, E-Z-DUO SP B2020, handles a pair of 20-amp. circuits.

will automatically be included in the plans. To help you decipher what the architect calls for in the plans, see Figure 13-1 for the common electrical symbols used on building plans.

Do You Need a Permit? Consult your local building department to learn whether a permit is required. Usually a homeowner is permitted to wire his own home, though there's a strong chance that you will have to first prove that you are well-grounded in electrical knowledge. If your area does grant you a permit to do your own work, you must still have the completed work approved by an authorized inspector. You will not be able to get a permit that allows a nonlicensed electrician (i.e., a moonlighter) to do the installation.

If your area does not require a permit, for your own protection, gain a full understanding of the basic safety rules for good installation as outlined in the National Electric Code.

Besides the National Code, arm yourself with a copy of local electrical requirements. In some areas, local requirements may be at variance with and supersede the National Code. If you are doing the job yourself, it is your responsibility to be familiar with such differences to assure a conforming installation. If it doesn't conform, the inspector can withhold approval until corrections are made per his or her instructions.

Materials. The installer is also responsible for verifying that the materials to be installed are approved by the the local power company. For one thing, all the materials you plan to use should be U.L. Listed. Don't take a salesman's word for it that a product has such approval—look for the stamp, "U.L. Approved." This symbol tells you that the item has been inspected and approved by the Underwriters' Laboratories as suitable for the purpose for which it is intended.

Armored (BX) and nonmetallic sheathed (Romex) cables are the most commonly used cables in home wiring. Of the two, Romex is easier to work with but its fibrous sheath is also far more subject to injury than BX cable. Romex is more flexible than BX but most codes have restrictions when it comes to bend radii (regardless of which cable is being used).

Nonmetallic sheathed cable contains a bared wire to provide a continuous ground. The flexible, galvanized steel casing of armored cable(BX) affords a continuous ground for protection against mechanical injury. Today, some BX cable also comes with a bare aluminum wire under its sheath to lower resistance and to provide still more ground protection. BX cable is the better choice when adding wiring to an older home, and the only cable you should consider using.

Both types of cables usually carry two or three conductors and are stamped with numbers relating to the number and size of wires. For example, a 3-wire cable using No. 14 wire will be labeled, "14-3."

Before buying either type, check with local authorities; in some areas, nonmetallic-sheathed cable is not yet acceptable.

Give careful thought to the size wire you use in your home. In older homes, it is common to find No. 14 wire used on branch circuits. Today, with greater electrical demand generated by the increased number of appli-

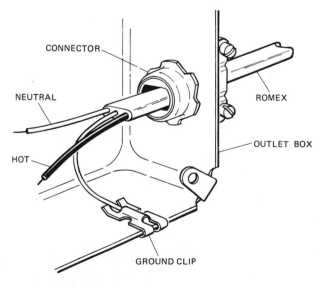

Figure 13-8 *Many local codes require grounded boxes and nonmetallic cable with a ground wire. A simple way to ground the wire to the outlet box is with the clip intended for this purpose. By using nonmetallic wire with a ground cable, you will have a continuously grounded system which will assure that the conductor will always be at ground potential thus reducing the danger of shocks should exposed metal accidentally become live (or hot).*

Figure 13-9 This newest CO/ ALR switch and receptacle from Leviton were the first wiring devices to pass strict U.L. tests for aluminum terminations. Terminals on both fixtures are for use with aluminum wire, copper, and copper-clad aluminum.

Courtesy Leviton Mfg. Co.

ances, a heavier gauge (No. 12) copper wire should be considered the minimum size to install. If you expect the load on a particular branch to be increased by the use of large appliances or equipment, the wire size should be increased accordingly.

Wiring Basics. If you plan to be your own electrician, here are some important fundamentals:

* All black and red wires are the hot wires in an electrical system. But, as can be seen in Figure 13-4, there are exceptions.
* To get 230 volts from a three-wire service, it is necessary to tap both hot lines. Each line carries 115 volts; thus the two in tandem carry 230 volts.
* If a white line is used to carry current, as in the switch setup shown in Figure 13-4, the white lines must be painted black. You will thus be flagged that the line is hot should you have to work in that box in the future.
* Although the white wire is the ground connection, the armor of BX and the bare wire in Romex also provide a continuous ground. Make certain the bare wire is connected to the grounding device now called for under the Code (Figure 13-8).
* In new construction, when running electric cable through studs, bore the holes at the stud centers so that the nails used on the wall covering do not penetrate the cable. If 2-by-3 material is used for studding

Figure 13-10 *Dimmer switch control can be used to replace ordinary switches. One type is used with incandescents, another with fluorescent fixtures. Dimmer switches are wired exactly the same as are conventional switches: the break is made on the hot side of the line; one black wire connects to the black feed, the other black wire to the black-wire fixture. The wattage capacity of the dimmer switch must always be greater than the total lighting wattage being controlled.*

on an interior, non-loadbearing partition wall, metal plates should be fastened to the stud faces to protect the cable from being penetrated by nails.

Some Rules in General. Along walls, duplex receptacles should be spaced no farther apart than 12 feet. This way, an appliance located at any point along the floor line will be within 6 feet of an outlet. The code also calls for an outlet in any wall more than 2-ft. wide. Outlets are generally placed 12 to 18 inches from the floor.

If outdoor, weatherproofed convenience outlets are not specified in your plans, consider installing one or more anyway. A great deal of living is done outdoors these days.

Ground Fault Circuit Interrupters. Since January 1973, the National Electric Code requires all 15- and 20-amp. outdoor receptacles in one- and two-family dwellings to be equipped with devices called Ground Fault Interrupters (called GFCI or GFI in the electrical trade). A GFI is also required for any receptacle within 10 to 15 feet of a swimming pool and for all equipment used with storable pools (Figure 13-12).

A GFI provides protection against serious injury or death caused by contact with damaged or defective electrical equipment (i.e., tool-insulation failure). An Interrupter monitors the currents in milliamps (ma) entering and leaving a circuit. If they aren't identical, it means that some current is leaking to a ground. If this happens when the tool user is grounded, such leakage means severe shock at best, electrocution at worst.

You can achieve total in-home protection by using GFCI breakers, but at roughly $50 per breaker the cost escalates rapidly (Figure 13-12). However, besides outdoor areas, you might consider GFCI protection at least for branch circuits serving the kitchen, bath, laundry center, and workshop.

Figure 13-11 *The dimmer shown is half the depth of conventional dimmers and can be installed using just a screwdriver. The 600-watt, U.L.-listed Trimaton has a rotary on-off action and is available at hardware and electrical supply stores. Leviton makes it.*

Figure 13-12 *A GFI (Ground Fault Interrupter) receptacle provides sure protection against ground fault; use of one is recommended for use on all circuits to bathroom, kitchen, laundry, and shop areas. GFI protection is already required by electric codes on all outdoor receptacles. The Sure-Gard duplex receptacle fits a standard outlet box and features an indicator light that shows when the device is operative. Decorative wall plates to suit receptacle are by the same maker, Leviton.*

6250-3

6602

6156

6151

Figure 13-13 *Since dimmer switches conserve energy, here are several types you may want to consider using in your home: number 6602, Trimaton dimmer shown on page 265; 6151, a replacement socket that easily converts any lamp into an infinitely variable light source; 6156, a table-top dimmer that controls table, pole, or swag lamps; and 6250-3, a lamp-cord dimmer that converts any table or portable incandescent lamp into a mood-setting dimmer lamp. The numbers indicated are the manufacturer's catalog numbers. All switches shown are by Leviton Manufacturing Company.*

Electrical Materials. If quality electrical materials are not readily available locally, large mail-order houses such as Sears, Roebuck and Company and Montgomery Ward, offer everything needed for a house wiring system. In fact, for only 50¢ Sears offers a profusely illustrated electrical booklet, called simply, "Electrical Wiring," which outlines basic installation instructions.

HOW TO HAVE POWER WHEN THERE IS NONE

If your electrical demands are minimal or your home is far removed from power company lines, you may have to supply your own electricity. Since utility companies charge by the foot when running lines into remote areas, the cost of a commercial installation might make such a hookup impractical.

You can get along on a generator if your needs are slight. For example, if you require electricity for merely lighting and a hot-water heater—with your other needs provided for by liquid propane gas (LPG) and/or fireplaces, a generator may provide all the electricity you'll ever need.

In fact, even if you are connected to a utility company you may want to add a generating system of your own as insurance against the brownouts and blackouts that are almost inevitable in the country after heavy storms and snowfalls.

To determine the size of the generator you must buy, add up the total wattage you expect to consume. In most cases, a unit capable of delivering 3,000 watts will satisfy basic needs. To determine wattage, take the number of amps from the nameplate of each appliance and tool you expect the generator to handle and multiply it by 115 volts. To this figure, add the total wattage for lights to be in service. Finally, increase the figure you come up with by 20 to 25 percent to guarantee some reserve capacity. This total is the size generator you need in order to enjoy unflickering service (see Figure 13-14).

Figure 13-14 An economically priced generator, Model 130A22-1C from Homelite, incorporates a Tecumseh HS 50 engine and weighs 75 pounds. Priced at $350, the generator is ideal for do-it-yourself builders and for homeowners concerned about utility blackouts and brownouts. The generator has a 2,250-watt continuous rating and an output of 120 volts, 60Hz, single-phase, alternating current.

Never buy a unit that is too small; power up properly because the cost factor is a small consideration. With an undersized generator, you stand a strong chance of damaging all motors if too many appliances are in use at the same time.

Depending upon the type chosen, you can expect to pay about $800 for a 3,500-watt generator. Some are fully automatic—starting up whenever power is called for and shutting off when use ceases. Others are controlled by switches.

Though the connection between the cabin or house and the generator needn't be as elaborate as it would have to be to suit a power company, all wiring done inside and out should be installed to satisfy the demands of local and national codes.

Finally, don't buy standby equipment (generators) with the thought of putting the power companies out of business; over the long haul, the power that the utilities supply is markedly cheaper.

GENERATOR CAPACITY DETERMINATION CHART

Will run at one time	1;250 w.	2,000 w.	3,000 w.	4,000 w.	5,000 w.
Automatic washer					X
Freezer			X	X	X
⅓ hp furnace fan	X	X	X	X	X
⅓ hp sump pump		X	X	X	X
Refrigerator	X	X	X	X	X
Television				X	X

Continuous-duty power plants are designed for daily service with engines that run at 1,800 to 2,400 rpm. They turn a 3,600 rpm alternator. The slower engine speed means that the engine will last about three times longer than a comparable emergency unit with direct drive. The continuous-duty type should be your first choice if your needs are for a primary source of power.

Intermittent-use power units are for partial or full loads of power for interrupted periods of time. Wattage capacities of this type range from 1,100 to 5,000 watts. The units come with such features as oversized mufflers to cut down noise, constant voltage regulation, built in overload protection, and extra motor-starting power.

At any rate, a transfer switch is a must when you use all auxiliary power equipment. With it, you transfer high-line power to alternator power during a failure. The transfer switch prevents alternator power from escaping back into the utility line where a workman, who thinks the line is dead, can receive a severe or fatal jolt.

It cannot be said too often, nor too loud: *Installing a home electric system is not a job for a beginner.* To keep costs down, perhaps you can hire a local licensed electrician who will have you work alongside as a helper. If so, you'll come out dollars ahead because you will cut down working time on the job. (And, as always, time is money.)

On the other hand, if you can't find a licensed electrician willing to go along with such a setup, if you're a neophyte, don't think you can handle the installation alone. The diagrams and photos shown in this chapter are, by no means, all-inclusive. Rather, they are a small sampling of the vast amount of know-how needed to correctly install a home wiring system. Though you may gain even more knowledge by consulting the books listed in Appendix D, you will still very likely fall short of the know-how needed to wire your own home.

This is one area of do-it-yourselfing that is usually best left to the professionals.

14

Which Type of Vacation Home for You?

* Finding the home you are looking for * Manufactured housing—
"Prefabs" * Mobility—The American way: motor homes, mobile homes
* Homes manufactured for your site: Shell houses, panelyzed houses,
modular—or sectional houses *

Whether you buy or build, choosing the second home that will make you and your family comfortable and happy now, as well as in the future, takes some doing. Once you have narrowed your search to a particular geographical area and have selected a site, you can focus on finding a house that will successfully meet the demands of your family.

FINDING THE HOME YOU ARE LOOKING FOR

To make the house-hunting chore a lighter one, you can do one of two things:

1. Arm yourself with enough solid building information to enable you to recognize a shoddily built house when you see one—and quickly pass it by.
2. Allow enough time for looking at houses or architect's plans if you decide to build. At this stage, you should not be rushing your decision.

To further simplify the task, try to break down the sometimes overwhelming number of considerations into three categories:

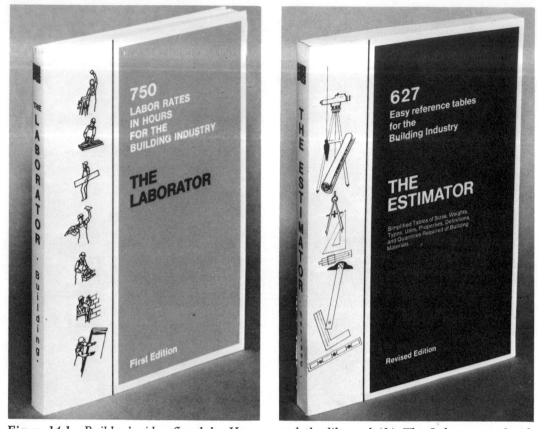

Figure 14-1 Builders' aids offered by Home Building Plans Service (see Appendix B for the address) include: (a) The Estimator ($4.95) contains information on the use of 3,000 building materials including their properties, values, and the like and (b) The Laborator, *a handbook of easy-to-read tables to help determine labor time for 140 different building functions. This edition covers most modern procedures ($3.95).*

1. *Economics.* Have you accurately—and honestly—calculated the amount you can afford?
2. *Taste or esthetics.* How is the house in question styled architecturally inside and out? Is it what you want? Or, at least, does it come close to the dream house you envisioned at the start of your search?
3. *Personal involvement.* Have you made up your mind regarding the degree of involvement with the house as a do-it-yourselfer? A complete do-it-yourself operation—i.e., building your own house—means that you will have to forego at least one season's use of nearby recreational facilities. On the other hand, many handy persons consider the books more than balanced with the number of dollars saved by family involvement in the construction of their house. Such savings often let you build more house for the money.

Eight sides—eight views . . .

Figure 14-2 *This octagonally shaped home is perfectly suited for location on a piece of high ground—perhaps a bluff or rolling hill—where breath-taking vistas surround the dwelling. The house shown has heavy beams supported by peeled poles and a massive stone fireplace to add drama to the living room. To keep exterior maintenance to a minimum, handsplit shakes are suggested for the roof and 1-by-6 tongue-and-groove siding goes on walls both vertically and horizontally. Total living space is over 1,900 sq. ft. Structurally a sophisticated house, it is not an easy one for an amateur builder to try on a first attempt. Plans for this home are available from the source shown above.*

If neither buying nor building appeals to you, manufactured homes offer an alternative. If flexibility is important, for example, your search will probably center quickly on mobile homes—with and without engines. If fast erection of a home is essential, one of the other types of manufactured homes—shell, panelized, or modular—is likely to appeal to you. Those wishing minimum maintenance and involvement should zero in on a condominium. If money is no object, perhaps you'll choose to have an architect custom-build your place. Those on the opposite end of the economic rainbow will probably opt to go with a do-it-yourself structure built from stock plans.

The important point, however, is simply that any one of these homes is sure to give satisfaction if it's quality built.

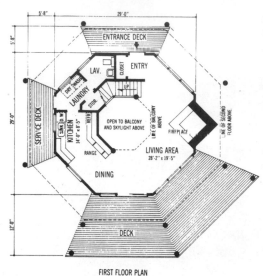

FIRST FLOOR PLAN
697 SQUARE FEET

Figure 14-3 A good design feature: Almost every part of the house enjoys an exterior wall. Also, the first floor living area is extended by three decks outside. Inside, the first-level design gives a studio-like open effect; and kitchen, bathroom, and entry are integrated to insure privacy as well as convenience.

Second-floor bedrooms are connected by a balcony hallway, access to the first level is via an open staircase. Notice the compartmentalized second-level bath layout—to assure greater privacy.

Plan No. WWPA 4751-87, Western Wood Products Association

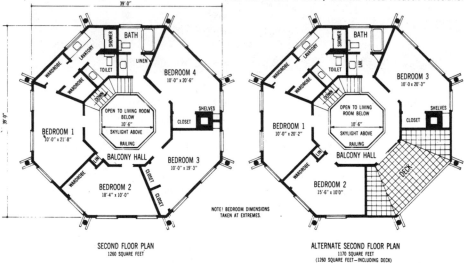

SECOND FLOOR PLAN
1260 SQUARE FEET

ALTERNATE SECOND FLOOR PLAN
1170 SQUARE FEET
(1260 SQUARE FEET—INCLUDING DECK)

MANUFACTURED HOUSING—"PREFABS"

Technically, the word "prefab" includes all factory-built dwellings. Basically of five types—(1) motor, (2) mobile, (3) shell, (4) panelized, and (5) modular—the range of quality available in each type is quite wide. Fast-buck operators mask the true value of a home by clouding the issue with all sorts of supposed extras. Under such smoke screens it's often difficult—if not impossible—for unwary and inexperienced buyers to pick the house that will give the most for the money.

Four-stager lets you think big but start small . . .

The starter-unit here is the octagonal-shaped structure at center which consists of 556 sq. ft. of living space. The 13-by-15-ft. bedroom-and-deck modules can be added a season at a time.

When all five sections are built, the house boasts 1,284 sq. ft. of living space inside and out. The massive fireplace in one corner gives a touch of elegance and comes in handy on chilly evenings.

The bedrooms can be added in any combination as the need arises; the bathroom between bedrooms one and two is optional but, if it is installed offers additional privacy and convenience.

Notice the wood deck at rear; from it, youngsters enter a house-saving mudroom, and then a bath with shower.

Figure 14-4

Western Wood Products Association photos

Figure 14-5

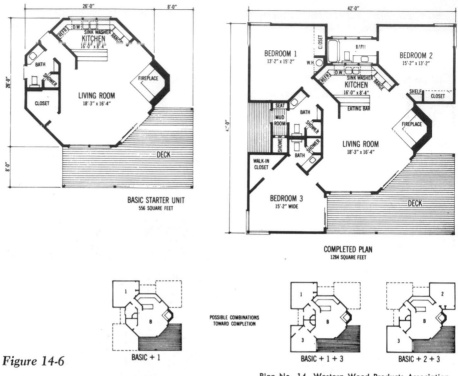

Figure 14-6

Plan No. 14, Western Wood Products Association

If you have any doubts call in a local architect and ask him for an opinion on the prefab you have under consideration. The expert advice is well worth the nominal fee, but you can save yourself that fee by sticking with quality manufacturers.

In no way a new concept, this house-building approach has been successfully attempted by big outfits all over the country. No one seems to know for sure just how many prefab manufacturers there are in the country at the moment, but most experts in the home-building field put the number at somewhere between 50 and 75.

Supposedly, prefabs should be cheaper than stick-builts because they are constructed by lower-paid factory personnel. But, contrary to popular opinion, monetary savings isn't the primary reason for selecting a prefab. In fact, many prefab builders admit they cannot compete price-wise with the small local builder whose office is the cab of a pickup truck. Transportation of the finished product often wipes out any savings on labor. Thus, because of shipping costs, most makers limit their sales area to within a 300- to 500-mile radius of the factory. Any greater hauling distances push the selling price clear out of sight. (Despite this fact, however, prefabs have been delivered to every part of the U.S. and out of it as well.)

Nevertheless, you can figure it will cost about $5 per sq. ft. less to put

Pretty, inexpensive cabin . . .

Perched on poles, this cabin offers a modest 896 sq. ft. of living space, which is more than adequate for a sports-loving couple. The exterior is finished entirely with wood treated with preservative and allowed to weather naturally.

Figure 14-7

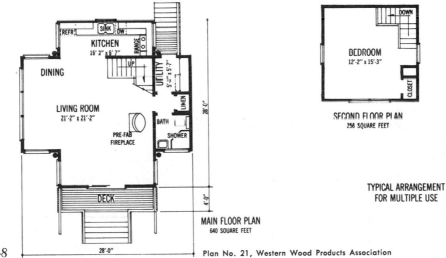

Figure 14-8

Plan No. 21, Western Wood Products Association

The first floor is left wide open and free of space-consuming interior walls. The kitchen is tucked neatly out of the way in an alcove and the second-level bedroom is reached via an open staircase. If poles are undesirable, plans for a continuous perimeter foundation for this model are available.

If land is at a premium, this design is well-suited to a cluster application (see Fig. 14-10). As shown, four couples can split the cost of the property, but arrangements can be worked out to suit groups of two, three, or more. Common decks connect the structures, but privacy is assured by the correct layout of the houses. Such cluster grouping can also be considered by those who wish to derive additional income from their second-home investments.

Figure 14-9

Western Wood Products Association photos

Figure 14-10   Cluster grouping, see Figure 14-8.

together a prefab than it would a stick-built structure of similar quality. And contrary to misconceptions about available styles, you'll find a wide range of architectural styles to choose from. In fact, since prefab prices range from $15,000 to around $75,000, just about all tastes can be satisfied with a manufactured home.

The major difference between prefabs and stick-builts is the quality of materials used. A review of prefab specifications and an inspection of several manufactured homes will reveal that, for the most part, better materials are used throughout. For example, the lumber is generally kiln-dried; exterior doors are usually solid (instead of hollow) core. And some prefab makers install double-insulated glass in windows as standard practice.

Prefabs are therefore increasing in popularity because they offer a reasonably economic way to get into a new, customized house in a hurry. There is a wide selection of homes to choose from and most makers will make an almost unlimited number of changes permitting potential buyers to customize to their heart's content. You can ask for and get extra closets, balconies, bathrooms, partitions, and different materials throughout. Since walls and rooms can be repositioned, the buyer can shape the house to suit personal needs perfectly. The buyer will, of course, pay for any added space and extra or higher-grade materials.

Some companies tack on a charge for redrawing the plans. In general, if a company does level a charge for tinkering with plans, it is obviously less expensive to stay with one of the standard offerings.

A modest-size expandable: *The design here suggests contemporary barn style because the roof line hints of a Dutch gambrel. Notice that there are several expansion options: Stage No. 1 gives 320 sq. ft. of living space containing kitchen, bath, and living area, while the deck and tilted railing add livability and interest. (See Figure 14-12.)*

You can then choose to add the bedroom or living room side next as your needs demand. This plan may be built on a pole foundation in modules but, if preferred, perimeter foundation plans are also available for the complete unit.

Figure 14-11   Plan 24.   Western Wood Products Association

Figure 14-12

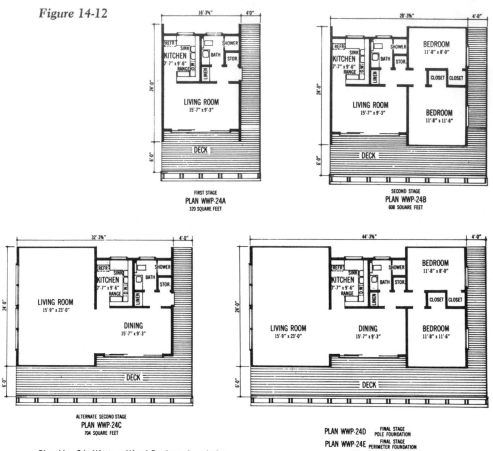

Plan No. 24, Western Wood Products Association

Do-it-yourselfers out to get the most house for the least money build from stock plans. The plans offered by reliable architectural firms are top quality and every bit on a par with what you might expect to get by hiring your own local architect—except that the house will not be specifically designed for your family. Stock plans are low-priced, complete, and—if bought from a reputable plans firm—acceptable by local building departments.

A popular misconception about prefabs is that they are nothing but look-alikes. Though admittedly just a sampling of what is available in prefabs today, the photos on these pages prove that the component system is actually very versatile. By simply mixing the various components (or modules) offered by manufacturers, extensive custom detailing or a major change is often made possible. Happily, you will find that the majority of prefab makers will work with you on this score. But keep in mind that the more you customize a house design, the more you will pay for the finished product.

Though in many cases you buy your prefab from an authorized local

Roomy chalet for sports buffs . . .

The plan shown for this structure is just one of three options available for interior layout. All versions feature two large bedrooms upstairs along with bath and storage areas. The basement provides a garage, storage room, and work room (which could easily be adapted for use as a family room).

The home features a prefab fireplace in the living room and a full bath on the main level. A generous amount of space available for sleeping makes this layout a good selection for skiers (who usually seem to have lots of friends who also like to ski).

Figure 14-13

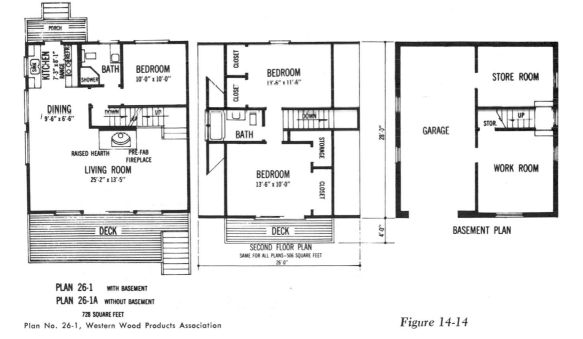

PLAN 26-1 WITH BASEMENT
PLAN 26-1A WITHOUT BASEMENT
728 SQUARE FEET
Plan No. 26-1, Western Wood Products Association

Figure 14-14

dealer, there are some manufacturers who will deal with you directly. An obvious big advantage that a quality prefab has over a stick-built house of comparable quality is the speed with which one can be erected. If the job is properly coordinated, the project—from start to finish—can be easily completed within one month.

On the following pages, a number of typical vacation homes are shown—by no means all that is available in vacation homes. (For other manufacturers, write to one or more of the associations listed in Appendix E.) For quick identification, all photos are tagged with firm names; for the full addresses of manufacturers and stock-plans services, see Appendices A and B respectively.

Luxury lodge for high country . . .

Based on the shape of the traditional western barn, this spacious lodge and ski house (the total living space is 2,220 sq. ft.) provides all the comforts for those seeking pleasure in winter sports. There is a sheltered ground floor access from the carport, and roomy storage to the left as you enter. The first floor level contains a 14-by-20-ft. living room with a vaulted ceiling and open kitchen/dining area. There's also a master bedroom that can be used as a den if preferred. The three bedrooms on the second level are grouped around a full bath. The balcony overlooking the living room can be used as extra sleeping space should you have an unexpected crush of weekend guests.

American Plywood Association
Figure 14-15

Figure 14-16

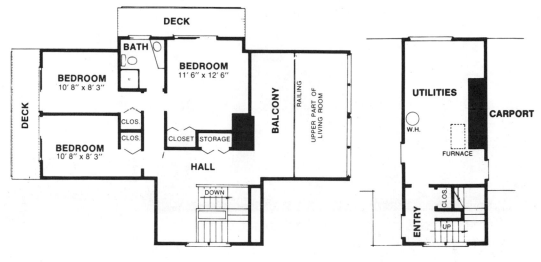

Figure 14-16   Continued

Plan No. 120, American Plywood Association

Figure 14-17

A low-cost second home . . .

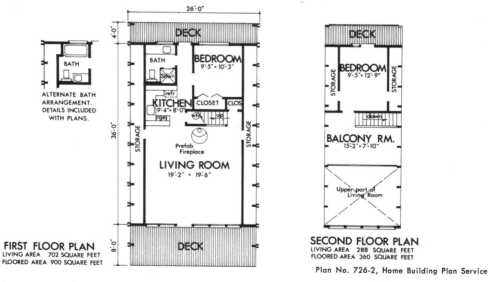

BATH

ALTERNATE BATH
ARRANGEMENT.
DETAILS INCLUDED
WITH PLANS.

26'-0"

DECK

BATH

BEDROOM
9'-5" × 10'-3"

refr

KITCHEN
9'-4" × 8'-0"

CLOSET   CLOS

rge

up

Prefab
Fireplace

LIVING ROOM
19'-2" × 19'-6"

STORAGE

STORAGE

36'-0"

4'-0"

8'-0"

DECK

FIRST FLOOR PLAN
LIVING AREA   702 SQUARE FEET
FLOORED AREA 900 SQUARE FEET

DECK

STORAGE

BEDROOM
9'-5" × 12'-9"

STORAGE

down

BALCONY RM.
15'-2" × 7'-10"

Upper part of
Living Room

SECOND FLOOR PLAN
LIVING AREA   288 SQUARE FEET
FLOORED AREA 360 SQUARE FEET

Plan No. 726-2, Home Building Plan Service

Figure 14-18 The A-frame design has been a favored second-home style for a decade or more. There are good reasons why this design enjoys such popularity: (1) Since its shape is exactly the opposite of the box-like structures that most of us live in at home, the drama such a dwelling offers gives a real sense of departure from our everyday lives; and (2), from a practical standpoint, it is one of the most economical homes that you can erect. Because roof and walls are one and the same, considerably less material is required to build an A-frame.

This modest version has 900 sq. ft. of space with 702 sq. ft. usable as living space. The cost to build this structure—depending upon the materials you decide to build with and the number of extras you install—is very low. By building it yourself, in fact, you can move in for less than $10,000.

Chalet-type dwelling—with or without basement . . .

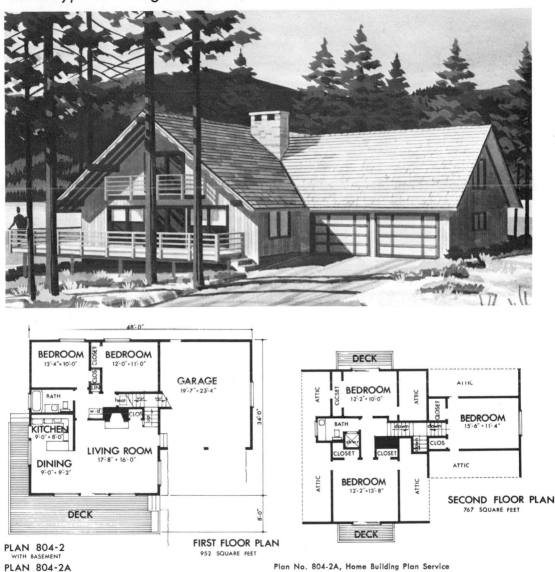

PLAN 804-2
WITH BASEMENT

PLAN 804-2A
WITHOUT BASEMENT

FIRST FLOOR PLAN
952 SQUARE FEET

SECOND FLOOR PLAN
767 SQUARE FEET

Plan No. 804-2A, Home Building Plan Service

Figure 14-19 Through careful design, the architect here has produced a modest first-floor area of 952 sq. ft. and a compact second-floor plan of 767 sq. ft.—yet there are five full-sized bedrooms to assure maximum privacy. There is also abundant storage space, built-ins, and many of the conveniences most expect only in their first homes. Plumbing is provided for two complete bathrooms; and a laundry washer and dryer has been tucked into one corner of the central hall on the main floor. If desired, this home can also be built with a full basement; to do so, specify plan number 804-2 (with basement).

For snow-country lovers . . .

Figure 14-20 *The exacting concern for construction detail in this plan is revealed by the use of various wood products. Notice the fireplace chimney, sheathed in resawn plywood and batten strips, against the dramatic textured siding of the red cedar shingle siding. Another good example is the balustrade used to enclose all decks and porches; though modern in design, a strong feeling of Swiss chalet is achieved.*

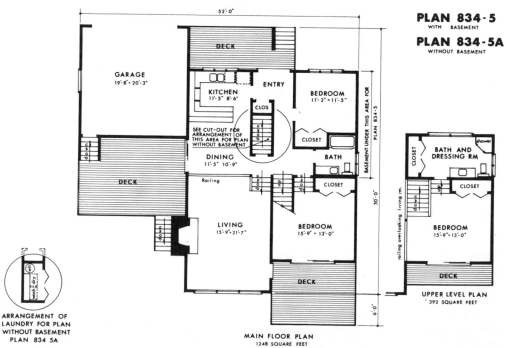

Home Building Plan Service

PLAN 834-5
WITH BASEMENT

PLAN 834-5A
WITHOUT BASEMENT

ARRANGEMENT OF
LAUNDRY FOR PLAN
WITHOUT BASEMENT
PLAN 834 5A

UPPER LEVEL PLAN
392 SQUARE FEET

MAIN FLOOR PLAN
1248 SQUARE FEET

MOBILITY—THE AMERICAN WAY

Motor Homes. Many sociologists consider mobility to be a peculiarly American trait. Until the fuel crisis of the mid-seventies, in fact, the number of motor homes on the highways increased each year. And even with the high cost of gasoline these days, a motor home is still worth your attention when you consider that your living quarters are with you when you reach your destination. In fact, gas costs can mean very little if your plans are to drive to a site and remain there for the summer.

There is no arguing the advantages to be gained by combining travel expenses with living quarters—especially when the latter can be as generously sized as 8 ft. wide by 8 ft. high and 24 ft. (or more) long. For anywhere from $14,000 to $25,000, you can own a fully equipped motor home capable of housing six or seven, complete with galley, bathroom with shower, dinette and storage space.

Mobile Homes. The basic prefab is the fully furnished mobile home. An updated version of campers and trailers of yesteryear and a direct descendent of the Conestoga, modern mobile homes are considerably improved. Assembled at the factory, they are hauled to the building site by truck and then positioned on a foundation or piers for a permanent or semipermanent stay. Utilities and sewage disposal are then connected.

Trucked to your site completely ready for instant vacationing . . . .

Figure 14-21 *Most of the features for all models in the Champion Special and Deluxe series are the same. The principal difference is that the Deluxe version includes a cathedral-type ceiling in the living room; more and larger lattice-work windows; additional carpeting, and a beamed living room ceiling.*

The manufacturer maintains 60 factories across the United States, making buyer inspection of models fairly accessible for those interested in mobile homes. Surprisingly, homes by this manufacturer include dry-wall construction inside.

Champion Home Builders Co.

Figure 14-22 Bathrooms are roomy with a tub and shrower area constructed of easy-care material. The vanity boasts a one-piece top. Optionals for the bathroom include toilet-tank set with rug, washer, and dryer (in a separate utility area outside bathroom wall), and linen cupboards above the washer and dryer.

Sleek, elegant—and mobile . . .

*Figure 14-23 34-footer, labeled Penthouse Fifth Wheel by Monitor, gives all the portability of a travel trailer, and the permanence and living convenience of a vacation cottage. Like many mobile homes, this model offers numerous standard conveniences and a selection of luxury optional extras. All Wickes units come prepared for later addition of air-condi-*tioning and television installation.

This home sleeps four people with two single beds as standard and a freestanding sofa hide-a-bed. Built on a 7-in. frame, it has tandem axles with 12-in. brakes and shock absorbers on each wheel, the latter of which is claimed to make the towing easier.

Available in many sizes, the most popular mobile homes boast about 1,000 square feet of living space, consisting of kitchen, full bath, dining area, living room, and two (or more) bedrooms; such a model is capable of housing six or seven people. The price for all this instant luxury is in the neighborhood of $8,000 to $10,000. But there are mobile homes around for under $5,000, just as there are luxury models selling for $15,000 and up.

For many, the best bet with a mobile home is to locate in a mobile-home park, either privately or state-owned. The usual course in such communities is to rent the land rather than buy it. Rentals are generally figured on a monthly basis and the fee varies with the size of site, the services offered by the park landlord, and the facilities. The rental fee includes connections to the park's water service and waste disposal system; but you pay for the electricity you consume and your telephone charges. Depending on geographic area, you can expect to pay anywhere from $4 to $125 per month for a decent site in an acceptable park.

Once you are settled in, you may decide to add other amenities to your new home. Perhaps you'd like to tack on a small addition to serve as a family fun room; or build a deck or carport. If such extras are in your plans, make certain they will be allowed before signing on with a park. Some parks don't permit such appurtenances.

Figure 14-24 An electric fireplace is one of the many optional features available; other luxuries you can add—if your tastes demand and budget permits—include monomatic toilet with dual holding tanks for self-containment; an AM/FM stereo tape deck with four speakers; an intercom system; a rear entrance door; and an eye-level oven.

The manufacturer offers a wide selection of interior fabrics and colors so that the buyer can create the environment liked best.

Typical floor plans for mobile-home living . . .

WICKES HOMES, For Living and Leisure

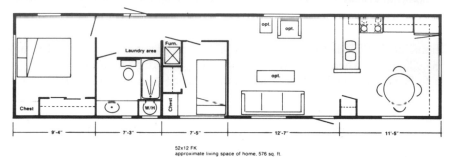

52x12 FK
approximate living space of home, 576 sq. ft.

Figure 14-25 *The standard width for mobile homes is 12 ft.; this model is 52 ft. long, and its approximate living space is 576 sq. ft.*

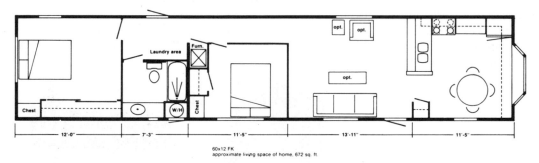

60x12 FK
approximate living space of home, 672 sq. ft.

Figure 14-26 *A 60-ft. version boasts 672 sq. ft. of living space; the optional bay window on one end is available on all Wickes floor plans.*

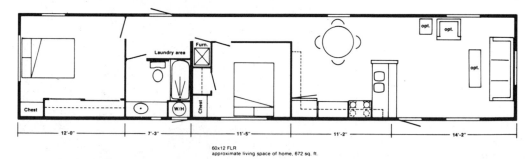

60x12 FLR
approximate living space of home, 672 sq. ft.

Figure 14-27 *A same-size home but with space utilized slightly differently. Here, the living room is moved to the end of the trailer, the bay window is dropped, and the kitchen-dinette area shifted next to the bedroom. Notice that regardless of layout, front entry is into the living room. The lengths indicated for the three floor plans shown include about 42 in. hitch length.*

Turn yourself loose in a 5th wheel . . .

Figure 14-28   Extra living space is gained at a vacation site via two tip-out rooms which can be added at any time to the 34-ft. Park Model by Monitor.

Figure 14-29   Sleeping quarters are roomier and more luxurious than you might suspect. This huge-size bedroom comes furnished with freestanding bed and chests and the room has its own private bath and dressing area. The head of the bed—beneath a sloped ceiling—is in the tipout room mentioned above.

Many—but not all—mobile parks include recreational facilities in your monthly fee. If so, you'll be spared additional expenses for joining tennis, golf, swimming, and similar clubs.

Mobile home popularity on the move. Primarily because of the soaring building costs and unstable mortgage interest rates, mobile homes currently account for more than half the family dwellings built in the United States. That claim is backed by figures released by the Mobile Homes Manufacturers Association (MHMA). According to this group, during 1974, 55 percent of the 1.1 million homes built in this country were mobile units. And the demand for this kind of housing is growing. In early 1975, practically all homes priced under $15,000, and roughly 80 percent of those under $20,000, were of the mobile variety.

Thus, it's safe to assume that the majority of today's home buyers are looking for low-cost housing more than they are mobility. This assumption is backed up by another revelation from the MHMA that "a very high percentage of mobile homes now being purchased are permanently sited."

It logically follows, then, that the number of mobile-home parks across the country is in the ascendency too. Many areas that formerly frowned on such developments are taking second looks at their zoning laws, with the result that mobile home settlements are springing up where they've never before been permitted.

From a homeowner's point of view, you should confine your search for a site to those areas with strict but fair zoning laws that are rigidly enforced. Such areas are not likely to attract unscrupulous mobile-park operators.

It has also been proved that reputable owner-operators are good risks to create sites that are comparable in quality to the better housing developments. To make certain you pick such a park, check out the community you are considering with the local building department. This arm of local government will be completely familiar with the attitudes of the owner-managers.

HOMES MANUFACTURED FOR YOUR SITE

Prefabs are designed and built by firms specializing in residential and condominium construction. They are partially put together at the factory for delivery to the jobsite.

Most prefabs are sold through builder-dealers, each having a specified area, and are not aimed at the do-it-yourself market. The purchase price includes delivery to your property and erection on foundation or piers, which you supply and pay for. Some manufacturers sell the house erected and completed only to the shell stage. Such an arrangement is perfect for the handy homeowner who wants immediate use and is willing to finish the inside.

A prefab arrives at the jobsite via a trailer equipped with a crane for the unloading and placement of parts. The manufacturer-trained crew puts the house together literally in a matter of hours—usually in two working shifts. In almost all cases, you are able to move into your new home a week after its arrival at your property.

A quick rundown of manufactured homes:

Shell Houses. A shell is exactly what the name implies—a structure consisting of walls, rough flooring, and a roof. The house is closed in to the weather (that is, finished on the outside), and exterior doors and windows are included in the purchase price. Inside is another story. You can figure on looking at open stud walls, exposed rafters, and plywood subflooring.

The usual purpose of a shell is to get the house up as fast as possible so you can get almost immediate use from it. The finish work is then generally worked on over a period of years out of current income. Since the shell can be erected for about $5,000, this approach keeps down the size of the mortgage.

To find shell-house dealers, look in the Yellow Pages under "Builders," "Contractors" and "Houses." You can also get leads on reputable dealers from local businessmen, bankers, and the lumberyard.

Generally, sales are handled by local authorized dealers who represent

Today's log cabin; a pleasant way to rough it. . . .

Great flexibility is a strong design feature of this log building; it can be used as a home, hunting lodge, chalet, or lakeside cottage. Called The Laurentide, the dwelling has five closets on the main floor plus a full-size utility room.

The parts for the log building come precut; and because the building is a simple rectangular shape, it can be erected in minimum time by a do-it-yourselfer with some experience and a healthy share of common sense. The first floor can be completed to provide an initial 962 sq. ft. of living space; the second-floor loft can be finished off at a later date to add another 572 sq. ft. of good country living. A good feature is the inside/outside fireplace; during warm weather it can be used for outdoor cooking and in the cold months it can be used to ease the heating bill by burning local firewood.

Figure 14-30

The Laurentide, Ward Cabin Company

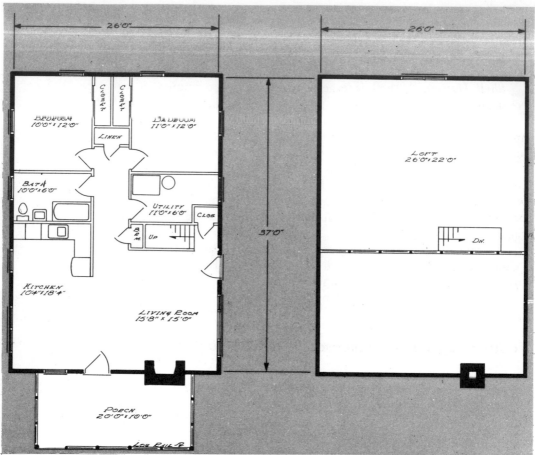

Figure 14-31

Log cabin floor plan (see Figure 14-30)

various manufacturers. In some cases, the dealer/builder will erect the structure upon your foundation walls or piers; others prefer to build the underpinnings themselves. At any rate, make certain it is clearly understood just who will take care of the foundation work before signing the contract. Also, if you choose to have the dealer/builder perform any work beyond the shell stage, make certain you have a written contract covering all phases of the work. The contract should also include an itemization of costs for the work.

Under no circumstance should you contract for a shell house without inspecting at least one actual model offered by the dealer builder. You will find that in addition to a wide selection of available shell styles, there is also considerable difference in quality from one maker to the next. Make certain the house you select will pass muster in your area; that is, it must be built so it is acceptable under the local building code.

Manufactured houses—a fast route to a quality, second-home ownership . . .

Many mistakenly think that all prefab houses look alike. Actually, one of the advantages of a prefabricated house is the versatility of component construction which allows considerable leeway when it comes to custom detailing.

On the following pages is a sampling of just what is available, and what you can do to individualize a typical manufactured house. For greater detail on any home shown, write the manufacturer. For other makers, write to the National Association of Homebuilders (see Appendix E for the addresses).

How a prefab house is built—from rough materials to moving-in:

Figure 14-32   A wide-angle view of a house factory indicates the scale of such an operation. At the center, a factory worker is assembling materials for a gable end wall. In the foreground, another worker checks out trim and molding for one-house shipment.

Figure 14-33 *A solitary worker operates the machine to assemble component members of the truss roof system used in Kingsberry homes.*

Figure 14-34 *An automatic nailing machine—note the nails in containers on drum. In this photo, sheathing is being fastened to the wall studs of the exterior wall. All large sections are machine-fastened.*

Figure 14-35 *Smaller sections of sheathing—beneath windows and over doors, for example—are cut to size and installed by factory technicians using power nailers.*

Figure 14-36 Paint is applied to various house members by a flow-coat machine. Paint that doesn't land on sheathing being coated is simply recycled and used on later pieces.

Figure 14-37 The foundation and piers are supplied by others (i.e., the owner). When a panelized house arrives at the jobsite, the foundation is carefully checked to make certain it conforms to the manufacturer's drawings and specifications for that dwelling. Once this is checked out, house erection can commence.

Figure 14-38 *A flooring system is installed on foundation walls; sub-flooring goes down using adhesive and nails.*

Figure 14-39 *Time isn't wasted by fully unloading trailer and placing panels taken from a stockpile. Instead, panels are so loaded that each can be placed in position as it is removed from the truck.*

Figure 14-40 A partially-erected dwelling. Notice that insulation and windows are already in existing walls. Both of these steps are handled at the factory.

Figure 14-41 When all walls are placed—interior partitions as well as exterior load-bearing ones—the truss roof goes up.

Kingsberry Homes Photos Courtesy of Boise-Cascade Corporation

Figure 14-42 A typical prefab dwelling is up and closed-in to the weather on the first day. It took a seven-man crew one eight-hour day to get this home to this stage of completion.

Figure 14-43 *Typical factory-built houses from this manufacturer include the Burlington (a) model shown in the photographs, pages 293-97, the Wayfarer (b), the Hatteras (c), and the Roxboro (d).*

Precut Houses. As the name suggests, these are houses that are precut— but not assembled—in the factory. Using precision methods and equipment, all framing members are precisely cut and shipped to the building location.

The price for a precut varies depending on how involved you will be as a do-it-yourselfer. You can, if desired, buy the parts, have them shipped to the site and do the building yourself. The house will probably go up faster than it would if stick-built, but keep in mind that you'll have to provide security for the materials parked on the jobsite. Precuts can be bought for as little as $1,500 for a modest cabin; most buyers, however, choose more luxurious ones, which can sell for as high as $50,000 or more.

A Panelized House. This type of dwelling consists of wall sections, put together on an assembly line, that are not completely finished. For example, exterior wall sections are usually completely finished on the outside and left with studs exposed on the inside. The interior partitions may or may not be fully closed in. These panels are then fastened together on the jobsite.

Not all panelized-house manufacturers will handle erection of the panels. If you want this done by others, be sure the point is clearly understood before you buy a panelized house.

Panelized house—up in a jiffy . . .

Open-plan living in the Birmingham model by Weston Homes permits maximum use of living space with an unimpaired choice of floor and wall areas. Some interior walls are covered with prefinished paneling, others are clad with seamless drywall. The rooms are a generous size, as can be seen in Figure 14-49. This model costs about $15,000 (exclusive of the land and foundation beneath the house).

Figure 14-44 *The erection crew uses a crane to unload the wrapped component parts consisting of floor and roof panels, interior and exterior walls, and the house mechanical core (i.e., utilities, heating, kitchen, etc.).*

Figure 14-45 *The large 4-by-12-ft. insulated, stress-skin floor panels are installed by the crew in a minimum amount of time. The home shown is erected over a crawl-space, but those built over a full basement get floor panels which come with a prefinished ceiling on the underside for installation over that space.*

Figure 14-46 *Wrapped bathroom/kitchen mechanical core—including cabinets—is lowered into position with plumbing, heating, and electrical systems factory-installed and ready for quick on-the-job connections to water, waste, and electrical lines.*

Birmingham Panelized House, Weston Homes, Inc.

Figure 14-47 *A crane lowers an exterior wall panel into place for fastening. The exterior walls feature prestained rough-sawn panel with board-and-batten design. Notice the already installed sliding windows (complete with storms and screens).*

Figure 14-48 Wood paneled interior walls are fitted to create rooms as designated in the floor plan. Since wall sections are delivered with wiring in place, make certain your local building department accepts such structures.

Birmingham Panelized House, Weston Homes, Inc.

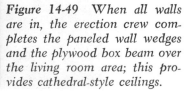

Figure 14-49 When all walls are in, the erection crew completes the paneled wall wedges and the plywood box beam over the living room area; this provides cathedral-style ceilings.

Birmingham Panelized House, Weston Homes, Inc.

Figure 14-50 *Individual 4-by-14-ft. roof panels go on next and the roof is then completed with the application of asphalt shingles. This model was closed in (sealed to the weather) by the trained crew in a single work shift.*

Figure 14-51 A practical and well-planned kitchen boasts an ample number of cabinets. These come prefinished.

Figure 14-52 A cathedral ceiling design allows individualized room planning, optional clerestory windows. The latter add decorator effect and permit maximum possible use of the room's wall area.

Birmingham Panelized House, Weston Homes, Inc.

Figure 14-53 A finished ranch home. A generous roof overhang and the wood shutters give the home a first-class look. Attention to such details is an integral part of Weston planning.

Modular—or Sectional—Houses. Completely built in the factory and then placed in position on the foundation, this type of structure has all wiring and plumbing in the walls. Because of this fact, it is neither universally nor readily accepted yet. The major objection to this type of factory-built house is that, because all utilities are in place (covered and out of sight), the local building department cannot inspect to assure conformance with local codes.

Though modular homes are usually shipped in much larger sections than other types of prefabs, highway laws do restrict shipment of modular sized pieces. Each must be less than 14-ft. wide and under 64-ft. long. This restriction, however, does not create unsolvable problems. Manufacturers simply design their houses in sections to conform to highway laws and assemble the house at the jobsite.

A modular home goes together very quickly once construction starts. Generally, it is just a matter of days before the house is ready for occupancy.

Depending upon the architectural style of your home, a modest model can run from $3 to $5 less per sq. ft. than a conventionally built house. In dollars and cents, that means that you can save anywhere from $3,000 to $5,000 on a 1,000-sq.-ft. house.

A prefab is a quick and easy way of getting into a second home. And if you assume some or all of the finishing jobs yourself, you can save a substantial amount of mortgage money.

A *modular house at a modest price . . .*

Figure 14-54   Mountain Haus, Vacation Land Homes, Inc.

Mountain Haus is a planning concept achieved by Vacation Land Homes, Inc. Basically, the house is designed using modules of 12-by-24 ft., 14-by-24 ft., 14-by-28 ft., 14-by-32 ft., and 14-by-40 ft. With these five modules, the maker places them in groups of two to five units to develop an almost unlimited number of floor plans. The various module sizes include two bedrooms to the module; a kitchen and one bath; one bath and one bedroom; and one living room and one dining room.

Designed especially with the do-it-yourselfer in mind, Mountain Haus can also be purchased for erection by the manufacturer's skilled crews.

Most important, you must evaluate your leisure-time goals, the needs of you and your family, and the possibility of either greater or lesser future needs. Once you know what you are looking for, take your time and make a selection from the great number of factory-built dwellings available today.

Figure 14-55

Mountain Haus, Vacation Land Homes, Inc.

Modular-home sections are fully assembled at the factory; here a two-man team makes quick work of putting together an interior wall. Units are completed at the factory for jobsite assembly.

Figure 14-56

Figure 14-57

Mountain Haus, Vacation Land Homes, Inc.

Figure 14-58 *Finished components are wrapped and stacked on a trailer for delivery. Notice the truck-mounted crane to speed up jobsite assembly.*

15

Condominiums—to Share or Not to Share?

What is a condominium? * *Condominium maintenance* * *How condos operate* * *Buying into a condo* * *Condominium checklist* * *Other points to consider* * *The federal government and condos* * *How to find a condo* *

As recently as the mid-1960s, the word condominium, or "condo," meant very little, if anything, to many potential home buyers. And even when condos were finally accepted and recognized as a logical and natural step in the evolution of homebuilding, few of those looking for a second home felt that such an arrangement suited their needs. But diminishing land resources and constantly escalating building costs have changed attitudes toward "joint or concurrent dominion" ownership.

As a result, for many people today the condo is the only way to own a second home. (Nevertheless, a condo is very definitely *not* the answer for many others.)

You owe it to yourself to at least investigate the present and future advantages of this type of real estate ownership. And, make no mistake about it, there are advantages.

Condos have met with phenomenal growth and acceptance in recent years. According to the National Association of Home Builders (NAHB), condominium construction in 1970 accounted for roughly 11 percent of all new residences built that year.

307

Seaside suaveness . . .

California Redwood Association

Figure 15-1 Vacation condominiums are springing up near the shore for those who favor boating and swimming. This townhouse project is completely oriented to the outdoors: Redwood plywood siding assures rugged weatherability and good looks as the structure turns a handsome silver with age. In a condo setup such as this, all owners have dock privileges. And if your condo bylaws permit, you can rent out your unit when you don't use it to help pay the tab for your second home.

WHAT IS A CONDOMINIUM?

In simplest terms, a condominium is a family unit in a large residential complex, in which the apartments or units are individually owned and (only occasionally) rented. Condominiums always have ground rules to live by and a single, central administration to manage the complex.

A condo can be practically a break-even investment under certain conditions. For example, if you use your apartment for only a few weeks during the year, you can arrange with the management to rent it out to others for the time you are not there. Under these circumstances, your condo may qualify as rental property and provide you with tax advantages. If you are buying to gain such an advantage, in part or whole, discuss all details with a lawyer and/or accountant before committing yourself to a purchase.

Depending upon the condominium development, your apartment unit may be in a high-rise structure or in a row of townhouse configurations, joined together in series of two, three, or more entities. Generally, in the leisure or second-home condo settlements, the individual units are more like

Figure 15-2 Architects James Morton and Henrik Bull and the Moana Development Company achieved their goal of providing vacation pleasure for hundreds of families with minimum disturbance of trees or shoreline in this condominium development. Planned as a comparatively low-density community (seven units per acre), Tahoe Tavern Properties sparkles with informal design, low-rise buildings, and extensive and careful landscaping—all geared to a relax-and-have-fun atmosphere.

Built for year-round use, all units are enjoyed during all seasons by owners and tenants alike.

California Redwood Association

homes than apartments. But, to conserve land and facilitate more efficient heating and cooling, the individual residences are usually built in several levels instead of ranch-house style. (Note: This can be a disadvantage for the infirm.)

CONDOMINIUM MAINTENANCE

The most appealing aspect of condo ownership, and the one most talked about, is the freedom from work—someone else does all those pesky maintenance and repair chores. You're guaranteed more time for leisure living and recreational pursuits. As a part owner of the condominium corporation, you pay for such relief by way of a monthly charge, usually levied in proportion to the value of your property.

On-the-grounds personnel maintain all equipment and services (except those inside each dwelling) and outside work, such as landscaping and the like. You'll have no grass to mow, leaves to rake, or snow to shovel. Similarly, mechanical problems, such as stopped-up water lines and overflowing septic tanks, will be handled by others.

The same staff is also available for owner jobs at reasonable cost. Thus, if it's not your bag to handle your own maintenance chores inside your apartment—or if you have no desire to take on do-it-yourself improvement tasks—you will likely have qualified people around at reasonable rates.

A year-round staff offers one other big advantage—peace of mind when you're away from the premises. Obviously, a condo is far more protected against intruders than a single-residence dwelling off by itself in the woods.

Another big advantage of condominium ownership is the access you have to many recreational facilities. Most vacation-area condos offer golf, indoor and outdoor tennis, year-round swimming pools, horseback riding, boating, skiing, hiking, and camping—you name it. Unless your funds are unlimited, there's no way to match the activities package going it alone in a house by yourself.

HOW CONDOS OPERATE

Basically a group concept, the owners pay for and share all recreational facilities and services in common. Each owner is levied a fee, which pays a management group to operate and maintain the grounds and equipment. The management group usually reports to a supervision group comprised of members elected by all the owners in the condominium.

Given the abundant services and facilities, you must ask—and answer—yourself whether you are willing to share all the facilities *all the time*. There's little doubt that a condo gives you more recreational facilities than you could hope to attain by living by yourself, but remember others have paid for—and will use—these facilities too.

Further, condominium living automatically imposes a list of do's and don'ts. For example, your group will undoubtedly have bylaws pertaining to children, guests, vehicles, and the like—questions that don't enter the minds of those living on their own property.

BUYING INTO A CONDO

Many money experts agree that putting your money into a condominium is an excellent hedge against inflation. The long-range forecasts for condominium development are extremely favorable in terms of future market values and resale potential. Such forecasts should turn out well for you provided the condominium you invest in is professionally planned, well managed, and in a highly desirable location for vacation or retirement living.

You purchase a condo in the same manner as you do a house: You either pay cash or take out a mortgage. Each owner arranges his or her own financing and pays property taxes and monthly mortgage payments. Usually, pinning down a mortgage is somewhat easier, particularly when the condo is well-managed. Because consistency of value is more-or-less guaranteed by good management, most banks lend money more quickly on a condominium than on a single residence of similar value.

You are at liberty to sell your property at any time without the approval of the corporation or other owners as long as your buyer agrees to abide by all legal regulations applying to your community. For practical reasons, such an agreement is generally required in writing.

Sunriver—A Spectacular Condominium: Sunriver, which is located just 15 miles south of Bend, Oregon, began as the joint dream of Oregonians John Gray and Don McCallum. Together with a staff of ecologists, these men created a vacation community in the midst of an unspoiled, virgin landscape.

The community consists of 5,500 acres—through which 8 ½ miles of the Deschutes River wanders. The developers' biggest concern was to assure that the balance of nature remain intact: For that reason, meadows, marshes, and riverbanks were left untouched so they would remain the home for their wildlife inhabitants.

Sunriver boasts a top-efficiency sewage system to prevent pollution from the development; and all utilities are planted beneath the ground to preserve the look of the surrounding woods.

The houses and lodges are styled to blend with the environment too. Constructed for the most part from native Northwest woods, the buildings have a very real sense of belonging, rather than invading—a design point all too often overlooked these days.

Figure 15-3 *Those who want condominium conveniences—but don't relish the thought of townhouse or apartment living—can choose to erect a single-family residence in some developments. This home is one of the typical structures permitted at Sunriver. The choice of homes in any quality development is restricted to those models offered by the builder. Such bylaws and rules prevent the intrusion of unseemly, or "far-out" architecture and inferior building materials which, over the long haul, would lessen the property values for all.*

For continuity of design throughout Sunriver, natural woods are heavily used on residential dwellings as well as on other buildings. Green belts and common areas are strategically placed throughout the entire 5,500 acres of Sunriver; open space is assured because the planned unit-development will restrict population density. Trees and green belts will not disappear at some future date to make way for more housing.

Figure 15-4 *Alone in a crowd. This handsome, contemporary single residence is highlighted by Western Red Cedar siding—another offering in a skiers' paradise, the Sunriver resort. In the background is Mt. Bachelor.*

Figure 15-5 *A third single-residence structure emphasizes the thought that went into architectural planning here. Though dwellings all blend with their surroundings, each has individuality.*

Figure 15-6 For those who prefer a stark, contemporary look, Sunriver offers this Pole House. Contrary to the popularly held opinion that all dwellings must look alike in a condominium community, builders of quality condos give a choice of three, four, or more living units to select from.

Figure 15-7 A ranch cabin designed by Zaik/Miller/Butler AIA of Portland, Oregon. The architects drew their design inspiration from nineteenth-century central Oregon ranch houses, noted for their barnboard construction, peaked corrugated galvanized metal roofs, and exterior stove pipes.

Figure 15-8 These cabins are comfortably and sturdily built and fashioned mostly from natural materials—native woods and stones. The rough-hewn poles inside and out, for example, are created from whole lodgepole pines.

Figure 15-9 Sunriver's shopping-center complex is centrally located with its buildings designed to look more like dwellings than stores—the commercial look was studiously avoided here. Attention to details is what makes all structures in this community pleasant to look at. For instance, notice the laminated beam in the open area under the roof. Such quality in detail work elevates this community from ordinary or run-of-the-mill developments.

Figure 15-10 Unique shops open onto a central, pine shaded mall.

Figure 15-11 Many condo developments include at least one championship golf course. The eighteenth hole at the Oregon development is shown here; the main lodge, which houses locker rooms, the social center, and a restaurant, is in the background.

Figure 15-12 *This massive and impressive structure around which the community's social life centers, The Lodge, is built primarily of local stones and woods. The grounds are kept extra-clean by a year-round maintenance staff. Salaries for the staff are provided by monthly charges levied upon the property owners.*

CONDOMINIUM CHECKLIST

To protect your investment, there are several aspects of condo ownership you should look into before plunking down your hard-earned dollars:

1. Check the background of the managing corporation to determine its track record. Evaluate its professional qualifications to operate a condo.

2. If the community that you are considering is a new one, check out the builder and the contractors involved. Your lawyer and the local bank can help on this score.

3. If the condo has been in existence for a period of time, carefully assess its financial record; if the group is well-handled, management will be proud to reveal these records to you.

4. Make certain you read and understand the condo's master declaration and bylaws before signing any papers. If you have youngsters, for example, does the group have health regulations and safety laws to protect you and

your children? Are small children supervised at the various facilities to assure their safety?

5. Find out whether there are any restrictions to your selling or renting your property.

6. Try to determine how much of a voice you will have in the conduct of community affairs.

7. Itemize your assessments (costs) and then weigh these figures against what it might cost you to buy or build a similar private home.

8. Make certain you have a lawyer check into your personal liability in the event the development fails financially or becomes a defendant in a lawsuit.

9. At any rate, before signing any papers or turning over any monies, discuss the condominium with your lawyer (and/or accountant if tax advantages are of concern). Obviously, an expert's advice is a must here.

THE FEDERAL GOVERNMENT AND CONDOMINIUMS

The condominium market, at present, is closely regulated in relatively few states. At the same time there have been widespread complaints of unfair and hidden fees, long-term control by builders, and other problems.

Since the condominium business is booming, and condo developments are expected to make up half the nation's housing supply in the next 20 years, many consumers feel that condominium sales should be regulated by the government. Builders, of course, disagree. At the same time, others are concerned that federal involvement will, in fact, drive up prices, primarily because builders will simply pass-on to consumers any regulatory expenses.

In the mid-seventies, a number of legislative proposals were introduced in Congress aimed at giving the government substantive regulatory powers. At the least, these bills would compel developers to make full disclosure of relevant facts.

Though this area is currently being studied by legislators, the Federal Trade Commission and H.U.D., regulatory steps are not expected to come for a while, but come they will, according to those who claim to be in the know. It's merely a matter of time.

HOW TO FIND A CONDO

To learn if any condominiums are under construction or in the planning stages in the area in which you plan to settle, consult the same reliable sources you would in looking for a private house. Local businessmen, bankers, realtors, and attorneys are usually aware of any condo activity in the immediate area. You can also check advertisements in the real estate sections of most Sunday newspapers.

The same local businessmen can give you an almost instant reading on the quality of an active condo operation too. That is, they can be expected to reliably evaluate whether the operation is legitimate or simply a fly-by-night scheme.

As in any venture that means a large commitment of capital, you must proceed slowly and with the help of experts in building, real estate, law, taxation, and accounting. By following your common-sense, you should be able to make a wise decision of lasting satisfaction.

16

The Basics of
Kitchen
and Bath Planning

Kitchen talk * *Overall kitchen planning: location, floor plan, kitchen shapes, equipment placement, appliances,* * *Planning work centers* * *Styling a kitchen* * *Planning a bathroom* * *Bath location* * *Bath ventilating* * *Bathroom noises and privacy* * *Heating* * *Lighting* * *Room layout* * *Bathroom fixtures* * *Bathroom trim and fittings* * *Finishing a bathroom* *

For obvious reasons, the kitchen and bathroom are the two most expensive rooms in your home. Both rooms are furnished as soon as installation is completed, and both require heavier investments in plumbing, heating, and electrical work than any other room in the house. Yet many homeowners, unless they purchased spanking-new homes, had little choice as to the locations of these rooms in their primary homes and the arrangement of fixtures within them. Those who bought their primary homes second-hand had to take these rooms as they came.

Whether buying or building your second home, you have the opportunity to create a bath and kitchen that reflects your preferences and tastes. So by all means give these rooms the thought and attention they deserve.

Few vacationing housekeepers care to leave behind the conveniences they have in their primary homes. No matter how rustic or informal the setting may be in your second home, you and your family will very likely want at least the kitchen and bath to be as up-to-date as the budget allows. The kitchens and baths discussed in this chapter, therefore, are based on the assumption that your home has either gas, electricity, or both supplied by the power company. Lacking these utilities, you have little choice but to equip and live with a kitchen as discussed in Chapter Seven under "Tenting Out."

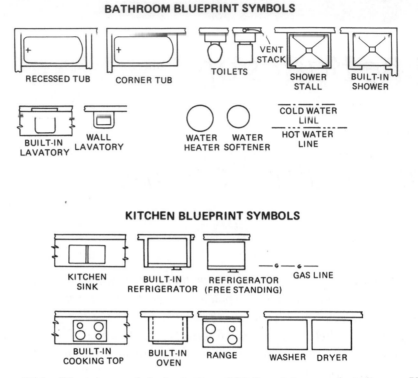

Figure 16-1 *Blueprint symbols for bath and kitchen fixtures and appliances. Use these symbols if you are preparing your own floor plan.*

For openers, keep in mind that once you have fitted these rooms with cabinets, appliances, fixtures, and the like, there is little you can do to change either room's efficiency or looks without spending a sizable sum of money. But if your planning is sound from the beginning, there isn't even the remotest possibility of discontent.

KITCHEN TALK

To assure that your design thinking is on target, start by deciding just what kitchen style you prefer to live with. Your personal interests will influence your choices: For example, are you an active homemaker? Is your family large or small? Or, are you an extra-sophisticated gourmet chef whose idea of bliss is a cooking session in a well-planned kitchen? In these cases, your interests are best served by a kitchen that's both step-saving and easy to care for.

On the other hand, if cooking is more a chore for you than fun, then esthetics, accessorizing with colors, and the like will probably be more important as far as you're concerned. If this is the case, in all likelihood you will

Figure 16-2   Kitchen architectural standards. Dimensions are important in kitchen-cabinet installation; any variance from conventional working and reaching heights and depths will result in a kitchen that is uncomfortable to work in. Base cabinets must be set level; use undercourse shingles to shim if necessary. Fasten the cabinets to wall studs using the proper size wood screws through rails at the rear of the cabinets. Hanging wall cabinets must also be plumbed and leveled before securing with screws.

An enclosed soffit over the hangers is made by building a ladder-like structure of 1-by-3 furring and covering with plasterboard or paneling.

KITCHEN ARCHITECTURAL STANDARDS

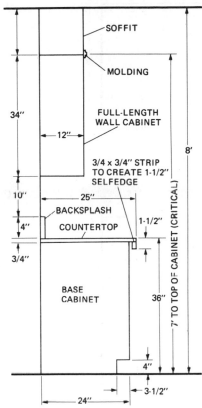

have to sacrifice some functional convenience in order to achieve "the look" you have your mind set on.

Early in the game, you should decide just what you prefer as far as decor goes. Do you consider the profuse use of natural wood a must, or would you rather look at bright, bold colors in both solids and patterns? Should walls be paneled, papered, or painted? Ceiling treatment? And how about floor covering? These are all design decisions you will have to make.

The size, ages, and lifestyle of a family should be carefully considered when planning a kitchen. A large family with small children, for example, is in the kitchen a lot more than a family with kids that are grown. Further, will your youngsters be at your second home for the entire vacation season? Or will several or all of them be off on trips of their own? Will they have friends staying over for extended visits?

Take into account your family's dining habits. It makes a difference whether you all sit down to formal meals at prescribed times, or various members of the family straggle in and out of the kitchen at all hours of the day for quickie snacks.

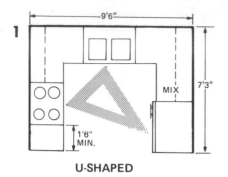

U-SHAPED

L-SHAPED

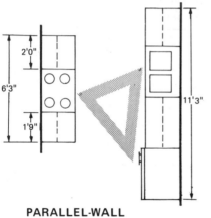

PARALLEL-WALL

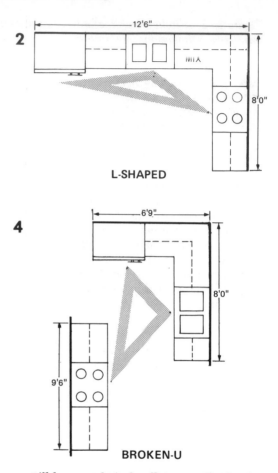

BROKEN-U

Figure 16-3 *Four typical kitchen arrangements.* In all likelihood, your kitchen will bear a strong resemblance to one of these shapes. The U-shaped is the most efficient, while the broken-U is the least desirable. The arrangements illustrate good placement of equipment and the minimum amount of counter space required for working comfort.

1. **U-shaped kitchen:** Here the sink is placed at the middle, with food storage and cook centers to both sides. The basic work triangle consists of three relatively short equal-length legs. This, plus the fact that no through-traffic interferes with the triangle, is what makes this the most desirable shape of all for a kitchen. 2. **L-shaped:** If an island or peninsula were added, this would become a U-shaped kitchen. If not, you

can still have a relatively efficient work triangle. The width of each work area shown here is based on recommended counter widths (see Figure 16-2). 3. **Parallel-wall arrangement:** If you must live with this kitchen, try to locate doors so traffic does not interfere with the work triangle. 4. **Broken-U kitchen arrangement:** In this floor plan, the range is located in an "island"; alternate choices would be to put either the refrigerator or the sink into this run of countertop. The broken-U floor plan is often found in older homes; in new home construction, creation of such a shape should be studiously avoided. As can be seen, the work triangle is inefficient, and in the plan shown the storage is minimal.

And your architect, if you are working with one, should be just as familiar with the answers to these questions as you are.

OVERALL KITCHEN PLANNING

In broad terms, there are seven considerations when planning a kitchen:

1. Room location,
2. floor plan,
3. room shape,
4. equipment placement,
5. appliances,
6. work centers, and
7. styling.

1. Location. Depending on how you acquire your second home, you may or may not be able to control kitchen location on the floor plan. If you opt for an older home, for instance, there is little you can do without getting into a major remodeling project—tearing out walls, building an addition, or the like. If you are building from stock plans, the architect has already specified where these rooms are to be placed; shifting them about at this stage can only cause an appreciable increase in building costs. In short, unless you are working with an architect to customize your house, the time to evaluate kitchen location is before you ever buy.

Here's what you should think about when looking at houses and stock plans:

a. Does the kitchen have an exterior door with access to the garage or carport? Such an arrangement is more than a luxury when it comes to hauling in groceries from weekly shopping trips. An exterior door in or near the kitchen also saves trips back and forth over carpeted floors in other rooms. You can also consider it a plus if there is easy access to your patio or deck from the kitchen; it's a bonus if your lifestyle calls for frequent entertaining or dining out on the deck.

b. If possible, the kitchen should be adjacent to and overlook the main activity area—i.e., the family room. Housing experts estimate that approximately 50 percent of your time is spent in the kitchen, thus, it makes sense to spare yourself any extra steps to check the children's activities. You'll also appreciate having the family room close by the kitchen even if you do not have small children: When you have guests in, you can be part of the crowd no matter how much time you have to spend in the kitchen. For these reasons, an open kitchen is usually the first-choice for leisure-home buyers.

2. Floor Plan. Most kitchen planning experts agree that the total square footage in a kitchen should be no less than 100 sq. ft., and no more than

150–160 sq. ft. If these figures are hard to visualize, keep in mind that 100 square feet is a modest 10 by 10 ft. That's not much space if you want a completely equipped kitchen.

On the other hand, a kitchen can become inefficient if the work centers are spread out too much. As floor space increases, the distance between the primary work centers—the sink (washing and preparation), the range (cooking), and refrigerator (storage)—usually increases. Ideally, the three work centers should create a triangle whose three sides add up to not more than 22 feet. The more you enlarge this triangle, the more you pay in the form of increased steps and wasted energy.

To place equipment most efficiently, doors and windows must be located with care. A lot of wall space broken by unnecessary or misplaced doors and windows creates an inferior layout.

3. Kitchen Shapes. At first, "shape" may be misinterpreted to mean "floor plan." It doesn't. Instead, the floor plan usually refers to the location of the room in relation to the other rooms of the house; and sometimes interior designers use the phrase to define equipment layout in the room. The shape, on the other hand, is the outline of the room itself; obviously, therefore, shape plays a very important part in finalizing the location of equipment in the room.

Not all kitchen arrangements are equally efficient. The U-shaped kitchen, for instance, is the most efficient: The big advantage is the control that you have over the distance between the work centers. Often, you can create a U-shaped kitchen where you would ordinarily have an L-shaped room by adding an island or peninsula to the cabinet run. For maximum efficiency, a U-shaped kitchen should be no narrower than 10 feet between the faces of opposite base cabinets.

Here's how other kitchen arrangements stack up in comparison:

Corridor (parallel wall) kitchen. With this shape, a work arrangement almost as efficient as the U-shape can be created. But, more than likely, you will have a time of it resolving the problems created by the traffic through the room. A corridor arrangement is generally dictated by the placement of doors at both ends of the room. The result is usually congestion in the work area at the busiest time of the day. This, of course, is unsafe as well as annoying to the cook.

One-Wall kitchen. If the room is small or narrow, a one-wall kitchen is probably your only choice. Reconcile yourself to the fact that cabinet storage space will be minimal, and that it is impossible to create an efficient work triangle.

In a one-wall kitchen you have no choice but to live with long traffic patterns. However, if the distance from one end of the cabinet run to the other is not too great—somewhere around 10 ft.—the kitchen equipment can still be arranged rather efficiently (see Figure 16-4).

Broken-U Arrangement. This kind of kitchen is commonly found in older homes in which the wall placement dictates the positioning of the

ONE WALL KITCHEN

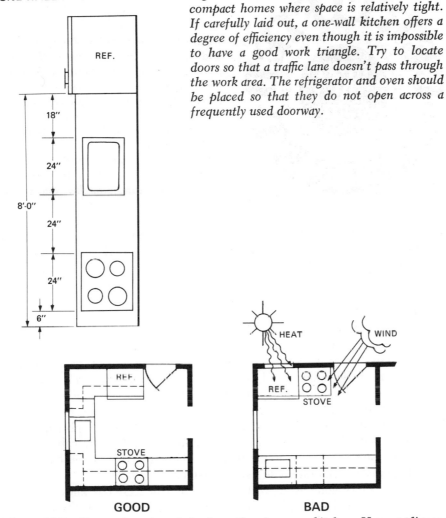

Figure 16-4 One-wall kitchens are found in compact homes where space is relatively tight. If carefully laid out, a one-wall kitchen offers a degree of efficiency even though it is impossible to have a good work triangle. Try to locate doors so that a traffic lane doesn't pass through the work area. The refrigerator and oven should be placed so that they do not open across a frequently used doorway.

GOOD　　　　**BAD**

Figure 16-5 Keep energy in mind when planning your kitchen. How appliances are positioned affects their efficiency. For example, a refrigerator near a radiator or in the direct sunlight has to work much harder than necessary. Similarly, a stove near a doorway or opened window overworks to keep hot.

cabinet runs. By far the least desirable kitchen arrangement, it should be scrupulously avoided in new construction.

4. *Equipment Placement.* To effectively locate equipment, you should evaluate your family's pattern of living as well as your work habits. List all those things that both please and annoy you in your primary-home kitchen. Hopefully, you can then duplicate the good features and eliminate the bad in your leisure-home kitchen.

Figure 16-6   When shopping for kitchen and bathroom cabinets, look for the certification seal of the National Kitchen Cabinet Association. The seal—carried on the insides of doors and drawers—assures that the cabinets meet construction and performance standards of the American National Standards Institute (ANSI). To earn the seal, cabinets must pass stringent tests of their ability to withstand hard use, moisture, scratches, and stains.

Other features in a kitchen. For many, a planning center is a must—an organized location for paper work, menu planning, check-writing, and the like. You also have to decide whether you want a phone in the kitchen, and, if so, whether it should be a wall or countertop model. Also, will your budget permit such creature comforts as built-in intercoms, warming trays, toasters, and the like? These features should be considered now when their installation is least expensive.

Before laying out any money, put your ideas down on paper. Measure the room exactly and make an easy-to-read scale drawing of the room. Include the locations, heights, and widths of all doors and windows; this is important when it comes to figuring which cabinets to install. Professional kitchen planners make up their drawings using ½-in. scale; you are well advised to work in the same size. With the room accurately drawn on graph paper, you can then proceed to lay out the work centers, i.e., kitchen cabinets and appliances. Since you are working in scale, check the legs of the basic work triangle to make certain it doesn't get too large.

When you've gone as far with drawing as you feel your knowledge can take you, visit the local cabinet shop to go over the plan with the expert-in-residence. Besides making certain that the layout is efficient, he or she can give you a pretty good estimate of what your cabinetry and other equipment is going to cost.

5. Appliances. Over the long pull, you come out ahead if you buy quality equipment from reputable dealers. Unknown brands, as well as "handyman" and "builder" specials, more often than not leave the buyer with the short end of the stick.

Today all appliances are available in a variety of colors, as well as in the traditional white, to suit all decors. The more expensive models boast fronts that can be fitted with rectangles of paneling or plastic laminate, which makes them virtually invisible in the row of cabinets into which they are installed.

When buying an appliance, remember that the more extras you add on, the more you pay initially and the more you pay in the long run for repairs and service. *Every* appliance performs the basic task for which it is intended. For example, a brand-name dishwasher washes dishes even if it is the manufacturer's bottom-of-the-line model. Though the same dishwasher, outfitted with all kinds of extra cycles, costs $100 or so more than the first model, it doesn't wash dishes any better than its lower-priced cousin. All it does, however, is make your task somewhat easier, a convenience for which you will pay because that elaborate gadgetry contains wear-points that require periodic servicing.

Refrigerators and freezers. Due mainly to more efficient insulation, refrigerators today have increased capacity while fitting into the same floor space that the older units occupied. Superior insulation allows the walls to be thinner, and the saved space creates greater capacity.

An important point to remember when selecting a refrigerator is whether the door opens to the right or left: The door, of course, should open so that contents can be transported from the unit in a direct line to a nearby countertop.

If your family's eating habits demand, you might consider installing a combination refrigerator-freezer in your second home. These come as two-door models with the freezer compartment door located horizontally across either top or bottom. There are also units as narrow as 30 in. that come fitted with two vertical doors.

Figure 16-7 A freezer over the refrigerator in a Coldspot model from Sears permits a lot of food storage in relatively few cubic feet of space. This model boasts epoxy-coated shelving that, it is claimed, resists abrasion, corrosion, humidity, staining, and repeated cleanings.

Figure 16-8 *Appliances with extras are available too. Sears has added an ice cube maker to several of its latest models in the Coldspot line. Optional extras add to the cost of the appliance, but in no way increase efficiency of the unit to do its basic job.*

Like all appliances, refrigerators with a host of extras are also available. At extra cost you can pick adjustable shelves, automatic ice-makers, chilled water in the door, no-frost models, crushed ice and ice cubes, and models with a meat-keeper that will store meat for a week without freezing.

Sinks. If you haven't bought a sink lately, you are likely to be surprised at the variety of styles, shapes, and sizes now available. The most commonly installed kitchen sink is the single-bowl type but, depending upon your work habits, you may prefer a double- or triple-bowl at your vacation home.

Sinks come in stainless steel and porcelain in a variety of decorator colors. If you have the counter space and can afford the expenditure, you might give some thought to putting in a pair of sinks. Two sinks are a great convenience in any kitchen where two people frequently work at the same time.

If you are not on a septic system, and the municipality permits such discharge into its sewage lines, you can choose a sink with a separate opening for a garbage disposal unit. Usually, this type of sink has a step-down styling; vegetables are washed and peeled in the upper-level sink, and the cuttings are then simply pushed and rinsed into the disposer opening.

While your thoughts are concentrated on the sink area, inspect some of the newer items now available for installation on the sink. Disregarding appearance, most of these extras are practical—not just luxury items: in way of examples, an instant hot-water dispenser (great for tea and instant soups), detergent and hand-lotion dispensers, and a water spray head on a flexible

Figure 16-9 A useful addition to any kitchen is a bar sink. The stainless steel model shown measures 15 by 15 in. and has a soft-satin bowl finish, flush fittings, and a sound dampener. This Harvest bar sink by American-Standard, shown with an Aquamix bar fitting and gooseneck spout, is available with either one, two, or three holes in the fittings deck.

Figure 16-10 Before installing an in-sink disposer, make certain your municipality allows them. Do not use a disposer if your waste goes to a septic field.

Typical sink fittings (faucets) . . .

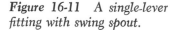
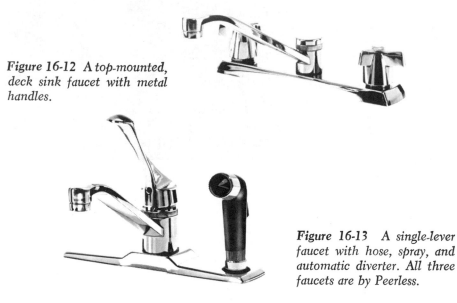

Figure 16-11 *A single-lever fitting with swing spout.*

Figure 16-12 *A top-mounted, deck sink faucet with metal handles.*

Figure 16-13 *A single-lever faucet with hose, spray, and automatic diverter. All three faucets are by Peerless.*

hose. In order to install any of these sink-mounted items you must purchase a sink that accepts them. These features are simply mounted in holes in the sink (provided when a factory-stamped knockout plug is removed).

The final touch for you may be a trash compacter. One of these can save you a lot of trips to the municipal dump.

Ranges and cooktops. As can be seen in the photographs on these pages, there are a number of ranges to choose from. The right one for you depends on the space available in your kitchen and your work habits. All versions are sold in both gas and electric models.

A wide array of extra features are available on both types of ranges—griddles, automatic timers, lights, special broiling devices, rotisseries, barbeques—some even have built-in ventilating systems. Finally, many ranges

Figure 16-14 *Double-oven in this GE cook center features one oven above and a second below the cook range.*

This drop-in cooktop fits into the cutout in a kitchen countertop. Both the electric and gas models shown are from Sears.

Figure 16-15 *Electric cooktop.*

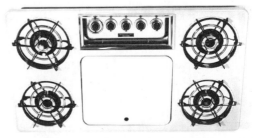

Figure 16-16 *Gas cooktop.*

Figure 16-17   This double wall oven is mated with a countertop cooktop; the oven is installed in the wall cabinet which gives storage space above and below it.

come with continuous cleaning or self-cleaning benefits, though the latter have dropped somewhat in popularity recently because of the high cost of gas and electricity.

If your preference is for a wall-mounted oven, you'll find that these come in both double- and single-oven styles. Once again, your way of working and eating should decide which is better for you. Obviously, if you do a lot of cooking and baking, the double-oven model should be your choice.

6. Planning Work Centers. There are three primary work centers in a kitchen:

Food storage consists primarily of the refrigerator, but can also include a pantry or cabinet storage. For maximum convenience, the storage center should have from 18 to 24 inches of counter space on the latch side of the refrigerator door. There should also be adequate counter surface conveniently close to cabinets used for food storage.

Food preparation—the sink. Since much kitchen activity occurs at the sink center, there should be 36 inches of counter space on both sides of the

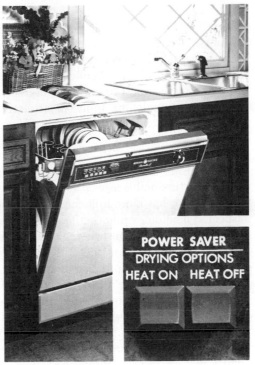

Figure 16-18 The energy crunch has triggered efforts by appliance makers to cut down consumption by their kitchen appliances. GE's Power Saver option on this dishwasher is claimed to save up to 40 percent of the power needed for a normal cycle. The idea is to turn off the heat when the wash cycle is completed, crack the door, and allow warm air—instead of an energy-consuming element—to do the drying.

sink. You'll need at least that much space for stacking dishes, handling foodstuffs, and other sink-related activities.

Cooking center—the range and oven. For safety reasons, make certain you have a minimum of 24 inches of counter adjoining one side of your range. If you should have to put down a heated pot or roasting pan in a hurry, a nearby counter can avert a tragedy.

The complete kitchen boasts other centers as well. Ideally, for example, you'll have the space to install a mixing center, consisting of about 40 inches of counter space close to a cabinet where all mixing utensils are stored.

A serving center is most often located near the cooking center, or it can be an island or other counter that makes the transfer of food from cook center to table more convenient.

7. *Styling a Kitchen.* No one wants a kitchen with "the blahs." But what can you do to make sure yours won't end up being dull or unappealing? There are many things you can do.

One step is the proper use of color. Bright, gay colors are stimulating and do much to create an impressive room with a happy look. But don't make the mistake of thinking that because a touch of bold is good, that a lot of bold is better. "Tain't necessarily so." On a moderate basis, colors can make a room exciting and imaginative. But living with hues on a daily basis can be mind-boggling.

It is possible, however, to use strong colors in a kitchen without creating a nerve-jangling effect. For example, in place of an overpowering, brilliant turquoise, consider using instead a soft, forest green or subtle colonial blue. You can also bring exciting—but tamed—reds into play but, as a rule of thumb, the use of warm colors should be kept to a minimum in what is ordinarily the warmest room in the house.

You may prefer to apply an attractively patterned wallcovering. With the advent of prepasted products, wallpapering is no longer the sticky mess it used to be. For practical reasons, select one of the fabric wallcoverings. These no longer have the shiny oilcloth look; rather, they're available in several finishes including some that look exactly like quality wallpaper. And most are extra-durable as well as washable.

The floor has more influence on the look of the kitchen than you might suspect. Therefore, while the floor-covering should be selected with care, it is the one part of the room where you can afford to be a little adventurous with a strong color. To be on the safe side, key your floor selection so it complements the color used on the countertop surface.

Lighting can make all the difference in the world, too. Make certain you have an adequate number of fixtures, both fluorescent and incandescent. You need good lighting for efficient working conditions as well as for mood lighting. Consider treatment of the windows both from the standpoint of function and appearance. If there is adequate artificial light in the room, shades may be just the thing; if so, pick bright colors or attractive patterns. They'll add a decorative touch. If you prefer letting sunlight filter in rather than shutting it out completely, you may decide on bamboo or slatted Venetian blinds.

The final touch in your kitchen is the highlighting by decorative accessories. Whether your home is decorated in contemporary, traditional, or early American decor, the small items will either make or break the room. Perhaps more than anything else, these reflect the tastes of the owners. Accessories needn't be elaborate. An antique jug here, a cooking utensil there, an arrangement of living plants may be all you need in the way of decorative touches.

Professional Help. Give serious thought to putting the entire kitchen-design problem in the hands of a qualified kitchen specialist. A specialist is especially capable and qualified. Unlike home remodelers, builders, plumbing contractors, even many architects and interior designers, a kitchen specialist has the specific know-how when it comes to kitchen planning. Even relatively handy people must be considered inexperienced at kitchen installation, compared with a specialist. Thus there is little doubt that a kitchen specialist can come closer to producing your dream kitchen than you can on your own. Though some kitchen remodelers take on other rooms, such as bath and family "rec" rooms, most of them stick to the room they know best.

In the long run, a professional saves you time and money. By using a professional, you relieve yourself of the scores of details involved in every kitchen job. You don't have to research kitchen-construction details or spend an inordinate amount of time planning and coordinating the work schedule for the various trades. Also, mistakes made in planning the kitchen are often costly ones, and the risk of erring on a kitchen project is greater than for most building or remodeling projects. If you make an error on a kitchen cabinet, for example, you'll have to live with it—that is, absorb the cost. Why not therefore let the specialists make and correct their own mistakes?

Kitchen Ventilation. In today's airtight homes, a kitchen exhaust fan is no longer considered a luxury: One should definitely be included in your kitchen planning.

Of the two types, ducted and nonducted, the first removes all odors, smoke, and moisture from the air to the outside. Once a ducted fan has done its job and removed air pollutants, it should be turned off to conserve energy. A large kitchen fan left running for a half-hour or so will lower the house temperature considerably. Nonducted hood fans, on the other hand, will not lower room temperature. These draw in contaminated air, process it through charcoal and screen filters, and return the same air to the room. Used primarily when it is impossible to install a ducted hood fan because of range placement along an interior wall, nonducted hoods are also commonly installed in the cabinet over built-in wall ovens.

Figure 16-19 This ducted hood with a custom look from Nutone Division of Scovill, can be used with any of ten different power units—three are inside-mounted and seven are exterior-mounted. The latter type puts the fan and its noise on the outside of the house; this is a significant improvement in home venting.

Figure 16-20   This nonducted fan from Nutone is designed for installation where ducting is not feasible. Three hard-working filters include a washable aluminum-mesh grease filter, a fiberglass smoke filter, and a charcoal odor filter. The hood also features twin lights enclosed in tough Lexan plastic.

Though markedly less efficient than a ducted hood fan, a nonducted hood is a better choice than a wall-mounted exhaust fan that is a number of feet away from the cook range. If you must use a nonducted hood, consider pairing it with a wall-mounted exhaust fan. The hood fan can be used to remove pollutants from the air and turned off. The wall exhaust fan can then be turned on to remove heat, moisture, and odors.

The Home Ventilating Institute recommends the following standards of air changes for wall or ceiling fans. In the kitchen, the fan should be rated as capable of 15 air changes per hour; in the bathroom, 8; in the family, recreation, or laundry room, 6.

To figure the ability of a wall or ceiling fan to deliver the needed air movement (the CFM, or cubic-feet-per-minute capacity), multiply the floor area (assuming an 8-ft. ceiling) by the appropriate factor, as follows: kitchen, 2; bathroom, 1.07; family recreation or laundry room, 0.8. Thus, for example, a 100-sq.-ft. kitchen requires a 200-CFM fan.

A different criterion applies to range hood fans. The recommended minimums are 40 CFM per lineal foot of range hood for placement along the wall, and 50 CFM per lineal foot for peninsula or island placement. In most cases, you are well advised to install a hood fan with a rating that is higher than the minimum that you compute.

Figure 16-21 No overhead hood is required with Jenn-Air's exclusive surface ventilation system. This system draws smoke and cooking odors through an exhaust vent in the center of the range, and vents them to the outdoors. The continuous cleaning oven is also power-vented to exhaust heat and smoke outdoors.

Figure 16-22 A centralized radio intercom pipes music throughout the house via twenty remote speaker locations, offering convenience because calls can be answered from all speakers. This model by Nutone also has auxiliary jacks in the master station for adding a record changer and an eight-track tape player if desired. For convenience sake, the master station is generally located in the kitchen.

Figure 16-23 Because they require less maintenance, kitchen cabinets covered with a high-pressure laminate such as Formica® are installed by many homeowners. With this surface, rubbing and polishing are eliminated, and surfaces clean up with a damp cloth.

Features you may want to add to your kitchen . . .

Figure 16-24 A slide-out cutting board.

Figure 16-25   Slide-out shelves.

Figure 16-26   A hostess cart.

Photos: Long-Bell Division/International Paper Co.

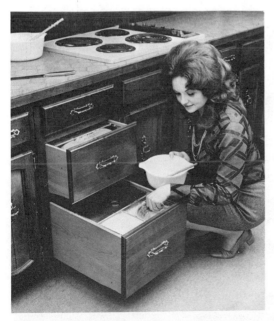

Figure 16-27   Bread and flour drawers.

Figure 16-28   A slide-out lid and tray rack.

Photos: Long-Bell Division/International Paper Co.

Figure 16-29   A 90° *lazy Susan* (*base cabi-net*).

Figure 16-30   A 45° *lazy Susan* (*wall cabi-net*).

Figure 16-31   Bold patterns of wallpaper and shade blend harmoniously with woodgrained cabinets by H. J. Scheirich Co.

Figure 16-32 In this section of a one-wall arrangement, note the use of recessed eyeball lights overhead. Good lighting is a must in a working kitchen.

Figure 16-33 Let your imagination run wild in your leisure home. Here, the dining area is separated from the kitchen by a good-sized "potting shed," which also provides storage. The decor in this setting was selected with an eye to Mother Nature—so rich wood tones play against the highlighted Tiffany glass in the lamp and window panels. The clay pots become as decorative as they are functional; and wicker, cane, and straw complete the natural pageantry of accessories. Walls, which appear to be authentic brick, are actually clad with sheet-type brick. The floor is protected by GAF Sure-Stik vinyl asbestos tiles in a quarry-tile motif. The room design is by Virginia Frankel, AID.

Figure 16-34 This warm and friendly kitchen/dining room emphasizes today's easy-going lifestyle. Outdoors is interchangeable with indoors—bleached woods, wicker baskets, stainless flatware, cook-and-serve casseroles, plastic utensils, and perky paper products underscore the simplified approach to living you should aim for in your second home. Designer Abbey Darer created this Scandinavian look by starting with Gafstar Deluxe no-wax cushioned vinyl flooring. Called Ambrosia, the floorcovering provides a soft splash of yellows, blues, and white.

PLANNING A BATHROOM

Like the kitchen, the bathroom should be furnished with care. Allow enough time to choose fixture styles as well as colors—and more importantly, to evaluate your service needs—so that you can utilize the available space most effectively.

In years past, bathrooms received little or no attention from the designer. The layout was more or less haphazard, consisting simply of positioning the three fixtures so that they could be easily connected to the water and waste lines. Usually, walls were clad with square or rectangular ceramic tile, and the floor was treated with octagonal tiles, generally white.

Happily, that picture has changed. Fixtures now come in an accommodating selection of styles and colors, and materials for floors and walls are just as exciting. A modern bathroom has new status; it is now possible to plan and execute a bathroom with taste and flair.

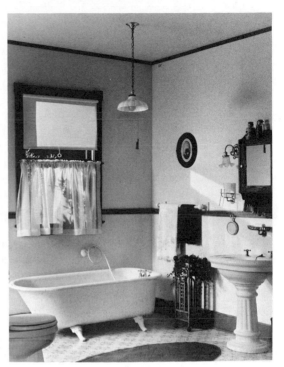

Figure 16-35 Typical bath in an older home: Though charming and nostalgic, it leaves much to be desired as far as comfort is concerned. The curtains flutter because of drafts around an old window, lights dim due to inadequate wiring, clinical walls look cold, and the floor is cold underfoot.

Figure 16-36 The same room, remodeled with today's new colors and materials, moves out of the past and into the present. To begin, the cold-looking walls were covered with a pink and orange shell vinyl design by General Tire called Coral Reef. The outside of the tub and leg-hiding moldings below are painted purple, and the new window is dressed with shutters. To complete the setting, a divider to conceal the toilet, shelves, theatrical lighting, and a bathroom rug, related to the color scheme, were added.

Bath Location. If you are building from stock plans or erecting a manufactured house, there is little you can do about the bath location. That's why it is so important, whether buying or building, that you analyze *all* your service needs before committing yourself to a particular house. Where the bathroom is located in the floor plan should carry as much weight, when making a purchase decision, as the size of kitchen or the number of bedrooms.

Conversely, if you are custom building, make certain that you discuss all the factors concerning bath location with the architect, who will consider all of the intangibles and decide which location is the best for you. Discuss whether you want the bath to be an exterior room (on the perimeter of the house) or an interior room. With advantages and disadvantages to both, the best kind for you is determined by your family's lifestyle and the total number of bathrooms in the house.

For example, with good planning, an adjunct bath to the master bedroom might be fitted with a second door so it can also be used as a powder room when you are entertaining. Or, if your home is served by two or more baths and your long-range plans include a swimming pool, consider placing one of the bathrooms on the building perimeter so it can double as a shower and dressing room. If there are many small children in your family, it may be practical to install a bath with multiple lavatory facilities. A bath intended for such use should be situated to serve primarily, if not exclusively, the youngsters' rooms.

Bath Ventilating. Building codes require that all baths be vented. If the room is located on the perimeter of the building, a movable (that is operable) window satisfies the requirement.

Interior bathrooms, however, must be mechanically vented. A bathroom exhaust fan should be sized to suit the room using the formula spelled out in the section on kitchens. If the fan switch is wired into the light switch, the fan switch can be left to go on and off automatically with the light switch. For practical reasons, a fan switch with variable-speed settings makes sense; this type lets you select an air speed to suit particular demands.

To be effective, an exhaust fan must be supplied with a steady supply of fresh air. This "makeup air" replaces the air drawn out through the exhaust fan. In most cases, makeup air is supplied by creating a gap between the door and floor.

Bathroom Noises and Privacy. When installing a bathroom, consideration should be given to acoustics. Sounds emanating from a bathroom—whether mechanical or human—are easily identifiable and often a source of embarrassment. Most people try to mask such embarrassing sounds with another noise such as running water or an exhaust fan.

Noises escape easily from bathrooms because of their design. To assure cleanliness and waterproofing, most materials used in a bathroom have hard surfaces and therefore reflect noises. Happily, designers and manufacturers have turned their attention to this problem, and materials are now becoming available to help to reduce sound levels by absorption. Carpeting especially designed for use in bathrooms is one such product. Just make certain you pick a type that can be cleaned frequently and with relative ease.

There are several other measures you can take to cut down noise emanations. For one thing, excessive undercutting of the bathroom door to provide makeup air for venting, aggravates the noise situation to a great degree; a proper ventilation system, however, allows a tighter door fit which proportionately reduces noise transmission. Wrapping pipes with insulation will also muffle sounds somewhat, but for even greater privacy, use blanket or batt insulation in bathroom walls. To get maximum soundproofing, you can frame bath walls with double-studding and weave insulation horizontally between studs. You should also plug holes in the walls (through which pipes pass) with a sound-absorbing material. Closets, window drapes, and the like also help to muffle sounds; this, of course, also increases privacy.

Heating. The size of a bathroom room heater (that is, a radiator or vent) is calculated using the same formula applicable to every other room in the house. Thus, the heating unit will provide you with sufficient comfort most of the time—but not all of the time, such as when you are showering or taking a bath. Thus, because of nudity, wetness, and a considerable drop in temperature when stepping from tub or shower, it is desirable to have a supplementary source of quick heat in the bathroom. Generally, such heat is provided by a wall- or ceiling-mounted electric space heater.

Several types of bathroom heaters are available, with and without blowers; which one is best for you is mostly a matter of personal preference. However, the unit you select should at least be U.L. Listed, and it should be installed so that there is no chance of a person accidentally burning himself by making contact with the heater.

Room heaters also help to dissipate moisture which would otherwise condense on the walls and ceiling.

Lighting. Besides overall illumination in a bathroom, you need supplementary lighting for special purposes; the obvious ones are for grooming and shaving at the dressing table and lavatory. Lights at these locations should be carefully positioned to avoid glare and strong shadows. Even the bulbs used in a bathroom should be chosen with care to avoid color distortion.

Special lighting may also be called for if the overall room lighting is inadequate. Many stall showers and enclosed bathtubs, for example, would be safer if better lighted. Here, the fixture must be waterproof.

At any rate, do not depend upon a window as the primary source of light. At night, of course, no light comes in via the window and during the day, privacy may demand that the shades remain drawn.

Room Layout. Three factors determine how you lay out your bathroom:

1. room size,
2. location of waste line, and
3. other uses you may want to get from the room.

Adequate lighting is a must in bathrooms . . .

Figure 16-37 Good-looking bath fixtures don't have to be expensive. Attractive, but low-cost, lighting called Lightline features satin-glass globes and a pewter finish. A 72-in. swag chain lets you put the light where it's needed.

You may have to manipulate space a bit if you plan to use the bathroom as a steam, sauna, dressing room, laundry center, or the like. Draw the room in scale on graph paper, and then, using scaled drawings of room fixtures, move the fixtures about in an attempt to achieve maximum room efficiency. At this stage, if you find that you have the room, consider installing a bidet. If so, locate this fixture next to the toilet for the sake of convenience.

For economy in plumbing, bathrooms are generally located side-by-side with the kitchen; thus, common water and waste lines serve both rooms to reduce plumbing installation costs. In two-level homes, the same reasoning generally dictates the placement of the bathroom directly over the kitchen. For similar reasons, if bathrooms are installed back-to-back, the fixtures should be located on the common wall. Be careful here, though: Many codes require all fixtures served by a vent stack to be within a 6-ft. radius of that stack. Check your local code to be safe.

Bathroom Fixtures. The sink (or washbasin). Basically of two types—wall-hung (often partially supported by a pair of legs) and counter (that is, dropped into a countertop over a cabinet called a vanity)—a wide selection of sinks are available today.

Either type of washbasin can be a stainless steel, porcelain enamel over cast iron, plastic, or vitreous china. The last type is the most commonly used bathroom sink in residential dwellings.

The wall-hungs are available in a variety of sizes and shapes—some as small as 12 inches wide, others more than 30 inches in width.

When you shop for counter-surface sinks, you may be surprised by the number of shapes, styles, and colors available. You can buy these round, oval, and rectangular. Some are mounted using a setting (Hudee) rim, while others are self-sealing.

Figure 16-38 A pedestal lavatory, by American-Standard, is available in brown, blue, gold, bayberry, bone, fawn beige, and white. Called Elisse, the sink won an award for design from the New York Museum of Modern Art—where it is now on permanent display.

The tub. The most commonly used tub is the rectangular type, which comes in lengths of 4½, 5, 5½, and 6 feet and in widths from roughly 28 to 32 inches. A tub can be purchased to suit perfectly the spot it will occupy. For example, you can buy a tub with both ends open for recessing in a niche, with one end open for a corner installation, or with both ends closed if the tub must be freestanding along a wall.

Although tub openings usually follow the outline of the tub, some are contoured—that is, the oval is angled slightly within the tub outline to create ledges for sitting or storing supplies.

The receptor tub is more or less square, generally either three or four feet. Intended to serve as a modified bath as well as a shower base, they are frequently installed where space is at a premium.

A sunken tub is somewhat more elegant than most and has strong appeal to those with a sensuous inclination. Before making the decision to install one of these, however, be aware that they do cost more initially and require more work and expense to install.

Today, tubs are made of porcelain enamel over cast iron or enameled steel (less expensive, but noisier). Relatively new ones on the market, made of reinforced or acrylic-faced fiberglass, are gaining in popularity because they eliminate mildew problems and the age-old chore of periodic grouting at the

A tub recess kit is designed for do-it-yourself remodeling and new construction jobs. The kit contains all the necessary material for a standard 5-ft. tub recess area—paneling, precut moldings, nails, caulking, and adhesive. They're available at local building materials suppliers.

Figure 16-39   To install the "bath-in-a-box," the do-it-yourselfer establishes guidelines for the edge moldings, caulks the tub rim along the wall, and then fits and installs the tub moldings.

Figure 16-40   A 5-ft.-wide back panel is fitted, and adhesive is applied to the wall and to the panel back. Corner- and top-edge moldings are fitted, caulked, and applied next.

Figure 16-41   The side panel goes up with openings already cut for the plumbing pipes. Tub and corner moldings are then caulked, and additional caulking waterseals the plumbing openings.

Figure 16-42   Finally, the Marlite panel is coated with adhesive and fitted into place.

Figure 16-43 *After the harmonizing tub and corner moldings are caulked, edge moldings are fitted and applied, and the plumbing fittings are replaced. The final step is to clean off the excess adhesive and caulking.*

wall-tub joint. Some makers now offer tubs complete with wall surround, which arrive at the jobsite in one or more pieces—depending on the maker —and eliminate entirely the problems noted above, which are so common with tiled bathroom walls.

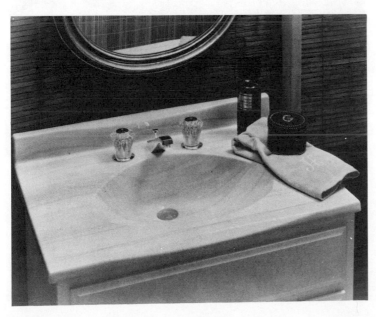

Figure 16-44 *A molded one-piece oval sink top eliminates the joints between sink and countertop. The version shown is by Kohler Company..*

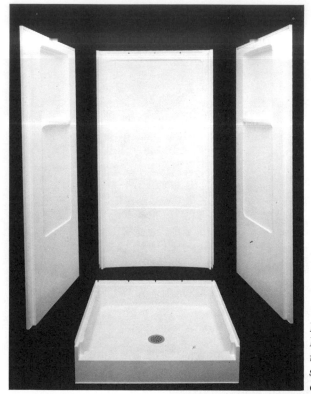

Figure 16-45 *Kit from Owens/Corning Fiberglas helps speed up bath installation, comes as shown. The manufacturer supplies complete installation how-to data with all units it offers.*

Figure *16-46 One-control faucet, Centura (Kohler Co.), features push-pull control. It's chromium-plated.*

Toilets. Usually of china, you can pick either a wall-hung or standing model. Wall-hungs are generally off the floor and greatly facilitate cleaning, though they require extra carpentry in the wall to provide an adequate support hanger.

Although a toilet is available with a flushometer or power flush, which obviates the need for a tank, you are probably better off buying the two-piece tank type. Admittedly, the power-flush toilet eliminates working parts and a great deal of servicing, but it is noisy; it also requires very strong water pressure, a luxury not always available in rural locations. On the other hand, the two-piece type, with a tank that contains clean water for flushing, is the quieter of the two types.

Toilets come with extra features: these include built-in ventilating systems that eliminate odors before they reach the room; a nonoverflow toilet; and a water-saving toilet for the ecologically-minded.

The bidet, designed expressly for perineal hygiene, wasn't even considered for use in most American homes until recently. Happily, misconceptions and unjust taboos concerning it are disappearing, and the fixture is being installed in a growing number of new homes.

Bidets, manufactured by most bathroom fixture makers in colors and styles to suit the other fixtures in the bathroom, look like seatless toilets. For convenience, locate the bidet next to the toilet.

Figure 16-47 Good bath idea number one: Kohler's 34-by-36-in. shower cove. It boasts roomy corner ledges for soap and toiletries, as well as rounded corners for easy clean-up.

Figure 16-48 Good bath idea number two: A fiberglass bath module offers freedom of design and construction. One-piece modules are tough, sturdy, and easily moved by two men. Called "Walls 'n All" by Kohler Co., construction eliminates seams, crevices, and hard-to-clean grout.

Figure 16-49 A dry sanitary toilet, called Destroilet, is simply a toilet and an incinerator contained in one small unit. Specifically designed for efficient disposal of human waste, the system can be used anywhere that there is a source of 115-volt electricity and a supply of either bottled or natural gas. Unit is recommended for use where septic systems are impractical, where waste disposal is a problem, or where the danger of pollution exists.

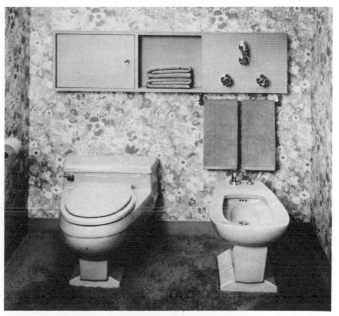

Figure 16-50 *Bidets provide the ultimate in personal hygiene. A companion to the toilet, a bidet is a fixture for use in cleaning the perineal area of the body after using the toilet. Installation of a bidet does not require extensive additional plumbing. The Barcelona Bidet by Eljer, with matching toilet, is shown.*

Figure 16-51 *Good bath idea number three: If possible, install an accordion door between the toilet-bath and vanity areas. The door can be quickly pulled into a closed position to hide an untidy tub that kids left behind.*

Stall showers. A typical shower unit measures 2½ ft. square by about 6 ft. in height. The standard shower is a two-piece design that includes a receptor base of metal or precast terrazzo and enameled metal sides.

Growing in popularity these days—and not without justification—are the one-piece showers of fiberglass-reinforced plastic. These units come complete; you simply set them in place and make the connections to the rough plumbing (that is, the water and waste lines).

DO'S AND DON'TS OF BATHROOM FIXTURE CARE

DO wash fixtures regularly with soap and water.

DON'T use harsh abrasives to clean fixtures; abrasives scratch.

DO wipe up immediately any medicines that contain acid substances; these can cause permanent staining.

DON'T overload the medicine cabinet; items may fall from it and damage the lavatory.

DO use a bathmat to protect the tub's finish if you must stand in the tub to clean the walls.

DON'T use photographic chemicals in bathroom; these have potent staining ability.

DO repair drippy faucets quickly. Constant dripping can create hard-water mineral deposits leaving a permanent stain.

DO use naphtha-based laundry soap—plus a dash of kerosene—to remove a stain from the lavatory basin that soap and water don't remove.

DON'T use cleansers with an acid or bleach base—these dull the fixture's gloss, eat into the surface, and encourage future staining.

(Excerpted from "The Eljer Plan" booklet.)

Bathroom Trim and Fittings. Lately, bathroom hardware manufacturers have gone all out to improve both the quality and service of bathroom fittings. For example, there are now washerless cartridges, single-control faucets, push-pull controls, and lever controls. And in the shower, though the idea of mixing valves has been around a while, new versions are better than ever.

Bathroom hardware is an important part of your overall decorating scheme. To help you effectively create a particular mood, you can choose finishes from chrome, pewter, and brass as well as from solid brass, gold, ceramic, and crystal-like acrylics (plastic). The newest entry in the bath-trim field are handles and waterspouts of brightly-colored plastic.

Finishing a Bathroom. Probably more than any other single factor, attention by designers in recent years has definitely elevated the bathroom in decorating status. What was considered a necessary evil of sorts—that is, an outhouse moved indoors—not too many years ago, is often one of the most attractive rooms in today's homes. Most building and decorating experts agree that the breakthrough in bath design and decorating was made possible by the introduction and acceptance of the counter-surface lavatories. These, while eliminating freestanding and wall-hung sinks, also created the need for ready-made cabinets into which the washbasins could be dropped.

This new bath furniture opened up new opportunities in bath decor through sophisticated cabinetry. Equally important, vanities provide much-needed storage space. As a result, there are now vanities in styles ranging from extra-simple to super-sophisticated. Happily, there are also many quality-built, well designed cabinets to choose from in a reasonable price range.

You should also be aware that many cheaply built, bottom-of-the-line vanities—which are certain to cause more of a headache than pleasure—are on the market. Constructed of either wood or metal, a well-built vanity is finished to provide maximum resistance to damage from moisture and water. The top is generally of a high-pressure laminate (such as Formica®) over a plywood or particle board core. Other materials often used for tops include marble, slate, flagstone, and ceramic tile.

Great bath ideas you may want to copy . . .

Figure 16-52 Clean lines, simplicity of design, and low-cost white fixtures make this bath an easy room to live with. Walls are covered with board paneling applied vertically over furring strips.

Figure 16-53 A contemporary bath by Eljer. Notice the paneling motif applied to the large vanity and surrounding the tub; this repeats the texture and pattern of the walls.

Figure 16-54 For extra durability, you can use ceramic tile. In this room suggested by the Tile Council of America, the unusual scoring of standard-size wall tiles creates a neat, linear look. This feeling is gracefully enhanced with inserts of decorative wall tiles. White octagonal tiles alternate with blue and white square-dot tiles to cover the spacious floor with a contrasting, crisp pattern.

Figure 16-55 Something to dream about: If your bathroom is living-room sized, you can consider creating the illusion of a sunken tub by framing the bathtub with lumber as shown. For looks, lumber should be either all-heart redwood or high-quality birch. To avoid unpleasant stains, seal the wood with a waterproof finish.

When deciding on a material with which to clad your bathroom walls, choose one that gives maximum resistance to steam, moisture, and water. Because of this criterion, ceramic-tile walls have long been a favored material for use on bath walls and floor. If you decide to go with tile, pick a high-glaze type for the walls. For safety, though, floor tiles should be of a type with a skidproof glaze surface.

Less expensive than ceramic tile, yet sturdy and durable, are laminated panels of hardboard that come in 16-in. (or wider) panels. Installed with connectors at all joints to keep out water, hardboards are manufactured in many colors and patterns to simulate wood, marble, stone, and other natural finishes; the latest entries also include patterns of pop and deco art and colonial motifs. Laminated hardboards are installed over plasterboard using mastic and a minimal number of nails. The vinyl-clad metal grid system that keeps water out of the joints also serves to hold the panels in place.

A new development for bathroom walls is the high-pressure laminate wall systems (the same material that's used on countertops, but thinner). Made up in prefitted wall panels, installation is relatively easy and certainly within the range of a do-it-yourselfer's skills.

Using Colors in the Bath. When it comes to picking colors, use the same criteria as for the kitchen. Don't consider the bathroom any different, for that matter, from the other rooms in your home. Don't hesitate to make effective use of bright or even bold colors, but follow the guidelines of most professional decorators when splashing color here and there: *Be bold but don't overpower.* In other words, don't get carried away with a color or pattern because it is eye-catching on a one-time basis. More important, ask yourself if you will be able to live with the color or decorating scheme on a daily basis.

Both the kitchen and bath, more than the other rooms in the house, serve very functional purposes. Therefore they must first be laid out for top efficiency, and secondly for esthetic appeal. There is no reason, however, why they cannot be just as attractive and pleasant as the rest of your home.

17

Closing Down Your Leisure Home at End of Season

* Where to start * Protection against vermin * Keeping pests out * Theft and vandalism * Plumbing * Electric and gas * Final close-down steps *

For those who use their vacation homes during the warm months only, Labor Day more or less marks the end of season. Shortly after this holiday, most schools reopen, and the intervening week or so at the primary home is needed to get the kids outfitted for the coming school year. But before leaving for the winter, you have to take several measures to assure your coming back to the house as you left it.

In fact, there are several things that you must protect your property from, such as damage or loss caused by:

* pests (vermin),
* vandalism and theft,
* weather and elements, and
* fire and damage from utilities.

Since there are many details to be remembered, a checklist of all of the closing-down steps is sensible. Chores should also be split up and assigned to each member of the family; there is no reason for Mom and Dad to do all the work. By organizing and working from such a list, you will not only speed up the task, you will also minimize the possibility of forgetting an important item. And in the spring, you simply reverse the steps on the list to get the house ready for the summer.

WHERE TO START

For one thing, sometime during the summer, discuss your homeowner's insurance policy with your insurance agent to learn whether any conditions must be met to assure your policy remaining in full force when the house is closed down.

Outside the House. At summer's end, begin by making a careful inspection of the grounds. Look for and remove any dead branches or limbs leaning dangerously toward or close to the house. Besides the chance of physical damage from limbs downed by storms, overhanging branches are favored entry routes by squirrels, raccoons, and other pests.

There are other steps you should take outside too; here's a quick rundown:

1. Clean out all gutters and leaders.
2. Repair and replace any loose roof shingles.
3. Point up (patch loose mortar joints) any loose chimney bricks.
4. Clear any accumulation of debris from the crawlspace area.
5. Check garbage cans and make certain that all of them are fitted with tight-fitting covers. Scrub the cans with soap and water, rinse them with disinfectant, and store them out of the weather. (Throw out damaged and uncovered cans.)

While outside, you can put your boat to bed too. If possible, your boat should be drydocked in either of three ways:

a. at the local marina,
b. at your year-round residence, or
c. on your vacation-home property.

The first two methods obviously simplify your chore immensely. But, if you elect to do the winterizing at your vacation-home property, follow these simple guidelines:

1. Pick an area near the house on the opposite side from prevailing winds.
2. If your boat is a small one, you can store it on sawhorses. To do so, flop the boat and lash it down securely with stout cords.
3. Once your boat is stowed, check your dock, mooring lines, and accessories for any loose gear that may be stored in and lashed to the boat.
4. Larger boats can be stored on a trailer, but you must provide maximum protection against weather damage and vandalism.

PROTECTION AGAINST VERMIN

Rodents just love to occupy a vacated home. Because they are comfortably protected from both weather and predators, pests find an empty house a delightful place to rear their young. Unfortunately, they can—and usually do —create an unbelievable amount of damage once they've gained entry: Curtains, mattresses, pillows, and the like all provide dandy lining for nests. A heavy infestation of pests over a single winter can create damage adding up to thousands of dollars.

For maximum protection against such a disaster, start by cleaning out all foodstuffs. The usual solution is to keep all foods in tightly sealed metal containers or glass jars to protect against mildew as well as rodents. Any foods packed in cardboard containers (cereals, flour, and the like) not only serve as prime attracters for rodents, they will also bring on weevils if left undisturbed for a period of time.

If you plan to use your cabin on weekends and intend to leave food in the house, you are well advised to line at least one cabinet and its drawers with sheet metal or aluminum to serve as a pest-proof food pantry. A fast and easy way to gain such a food storage area is to purchase a ready-made bread box that can be simply dropped into a deep drawer. Measure the drawer first—or, bring it with you to the cabinet shop for a custom fitting.

If you will not use your cabin at all over the winter, remove *all* foods from the premises. If you can't use them at home, throw them in the pile of debris to be hauled to the dump before you leave for good. This includes, of course, any liquids in jars and cans. In cold snow country these may burst their containers when temperatures drop below freezing.

Keeping Pests Out. Pests enter a home through the slightest of cracks. Enlarging a small hole around a pipe entering a house from below is a simple task for a rat. The usual protection is to securely anchor metal collars around all pipes that enter a home from the crawlspace. Given a place to stand and operate from, rats will chew their way through any wood surface. Unfortunately, a foundation-wall ledge usually provides a convenient place for them to park while gnawing their way through the subfloor and floor above. Thus, keep your crawlspace cleared of all debris and fill in, if possible, any areas below the joists where rats may get a toehold.

Flues and stovepipes should be tightly capped: These too provide a favored method of entry for vermin—and birds, which also do a great deal of damage. You can fashion a chimney cap from galvanized sheet metal. Make certain the cap is tight-fitting and securely fastened to the chimney. As soon as you cap your chimney, post a large sign in your fireplace flagging you to uncover the chimney before you light a fire next spring. If your stovepipe lacks a screened hood, a 2-lb. coffee can makes a perfect cap. Finally, close all dampers for extra protection. (Capping unheated chimneys and stovepipes also protects them from rust.)

The odor of camphor will do much to discourage entry by pests because they simply do not like the smell. As a final protective measure, scatter a liberal number of mothballs in every room of the house. Use mothballs, instead of flakes, because they are easier to clean up when you return; place them between mattresses and springs, under chair cushions, and in other likely nesting spots. But keep in mind that camphor evaporates when exposed to air; thus you may wish to have your caretaker replenish the supply every six weeks or so.

In any event, do not set rodent traps: Decomposition over the winter can cause an odor that will be difficult to eliminate. Neither should you sprinkle poisons about. The risk of forgetting about them next spring, and their being found and ingested by a small child or family pet, is too great.

THEFT AND VANDALISM

Actually, there is very little that you can do to protect your property from thieves, especially if your place is off by itself in the woods.

If you have year-round neighbors, their presence will do much to discourage illegal entry—especially if your place is protected so that the culprits will be forced to make undue noise to gain entry. For that reason, you should invest in top-quality window and door locks; these offer considerably more protection than the bottom-of-the-line models. Although slick professionals have both the know-how and tools to overcome any lock, the more sophisticated safeguards do discourage kids, amateurs, and hunters who are simply looking for shelter or a place to sleep. Unfortunately, when the nonprofessionals gain entry, they often cause as much damage and dollar loss as their professional counterparts.

You can usually hire a local resident who, for a nominal fee, will keep an eye on your place during your absence. To avoid any chance of misunderstanding, discuss and agree upon the fee and the chores. In fact, it might be a good idea to type up a list of duties and indicate the agreed-upon wages. Both parties should initial the agreement and receive a copy.

In the final analysis, the smartest move you can make is to leave nothing of great value behind. That's what thieves are after and if you leave shades up so potential burglars can make a visual inspection through your windows, they'll generally pass the place that is lacking expensive TV sets, hi-fi units, and the like.

PLUMBING

If the temperature in your area drops below freezing each winter, you will have to drain all lines to avoid bursting pipes. Even if your home is in a warmer climate, you still ought to close down the plumbing; if a pipe should burst (that is, a soldered joint break open) during your absence, the cost of the resulting water damage to both furniture and home could be truly monumental.

Shut off the water supply main and drain all lines. Open the valves on all fixtures, drain the fittings at their lowest points, and leave the valves open. If the fixture lacks a valve (or plug), leave the faucets in the full-open position. If a small amount of water remains in the valves, it can be removed by rigging a section of hose to the outlet (pressure) side of your vacuum cleaner and blowing out the fixture. If your vacation home is closed while the temperature is still moderate, any small amounts of water remaining in fixtures will evaporate prior to arrival of freezing temperatures. Drain or siphon water from the toilet tank and remove every last bit with a sponge.

Pour about one cup of permanent-type antifreeze in every trap in the house. (Don't forget the bathtub has a trap too.) Pour two cups of permanent-type antifreeze in the toilet bowl. If you have a dishwasher, add a small amount of permanent-type antifreeze to it since a small amount of water remains in most dishwashers. If this water is allowed to freeze, there is a strong chance that the washer's gaskets will be destroyed; and, that repair is troublesome and can be expensive.

The water pump and wellpoint systems vary depending upon the type of installation. The first time around, your best bet is to have your plumber show you what to do to close down the water system. Make it a point to write down all the steps so that you'll know exactly how to repeat the job the following year.

If you'd rather not close down your water lines yourself, you can ask a plumber to handle this chore for you. Whether closing down the system in the fall, or reactivating it next spring, a plumber will charge about $50 for each visit.

ELECTRIC AND GAS

If your house is serviced by electricity, power should be shut off at the main (on the entrance service panel) unless some appliance must be kept in operation. If current must remain on, all nonworking appliances, lamps, and the like, should be unplugged from their outlets because of risk of animals gnawing at the wires.

Natural-gas appliances should be shut down to pilot-light operation; today, approved appliances have built-in safeties (shut-offs) should a malfunction occur. Older appliances do not have such protection and should be turned off entirely.

LP gas appliances can be entirely shut off, and the LP tank should be shut off too.

FINAL CLOSE-DOWN STEPS

Make certain your refrigerator is thoroughly washed down and its door left in a propped-open position. Failure to leave the door open will create a heavy, musty odor that will be almost impossible to eliminate later.

Before leaving, make a final check to assure that all combustible materials—paints, solvents, cleaning fluids, and the like are removed from the house. Similarly, if matches must be left behind, they should be stored in metal cans fitted with covers—there's always the possibility that hungry vermin will start a fire by gnawing on a wooden match head.

Next, check all windows, screens or storms, and doors to make certain they are securely locked.

And, finally, close and lock the front door—and look forward to next year!

18

This and That About Leisure-Home Living

*Decks, terraces and patios * Patio shape * Patio materials *
Fencing * Fence materials * Getting garden ideas * Landscaping:
the environment around your home * Piers and floats * Float materials
* Outdoor lighting * Basics of outdoor lighting * Types of fixtures
* Ideas for lightscaping: automation, accent lighting, eliminate hazards,
lights for dining, lawn games * Low-voltage light systems * Security
—uptight or out of sight? * Protection against vandalism and theft *
What about locks? * Types of locks * Burglar alarms * Fire
protection * Vacation-home lifestyle * Life at home *

Once you've settled into your new second home, only you will know for sure whether your work is finished. Your preferred lifestyle (and that of your neighbors) will pretty much determine the amount of work you'll want (or have) to do around the property. One thing is fairly certain, however: If you plan ultimately to retire to your second home, now is the time to put in the extras (the pool, patio, and the like)—not later, when you are forced to live on a fixed income.

If you do need more living space and gain a great deal of satisfaction from outdoor living, as many people do these days, you will find that in a deck, terrace or patio. One or the other is sure to rank high on a list of things to add to your leisure home. Whether you want a transition area from house to nature, a sun trap, or an extension of indoor living, a deck is unquestionably the least expensive way to gain more living space.

Western Wood Products Association

Figure 18-1 *A leisure-home setting on beautiful Puget Sound, in western Washington. Notice the profusion of decking, which is common to homes located near the shore. Deck is laid with grid-like pattern—the planking in each section runs perpendicular to the planking in sections it abuts.*

DECKS, TERRACES, PATIOS

The words—"deck," "patio," and "terrace"—don't mean exactly the same thing. Practically, they are one and the same, but architecturally there is a difference. Here are the definitions accepted by most in the building industry:

* A *deck* is a flat, floored, roofless area adjoining a house which may or may not jut out from the house.
* A *terrace* can be any relatively level area either paved or planted (that is, a lawn) adjoining a building.
* Architecturally, a *patio* is defined as an inner court open to the sky, or a recreation area that adjoins a building. Thus, patios are usually paved with one of many types of materials. Also, patios are generally especially well-suited for outdoor dining.

California Redwood Association Photo

Figure 18-2 *For safety on this hilly site, architect Philip P. Conley specified screening between deck and railing on the fence surrounding the house.*

By any name, all are intended to serve as fair-weather extensions of indoor living space. For example, a deck is often used for Sunday morning brunches and informal family dining, as well as for barbecues and parties. For the sake of clarity here, the word deck when used, will imply an outdoor family room of any type.

Firmly entrenched as part of the American lifestyle, outdoor living is greatly enhanced by a deck. In fact, the majority of architects consider a patio or terrace an integral part of a vacation home's design. Often called "outdoor family rooms," decks bring with them a way of life that most of us consider indispensable for vacation living. This feeling becomes obvious when you study the floor plans for the homes shown throughout this book; practically every one of them features a deck.

Functionally and esthetically too, these outdoor areas are intended to serve a role as part of planned living space. More often than not, a deck is the architectural element that makes a home design work. In many cases, if the deck is eliminated, the home's architectural lines are effectively destroyed.

Architect: Ron Senna
Owner: Louise Rigg

Figure 18-3 Wrap-around decks are usually an integral part of architectural design. Here, an unusual railing effect is created from a combination of plywood and lumber while the decking is of two different widths of boards.

Many outdoor-living buffs who literally live on their decks choose to erect a roof so that they can use the area no matter what the weather. Similarly, if your plans call for a lot of outdoor night life, you'll want to screen in the area between roof and floor to keep out mosquitos and other night-flying insects.

If a deck is not indicated in your house plans and you'd like to add one, there are some rules-of-thumb you can lean on to choose the best location:

* A small deck can be installed next to an entry but, if privacy is important, add a privacy screen (built in conjunction with the platform).
* Any deck intended primarily for use as a dining area should be located to assure maximum efficiency between it and the kitchen. In order to enjoy outdoor eating, service from the kitchen should be as effortless as possible.

Typical do-it-yourself raised deck . . .

A raised deck is called for on hilly sites common to vacation home properties. Details for building a typical raised deck are shown in Figures 18-4 and 18-5. Three basic suggestions when building an attached deck such as this include: (1) To make certain the deck is properly footed and anchored to provide adequate rigidity; (2) To check the local building code because construction of such a structure falls within it; and (3) To get the longest life from your deck, treat all wood members with a preservative and use only noncorrosive nails and fasteners for all construction.

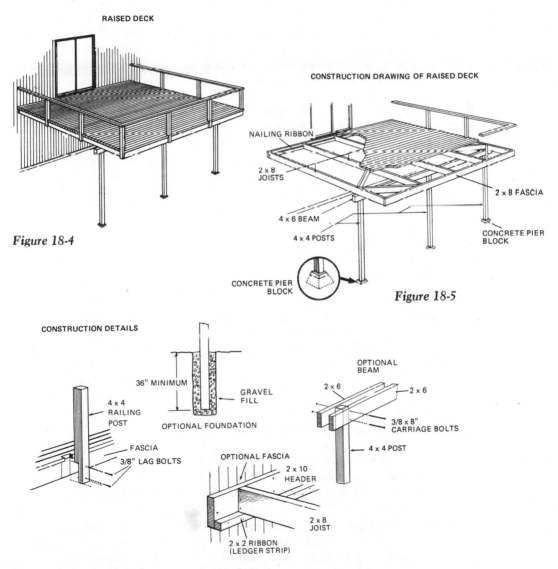

Figure 18-4

Figure 18-5

Figure 18-6 Good deck construction techniques.

Drawings Courtesy Western Wood Products Association

* Use a multilevel deck if the terrain demands one; the design can be modified to suit the land. But remember, since strength is important for any deck, it is extra important when it comes to decks built on hilly ground. Ask your local building department to look over your proposed deck plan to make certain it is a structurally sound one.

* Carefully plan the deck's location. Sun and wind are the dominant elements to consider when it comes to planning an outdoor family room. Since strong winds from the northwest can be expected during autumn, winter, and spring, it is therefore best to locate dining and entertaining patios on the south or southeast side of the house. If your patio must face southwest, try to place it so that tall trees will cast shade on it during the late afternoon hours. You can also consider installing a windbreak such as a fence, storage shed, or garage to gain protection from heavy winds.

Before you start to build your deck, check local building codes to determine whether or not a permit is required.

Patio Shape. Once you have picked the location, you must decide on the shape. You can, of course, erect an exotic shape, such as an initial inside a heart, but by and large you would be wise to stick to one of the simpler geometric shapes, such as a circle, square, or rectangle. In any event, try to coordinate the look of your garden plan, deck, and house, or the overall effect might be disastrous.

Patio Materials. What to pave your patio with is your next decision. Since so many different types of materials are available for decks and patios and almost all of them can be tailored to fit any design or pattern, your major consideration may be simply how much money you want to spend.

Concrete. Even if you simply install a slab of concrete, there are a number of ways you can pour a concrete slab to create different looks. A slab can be contained in a gridwork of stained 2-by-4 lumber; color can be added, or stone aggregate can be exposed to create a texture, among many other options. If preferred, a slab can be covered with one of the outdoor carpets intended for such use; these come in green and in a texture resembling turf, or in gaily striped, colorful patterns for the bold and adventurous.

Wood. If you build your deck with wood, follow these simple rules to increase the longevity of your investment:

* Use either cedar or construction-heart redwood anywhere the wood comes into contact with the ground. These woods are also recommended for use as any member of the structure that's within 6 inches of grade.

* For decking, railings, benches, and the like, choose construction-common redwood, well known for its superior resistance to attack by termites. But Idaho pine, Douglas fir, or Engelmann spruce have greater rigidity and strength.

TYPICAL PATIO PAVING MATERIALS

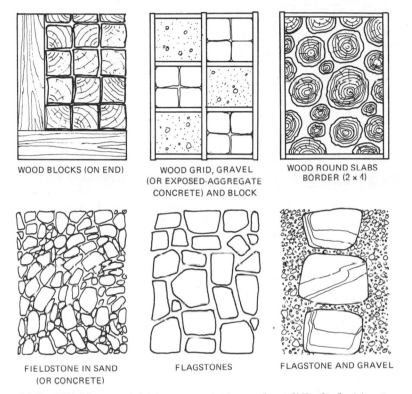

WOOD BLOCKS (ON END)

WOOD GRID, GRAVEL
(OR EXPOSED-AGGREGATE
CONCRETE) AND BLOCK

WOOD ROUND SLABS
BORDER (2 x 4)

FIELDSTONE IN SAND
(OR CONCRETE)

FLAGSTONES

FLAGSTONE AND GRAVEL

Figure 18-7 *Which material to use on a patio can be a difficult decision to make because of the variety of materials available. You will simply have to decide which you like best and whether you can afford it. The types shown here can all be installed by a do-it-yourselfer, but you are well advised to visit your local library to do some research on patio construction.*

* No matter which wood you use, treat the entire deck with a wood preservative such as creosote. On redwood, use a water repellent to help stabilize the wood's color at buckskin tan. Before applying a wood preservative, take the time to read the maker's instructions on the can and follow them to the letter. *Make certain you wear safety goggles and protect your skin when using creosote, or other wood preservatives.*

* Use only corrosion-resistant nails and fasteners to assemble a wood patio, or it will soon be covered with ugly, black rust marks. Stainless steel or aluminum alloy nails are recommended. Top-quality hot-dipped galvanized are also acceptable if the galvanized coating is not damaged during nailing. Though noncorrosive nails cost slightly more

PATTERNS FOR BRICK PATIOS

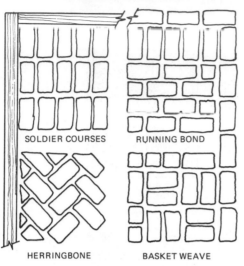

SOLDIER COURSES   RUNNING BOND

HERRINGBONE   BASKET WEAVE

Figure 18-8 Next to wood, brick is probably the most popular patio-paving material. Bricks can be laid to form patios of literally any shape or design, and they are relatively inexpensive. If the patio bricks are set in sand—rather than in concrete—only minimal pitch is required. Border, or surround, for brick patios is usually constructed of redwood or used railroad ties. To locate the latter in your area, look in the Yellow Pages under "Ties, Railroad."

than ordinary ones, their superior performance more than justifies the extra expense.

Do not use plain iron, steel, or cement-coated nails, or nails galvanized by other than the hot-dip process. When these fasteners come into contact with moisture they corrode and lose their holding power.

Bricks. There are many reasons why bricks have always been a favorite patio material. Extremely versatile, they can be laid to suit almost any form or design. They are, further, relatively inexpensive, easy to install, perfectly termite proof, and obviously long-wearing.

For patio paving, use only "hard-burned" bricks and pass up the cheaper, less durable ones. You may work with either glazed or unglazed bricks (with a rough finish). Order all your bricks at one time because colors vary from one batch to the next. Sizes also may vary slightly from dealer to dealer.

A brick patio can be laid in sand (a fairly simple chore) or in concrete (a method that may require some professional help).

FENCING

Once you have completed all construction on your property and there will be no need for trucks or other large equipment to enter, you may consider installing a fence.

In many parts of the country, local and state laws and building codes impose restrictions on fences. In all likelihood, you will be limited as to how high you can build along your property line. To be safe, check local code requirements.

Figure 18-9 *Building purists rightly claim that there is no such thing as a purely decorative fence, that a fence must function in some way. In this house design by architect Robert Goetz, Tuburon, California, the strong horizontal railings and the pattern of the vertical balustrades interplay effectively with diagonals of house roof lines and siding. Besides serving as the connecting element between the house and ground, fencing also assures safety for deck users.*

California Redwood Association

Figure 18-10 *The other side of the Goetz residence is amply endowed with livable deck too. Here, space is utilized for outdoor dining and entertaining. Notice the steps leading to the attached pier.*

When you investigate the local codes, you may also find that fences must be placed a minimum distance inside property lines. Make certain any fence along your property line is, in fact, *on your property*. Countless neighborhood feuds have been caused by carelessly placed fencing.

Codes generally define fence construction as well: For instance, you may find that the law specifies that fence design must allow at least 40 percent visibility *through* the fence (thus eliminating solid walls).

Fence Materials. Materials for a fence are determined by three factors:

1. esthetics,
2. the primary purpose of the fence, and
3. money.

1. *Esthetics,* of course, means that the fence should harmonize with your garden scheme and home architecture. Failure to recognize the need for this coordination of design is almost sure to mean a fence that will be an eyesore and a resultant source of discontent in the neighborhood.

2. Remember the fence's *primary purpose* when it comes to choosing the materials too. Obviously, a fence to contain small children or pets must be built differently than one intended to serve as a property divider only. A fence intended to provide privacy can be built so breezes will not be stopped completely. Similarly, a fence meant to discourage trespassing can be fashioned of materials that will not shut out the sun.

3. If *money* isn't tight, you can choose the material that best suits the first two conditions. But if you're counting pennies, you will have to be content with an affordable material that comes the closest to doing so.

Getting Garden Ideas. Some of the many sources for good ideas regarding patios, gardens, and fences are listed in Appendix B. Additionally, most home building centers dispense such literature free of charge or at nominal cost. Finally, all well-stocked libraries have a number of garden and deck books on their shelves.

LANDSCAPING: THE ENVIRONMENT AROUND YOUR HOME

How you arrange your leisure-home property has a dynamic effect on the way you live. Thus, you may be wise to call in a landscape architect to help you with the planning and/or development of your landscaping program—including decks and fences.

Generally, you pay landscape architects a fee for their services just as you do a lawyer. The landscape architect does not get commissions or discounts from contractors or from materials dealers; but the fee may be based on a percentage of the total amount of monies paid to these suppliers. Landscape architects use different methods to compute their fees:

Fences are always designed to serve some function, thus style is generally created by fulfilling certain needs. In Figure 18-11, the fence also serves as a privacy screen and patio bench. By extending one section of the fence outward from the patio, plantings can be installed to create a living wall.

In Figure 18-12, a fence constructed of sturdy lumber is intended to serve primarily as a windbreak. Spacing of boards permits passage of some breeze, but the gale-like effect of heavy winds is diminished. Such windscreens are strategically placed to minimize the effect of prevailing winds on patios and decks.

Figure 18-11

California Redwood Association Photos

Figure 18-12

Figure 18-13

Better utilization of space is the result of this fence structure designed by California landscape architect Grant Jones. The fence serves as a privacy screen as well as a garden focal point. Actually, the structure is a pair of fences under a roof; in between, a potter's studio is comfortable, yet fully hidden from view. The A-shaped, skylight roof assures adequate natural light for the pottery-shed user.

California Redwood Association Photos

Figure 18-14

1. the fee may be calculated on an hourly basis for the time devoted to the job;
2. a percentage of the total cost of planting and building may be charged; or
3. a lump sum may be quoted and agreed upon in advance.

Since fees vary considerably depending on the individuals and the type of work to be done, it will probably pay you to call on more than one landscape architect for price quotes.

A landscape architect that I have worked with charges from $400 to $500 for a complete plan for a typical suburban property. If he executes the plan, which includes the hiring and supervision of contractors and suppliers, he then charges 10 percent of all the installation costs. The advantage of this arrangement to the homeowner is obvious. For an initial modest fee, you have a complete landscaping plan. If cost is a factor, you can then elect to implement the plan over a period of years, and pay the architect a percentage as each phase is completed.

To find landscape architects in your area, check the Yellow Pages or write to the American Society of Landscape Architects (see Appendix E).

PIERS AND FLOATS

Obviously, only those whose property abuts calm water need either of these. For any one of several reasons (for water-skiing or take-off, sunbathing, diving or swimming, or boat-mooring), you may decide that a pier or float is desirable for you.

A pier is a platform over water, permanently fixed at one level regardless of tidal action. Pier design is flexible and all piers are built on either concrete or wood piling. Since both the necessary knowledge and tools are specialized, building a pier is not a job that a typical homeowner can tackle with relish. The wisest move is to call in a professional pier-builder.

A float, on the other hand, though anchored in place, bobs about on the water. Enough slack is left in the anchor or mooring line for the float to rise and fall with the tides. In general, floats do not have a very long lifespan. In fact, a float commonly becomes water-logged and rots from below in five years or so. For this reason, a float should be built in sections which can be hauled out periodically for a bottom scraping and painting.

Float Materials. The choice of flotation material depends primarily on what's available locally. Ideally, the material should be low in cost or free, and it should be able to remain buoyant over a long period. Besides logs, floats are often constructed of empty 50-gallon drums and of plastics.

Though kiln-dried logs (especially cedar) make a good float, logs tend to soak up water rapidly with the result that the float will probably be awash in two or three years.

Figure 18-15 *A pier is permanently installed at a fixed elevation over water. The ladder at the right is for use by boaters at low tide. An unusually shaped pier such as this one gives greater versatility of use. For example, the area between the ladder and railing can be used for water skier's takeoffs. And for mooring, a boat can be brought in and docked on either side depending upon wind and tidal direction.*

Fifty-gallon drums corrode rapidly in salt water, and in fresh water if left immersed year-round. The smartest way to build a float bouyed by drums is to first put together the frame and then push the drums beneath it until the desired bouyancy is achieved. (With too many drums, the float bobs about like a cork, making it difficult if not impossible to use.)

Foam plastic, such as Styrofoam, is impervious to water and is not bothered by marine life or salt water. It does, however, dissolve when it comes into contact with gasoline, but a protective coating can be applied to protect the foam from such damage. This sealer is a must if you plan to moor a power boat at your float.

Before building pier or float, you are legally required to get a permit for building over navigable water, available from the District Engineer, U.S. Army Corps of Engineers. The Corps also offers a pamphlet that spells out all details concerning such construction.

OUTDOOR LIGHTING

Not too many years ago, outdoor residential lighting consisted of little more than a few floodlights around the property in rather bare-looking luminaires (fixtures). Generally, such functional lights were affixed to buildings or perched on poles to provide broad, general illumination for safety and security at night.

A third consideration, beautification, now plays an equally important role in outdoor lighting. "Lightscaping" is actually an extension of your indoor lighting, but, if done properly, it can add new dimensions to your home environment to create, in effect, a totally new living area.

And don't think that lighting the outdoors automatically means that you will be using energy capriciously in these energy-conscious days. For one thing, when exterior lights are in use it means that the family is outdoors and that indoor lights can be turned off or used minimally.

Basics of Outdoor Lighting. Some basic principles will eliminate the mystery to successful outdoor lighting. Primarily, it is important to avoid flat lighting. Instead, place lights to create scenes with highlights and shadows of the sort found in a painting or charcoal drawing. Usually, a touch of light here and there, cast by the appropriate luminaire, creates a nighttime setting with charm. A good way to determine where to place lights is to work with portable lamp sockets and extension cords. Using these, you can fiddle with a number of different arrangements until you find the setup you like best.

When locating outdoor lights, make certain that you consider your neighbor's privacy and wants too. Poorly placed lights that illuminate the property of others—when and where it's not wanted—are sure to cause hard feelings. Make sure that your lighting system won't be the cause of a neighborhood squabble.

Types of Fixtures. Shielding luminaires are often used today even though they are less efficient—that is, slightly more expensive to operate. On the plus side, however, they do eliminate irritating glare while providing illumination where it's wanted. Local (or spot) and border lighting are usually based more upon esthetics than on the ability to see.

Incandescent fixtures for outdoor use are available in color if you want to emphasize garden colors, attract or repel insects, or create special-effect foliage lighting. Currently, many installations use incandescents in a floodlight holder with built-in reflectors (PAR). Some holders shield the entire lamp so indoor lamps may be used. Others that protect just the lamp base require outdoor (weatherproof) lamps.

You can use fluorescents outdoors provided you meet three criteria:

1. use only weatherproof luminaries,
2. make certain that the ballasts and luminaries are designed for use at below-freezing temperatures, and

3. if lamps are exposed to temperatures in the 32° to 50°F. bracket, enclose them.

High-intensity discharge (HID) lamps are used for floodlighting larger areas; these are not commonly used in residential outdoor lighting.

No matter which fixtures you use, *play it safe*. All electric fixtures and wiring used outside must be designed for outdoor use and installed in conformance with the National Electric Code as well as with the requirements of your local building department.

IDEAS FOR LIGHTSCAPING

Automation. Consider the advantages of installing equipment that turns lights on and off automatically. Such equipment is relatively inexpensive and can save many dollars over the course of a lighting season by completely eliminating wasted electricity.

Accent Lighting. Trees, shrubbery, and other accent or focal points in the garden can be mood-lit by directing accent lights from above or below. This type of lighting is usually best used in addition to soft-tinted, directed, or reflected lighting. Since overall floodlighting tends to "whitewash" a garden, accent lights are the best tools you have for avoiding that much-dreaded look.

Eliminate Hazards. Light all walks, steps, and paths to avoid any chance of missteps and falls with their probable injuries. Don't use overly bright or glaring luminaires on steps because such lights are likely to blind step users. Ideally, step fixtures have concealed bulbs yet cast the desired safety lighting on the steps. Another way to avoid glare is to hide luminaires behind shrubbery and the like.

Lights for Dining. On a patio, it is desirable to have lighting that draws everyone together into a group. You should aim to create a lighting scheme that gives good visibility without any harsh or irritating light. There should also be some transitional lighting on the fringe of the dining area so that the change from lighted to dark areas is not too abrupt.

Lawn Games. Most games will be adequately illuminated if you use a pair of poles 18- to 20-feet high with two or more 150-watt flood lamps per pole. For net games, position the light poles approximately 3 feet from both ends of the net. No matter what game you are illuminating, make certain the luminaires are placed so that they do not shine into the player's eyes.

Low-Voltage Light Systems. Basically, there are two advantages in a low-voltage system—economy and safety.

Low-voltage systems mean economy because they use low-wattage bulbs that are intended for accent lighting and that consequently require less electricity. Further, the equipment is also lower in price than comparable high-voltage equipment. Finally, you can save on installation charges because the installation is easy enough to make this a do-it-yourself task all the way.

General Electric, Nela Park

Figure 18-16   *Functional night lightscaping also adds drama and charm to your yard setting. Here, in a courtyard and rock garden viewed from the roof, illumination in the foreground on the bench, rocks, and ilex plants is from deep-shielded "moon light" fixture using a 100-watt blue-white PAR lamp. In the background, small low-voltage spotlights can be seen under overhang illuminating planters and rock garden area. The light on the decking comes from a prismatic wall fixture with two 50-watt A-Bulbs.*

Safety is excellent because the transformer, the heart of the system, reduces voltage from the standard 117 volts to 6 or 12 volts, rendering dangerous or fatal shocks impossible. Some transformers, simple devices, come with timers that automatically turn lights on and off.

It is important that you use the proper size transformer. To determine the right size, add up the total wattage of all fixtures and select a transformer that closely matches the load. In any event, the load wattage should not be

General Electric Company, Nela Park

Figure 18-17   *Lights let you enjoy your private facilities at all hours. Blue-white incandescent downlights here accent the texture of the Mexican brick while standard incandescent downlights highlight the plantings in front of the playroom. Also notice the wall illuminated by lights recessed in an overhang at the left.*

Electrical Safety

* Work on your electrical system only when the ground is dry.
* Control all outdoor circuits by a switch. Turn off all current to the outdoors when working on the system.
* For yard lighting, use outdoor-type equipment only. Such equipment has waterproof cords, plugs, sockets, and connections. Buy only equipment that is U.L. Listed.
* Use tape on all temporary connections and elevate them to keep them out of puddles—because circuits should be tested before they are buried.
* If equipment comes with seals, gaskets, or rubber rings, use them. These are intended to keep moisture out of the sockets.
* Unless you are experienced at electrical work and familiar with the codes, leave permanent outdoor wiring to the professionals. Use ground burial cable (type UF) in trenches to get power to luminaires.
* Remember that under the electric code all outdoor circuits must be protected by a Ground Fault Circuit Interrupter (GFCI).

Figure 18-18   **Figure 18-19**

Used creatively, night lighting will beautify your property as well as make it safer. Low-voltage lights here are directed at a decorative fence and plant which serve as focal points during evening hours. Intermatic Inc. Photos

less than half the transformer's rating, nor more than the transformer's capacity.

The best outdoor lighting is obtained by combining regular-voltage equipment for lighting broad areas, with low-voltage equipment for small areas and for accent lighting.

SECURITY—UPTIGHT OR OUT OF SIGHT

In particular, you should be concerned with (1) loss from vandalism or theft and (2) loss by fire. Both are of real concern to leisure-home owners who must leave their properties unprotected for varying periods.

Protection Against Vandalism and Theft. At this stage, you will realize the wisdom of having taken local protection into consideration before you ever invested a dollar. Now you should take the time to learn exactly what protection you are getting for your tax dollars. Check with your local police department to learn the frequency with which a patrol car passes your property. Does the car make a pass like clockwork or are patrols intentionally staggered so others can't set the stage with a stopwatch?

Find out whether the local police suggest your advising them when you leave your second home so they can give your property some extra attention. The local police are just as eager as you are to keep the crime rate down; thus you are well advised to follow whatever suggestions they have regarding the security of your home.

Also let several of your neighbors know each time you leave your property for an extended period. If any activity is noted on your property, they will know to call the police department. Further, a neighbor with a key to your home can assure that papers, mail, and the like don't pile up outside your house; and, in the event there is any suspicious activity noted, he or she can admit police to the premises.

Look at the problem this way: Burglars want fast and easy hits. Ideally, they like to quickly and quietly gain entry, select what they want, and depart unnoticed. Thus, your task is to make that sequence as unlikely as possible in your home. Since the two worst enemies of any burglar are light and noise, you can take some action.

You can rig outdoor lights to operate automatically during your absence. Lights can be timed or programmed to come on at dusk and go off at sunrise. This can eliminate any dark areas and shadows for burglars to operate or hide in.

What About Locks? Granted, the old saw, "Locks are made for honest people," is largely true. A skilled burglar *can* get into just about any house—under the right circumstances. In the final analysis, however, you get what you pay for when it comes to lock devices for the home. Today some fairly sophisticated locks are on the market, making the burglary business tougher than ever.

Your first line of defense against thieves at your leisure home is with judiciously selected, quality locks.

Security checklist. Here are some questions to help you determine how secure your home is:

1. Do all exterior doors on your house have locks?
   a. Are the locks of the type that have a springloaded latch (striker) that can be forced aside with a stiff plastic card? Or,
   b. Do locks have dead bolts?
2. If you bought an older home, did you think to change all locks after moving in? You have no idea how many keys the previous owner may have distributed—nor to whom.
3. Are exterior doors of solid wood or are they hollow core?
4. Are all hinges on exterior doors concealed from the outside? If not, the thief can simply push out the hinge pins and lift off the door.
5. Can any sliding glass doors or windows be lifted off their tracks from the outside?

6. Is every window protected by a workable lock?

Types of Locks. The lowest-cost door locks (the fast-setting type) have interior locking buttons, usually on the knobs. These have beveled striker (often referred to as latch) that slides in and out of the striker plate mounted on the doorjamb. If the doorjamb is of the nonrabbeted type (that is, the stop is nailed to the face of the jamb), the lock can be forced open by sliding a stiff, thin plastic card between stop and jamb. These locks offer very little protection.

For a few bucks more you can install the same lock with a deadbolt. Here, even if the striker is pushed aside, the dead bolt remains in the striker plate in the jamb and the door stays locked.

Mortise locks can be found in most older homes and in custom construction. This is the type operated with a key from the outside. A mortise-type lock has a dead bolt activated—that is, slid into or out of the striker plate—by either the key outside or a button inside.

Keyless locks, rather new in residential security, utilize a series of pushbuttons rather than a key, to avoid the risk of key duplication, as well as the chance of a picked lock. The most effective keyless locks are pretty expensive but worth considering.

Vertical bolt locks, good auxiliary locks, interact with a mating plate mounted on the jamb. The locking mechanism is a cylinder that can be key-operated from both sides of the door.

Sliding glass doors and windows. In one way or another, you must make it impossible to lift the window or door out from its tracks. Though there are many home-grown stunts for securing sliding doors—such as placing a thick dowel across the opening—your smartest move is to buy a quality lock intended for sliding doors and windows. These come with a locking mechanism that can be opened from the outside as well as inside. Sliding door locks can also be bought that will accept the same key that you use for the front and back doors.

Window locks. Generally, the locks that come on the windows provide adequate protection. However, since these locks are operable from the inside, a burglar can simply break or remove a pane of glass to get at the lock. For this reason, if desired, you can take the precaution of adding keyed locks to windows too. With these, a thief still will not be able to open the window, even after breaking the glass.

Burglar Alarms. You may or may not want to install one of these at your leisure home. A good burglar alarm is a sophisticated piece of equipment and requires an expensive installation. In order for the investment to be worthwhile, neighbors living within earshot year-round are a must.

If you decide to install an alarm system, carefully check out the system before buying. Since you do not want one that will give many false alarms, the detector's sensitivity should be adjustable and the alarm's circuit an easy one to test. Finally, if the system is to be 100 percent effective all of the time, it should include auxiliary battery power.

Fire Protection. In the country the water supply is usually inadequate for fighting fires. Thus it makes sense to prepare for any emergencies on your own. Obviously, if you live a great distance from municipal help, or there is only a minimal amount of it available, take precautions to provide as much of your own fire protection as possible. Your best bet is to consult with your local fire department regarding how much self-protection you should have from fires.

Many homeowners in rural areas consider a rooftop sprinkling system a worthwhile investment. The pipe and sprinklers are of the same type that are used in lawn-sprinkling systems—just make certain you do not use plastic piping.

Short of an automatic system, you can keep a healthy supply of water on hand as well as a number of fire extinguishers. When buying extinguishers, note the types of fires the various extinguishers are intended for. *Not all* extinguishers put out every type of fire; there are, however, extinguishers available to fight the three most common classes of home fires.

But for fire protection when you are absent you *should* consider installing a smoke and fire detection system. The alarm bell for it should be a loud one mounted outdoors so that your nearest neighbors can hear it easily if it sounds. Periodically, test the alarm and, for maximum security, wire the system to operate from battery power should electrical service from the power company be interrupted.

You can work at fire prevention as well as fire fighting. Work to eliminate as many causes of fire as possible in and around your home. According to fire authorities, carelessness with matches and smoking materials is the number one cause of home fires. Electrical failures rank number two. Thus, it makes sense to enforce safety rules in your home concerning all flammable materials. Follow the suggestions for such materials as outlined in Chapter 17 when closing your home for the season. And make it your practice to never overload electrical circuits.

Have on hand a family firefighting plan. To assure that all members of the family know their tasks in such an emergency, run through fire drills several times a year. Remember that one of the first things to do in event of a fire is to turn off the gas and electricity at the mains if at all possible. Every member of the family should know how to do both.

VACATION-HOME LIFESTYLE

When you move into your new second home, play your social life on the cool side for a while. You are sure to make new friends as soon as you move in, but if you are overfriendly at the start, you may regret it later on when you would prefer more privacy.

A new family in the neighborhood is commonly invited to all types of social functions. If you jump into every activity without thinking, it will be difficult—if not impossible—later to revamp your social life; you will be expected to keep up the pace you started with, or run the risk of ill will in the neighborhood. The result can be that it will be just about impossible for you to go into your backyard—alone or for a small family get-together—without some of your more zealous neighbors wondering why they weren't invited.

Many vacation areas are filled with folks who make socializing their summer avocation. Though this is fine for those who prefer such living, most of us who invest in country property have a specific desire to get back, or get closer, to nature—that is, to find a more relaxing way of life than we have in town.

If you prefer the quiet life over the party whirl, play it slow; you might even be a bit aloof with neighbors at the beginning. Give yourself a chance to get to know them well before becoming overly, and perhaps hopelessly, involved with them on a social basis.

Life at Home. In order to enjoy your vacation home to the fullest, there must be some cooperation within the family too. All are out in the country for a change of pace—including Mom and Dad. But the only way *everyone* will find it is if all the chores are shared by all the family.

Youngsters should be required to perform certain tasks each day, such as helping with housework, shopping, babysitting, and the like. And since in many family situations Dad will probably get out to the country only on weekends (aside from his vacation), the kids should pitch in on the chores he'd normally handle, such as cutting the lawn, raking leaves, and bringing trash to the town dump. He'll be much happier with his second-home life if he doesn't have to spend his weekends playing handyman.

By pitching in and sharing the workload, all will be able to share the advantages and fun of leisure-home ownership too. This, of course, is just plain, old-fashioned common sense. Since your common sense is probably what made you decide to buy or build a second home to begin with, keep it in gear on this score too.

If you have carefully evaluated your second-home area and all its aspects, you should be fully satisfied with your lifestyle "away from home." The measures outlined in this and other chapters of this book cover everything you must decide on—from social milieu to nail sizes—in order to be happy with your leisure way of life. If you are honest about your goals and means, you will undoubtedly make the right decisions.

19

Tools and Building Products You Should Know About

*   Hand tools   *   About hand tools   *   Power tools   *   About portable power tool motors   *   Grounding   *   Quickie course on lumber: Lumber sizes, Selecting and buying lumber, Board feet, How lumber is sold, Look for warp   *   Thoughts about building products in general   *

Most folks who plan to build their own second homes probably own at least some of the tools needed for the job. On the other hand, studies show that many inexperienced people, who own practically no tools, are jumping into all kinds of do-it-yourself activities—including projects as large as building a house.

Anyone who has the drive, ambition, and energy to tackle a project of this size and scope needs all the help possible. Good tools provide such help. Since you save a considerable amount of money by being your own builder, you should have no qualms about diverting some of that saved loot to acquire work-saving tools. Additionally, tools bought with care are a good investment; used and maintained properly, they'll retain their value (in some cases, even grow in value) over the years.

Safety first. If you are unfamiliar with power tools, make certain you take the time to learn correct tool usage before swinging into action on your job. You should never plug in a new tool before thoroughly reading the manufacturer's instructions that come packed with the tool. In the final analysis, the only sure way to avoid power-tool accidents is by using them the way they are supposed to be used. One quick method for learning the right way to handle power tools is by enrolling in an adult education (evening) course if the local school includes a workshop class in its curriculum.

Finally, make no mistake about it, safe use of tools is the user's responsibility. Rule number one is to keep your mind on what you're doing *every-*

Figure 19-1 A leisure home with pizzazz; a crisp, contemporary look made extra-appealing because of high-quality craftsmanship. To duplicate the look of careful workmanship, you will need a good understanding of how to work with hand and power tools.

time you handle a power tool. Number two is to avoid using any tool that makes you apprehensive: If it doesn't feel comfortable in hand, simply don't use it.

HAND TOOLS

Many of these are not yet—and, very likely, never will be—replaced or outmoded by power tools. For example, nothing on the market at this time does the job of the familiar and reliable hammer any better than the hammer itself. And as basic as the hammer is, you had better believe you need know-how to use the tool.

Besides knowing how to handle a tool, you should know which tool to buy and use. For example, a 20-oz. hammer with a ripping claw is ideal for framing carpentry. But the same tool would wear you out if you used it on interior, finished carpentry work where a 16-oz. claw hammer excels. Or if you plan on laying bricks, buy a bricklayer's hammer. Installation of wood shingles requires a sharp lath hatchet for trimming as well as nailing. And so on—you get the picture.

Basic hand tools

16-oz. curved-claw hammer, drop-forged steel head	Nail apron
	Keyhole or compass saw
20-oz. rip-claw hammer, drop-forged steel head	Coping saw
	Hacksaw
8-point crosscut saw	Miter box
6-point rip saw	Brace and set of bits
6-ft. zigzag rule extension	Block plane
25- or 50-ft. steel tape	Jack plane
Steel framing square	Set of wood chisels
Try square	Set of cold chisels
Combination square	Utility knife
Hatchet	Assortment of files, rasps, and shaping tools (such as Stanley's Surform tool)
24-in. spirit level	
48-in. spirit level	
Assortment of screw drivers including some Phillips-type and short, stubby models	Bevel square
	Putty knife
	Assortment of pipe wrenches
Awl	Sturdy toolbox
Nailset	

The above list is not by any stretch of the imagination all-inclusive. But it does Include most of the hand tools that you will need for the carpentry portion of housebuilding. If all specialty tools, such as a sledgehammer for staking-out chores, were included, the list would be stretched to a size of a small book by itself. There are good books on hand tools available at bookstores and libraries. Either consult one of these, write to the Hand Tool Institute, or see Appendix E for additional information on hand tools.

The above is a list of the basic hand tools you should have on hand before starting. You can increase the number of tools you own by ordering specialty tools as the job progresses. A painless way to do it is to add a tool or two to each materials order. Thus, when you order plasterboard, include the spackling knives that are recommended for the taping and jointing.

Don't skimp when it comes to buying tools. Adopt the attitude, whether buying a hand or power tool, to always buy quality. As tempting as they often seem, pass by the "leader items" that many lumberyards and hardware stores position up front by the barrel-full. These are, almost without exception, of inferior quality; they just won't last under the heavy use that you'll expose them to in the months ahead.

In fact, as uneconomical as these junk tools are in the long run, they are an even worse investment when it comes to safety. For example, high-

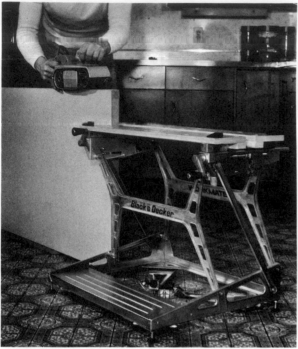

Figure 19-2 *This versatile tool from Black and Decker is sure to become one of a carpenter's favored tools. The portable work surface serves as a workbench, holding device or both, sells for about $90. Called Workmate, it has to rate as one of the handiest tools that you can add to your collection.*

Figure 19-3 *A starter toolbox from The Stanley Works includes hand tools for nailing, cutting, and shaping. Available at most hardware stores and building supply dealers, the set is labeled No. H895A.*

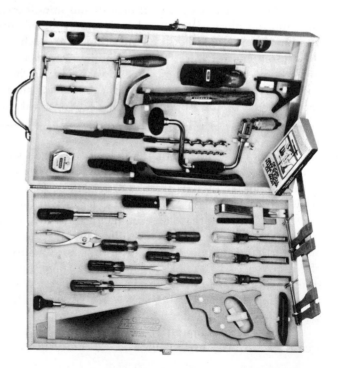

speed twist and spade bits that sell for a fraction of the cost of decent bits quickly break, dull, and fail. And the under-two-buck hammers that many merchandisers seem to dote upon are downright dangerous to use. You would be ill-advised to try to drive many large nails with one of these "toys." Personally, I twice witnessed pieces of their heads breaking off and flying about the room like shrapnel. If such a missile were to hit a human, it would at least be painful and at worst could cost an eye.

Buying a cheap tool is a poor way to save a couple of dollars. Buy the best and your tools will still be in service long after you've moved into your home.

About tool rentals. Don't get carried away—by all that money that you're saving by being your own carpenter—and capriciously buy every tool that strikes your fancy. There are some tools—such as a reciprocating saw or power hammer—that are helpful on one aspect of the job, but that you may never use again. In such cases, rent the tool from a local tool rental outfit for whatever length of time it is needed. Considering the value of such tools, you will find that rental fees are pretty reasonable.

Sometimes, however, renting a tool is not as easy as you might think. A small rental company, particularly in a remote area, may not be able to supply certain tools. In that case, try a rental outfit in your primary-home area. If that outfit does not allow the tool to be taken out of the area, check with contractors in the jobsite area. A local builder may be happy to make a few dollars in rental income on a tool if it is not needed for a while. If the contractor can't supply you with the tool you need, perhaps you can locate another source. If none of these possibilities work out, then at least you can console yourself with the knowledge that you have no choice but to buy the tool.

Power Tools. On any big project, such as building a home, time is an important factor. Often called "the energy savers," portable power tools save you plenty of that commodity.

Obviously, a power tool spares you the boredom of certain repetitive jobs—cutting 60 or 70 wall studs in one session, for example. But just because you are working with power, don't think you don't have to be concerned about the quality of your workmanship. The fact is, a power tool in careless hands magnifies the horrors of shoddy workmanship. An incompetent user also creates a good deal of wasted materials (that cost money). So by all means plan on working with power tools—but make certain you know how to handle them correctly first. If necessary, have the storekeeper demonstrate the tool and handle it yourself before buying.

In general, power tools are either electric- or air-operated. Any other types are used only by professionals. For that matter, since air-operated tools are connected to a compressor, they are not very often used by do-it-yourselfers. Electric portables, therefore, are the tools you will buy. They can be either plugged into a conventional 115-volt outlet or powered by a generator if you are building in the woods.

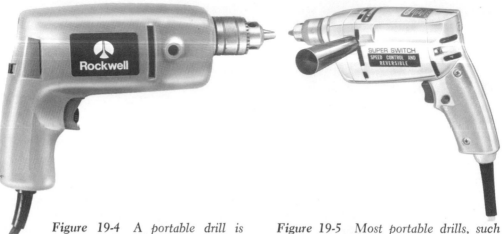

Figure 19-4 A portable drill is generally the first power tool purchased by fledgling do-it-yourselfers. Wise buyers select a model that features variable-speed control and reversing as does this ¼-incher from Rockwell.

Figure 19-5 Most portable drills, such as this Stanley No. 91061, come with an auxiliary handle that can be used on either side of the drill. The extra handle is handy for tough drilling in concrete and for long, tedious drilling chores.

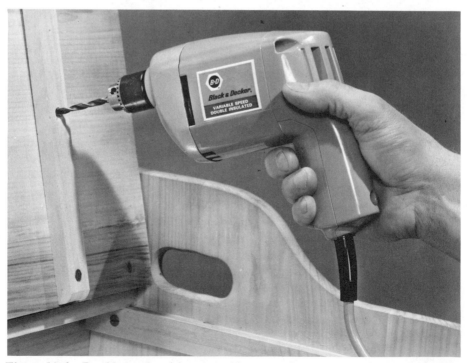

Figure 19-6 Double-insulated housing eliminates the need for a 3-wire cord and 3-prong plug, as in Black & Decker's Model 7014.

Figure 19-7 *A 7¼-in. circular saw is the best choice for most home handy-men. At 90°, the blade gives a 2⅜-in. deep cut; at 45°, you can cut through 1⅞ in. The folding sawhorses are a good job aid too. Like the saw, they are by The Stanley Works.*

Basically, each type of power tool is designed to do one job and one job only. But some makers offer tools supposedly capable of performing almost any carpentry job you might imagine. The manufacturer usually offers a basic power tool, generally a drill, that miraculously converts to hacksaw, circular saw, jigsaw—you name it. My opinion of such tools is not flattering; in fact, if I permitted one on the job it would probably be to cut the daily supply of hero sandwiches for lunch.

Avoid dual performers. Instead, buy a middle- or top-of-the-line tool, designed for a single function, from a major manufacturer. You will not likely be disappointed.

Two heavy-duty 7 ¼ -in. portable saws; one of these will save you more time on the job, possibly, than any other power tool. Quality-built tools such as these have a reliable blade guard for user protection and positive depth and bevel control for cutting accuracy.

Figure 19-8   *Rockwell's Model 4520.*

Figure 19-9   *Black & Decker's No. 7301.*

Figure 19-10   *A reliable chain saw is valuable during construction, particularly if you're building on virgin ground where trees must be cleared. You can also use a chain saw to cut framing members; cuts will be both accurate and fast.*

Figure 19-11   Stanley All-Purpose Saw No. 90459.

Figure 19-12 Rockwell's No. 4320. If you plan to do most of your own finish carpentry, a sabre saw is a must. With it you can cut scrolls, curves, intricate patterns in wood, plastics, aluminum. If your plans call for paneling a couple of rooms, a sabre saw will pay for itself on these projects alone.

About portable power tool motors. Series-wound universal-type motors are used in portable power tools for several reasons. For one thing, the weight, in relation to the motor's power output, is light; thus you get more punch per pound. Also, such motors may operate on either AC or DC, either 60 cycles or less, and either 115 or 230 volts.

Because of the variable power requirements, however, make it a practice to read a tool's nameplate to check its rating before buying any power tool. Make certain that the tool can be operated on the amount (115 or 230 volts) and type (AC or DC) of current available.

When using a power tool, try to avoid undue or prolonged overloading of the tool. Overload causes overheating, and constant motor overheating causes motor failure. If the tool *must* be used for a chore that overloads it, do so for short periods of time only, and then rest the tool. You can speed-up the rest time (that is, the cooling-off period) by running the tool without load.

Figure 19-13 You can use a rip fence on your sabre saw to produce accurate long cuts. The two-speeder shown, model 7514 by Black & Decker, lets you pick the best speed for the job at hand.

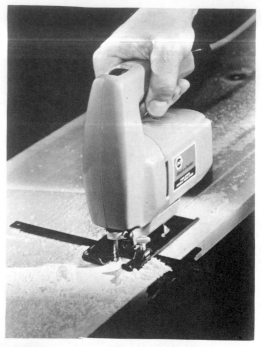

Figure 19-14 A rugged belt sander isn't a luxury, it's a must. With it, you can remove stock quickly by using a coarse-grit belt, or you can produce a mirror-smooth finish on wood by switching to one of the finer grits. The most popular belt sanders among homeowners are the models that accept 3-by-21-in. sanding belts. The bag on this one indicates that it's a dustless model.

Take the time to read the maker's use and maintenance instructions packed with tools. To get maximum service and longevity from a tool, you should follow all the manufacturer's suggestions for tool use and care.

Grounding. For safety, power tools today come with either a 3-wire cord and 3-prong plug, or a plastic, double-insulated housing. In the case of the 3-prong plug, the third prong on the plug is connected to the tool's metal housing via a green grounding wire. Thus it is important that any power tool with a grounding plug be used with an approved receptacle.

Figure 19-15 *Routers are probably the least understood—and most underrated— of all power tools. Yet they allow you to put the professional touch on a project. The edge of the board here is being dressed with an ogee cutter: The look is quite an improvement over the rounded-over corner you're confined to if you have to do the job by hand. When selecting a router, keep in mind that high speed is as important as h.p.*

In any event, you would be wise to consider using GFI receptacles or GFI circuit breakers in conjunction with power-tool work. These devices protect you from shock due to a ground failure (that is, current leaking to the tool's metal housing and diverting through the tool user if he contacts a ground such as a coldwater pipe). In fact, the National Code now calls for GFI-protected receptacles on all construction jobsites. (See page 264)

RECOMMENDED POWER TOOLS
(minimum)

7¼-in. portable circular saw with assorted blades—combination, carbide-tipped, rip, fine-tooth crosscut, and plywood

Figure 19-16 Stanley's Model 90092. Compact, lightweight router is easy to handle. Though its size makes it hard to believe, this model sports a ¾-H.P. motor capable of producing 28,000 rpm for productive job output.

Figure 19-17 It makes good sense to have a bench grinder on the job from the word go. You can turn to it to keep hatchets, knives, chisels, drill bits, and the like sharp throughout the life of the job without spending an additional cent. When your home is built, you can simply move the tool into your workshop area.

Figure 19-18 A pad sander is also a must; you will need one to prepare all surfaces that require finishing of one type or another. For a few bucks more, you can pick a dustless model. In the years ahead, you'll be glad you did.

Figure 19-19 This easy-to-install Ground Fault Circuit Interrupter is designed to fit in a standard electrical receptacle box for 115 volt 15 or 20 ampere (grounded branch) circuits. Device, manufactured by 3M Company, senses a difference in current entering an appliance and breaks the circuit almost instantaneously if the current differs by a hazardous level.

⅜-in. portable drill, variable-speed with reverse; with screwdriver attachments for drill

3-by-21-in. belt sander, plus an assortment of belts (fine to coarse grits)

Finishing (pad) sander, either orbital or straight-line type

Router—¾ or 1 h.p. motor plus an assortment of cutters (bits). Select carbide-tipped cutters if longevity is important.

Extension cords—the right size for the job, as shown below:

Distance from outlet (feet)	Wire size needed for 15-amp current
15	#14
25	#14
35	#12
50	#10

A QUICKIE COURSE ON LUMBER

Lumber Sizes. The familiar terms (that is, 2-by-4s, 2-by-6s, 1-by-8s, and the like) are really working names more than actual finished sizes. All wood is referred to and ordered by these *nominal* sizes. The *actual* sizes are slimmer in both thickness and width as can be seen in the chart below. Thus, a *nominal* 2-by-4 in reality measures 1½ by 3½ in. *actual*. The slimming down is a result of planing or finishing of the wood. The sizes for seasoned lumber are uniform throughout the U.S.

LUMBER SIZES

Nominal Size in inches	Actual Size in inches	Nominal Size in inches	Actual Size in inches
1 × 2	¾ × 1½	2 × 6	1½ × 5½
1 × 4	¾ × 3½	2 × 10	1½ × 9½
1 × 6	¾ × 5½	2 × 12	1½ × 9¼
1 × 10	¾ × 9¼	3 × 6	2½ × 5½
1 × 12	¾ × 11¼	4 × 4	3½ × 3½
2 × 4	1½ × 3½	4 × 6	3½ × 5½

Note: The dimensions above are for softwoods. Hardwoods, as a rule, usually run about ⅛ inch less in thickness and width than the nominal size. Thus, a 1 × 4 piece of dressed hardboard will measure ⅞″ × 3⅞″.

Selecting and Buying Lumber. Because wood offers such an infinite variety of color, grain, and natural characteristics, it permits an individuality in home-construction that is virtually unmatched by any other building material. Most lumberyards and building-supply dealers today carry an extensive selection of wood and wood products.

Because of the ever-increasing number of products from wood, more and more of these retailers are becoming, literally, wood information centers, providing considerable help to do-it-yourselfers. Booklets and other litera-

Figure 19-20   Grade Stamps. The function of grading is to provide identification so the user can purchase the right wood for the use intended. Here's what those stamps mean: (A) The official Western Wood Products Association mark on a piece of lumber assures its assigned grade. Grading practices of all Western Wood Products Association member mills are closely supervised to assure uniformity. (B) The permanent number assigned to each mill for grade-stamp purposes. (C) This is an example of an official grade name abbreviation. The official grade name gives positive identification to graded lumber. ("CONST" stands for construction grade). (D) This mark identifies the wood species. (E) This symbol denotes the moisture content of the wood when it was manufactured. "S-Dry" indicates seasoned lumber, while "S-Green" would identify green or unseasoned lumber. (It is recommended that S-Dry be used for all enclosed framing.)

ture are usually available at these places; included in this material you will find information that will help you make intelligent selections of material for various jobs. The dealer, of course, can also help you choose the lumber for various projects.

Of course, in the final analysis, price may have as much a bearing on your decision as does personal taste. To avoid foolish overspending or the unnecessary purchase of materials, there are several rules of thumb that serve as effective guidelines:

1. Buy the lowest grade of lumber that will satisfactorily do the job.
2. Measure accurately so that you don't overorder.
3. Carefully list your order in full detail to avoid confusion (see Figure 19-21).

Board feet. Prices quoted by a lumberyard will very likely be by the board foot. Thus you should know how to compute board feet so that you can accurately estimate the costs of a planned order.

Stated simply, a *board foot* equals a piece of lumber 12 in. sq. and 1 in. thick. To determine the number of board feet in any piece of lumber, multiply the piece's length in feet by its nominal thickness and width in inches, then divide by 12. For example, to find the board feet in one 2-by-4 that is 12 ft. long:

$$\frac{12' \times 2'' \times 4''}{12} = \frac{96}{12} = 8 \text{ board feet}$$

LUMBER GRADE STANDARDS

Select		Common		Structural
Okay for natural finishes	Okay for paint finishes	Okay for use without waste	Okay for use with some waste	
Grade A: Practically clear	**Grade C:** High-quality paint finish	**No. 1:** Tight-knotted	**No. 3:** Grade characteristics close to No. 2	**Construction:** Highest quality structural material.
Grade B: High quality almost clear	**Grade D:** Characteristics of both select and common	**No. 2:** Less restricted in quality than No. 1	**No. 4:** Lowest quality	**Standard:** Close in quality to construction grade.
				Utility: Poor quality. Usually requires added members (studs 12 in. O.C. for example, and midpoint blocking on walls higher than 8 ft.
				Economy: Lowest quality; do not use for structural members.

Select and **common** lumber are graded by appearance.
Structural is graded for strength.

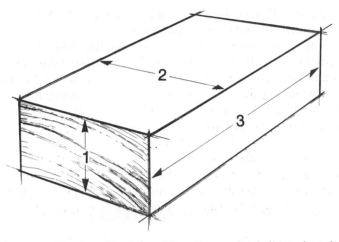

Figure 19-21 *Lumber is ordered by giving the nominal dimensions in the 1-2-3 sequence shown on the board above. Variation of standard practice used by lumbermen can cause confusion and improperly filled order. The chart, below, gives the correct sequence for ordering stock materials. If you require additional milling, such as surfacing four sides, that information is added to the end of the order. Thus, the example shown would then read 3/2" x 4" x 8' std. fir S4S.*

Here's the correct way to order lumber:

A	B	C
3	2" x 4" x 8'	std., fir

A = *Quantity wanted . . . three pieces*
B = *Nominal sizes in correct order . . . 1) thickness, 2) width, 3) length*
C = *Grade—standard—and species—fir*

Assuming two-by stock is selling for about $250 per 1,000 board feet, you can expect to pay about $2 (25¢ × 8) for this particular length of 2-by-4 lumber.

For large lumber orders, such as flooring and sheathing, where the lengths can be varied, the standard practice is to order by board feet. The lumberyard then ships random lengths of the particular-size boards that you ordered.

But don't arbitrarily order by board feet or your waste may be out of sight. For instance, suppose the project you're on at the moment requires 10 12-ft. lengths of 2-by-4. To order by either board feet (80) or total linear footage (120) would be a mistake. If you do, the supplier will ship random lengths and you'll end up with pieces under 12 ft. that you won't be able to use on the job. However, if you specify 10 12-ft. 2-by-4s, though the dealer may still give you 5 24-footers, they'll be cut to your needs.

How lumber is sold. All lumber is not sold the same way. Furring strips, for example, are usually sold in bundles of 10 same-size lengths. When furring a ceiling or wall, you simply measure and total the linear footage you wish to fur and order by total linear footage.

Other lumber is generally sold by the lengths. Moldings and casings come in lengths of 8, 10, 12, 14, 16 and 20 feet. Depending on the policy at your lumberyard, you can usually pick up a piece close to exactly what you need. If trimming the baseboard in a room measuring 10 × 16 ft., you simply order 60 lineal ft. of baseboard molding. (52 linear feet plus roughly 10 percent to allow for copes, miters, and waste.)

Look for warp. You will learn quickly when working with wood that trying to build anything with warped or cupped material is frustrating at best and money-wasting at worst. To avoid such an annoyance, try to pick your own material whenever possible at the lumberyard. Hold the pieces at arm's length and sight along both edges. If the board is warped, your eye will detect it.

Some yards, more than others, seem to stock an inordinate amount of badly warped and checked materials. Your best move is to simply avoid doing business with such retailers and buy your lumber elsewhere. Waste costs money—and you're the one footing the bill.

Installing ceramic tiles do-it-yourself fashion . . .

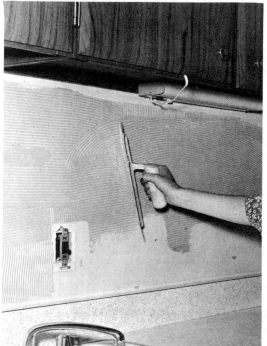

Figure 19-22 Pregrouted ceramic tiles from American Olean Tile Company make tiling easier than ever. To start installation, use a notched trowel to spread adhesive over plasterboard wall. The only preparation required is that the surface be cleaned, then roughened slightly with sandpaper.

Figure 19-23 *Next, sheets of tile—which have been pregrouted with a flexible silicone rubber —go up.*

Figure 19-24 *Making straight cuts in tile is easy using a simplified cutting kit. Score tile with carbide-tipped tool and position it over the raised metal strip of the board. To make a clean break, plastic template is placed over tile and hand-pressure is applied. Complete sheets of tile may be cut on the kit using the same method.*

Figure 19-25 *Irregular cuts and notches can be made with tile nippers, or with a pair of conventional pliers.*

Figure 19-26 *Install cut tile around electrical switches and the like. Notice two pieces of tile used above the notched piece being put into place. Most of the joint, and all of the notch, will be hidden by the switch-plate cover.*

Figure 19-27 Joints between sheets are grouted using a hand gun loaded with the same silicone rubber that's used in the sheets. The cartridge features a special nozzle designed especially to fit joints.

Figure 19-28 Next, joints are sprayed with denatured alcohol. Caution: Make certain room is well-ventilated during this step.

Figure 19-29 Finally, shape dampened joint with fingers, wiping frequently to avoid smears. Use a cheesecloth pad saturated with denatured alcohol for final cleanup—wiping along the joint, instead of across it.

Prefinished paneling makes a
world of difference . . .

Figure 19-30 Valley Forge Birch series from
Georgia-Pacific fits all decors from early American to contemporary. Of various selected hardwood, paneling in this series is typified by its
rich colortoning.

Figure 19-31 Riviera White Pine,
particularly suited for mountain
homes.

Figure 19-32 *Prefinished paneling with the look and feel of rough-hewn cedar is now available from Masonite Corp. Appropriately labeled Plainsman, the highly textured, deeply embossed hardboard sells for slightly less than natural wood. Available in three colors, gray, white and brown (shown), it's priced at about $12 per 4 x 8 sheet.*

Figure 19-33 *Deep, random-width V-grooves which duplicate hand laid tongue-and-groove plankings, encourages horizontal installation as in this family-room setting. Earthwood paneling, from Masonite's Forester series.*

Figure 19-34 Dimensional vinyl wall tiles in Dutch Garden pattern from Decro-Wall are toned in goldenrod and brown to blend with most popular color schemes. Each package of eight 12 x 12 in. tiles covers about 8 sq. ft.

Figure 19-35 Called Almanack, this random-plank paneling is embossed and printed to capture the grain of oak, in four oaken tones from U.S. Plywood's Weldwood Collection.

Figure 19-36 *The same manufacturer offers self-stick tiles in a variety of sculptured designs. Geometrix, shown, is a blend of uneven parallels and triangular dimensions. Tiles are usable indoors and out; of heavy-gauge vinyl, the tiles are washable, waterproof, non-flammable and easy to install.*

Figure 19-37   **Figure 19-38**

Tiled ceiling, Integrid by Armstrong, comes out looking like a one-piece installation because the 1 x 4 ft. tiles do not have beveled edges. This system can also be used to install Armstrong's 12 x 12 in. Decorator Chandelier tiles as shown in Fig. 19-38.

Floor coverings that a do-it-yourselfer can install . . .

Figure 19-39 *Solarian no-wax floorcovering from Armstrong boasts a Mirabond wear surface that keeps a high gloss—without waxing—longer than an ordinary vinyl floor. Pattern shown is called Roman Village; it's available in five colors: White, orange, green, blue, brown.*

Figure 19-40 *Floor of Place 'n Press tiles is easy for the do-it-yourselfer to install because adhesive is already applied. You simply peel off paper backing, position tile on floor and press it firmly. These tiles can be applied over any well-bonded, smooth resilient flooring, terrazzo, concrete and painted floors in good condition. Pattern shown is Regency Square by Armstrong Cork Co.*

Figure 19-41 *Resilient floor tiles with parquet wood pattern are also available. Chestnut Wood, a 12 x 12 in. parquet design in walnut or pecan is by Armstrong.*

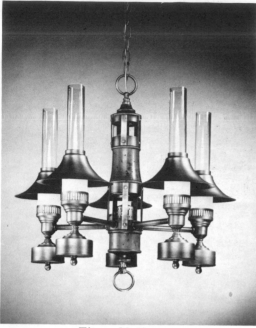

Figure 19-42

Figure 19-43

Choose light fixtures with care, they should add to the desired visual effect. These are well-designed, crafted with care, reasonably priced. Fig. 19-42, Nantucket style, is inspired by the romantic 1830's in American history when whaling fleets roamed the seas and the Island of Nantucket was the whaling capital of the world. In Fig. 19-43, the natural look of wood and contemporary styling are combined to create an up-to-date rustic feeling. Both are by the Residential Lighting Division of Thomas Industries, Inc.

Glidden Durkee

Figure 19-44 Wear Resistant finish floor paint can be used on concrete basement floors, porches and breezeways. If surface is properly prepared, it can also be used on wood floors, steps, handrails and ferrous metal surfaces. Low in odor, the latex paint contains no flammable solvents.

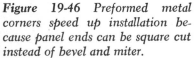

Figure 19-45 Bayside Lap Siding, a hard-board siding with the look of cedar shakes, comes in uniform 16-ft. lengths. Unlike the individual shingles, lengths are installed with the same speed as other lap sidings. One length covers 16 sq. ft., nailing is at 16 in. intervals, into studs. Masonite makes it.

Figure 19-46 Preformed metal corners speed up installation because panel ends can be square cut instead of bevel and miter.

Figure 19-47 Vinyl siding, with a "wood-grained" finish, is manufactured by Certain-Teed Products Corp. The manufacturer also makes vinyl soffit and fascia pieces to eliminate the periodic re-painting of these house members. The soffit and fascia pieces are available in the same three colors as the vinyl siding—white, yellow and pale green.

Figure 19-48 Man-made masonry paneling duplicates the natural appearance, texture and color veining of oven-fired brick. Called New Brookline, it's offered by the Roxite Division of Masonite Corporation. In three colors, white, buff and red (shown), it comes premortared for application in any kind of weather. Each 18-brick panel covers 3 sq. ft. An accessory, Edgebrick, is available for use on window ledges and as a cap on wainscotting.

Figure 19-49 Shingle side-wall, neat, goodlooking and enduring.

Red Cedar Shingle &
Handsplit Shake Bureau

Six ways to shingle a roof with wood . . .

Figure 19-50 Custom shake shingle roof application. Note shaped butt edges which are intermixed with square butt edges.

Figure 19-51 *Because of its varying look, this treatment has often been referred to as the "drunken shingler's roof." The Dutch Weave is achieved by a random doubling or superimposing of shingles throughout the roof area. It is a completely informal or casual application.*

Figure 19-52 *The Pyramid effect is obtained by superimposing two extra shingles at random throughout roof area. This application, obviously, is a variation of the Dutch weave and can be used in conjunction with the latter, if desired. To build the "pyramids," a narrow and a wide shingle are used one over the other as shown.*

Figure 19-53 *Thatch is one of the oldest and most popular variations of Red Cedar shingle applications. To do it, random weather exposures conform to hypothetical course lines. Normal deviation above and below the hypothetical course line should not exceed 1 in. Sometimes, depending upon the installer, extreme applications exceed this rule of thumb.*

Figure 19-54 *The Serrated shingle application accentuates the horizontal shadow line of the roof by uniformly doubling every 3rd, 4th, 5th or 6th course line. Spacing of the doubled course line should be consistent. If every third course is doubled, the serrated roof application will provide a four-ply roof. The top layer of the doubled courses can be laid with the butt edge flush to the undercourse or with a slight overhang. Here, the overhang is slightly exaggerated for purposes of illustration.*

Figure 19-55 Ocean Wave involves the application of two matching pairs of shingles laid at right angles to—and under—the principal course. The waves should be uniformly spaced throughout the roof to achieve a consistent pattern; the cross shingles forming the curvature should be about 6 in. wide.

Figure 19-56 This Independence "Shangle" by Certain-Teed is a heavyweight asphalt shingle with a style and texture somewhat similar to wood shakes. Available in four wood tones—Cedar bark, sawmill tan, weathered wood and black Forest—Independence shingles weigh in at 340 lbs. per square.

Figure 19-57 High-pressure plastic laminates are available in colors, finishes and textures undreamed of as recently as two years ago. Eldorado Leather by Formica® Corporation can be used for a countertop application because it coordinates with many popular colors found in appliances, fixtures and cabinetry.

Look what you can do with stock moldings . . .

Courtesy Western Wood Moulding & Millwork Producers

Figure 19-58 The warmth of a wall paneled in the traditional style is ideal for a mountain or lake retreat. This one was built by applying western wood molding screen stock and cap moldings over standard 4 x 8 ft. plywood panels. The entire wall was then sanded and finished with walnut stain and semigloss varnish.

Photos Courtesy Western Wood Moulding & Millwork Producers

Figure 19-59 *For an easy-to-do, goodlooking, vacation-home interior wall, consider using rough-sawn wood and stock lattice molding strips. The latter are stained dark brown and applied over joints between Western Red Cedar rough-sawn 1 x 12 boards. Treatment is attractive and requires little maintenance—an ideal solution in a leisure home.*

Figure 19-60 *Plain flush door is transformed to traditional paneled-door effect. It's achieved with wood batten molding pattern.*

Courtesy Western Wood Moulding & Millwork Producers

Figure 19-61 *Here, contemporary styling was given to this vacation home entrance door with pairs of small cove molding glued back-to back and applied in eight vertical strips.*

One for energy-saving . . .

Figure 19-62 *Second floor window of this beachfront house literally bounces the sun's heat away. Scotchtint sun control film applied to the window can lower inside room temperature up to 20°F.*

Figure 19-63 Half-completed window treatment dramatically shows how the sun control film keeps glare out of this waterfront home. Applied by trained, authorized dealer-applicators, the film repels up to 75 percent of the sun's heat.

3M Company

About moldings . . .

Moldings in architecture have survived for thousands of years. We know that ancient Greek designers used moldings to divide surfaces into smaller parts, to create interest and variety, and to produce highlights and shadows (today, this is often referred to as architectural shadowline). Since you are more than likely going to use some moldings in your new home, you owe it to yourself to possess at least a passing knowledge of moldings. You'll find the basics here, to learn more about moldings, write to the Western Wood Moulding and Millwork Producers (address can be found in Appendix E).

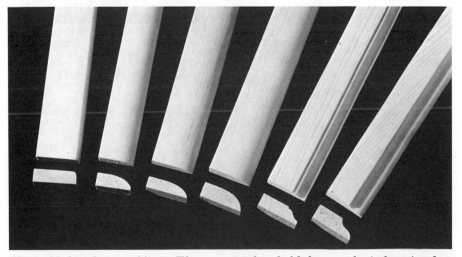

Figure 19-64 Stop moldings. These are used to hold doors and windows in place and to make tight joints. Several of the many-available stop shapes are shown.

Figure 19-65 Casing is used primarily around doors and windows, but can also be used for special decorating purposes. The reverse sides of these patterns are cut away (scooped out) to give a better fit over plaster edges, nail heads and other uneven surfaces.

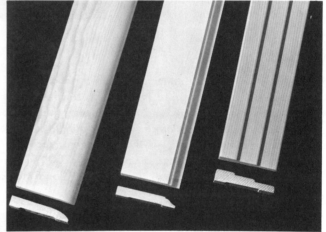

Figure 19-66 Base moldings are essential for interiors, many are similar to casings in design. Typical patterns are the streamlined (also called sanitary, bullnose and clamshell) on the left and the waterfall pattern at the right. Here, too, backs are cut away for a better fit over irregular surfaces.

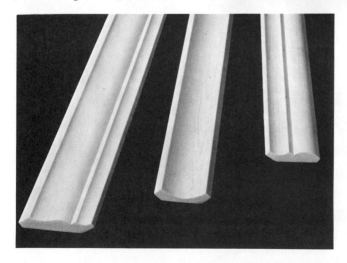

Figure 19-67 Three popular western wood moldings, from left, crown, cove and bed molding. Generally, for use on wall-ceiling joints, they can also be used in molding combinations to create special-design effects.

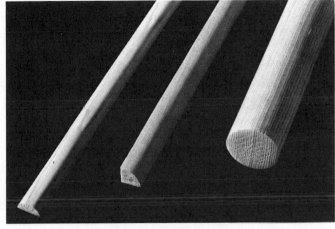

Figure 19-68 The rounds family —half-round, quarter-round and round (or dowel). These are three basic types of rounds which may be purchased in many sizes.

In the illustrations for this chapter are listed some—but by no means all—manufacturers of good quality building products. If you have any questions about a manufacturer's product, write direct for the answers. Many manufacturers also offer free literature, ranging from product catalogs to how-to instructions, for the asking. For that reason, the complete addresses of all manufacturers included in this book are listed in Appendix C.

Buying carefully should be your rule for all building tools and materials. Though you may, from time to time, stumble across a real buy, what you save by purchasing unknown and untested products is questionable at best. Experience has shown that it's more likely you'll be burned by "bargains."

Finally, keep in mind that the local dealer wants your business in the future as well as now. For that reason, reputable building-materials dealers generally give floor space only to proven products by manufacturers that are known to be winners. For your peace of mind, stick with these winners and you will be one too.

Enjoy your second home.

Reference
Matter

*   *Manufacturers of Prefab homes* * *Vacation-home plans* * *Building-products manufacturers* * *Good publications you should know about* * *Associations, government agencies* *

AUTHOR'S NOTE

The five appendices on the following pages include a cross-section of various associations, manufacturers, plans services and the like. Inclusion of any firm does not necessarily imply endorsement by the author (nor by Reston Publishing Company). To the best of my knowledge, however, all firms and organizations mentioned are generally considered to be leaders in their respective fields.

The information contained in Appendices A through E is intended to help the reader quickly narrow the search for information and/or materials—so that he can get on with the important business of buying or building his second home.

Appendix A

Manufacturers of Vacation Homes

For information on availability of manufactured homes (in your area) and prices, write to the makers at the addresses given. (Note: The manufacturers shown in boldface type have products shown elsewhere in this book.)

DOME STRUCTURES

O'Dome House, Tension Structures, Inc., 9800 Ann Arbor Road, Plymouth, Mich. 48170

LOG HOMES

Boyne Falls Log Homes, Inc., Boyne Falls, Mich. 49713
Carolina Log Buildings, Inc., Fletcher, N.C. 28732
Real Log Homes, Inc., Missoula, Mont. 59801
Vermont Log Buildings, Inc., Hartford, Vt. 05048
Ward Cabin Company, Box 72, Houlton, Me. 04730

MODULAR HOMES

Acorn Structures, Inc., Box 250, Concord, Mass. 01742 (Send $3. for "Acorn Houses, Planning and Information Kit".)
Vacation Land Homes, Inc., Box 292, Bellaire, Mich. 49615
Stanmar, Inc., Boston Post Road, Sudbury, Mass. 01776

MOTOR AND MOBILE HOMES

GMC Truck and Coach Division, General Motors Corporation, 660 South Boulevard East, Pontiac, Mich. 48053
Champion Home Builders Company, Box D, Richfield Springs, N.Y. 13439
Wickes Recreational Vehicles, Wickes Homes, Department JA, Box 97, Argos, Ind. 46501

PANELIZED HOMES (closed wall/mechanical core)
Weston Homes, Inc., Box 126, Rotschild, Wisc. 54474

PRECUT HOMES
Cluster Shed, Inc., Hartland, Vt. 05048
Cluster Shed, Inc., Fletcher, N.C. 28732
Timber Lodge, Inc., 105 West 18th Ave., North Kansas City, Mo. 64116

PREFABS
The Aladdin Company, Bay City, Mich. 48706
American Barn Corporation, 123 Elm St., So. Deerfield, Mass. 01373
Kingsberry Homes, Boise-Cascade Manufactured Housing Division, 61 Perimeter Park, Atlanta, Ga. 30341

Appendix B

Vacation Home Plans

Write to the firms listed at addresses shown below to request building plans, information and prices. Prices can vary depending upon the house selected and the number of plan sets ordered. This information will be spelled out in the descriptive literature you will receive upon requesting plan literature. (Boldface type indicates that homes from this source are illustrated elsewhere in this book.)

Custom architects can also be located in the local Yellow Pages directory.

PLANS SERVICE

Home Building Plan Service, 2235 N.E. Sandy Boulevard, Portland, Ore. 97232. The Laborator and Estimator (see chapter 14) are also available from this firm.

CUSTOM ARCHITECT

Architects Etcetera, 124 Southwest Yamhill Street, Portland, Ore. 97204

Appendix C

Building Products

All manufacturers listed have products illustrated elsewhere in this book. For more product information and prices, write makers direct.

APPLIANCES

General Electric, News Bureau, 38th Floor, 400 3rd Avenue, New York, N.Y. 10016

Jenn-Air Corporation, 3035 Shadeland, Indianapolis, Ind. 46226.

Sears, Roebuck and Company, Department 703, Sears Tower, Chicago, Ill. 60684

CERAMIC TILE

American Olean Company, Lansdale, Pa. 19446

ELECTRICAL HARDWARE

Leviton Manufacturing Company, Inc., 59-25 Little Neck Parkway, Little Neck, N.Y. 11362 *Electrical wiring devices, cord sets, dimmers, ground fault circuit interrupters.*

3M Company, 3M Center, Electro Products Division, St. Paul, Minn. 55101 *Ground fault circuit interrupters.*

Wadsworth Electric, 42-1 Wadsworth Avenue, Covington, Ky. 41012 *Service entrance equipment.*

ENERGY-SAVING PRODUCTS

3M Company, 3M Center, Industrial Tape Division, St. Paul, Minn. 55101 *Scotchtint.*

Andersen Corporation, Bayport, Minn. 55003 *Perma-Shield windows.*

FANS, VENTILATING

Kool-O-Matic Corporation, 1831 Terminal Road, Niles, Mich., 49120 *Attic power ventilator.*

Nutone division of Scovill, Madison and Red Bank Roads, Cincinnati, Ohio 45227. *Wide variety of exhaust fans for all rooms of the house including attic power ventilators; fan-heater and fan-heater-light combinations for bathrooms.*

FIREPLACE, PREFAB

Majestic Company, 245 Erie St., Huntington, Ind., 46750 *Woodburning and electric models.*

FIXTURES, KITCHEN AND BATH

American Standard, Box 2003, New Brunswick, N.J. 08903

Eljer Plumbingware, Wallace-Murray Corporation, 3 Gateway Center, Pittsburgh, Pa. 15222

Kohler Company, Kohler, Wisc. 53044

LaMere Industries, Inc., 227 North Main Street, Walworth, Wisc., 53184 *Destroilet.*

Owens-Corning Fiberglas, Fiberglas Tower, Toledo, Ohio 43654 *Molded tub and shower enclosures.*

Peerless Faucet, a division of Masco Corporation, Box 31, Greensburg, Ind., 47240 *Trim for bath and kitchen fixtures.*

FLOOR AND CEILING TILES

Armstrong Cork Company, Lancaster, Pa. 17604.

GAF Corporation (Floor Products), Building Materials Group, 140 West 51st St., New York, N.Y. 10020

HARDWARE, MISC.

Ajax Hardware, City of Industry, Calif. 91749

Amerock Corporation, Rockford, Ill. 61101 *Dor-Closer and wide variety of cabinet and door hardware.*

TECO, 5530 Wisconsin Ave., Washington, D.C. 20015 *Framing hardware.*

HEATING/COOLING (AIR CONDITIONING)

Airtemp Division, Chrysler Corporation, 1600 Webster Street, Dayton, Ohio 45404 *Heating, air conditioning, humidifiers, electronic air cleaners.*

American-Standard, Box 2003, New Brunswick, N.J. 08903 *Components for hydronics heating system and gas and oil fired furnaces.*

Lennox Industries Inc., Box 250, Marshalltown, Iowa 50158 *Total-comfort heating-and-cooling systems.*

Nutone division of Scovill, Madison and Red Bank Roads, Cincinnati, Ohio 45227 *Electric space heaters.*

INSULATION

Johns-Manville Corporation, Box 5705 RP, Greenwood Plaza, Denver, Colo. 80217

KITCHEN CABINETS

H. J. Scheirich Company, Box 21037, Louisville, KY 40221

Long-Bell Division of International Paper Company, Box 8411, Portland, Ore. 97207

United Cabinet Corporation, Box 420, Jasper, Ind. 47546

(*Note: Kitchen cabinet manufacturers listed above also produce bathroom vanitories.*)

BATH AND MEDICINE CABINETS AND LIGHTING

General Bathroom Products Corporation, 2201 Touhy Avenue, Elk Grove Village, Ill. 60007 *Bath cabinets and vanities.*

Intermatic, Inc., Intermatic Plaza, Spring Grove, Ill. 60081 *Low voltage luminaires.*

Nutone Division of Scovill, Madison and Red Bank Roads, Cincinnati, Ohio 45227 *Medicine cabinets with luminaires.*

Thomas Industries, Inc., Box 1643, Louisville, Ky. 40201 *Interior and exterior luminaires.*

MILLWORK (DOORS AND WINDOWS)

Andersen Corporation, Bayport, Minn. 55003

Caradco Window and Door Division of Scovill, 1098 Jackson Street, Box 658, Dubuque, Ia. 52001

OUTDOOR BASEMENT ENTRY

The Bilco Company, New Haven, Conn. 06505

PAINTS

Glidden-Durkee Division of SCM Corporation, 900 Union Commerce Building, Cleveland, Ohio 44115

PLASTIC LAMINATES, HIGH-PRESSURE

Formica Corporation, 120 East 4th Street, Cincinnati, Ohio, 45202

Nevamar division of Exxon Chemical Company, Odenton, Md. 21113

PUMPS (WATER SUPPLY MATERIALS)

Decatur Pump Company, Box 431, Decatur, Ill. 62525 *Burks Pumps.*

Jacuzzi Bros., Inc., 11511 New Benton Highway, Little Rock, Ark. 72203 *Water pumps (including the Aquagenie).*

Johnson Division, Universal Oil Products Company, Box 23118, St. Paul, Minn., 53165 *Red Head wellpoints for driven wells.*

ROOFING AND SIDING MATERIALS

Certain-Teed Products Corporation, Box 860, Valley Forge, Pa. 19482 *Roof shingles, vinyl siding, vinyl soffit and fascia system.*

GAF Corporation, Building Products Division, 140 West 51st Street, New York, N.Y. 10020 *Roof shingles and various siding systems.*

Georgia-Pacific Corporation, 900 S.W. 5th Avenue, Portland, Ore. 97204 *Wood sheathing and siding products.*

Johns-Manville Corporation, Box 5705 RP, Greenwood Plaza, Denver, Colo. 80217 *Various roofing materials, vinyl siding and accessories.*

Masonite Corporation, 29 No. Wacker Drive, Chicago, Ill. 60606 *Hardboard siding products, textured and smooth.*

U.S. Plywood, Division of Champion International, 1 Landmark Square, Stamford, Conn., 06921 *Plywood sheathing and siding.*

TENTING/LIVING OUT (ROUGHING-IT SUPPLIES)

The Coleman Company, Inc., 250 North Francis, Wichita, Kansas 67201 *Miscellaneous camping gear.*

Sears, Roebuck and Company, Sears Tower, Chicago, Ill. 60684 *Camping gear, Porta-Potti—available at nearest Sears store or catalog outlet.*

Zebco Camping Products, division of Brunswick Corporation, 6101 East Apache, Tulsa, Okla. 74101 *Wide variety of camping products.*

TOOLS

Black & Decker Manufacturing Company, Towson, Md. 21204 *Portable power tools.*

Homelite division of Textron, Inc., Charlotte, N.C. 28217 *Generators, chain saws.*

Rockwell Manufacturing Company, Inc., Power Tool Division, Consumer Products, Suite 303, 3171 Directors Row, Memphis, Tenn. 38131 *Portable power tools.*

The Stanley Works, 195 Lake Street, New Britain, Conn., 06050 *Handtools, portable power tools.*

WALLCOVERINGS

American Olean Tile Company, Division National Gypsum, 2075 Cannon Avenue, Lansdale, Pa. 19446 *Ceramic tile for walls and floors.*

Decro-Wall Corporation, 375 Executive Boulevard, Elmsford, N.Y. 10523 *Do-it-yourself plastic stick-on panels and tiles.*

The General Tire and Rubber Company, 1 General Street, Akron, Ohio 44329 *Ceramic tile.*

Georgia-Pacific Corporation, 900 S.W. 5th Avenue, Portland, Ore. 97204 *Prefinished paneling.*

Marlite Paneling, Division of Masonite Corporation, Dover, Ohio 44622 *Water-resistant paneling.*

Masonite Corporation, 29 North Wacker Drive, Chicago, Ill. 60606 *Prefinished hardboard paneling.*

Roxite Division of Masonite Corporation, 29 North Wacker Drive, Chicago, Ill. 60606 *Brick panels.*

U.S. Plywood, division of Champion International, 1 Landmark Square, Stamford, Conn. 06921 *Prefinished plywood paneling.*

Appendix D

Good Publications You Should Know About

Note: Orders for *all* booklets produced by the U.S. Government Printing Office should be addressed to:

Superintendent of Documents
U.S. Government Printing Office
Washington, D.C. 20402

Make checks and money orders payable to the superintendent. If desired, you can send for a price list of government consumer publications (Price List 86) —single copies are free, while multiple copies are priced at 10 cents each. Other publications listed below are available direct from manufacturers. (Some are free, others are reasonably priced.)

BATH PLANNING
"The Eljer Plan for a Better Bathroom", Eljer Plumbingware Division of Wallace-Murray Corporation, 3 Gateway Center, Pittsburgh, Pa. 15222 $1.00

BUILDING AIDS
"Laborator, $3.95; Estimator, $4.95; Complete Book of Home Decorating, $9.95; Build Your Own Home, a guide for subcontracting the easy way, $6.00 Home Building Plan Service, 2235 N. E. Sandy Boulevard, Portland, Ore. 97232

BUILDING KNOW-HOW
"Design for Low-Cost Wood Homes", Anderson, L.O. and Zorning, Harold F., U.S. Department of Agriculture/Forest Service, U.S. Government Printing Office

"House Construction Details", Burbank, Nelson L. and Pfister, Herbert R.; Simmons-Boardman Publishing Corporation, 30 Church Street, New York, N.Y. 10007

"House Construction: How to Reduce Costs", U.S. Department of Agriculture, Home and Garden Bulletin No. 168; U.S. Government Printing Office

"Low-Cost Homes for Rural America—Construction Manual", Agriculture Handbook No. 364, U.S. Government Printing Office

"Modern Carpentry", Wagner, Willis H., The Goodheart-Wilcox Company, 123 W. Taft Drive, South Holland, Ill. 60473

"Wood Frame House Construction", Agriculture Handbook No. 73, $2.25; U.S. Government Printing Office

"Electricity in the Home", free booklet from the National Fire Protection Association, 470 Atlantic Avenue, Boston, Mass. 02210

"National Electric Code", $5.50; National Fire Protection Association, 470 Atlantic Avenue, Boston, Mass. 02210

Nutone Book of Ideas, $1.00; Nutone Division of Scovill, Madison and Red Bank Roads, Cincinnati, Ohio 45227

"The Popular Mechanics Home Book of Electrical Wiring and Repair", Strand, Harold P., Hawthorne Books, Inc., New York, N.Y. $5.95 at bookstores

FIREPLACE

"Fireplace Ideas", $3. ppd. Majestic Company, 245 Erie St., Huntington, Ind. 46750

FLOORCOVERING KNOW-HOW

"Step Out in Style", free. Armstrong Cork Company, Lancaster, Pa. 17604

GENERAL REFERENCE BOOKS

"Handbook for the Home", U.S. Department of Agriculture, 1973 yearbook, U.S. Government Printing Office. $5.70

"House Hunter's Guide", The American Wood Council, 1619 Massachusetts Avenue, N.W., Wash. D.C. 20036 Free

"Popular Mechanics Complete Manual of Home Repair and Improvement" Hearst Books, 250 W. 55th Street, New York, N.Y. 10019 $8.95 at bookstores

KITCHEN PLANNING

"Kitchen Planning Kit", $1.00; Long-Bell Division of International Paper Company, Box 8411, Portland, Ore. 97207

MOBILE HOMES

"*Quick Facts*," Manufactured Housing Institute, Box 201, 14650 Lee Road, Chantilly, Va. 22021 Free

"*Your Mobile Home Buying Guide*", Wickes Homes, a division of Wickes Corp., Dept. JA, 401 West St., Argos, Ind. 46501 Free

PANELING HOW-TO

"*Your Guide on How to Panel a Room*", Masonite Corporation, Dept. I, 1909 E. Cornell Drive, Peoria, Ill. 61614

PLANS, IDEAS

"*Great Ideas for Second Homes*"—a 36-page color booklet describing 20 vacation homes. Available from American Plywood Association, 1119 A Street, Tacoma, Wash. 98401 Single copies, 50 cents; request Form T610.

"*17 Leisure Home Designs*", in color booklet from Western Wood Products Association, 1500 Yeon Building, Portland, Ore. 97204 $1.00

PLASTIC LAMINATES

"*Do-It-Yourself with Formica*", Advertising Distribution, Formica Corporation, The Formica Building, 120 East 4th Street, Cincinnati, Ohio 45202 35 cents ppd.

ROOFING

"*A Homeowner's Guide to the Selection of Quality Roofing*", Asphalt Roofing Manufacturers Association, SR & A, Box 3202, Grand Central Station, New York, N.Y. 10017 30 cents

VENTILATING

"*Certified Home Ventilating Products Directory—Air Delivery and Sound Levels*" (*Annual*). To order, send a postage-paid 8 x 10″ envelope, self-addressed, plus 50 cents to cover printing and handling, to: Home Ventilating Institute, 230 North Michigan Avenue, Chicago, Ill. 60601.

WATER AND WELLS

"*Manual of Individual Water Supply Systems*", Environmental Protection Agency/Water Supply Division, U.S. Government Printing Office. $2.20.

"*Water Supply Sources for the Farmstead and Rural Home*", Farmer's Bulletin No. 2237, Department of Agriculture, U.S. Government Printing Office 30 cents

"*Water System & Treatment Handbook, 4th Edition*", The Water Systems Council, 221 No. LaSalle Street, Chicago, Ill. 60601 Write for price

WOODS/MOLDINGS

An assortment of wood and molding literature is available free from Western
Wood Moulding and Millwork Producers, 1730 S.W. Skyline, Box 25278,
Portland, Ore. 97225

Appendix E

Associations You May Want To Write To

Have you ever been baffled about where to find a particular building product? Or wondered how a particular product is best applied? One of the quickest and surest ways to get the answers to these questions is by writing to the association that handles the product (or products) you're concerned with. To make it easy for you to do just that when it comes to building your second home, we've listed those associations which you are almost certain to want to know about.

BUILDING AND RESIDENTIAL PRODUCTS

ALUMINUM

Aluminum Siding Association, (ASA), 410 North Michigan Avenue, 9th Floor, Chicago, Ill. 60611

APPLIANCES

Association of Home Appliances Manufacturers (AHAM), 200 North Wacker Drive, Chicago, Ill. 60606

ELECTRICAL

American Insurance Association, 85 John St., New York, N.Y. 10038 (Formerly the National Board of Fire Underwriters.)

National Electrical Manufacturers Association (NEMA), 155 East 44th Street, New York, N.Y. 10017

National Fire Protection Association, 470 Atlantic Avenue, Boston, Mass. 02210 (For information on current National Electrical Code.)

Edison Electric Institute, 90 Park Avenue, New York, N.Y. 10010

HEATING AND COOLING

Air-Conditioning and Refrigeration Institute, 1815 North Ft. Myers Drive, Arlington, Va. 22209

INSULATION

National Mineral Wool Insulation Association, Inc., 382 Springfield Avenue, Summit, N.J. 07901

KITCHEN

American Institute of Kitchen Dealers (AIKD), 114 Main Street, Hacketts-town, N.J. 07840

National Kitchen Cabinet Association (NKCA), 334 East Broadway, Suite 248, Louisville, Ky. 40202

MOBILE HOMES

Manufactured Housing Institute (MHI), Box 201, 14650 Lee Road, Chan-tilly, Va. 22021

ROOFING

Asphalt Roofing Manufacturers Association, Room 1717, 757 3rd Avenue, New York, N.Y. 10017

TILE, CERAMIC

Tile Council of America, Box 326, Princeton, N.J. 08540

TOOLS

Power Tool Institute (PTI), 1803 South Busse Road, Mt. Prospect, Ill. 60056

WINDOW SHADES

Window Shade Manufacturers Association, 230 Park Avenue, New York, N.Y. 10017

INDUSTRY, PROFESSIONAL ASSOCIATIONS, GOVERNMENT

BUILDING

National Association of Home Builders (NAHB), 15th and M Streets N.W., Washington, D.C. 20005

National Home Improvement Council, 11 East 44th Street, New York, N.Y. 10017

CONCRETE

Portland Cement Association, Old Orchard Road, Skokie, Ill. 60076

GOVERNMENT
HUD, Department of Housing and Urban Development, 451 7th Street S.W., Washington, D.C. 20410
U.S. Government Printing Office, Superintendent of Documents, Washington, D.C. 20402

PAINT
National Paint and Coatings Association, 1500 Rhode Island Avenue, Washington, D.C.

PESTS
National Pest Control Association, 8150 Leesburg Pike, Suite 1100, Vienna, Va. 22180

PLUMBING
National Association of Plumbing and —Heating—Cooling Contractors, 1016 20th Strcct N.W., Washington, D.C.

REAL ESTATE
National Association of Realtors (NAR), 155 East Superior Street, Chicago, Ill. 60611

VENTILATION
Home Ventilating Institute, 230 North Michigan Avcnuc, Chicago, Ill. 60601

WATER
American Water Works Association, 6666 West Quincy Avenue, Denver, Colo. 80235
Water Systems Council, 221 North LaSalle Street, Chicago, Ill. 60601

WARRANTY PROTECTION
HOW Corporation, National Housing Center, 15th and M Streets, N.W., Washington, D.C. 20005

WOOD
American Hardboard Association, 20 North Wacker Drive, Chicago, Ill. 60606
American Plywood Association, 1119 A Street, Tacoma, Wash. 98401
California Redwood Association, 617 Montgomery Street, San Francisco, Calif. 94111
National Woodwork Manufacturers Association, 400 W. Madison Street, Chicago, Ill. 60606

Red Cedar Shingle and Handsplit Shake Bureau, 5510 White Building, Seattle, Wash. 98101

Western Wood Moulding and Millwork Producers, 1730 S.W. Skyline, Box 25278, Portland, Ore. 97225

Western Wood Products Association (WWPA), 1500 Yeon Building, Portland, Ore. 97204

Western Red Cedar Lumber Association, Yeon Building, Portland, Ore. 97204

Glossary of Terms

Acoustical materials: types of plaster, board, or tiles that absorb soundwaves; usually applied to interior surfaces.

Adhesive: Substance capable of holding two or more materials together; in construction, the term usually applies to various mastics, pastes, glues, cements, and the like.

Aggregate: rock, gravel, and sand, mixed with cement to make concrete.

Air-conditioning: the mechanical controlling of air movement, temperature, humidity, and quality (purity).

Air-dried lumber: lumber that has been piled in sheds. Its minimum moisture content is 12–15 percent, the average is somewhat higher, and the highest should never exceed 19 percent.

Alternating current (A.C.): the flow of electricity that reverses at regular intervals, in cycles. In lines serving residential dwellings, it flows at 60 cycles per second.

Amortization: periodic payment on the principal sum of a mortgage loan.

Amperage: the strength of a current of electricity, expressed in amperes.

Anchor bolts: bolts embedded in concrete that hold structural members (plates, sills) in place.

Appraisal: an estimate of the real or market value of a property; for example, a valuation based on comparable sales or reproduction costs, or the price a willing buyer would agree to pay to a willing seller.

Appreciation: increase in the value of property caused by improvements, additions, inflation, or other economic factors.

Apron: the casing nailed to the wall that butts against the underside of the window stool.

Armored cable: insulated conductor with a flexible, galvanized steel cover, that is, BX.

Assessed valuation: the value assigned to real estate by a taxing authority for property-tax purposes; usually a percentage of the property's market value.

Backband: a rabbeted molding used on the edge of a window or door casing for ornamentation or to increase the width (to hide joint).

Backfill: the replacement of earth after excavating.

Balloon mortgage: a long-term loan that is to be paid off in a lump sum at the end of a specified term (as opposed to a self-amortizing loan).

447

Balusters: small spindles capped by a horizontal member forming the railing for a stairway, porch, or balcony.

Bare-wire ground: the uninsulated wire supplied in most armored or nonmetallic sheathed cable. The Code requires its use at all outlets, and all boxes where cables are joined or terminated, to maintain ground continuity.

Base, baseboard: the board placed at the bottom of a wall next to the floor.

Base molding: trim molding on the upper edge of base or baseboard.

Base shoe: trim molding used to conceal the baseboard/floor joint.

Basement (cellar): the base story of a house; generally below grade.

Batten: a narrow strip of wood to conceal a joint.

Batter board: temporary framework used when laying out corners for excavating and foundation work.

Bay window: a rectangular, curved, or polygonal window (or group of windows) usually supported on a foundation extending beyond the building's main wall.

Beam: a structural member used between (that is, spanning a distance between) supporting walls, columns or posts.

Bearing partition (wall): a wall or partition that supports weight from above in addition to its own weight.

Bed molding: molding used where two surfaces come together at an angle, such as between the rafters and knee wall in an attic room.

Benchmark: a surveyor's mark on a permanent object fixed to the ground from which land measurements and elevations can be taken with accuracy.

Bevel: to cut a board to an angle instead of at a right angle, such as a board or door edge.

Bid: an offer to supply materials, equipment, labor, and the like at a specified price; or, the entire structure (in the case of the general contractor), or a section or portion of the job (in the case of the subcontractors).

Binder: the deposit paid to secure the right to purchase a home at the terms agreed to by both seller and buyer.

Blemish: a mark or other abnormality that detracts from the appearance of wood.

Board: lumber less than 2 inches thick.

Bonding wire: a wire that is sometimes used to bond the frame of electrical equipment or a grounded conductor to a water pipe.

Box: a rigid protective enclosure for wire connections, switches, and outlets.

Branch circuit: that portion of a wiring system including all cable, outlets, and switches wired through the same fuse or circuit breaker.

Bridging: pieces of lumber installed between floor joists to distribute the floor load more evenly.

BTU, British thermal unit: the amount of heat that will raise the temperature of one pound of water 1° F.

Builder: *see* Contractor.

Burial cable: an electrical cable designed for direct burial in underground installations. Conduit is not required with direct burial cable.

BX cable: *see* Armored cable.

C, thermal conductance: C is similar to the designation k but is used for a material of any thickness.

Casing: molding of various thicknesses, widths, and designs used to trim doors and windows. Casing spans joints between jamb and wall.

Caulk: to seal and make waterproof cracks around window and door frames and other fixed exterior protuberances.

Certificate of reasonable value (CRV): a certificate issued by the Veterans Administration specifying the maximum loan on a given property that it will guarantee to an eligible veteran purchaser.

Circuit breaker: a switch that opens automatically when more than a predetermined amount of current passes through it. Used instead of a fuse, it can be reset by hand after being tripped by an overload.

Closing, settlement at: a meeting of parties to either a mortgage transaction or a transfer of title of property at which the documents needed to accomplish these events are executed.

Cluster development: a group of buildings situated around courts, cul-de-sacs, or short streets—sited closer together than in conventional single-family plans to preserve open space for common usage.

Code: the National Electric Code was established and is periodically reviewed by the National Board of Fire Underwriters. The NEC is accepted as the minimum standard in many areas; except those areas which have more restrictive codes.

Collar beam: a beam connecting pairs of opposite rafters, usually well above the top plate. Sometimes called a rafter tie.

Column: an upright supporting member, either rectangular or circular in shape.

Common property: land and facilities shared by all the individual owners in a residential project and managed by an owners-association. In planned developments, common property usually includes tennis courts, pools, community buildings, and other amenities for residents' convenience and enjoyment.

CC and R's: conditions, covenants, and restrictions pertaining to a piece of real estate define the use that may be made of property and spell out any restrictions that may exist.

Condo (condominium): an apartment house or complex where individual units are owned rather than rented with each homeowner holding an un-divided interest in the common area and facilities. Dwellings are separately mortgaged; each member contributes a share of the expense of maintenance and operations of common facilities, which are administered by an elected board of owners.

Conduit, electrical: steel pipe or tubing through which wire conductors are pulled.

Contract of sale: a written and signed agreement by both parties involved in the transfer of real property as to conditions, price, and other terms.

Contractor: the builder who oversees all construction, supervises labor, and subcontractors, and delivers the house per the signed documents of sale.

Convenience outlet: a plug receptacle in a wall outlet.

Cooperative: stock ownership in a multi-unit project, entitling the stockholder to occupy, but not own, a dwelling unit. A cooperative is owned by all residents and operated by an elected board of directors. Property taxes are assessed on the project as a whole and there is only one mortgage (as opposed to individual mortgages and property taxes on each unit under a condominium agreement).

Coped joint: the end of one trim member cut and shaped so it will fit the contour of the trim it butt-joins at a right angle.

Corner bead: a strip of ¾-in. round or angular wood placed over a plastered or drywall outside corner for protection.

Cornice: a method of trimming where the exterior wall and roof meet.

Cove molding: three-sided molding with a concave face used to cover small angles (where two members meet at a right angle).

Covenant: a written agreement usually relating to land use, conditioning, or restricting. Generally, a covenant binds all subsequent owners.

Coverage: pertaining to roofing, it refers to the degree of weather protection offered by a roofing material. Depending upon roofing material, it can be single, double, or triple coverage.

Dado: a rectangular groove in a board or plank cut across the grain.

Deck: a roof surface or platform attached to and jutting out from the house.

Deed: the legal written instrument that conveys title to real property.

Direct current (DC): the flow of electricity in one direction, as from a battery, so that each wire always has the same polarity.

Discount points: *see* Points.

Door jamb (frame): the assembly of wooden parts that create the surround into which a door is fitted. Door jambs are designated as interior and exterior.

Drip cap: the molding applied over exterior window and door frames that directs water away from a structure to prevent any chance of seepage under the exterior face material (casings).

Drip edge: a weather-resistant metal edge installed along eaves and rakes to facilitate the shedding of water at the lower edge of the roof.

Dry rot: a general term, loosely applied to various types of wood decay. Paradoxically, "dry rot" is usually caused by excessive and lasting accumulations of water.

Dry wall: an interior wallcovering material that consists of plaster sandwiched between paper surfaces. Applied directly to wall studs, usually in ⅜- or ½-in. thickness and 4-by-8-ft. panels.

Easement: the right given by the owner of land to another party for the specific and limited use of that land.

Eaves: the parts of a roof that extend beyond an exterior wall, also frequently called overhang.

Encumbrance: any right to or interest in land that may subsist to another person, to the diminution of the value of the property.

Equity: the value of property in excess of all indebtedness against the property.

Excavation: a cavity formed by cutting and digging that serves as the basement for a dwelling.

Exposure: pertaining to shingles and siding, specifically, exposure to weather—the distance from the butt edge of one course to the butt edge of the adjacent course.

Fascia, facia: the vertical wood member that forms the outer face of a box cornice (nailed to rafter ends).

Felt: a tough, strong building paper saturated with asphalt. Most commonly used in 15- and 30-lb. weights.

Fenestration: the placement, arrangement, and sizes of windows and exterior doors in a building.

First mortgage loan: a first lien against property, generally contracted to provide financing for the real estate for a long period of time.

Flashing: strips of metal or roofing material used to make joints watertight on a roof—especially in valleys and where inclined and vertical surfaces intersect (such as roof and chimney, vents, and the like).

Flue: the lined space in a chimney through which smoke passes.

Fluorescent light: a type of lamp in which electricity arcs from one electrode through a mercury vapor to another electrode to produce invisible ultraviolet light. This, in turn, causes a phosphorescent material coating on the inside of the tube to glow and produce a strong, but well-diffused, light. The color depends upon the type phosphor used.

Footing: the spreading course (or courses) at the base of a foundation wall, pier, or column. The footing serves to distribute the superimposed load over a greater area.

Foreclosure: the legal proceeding by a lender that bars a mortgagor's right to redeem a mortgage when regular payments have not been made.

Foundation: the supporting portion of a structure below grade, including footings.

Framing: the timbers in a structure that give it shape and strength. Framing includes all walls (interior and exterior), floors, ceilings, and roof.

Front money: a sum that includes funds needed to pay for the land, permanent financing fees, legal fees, title insurance, and other closing costs not included in the construction loan.

Furring: narrow strips of wood, usually spaced 16 in. on center, that form a nailing base for another surface.

Fuse: a short metal strip designed to melt when more than a certain amount of current flows through it. It is installed in a circuit (in a service panel) to prevent serious overloading. Unlike a circuit breaker, when a fuse blows, it must be replaced with a new one.

Gable: the end of a wall or building that comes to a triangular point under a sloping roof; also, a type of roof.

Girder: a principal beam used to support concentrated loads at various points along its length.

Grain: the direction, size, and appearance of fibers in wood.

Groove: a rectangular groove in a board or plank cut with (in the direction of) the grain.

Ground: (1) *carpentry:* A strip of wood that assists the plasterer in making a straight wall and that also gives a surface to which the finish of a room may be nailed (e.g., the baseboard). (2) *Electrical:* The connection between an electrical wiring system, or any part of it, and the earth. The neutral (white) wire side of a circuit leading to this connection.

GFI, GFCI (Ground Fault Circuit Interrupter): a device installed in a circuit to monitor the current flow in both sides of a circuit. If a difference occurs, a GFI acts instantly to turn off current and avert a dangerous shock.

Gutter: a wood or metal trough affixed to the edge of a roof at the eave end to collect and conduct water.

Hardboard: a man-made building material manufactured of wood fibers and formed into panels having a density of 50 to 80 lbs. per cubic ft.

Header: a beam placed perpendicular—and nailed—to joists. Also, a doubled-up framing member that spans an opening (such as a window or door), sometimes called a lintel.

Heartwood: wood that extends from the pith or center of the tree to the sapwood. The cells of the heartwood no longer participate in the tree's life process.

Heating element: a component containing high-resistance wire used in appliances to generate a great amount of heat.

Hip: (1) a roof that rises from all four sides of a building. (2) An external angle formed by the meeting of two sloping ends of the roof, from the ridge to the eaves.

Home association: an incorporated private organization, operating under recorded land agreements, established to maintain the common property of a condominium or planned development and to provide various services for the common use and enjoyment of the residents.

Horsepower: the unit of power equal to 746 watts, used to rate motor capacity.

Hot wire: any wire conductor carrying power. In a two-wire cable, it is always the wire with the black insulation.

Incandescent light: a type of lamp in which electricity heats a tungsten filament to produce light.

Insulating glass: double-glazed window lights (panes); these obviate the need for storm windows.

Insulation, thermal: any material that is high in resistance to heat transmission and that is placed in structures to reduce the rate of heat flow.

Insured loan: a loan on which an agency (such as FHA, VA) insures the lender against the loss of some or all of the principal.

Interest rate: the cost of a loan, generally indicated as a percentage and included as part of the terms and conditions of a mortgage loan.

Interim financing: also referred to as construction loan and builder's loan, a loan to cover construction costs and other incidental expenses attributable to the construction period.

Jamb: the top and side members of a door or window frame that make contact with the door or window.

Joint tenancy: property owned by two or more persons with equal interest.

Joist: one of a series of parallel beams used to support floor and ceiling loads. The size is determined by the span from wall to wall. Joists, in turn, rest on and are supported by beams, girders, or bearing walls.

Junction box: a round or square box used solely to house wire splices, covered with a blank plate.

k, thermal conductivity: the quantity of heat that passes through a homogeneous material 1-in. thick and 1 sq. ft. in area in one hour's time (when the temperature difference between the two sides is $1°$ F.).

Kiln-dried lumber: lumber that is heat-treated to reduce moisture content to about 6 to 8 percent.

Kilowatt: 1,000 watts.

Kilowatt-hour: 1,000 watts of power used for an hour.

Knot: the base of a branch or limb that is incorporated in the body of the tree.

Lally column: a cylindrically shaped steel post used to support girders and beams.

Land contract: a contract used in some areas of the country to sell real property on an installment plan with a small down payment. The title remains with the seller until the terms of the contract are fulfilled.

Leader: often called downspout, a vertical pipe that carries rainwater from the gutter to the ground.

Lease: the contract whereby a piece of real estate is rented.

Lessee: the individual who contracts to rent property from another.

Lessor: the property owner who leases to a tenant.

Leverage: the ability to utilize borrowed money in order to purchase real property.

Lien: a charge upon property for the payment of a debt, that is, a lien placed by a subcontractor who worked to create or improve the property.

Line: the cable supplying power to the branch circuit.

Lumber, boards: lumber that is less than 2 inches thick but 1 or more inches wide.

Lumber, dressed: lumber surfaced at the mill on one or more sides, indicated as S1S, S2S, S3S, S4S.

Lumber, yard: the grades, sizes, and designs used in general household carpentry.

Main switch: the control at the service entrance that can disconnect all circuits at one time, fused to protect the entire service.

Manufactured home: a home constructed in a factory and assembled on piers or a foundation at the jobsite.

Masonry: can be either stone, brick, hollow tile, or concrete block bonded together with mortar to form walls, piers, or buttresses. Can also be poured concrete.

Master deed: the basic document used in the creation of a condominium, describing the division of the project into units and common elements.

Mechanical equipment: in building terms, all equipment under the general heading of plumbing, heating, air-conditioning, electrical, and gas fitting.

Mobile home: a fully equipped, factory-built home that can be hauled over the highway. At the site, a mobile home is usually placed on a foundation or piers.

Modular home: a manufactured home built in sections for assembly at the site. These have the appearance of stick-built homes.

Molding: patterned strips used to cover joints attractively.

Mortgage: a conditional transfer of property to secure a debt. The mortgage is terminated upon the repayment of the debt.

Motor home: a fully furnished, self-powered home on wheels often referred to as a van camper.

Mullion: the vertical member between two windows in the same frame (generally nonstructural).

Muntin: a fragile wood member that divides the sash on doors and windows. Each framed portion is referred to as a light.

NEPA [National Environmental Policy Act (1970)]: the first major United States legislation dealing with environmental concerns on a national level.

Neutral: the white wire in a service entrance (sometimes supplied as a bared wire) is always connected to the clamp terminal on the common ground strip in the panel. Also, all cable white wires.

Newel: the post to which the end of a stair railing (banister) is fastened. Also, a stiffening post at a landing.

Nominal size: the size by which lumber is sold but to which it does not necessarily measure.

Nonbearing partition (wall): a floor-to-ceiling wall that supports no load other than its own weight.

Nonmetallic sheathed cable: not accepted by all building codes, insulated conductors with a tough, fibrous cover.

Ogee: a three-faced molding with the profile of the letter S.

On center (O.C.): the measure from the center of one member to the center of the next (e.g., studs spaced 16 in. O.C.).

Open-end mortgage: a mortgage written so as to secure and permit additional advances beyond the amount of the original loan.

Option: the right to buy property at an agreed-upon price within a specified time. An option is binding upon the seller if the purchaser has given some sort of consideration, such as a deposit.

Outlet: a location on a circuit where electrical current is made available through direct connection or plug receptacles.

Panelized home: a factory-built home consisting, basically, of manufactured panels assembled at the jobsite.

Particleboard: a man-made building material that comes in panels consisting of particles of wood shavings and slivers bonded together with a synthetic resin or other added binder.

Parting strip: a rectangular wood piece used in the side and head jambs of a double-hung window to separate the upper and lower sashes.

Partition: a wall that subdivides space within a building, either bearing or nonbearing.

Penny, d: when used with nails, the term applies to nail length—common, casing, finishing and box nails. Originally, the term was a designation for the price per hundred.

Pier: a masonry column, usually rectangular in cross section, used to support other structural members.

Pitch: the inclination of a roof or stairs. The pitch is the rise divided by the span.

Plan: a drawing representing any floor

or horizontal cross section of a building, or the horizontal plane of any other object or area.

Plaster: a sand, lime, cement, and water mixture used on interior and exterior vertical surfaces.

Plat: a map or chart of a city, section, or subdivision wherein the location and boundaries of individual properties are indicated.

Plate, base, or sole: a horizontal member upon which studs stand.

Plate, top: a horizontal member to which the top ends of studs are affixed, and upon which the joists of the floor above rest.

Platform framing: a framing system in which the floor joists of each story rest upon the top plates of the floor below.

Plough: to cut a groove in a plank.

Plumb: exactly perpendicular or vertical, or at right angles to a level floor.

Plumbing: includes the installation of pipes, fixtures, and other apparatus for bringing in a water supply and removing water-borne wastes.

Plywood: a structural material consisting of sheets of wood glued or cemented together with grains of adjacent sheets at right angles. Each sheet is referred to as a ply (4-ply, for example).

Points: a point is a charge of one percent of the mortgage value, a onetime charge assessed by the lender to increase the yield from the mortgage loan and give a cash return that compares favorably with other types of investments. The government prohibits the buyer from paying points on FHA and VA insured mortgage loans.

Post: a structural, vertical member upon which other structural members —a beam or girder—rest.

Pre-cut home: a building whose parts are cut to exact size in a factory.

Prefabricated construction: a method of construction designed to cut down the time required for building on the site. Generally, all cutting and fitting is done at the plant, regardless of the type of prefab construction.

Principal: the amount of money borrowed from a lender.

Quarter round: a molding with a profile shaped like a quarter-circle.

Quitclaim deed: a document by which any and all interest in real estate is released or relinquished to another, without any warranty against the right of the parties to claim a higher interest in the property.

R-value: a measure of the ability of a material to retard the flow of heat.

Rafter: one of a series of parallel structural roof members designed and installed to carry roof load. On a flat roof, these are often called roof joists.

Rake: the inclined edge of a pitched roof over an end wall. Also, the trim members that form the finish between the roof and the wall at a gable end.

Receptacle: a wall outlet fitting for attachment plugs.

Reinforced concrete: poured concrete reinforced by the addition of steel bars or wire mesh.

Relative humidity: the ratio of the amount of water vapor in the air expressed in terms of the percentage of the total amount of water that the air could hold at the same temperature.

Resilience: the ability of a material to withstand temporary deformation (for example, when the stresses are removed, the material assumes its original shape).

Resistance: the forces present in wiring or other conductors that oppose the passage of current, as measured in ohms.

Ridge: the apex of the angle formed by a roof, or peak, where the common rafters meet (that is, where an external angle greater than 180° is formed).

Riser: the vertical stair member between stair treads.

Roof truss: *see* Truss.

Roofing: all materials affixed to the

structural members of a roof to make it waterproof.

Rough opening: any opening formed by the framing members.

Sash: wooden framework that holds the glass in a window.

Second mortgage: a mortgage placed subsequent to an existing mortgage. The second mortgage holder's interest is secondary to the first (existing) mortgage holder's.

Septic tank: a sewage-settling tank that retains sludge to foster sufficient decomposition by bacterial action.

Settlement expense: not the same as closing costs, these are charges that a buyer or seller has to pay at the closing. Settlement costs include insurance and tax payments, special assessments to municipal facilities for improvements and sales commissions.

Shakes: handsplit cedar shingles.

Sheathing: initial, structural covering over studs or rafters.

Shingle butt: the lower exposed edge of a shingle.

Short circuit: when the hot and neutral wires or normally grounded surfaces in a closed circuit touch each other due to worn insulation or loose connections, power takes a short cut to the ground, bypassing enough resistance on the way to blow the fuse or trip the circuit breaker.

Siding: the finish exterior covering on a house; many types are available.

Sill: the lowest member of the framing of a structure, the sill rests upon the foundation and supports the vertical framing members. The term also describes the lowest framing member of a window opening or exterior door frame.

Soffit: the underside of various members of a building, such as in staircases, cornices, or beams. The term is also used to describe drop or furred-down ceilings like those usually found over kitchen wall-cabinets (hangers).

Span: the distance between walls, columns, or other vertical structural members.

Specification: a written, signed document that spells out the kind, quality, and sometimes quantity of materials for a construction job.

Square: usually applied to roofing and some siding materials, this unit of measure refers to a 100 sq. ft. area—10 x 10 ft.

Stick-built house: as the name implies, this is a house that is built literally stick by stick, at the jobsite.

Stool: also frequently called sill-cap, a flat narrow shelf that is the top member of the interior trim at the bottom of the window.

Storm sash: the extra glass or window placed outside an existing window.

Structural lumber: lumber graded for strength into four classes: (1) construction, (2) standard, (3) utility, and (4) economy.

Stud: the vertical structural member placed as a supporting element in a wall.

Subfloor: boards or panels laid on floor joists over which the finish floor is placed.

Thermostat: a device—usually wall-mounted—that automatically controls heating and cooling by its response to changes in temperature.

Tie beam: a beam affixed to, and tying together, a pair of rafters to prevent them from thrusting walls out of line. *Also see* Collar beam.

Title: evidence, usually in the form of a deed, of a person's legal right to the ownership of property.

Toenail: to drive a nail, spike or rod at a slant. Also, to clinch or fasten with a nail so driven.

Tread: that member of a stair upon which the foot is placed.

Trimmer: a beam, or joist, to which a header is nailed in framing an opening for a stairway or chimney.

Truss: a structural element of a roof consisting of beams, rafters, and ties positioned to form triangles. A truss provides excellent, rigid support with a minimum amount of material.

U: the overall coefficient of heat transmission. The hourly rate of heat flow through all materials in a wall, ceiling, or floor.

Usury: interest in excess of the legal rate charged to a borrower for the use of money.

Valley: an internal angle or water runway formed by the intersection of two slopes in a roof.

Vapor barrier: a watertight material (such as polyethylene) used to prevent moisture from passing through structural elements and causing damage.

Vent: a pipe installed in the waste drainage system to provide circulation of air, and to protect trap seals from siphonage and back pressure.

Ventilation: to supply and remove air by natural or mechanical means.

Volt: as defined by International Electric Congress, 1893, a volt is that electromotive force which steadily applied to a conductor with one-ohm resistance will produce current of one ampere.

Voltage: the pressure or electromotive force used to start and move an electric current, as measured in volts.

Wallboard: large sheets fashioned from wood, pulp, gypsum, or other materials to provide a finish-wall surface. *Also see* Dry wall.

Wattage: the amount of electrical power flowing at a given point, as measured in watts.

Zoning: the division of a community into areas in each of which only certain designated uses of land are permitted for residential, commercial, or industrial purposes.

Index

Page numbers in **boldface** type indicate illustrations